Jesse

A Victorian Man

1832-1904

Written By

Glenn S Bowley PGCE. BSc (Hons). MIfL.

And dedicated to my patient proof reading wife... Elaine

Jesse. A Victorian Man. 1832-1904
Copyright © Glenn S Bowley 2010
All rights reserved.

Cover illustrations by: Glenn S Bowley
Published by: Glenn S Bowley

Inquiries should be addressed to
Glenn.S.Bowley@gmail.com

FIRST EDITION
First Printing (July 30th 2010)

British Library Cataloguing-in-Publication Data
A catalogue entry for this title is available from the British Library.

ISBN 978-0-9566122-0-5

Produced in the United Kingdom with the assistance of:
Jeremy Mills Publishing Ltd.
113 Lidget Street
Lindley
Huddersfield
West Yorkshire HD3 3JR
Office Telephone: 01484 463340
Office Fax: 01484 643609
www.jeremymillspublishing.co.uk

Email: **info@jeremymillspublishing.co.uk**

Contents

Introduction

Have you ever wondered why you were born, where you were born? And how people you have never met have some bearing on this question. This story is my answer to this question. If you decided to answer this question, your answer should be totally different from mine. If, like I did, you take the time to find out...!

So, here is my story, "Jesse." His decisions and his life affected mine....

Chapter One: My First Day.

Our tale begins in 1832 in a small village called Shalbourne. Shalbourne is a typical rural English village; it lies on the border between Wiltshire and Berkshire. In Shalbourne the villagers have many problems trying to make a living from the land, a lot of them are tenants who live and work on very small plots of land called strips. Some villagers do of course work the land for very poor wages on local farms who are owned by absent landlords, so called gentleman farmers. Either position makes for poor eating. The small holding that we are concerned with is made up of two strips of land and a small hovel of a cottage known and described as a country cottage with land for tax purposes. Since enclosure the land on this small holding has not made a profit nor has it yielded enough to keep the family from starvation. Many villagers have said things were better when the land was common land and everybody shared the yield.

To the front of this cottage, there is a yard. In the yard, there is a plough in need of attention, which is laid on its side. Two small boys are sat waiting patiently for their father to give them the signal to enter the cottage. One of the boys begins to cry, he can hear the sounds of his mother's pain, which begins to echo across the small piece of land, which is only half prepared for planting and, unless the plough is repaired it will stay that way. Eventually, as the afternoon drew on, there is a calm, which comes over the cottage and a tall, thin, gaunt looking man appears at the door with a small bundle of rags in his arms. He places the bundle on the old rocker which sits at the side of the front door and beckons the two small boys forward towards him. Quietly, he says, "look after your brother and don't go inside until I come back." Looking around slowly, he spots his wooden shovel resting against the old gate at the end of the yard. He walks down the yard quickly, picks up the shovel and without stopping proceeds through the gate and down the small leafy lane towards the church. The smallest of the boys asks quietly, "Has dad gone to work, who has died?" There is no reply from his brother as the stabbing sounds of their fathers digging begin to reach the yard.

Two hours later the man returns looking tired and slightly out of breath, when he reaches the gate, he places his hand on the gate post and coughs to clear his throat, with his dirty shirt sleeve, he wipes the beads of sweat from his forehead before continuing up the yard towards the front door where he pauses slightly before entering. He does this without saying anything to the boys, who are by now wondering what is going on inside the cottage.

The youngest of the boys ran towards the front door and tries in vain to open it, but the door has been bolted from the inside by a large piece of wood, which his father uses to keep out the landlord when the rent is due. The boy slowly slid down the door, eventually ending up on the floor in a bundle where he cries and sobs for those parental hugs that he usually got at that time of the evening before going to sleep in the corner of the cottage. The oldest of the boys had by now become so curious to find out what was going on inside the cottage that he had gone around to the side of the cottage and was stood on an old pitch fork which was leant up against the wall under the side window of the cottage. The window was pane-less but kept out the winter winds by means of two old wooden shutters, which met in the middle of the window. Where the shutters met there was a thin gap, just enough to see inside. Inside the cottage, the boy could just make out the candle lit shadows of old Mrs. Richardson, wet nurse and so called midwife and his father, who was stood by the side of the large bed at the back of the cottage. Mrs. Richardson quietly said, "never mind Tom, your young enough to marry again." and with that, she leant over the bed and began slowly pulling up a dirty blanket until it covered the taunt pale blue face of Tom's wife.

Just then a voice from the front of the cottage shouted, "you lad! What are you doing there?" Startled, the lad fell from the pitch fork onto the cobbled yard. It wasn't long before he found himself being viciously pulled by the arm and thrown towards the front of the cottage. "Little pigs have big ears!" was growled at the lad by a rather sinister looking figure. The figure, which was dark and rounded against the white of the yard wall, again began to bear down on the lad as he scrambled along the yard floor. Eventually, when the lad began to focus his eyes in the remaining light of the day he could just make out who the figure was, it was the local vicar. This vicar had a reputation among the local children of fetching young children what the vicar described as a 'side ditherer'. This was a blow of such magnitude around the back of the head or across the ear, that it literally sent you dithering sideward's.

When the lad realized who it was, he carried on scurrying backwards along the yard floor only quicker than he had done before, in fact, he moved so quickly that he ended up flat on his backside and had to be lifted to his feet by his brother. Both boys stood absolutely still as if they were made of stone. The vicar leant slightly forward and threatened them with a raised back hand as much as to say, "Don't you dare move!" After this the vicar turned and disappeared into the cottage, slamming the door behind him. By now the boys had backed themselves into the corner of the yard, they dare not move. The youngest boy quietly said to his brother, "Charlie, as the vicar come to give dad a side ditherer?" Charlie replied, "No, don't be silly, he's come to sort out mother, she's not feeling well. He'll surely say a prayer for her."

The night drew dark and the boys began to cuddle up to each other in the corner of the yard to keep warm. Suddenly there was a loud scream from the little bundle of rags, which was still lying on the old rocking chair. Both boys jumped to their feet and started to run towards the bundle, but before they reached the rocking chair Mrs. Richardson appeared at the door and said, "It's alright my little beauties you can't help the poor child." Both lads stopped suddenly and looked at her puzzled. Mrs. Richardson laughed and undid her blouse whilst saying, "You don't have the right equipment to start with." She

2

began feeding the baby whilst shouting back into the cottage, "I'll give you the first feed free Tom but after that you'll have to pay me for the rest. I'll do you one a day if that's alright with you?" A small grunt of acknowledgement was her reply as Tom walked towards the cottage gate with the vicar. "Well Tom!" the vicar said. "I'll send the rector up in the morning with the cart and we'll have a service at eleven. I take it you've already dug the grave." Tom replied, "Yes... at least I don't have to pay for that doing," "a perk of the job!" the vicar replied. He then turned to the boys and said, "you two inside and kiss your mother goodbye." Both boys disappeared quickly into the cottage and slowly walked towards their mother, who had just her freshly washed face showing above the bed sheet. Charlie pushed his brother forward and said, "Go on our Henry, kiss mother and be quick about it." Henry leant forward slowly, reluctantly, and kissed his mother's cheek. He then suddenly jumped back and shrieked, "core! She's as cold as mutton our Charlie." Charlie's head quickly rotated towards the door. "Quiet Henry or dad will surely clip us both," snapped Charlie. By now both boys were looking towards the door to see if the noise had raised the interest of their father, but it hadn't, he was busily talking to Mrs. Richardson about the baby. "What are you going to call the baby then Tom?" asked Mrs. Richardson, who had by now finished feeding the baby and was lying it down on the rocker again. Tom picked up the baby and sat down on the rocker, after a few rocks, he inquired, "What's your name Mrs. Richardson?" "My name?" she laughed. "Why, my name's Jessie. You can't call the baby that, he's a boy!" The vicar, who was just about to leave, shouted through the gate, "Yes he can, just leave out the 'i'. Tom and the baby can then use the name. I'll even christen the child Jesse." Tom smiled, "Jesse it is then!" He said as he slowly rocked backwards and forwards in the rocker.

Mrs. Richardson grabbed her shawl and said, "I'll leave you now Tom. I'll be back to feed young Jesse in the morning." "Must you go so soon?" asked Tom. Mrs. Richardson replied, "Afraid so, him in doors will be waiting for his tea." Tom looked directly at Mrs. Richardson and said, "Well if you must go, are you going through the village on your way home?" "Yes!" she replied whilst nodding her head. "Why? Do you want me to tell the rest of the family? Hannah's sister, Emma, will definitely want to know. She lives out towards Ham on Mill Lane doesn't she?" Tom, who was by now becoming choked with grief, quietly replied, "aye, let them all know, tell them, tell them all. And don't forget to tell them that the service is at eleven o'clock in the church tomorrow." Before Tom had finished speaking Mrs. Richardson had gone, she could be heard shouting back from half way down the lane, "night Tom, night. I'll see you tomorrow." her voice faded into the distance.

Tom was now left to the silence of the night, a tear ran gradually down his face as he stopped rocking, he looked down at Jesse, and cried, "This is your fault, all your fault." He stumbled forwards out of the rocker and onto his knees, he then bent over and placed the child on the cold cobble stones of the front yard, he got up, turned around and slowly walked back inside the cottage leaving the child where it lay. By now the tears were streaming down his face, he snapped at the boys, "get to bed!" The boys scurried across the room to the corner of the cottage where they slept on a small pile of straw and some old wheat sacks. Tom then slowly lay on top of the bed and cuddled the mutton cold body of his wife. He continued to sob and whimper late into the night, eventually dropping off to sleep in the early hours of the morning.

"Henry, Henry! Are you awake?" whispered Charlie. There was no response from Henry so Charlie got up and slowly creped across the room towards the door. Charlie managed to open the door without disturbing his father, he peered down the yard and there was the little bundle of rags in the middle of the yard. Charlie knew that the child was still alive because he could see the breath coming from the bundle, Charlie shudder with the cold as he began tip toeing down the yard towards the baby. He picked up the bundle and started back up the yard towards the door with the bundle closely held to his chest. As he reached the door, he looked up to find the doorway blocked by his father. Charlie said nervously, "we've got to bring the baby in dad. It'll die out here dad." there was a moment's silence. Then Tom turned and return to the death bed of his wife. Charlie returned to the corner of the room where he found Henry still sound asleep on a small pile of straw. He'd pulled a couple of sacks over his shoulders for warmth. Charlie carefully pushed Henry over a little without waking him and placed Jesse down on the warm straw where Henry had been laid. He then laid himself down beside Jesse and whispered, "Hello baby." He then pulled a sack over himself and slowly closed his eyes.

It was a long night and dawn seemed exceptionally quiet and was full of mist when it did finally arrive. Tom sat up on the end of the bed, he looked towards the children who were huddled together in the corner of the room and shouted, "Charlie! Henry! Get up." There was very little movement from the boys, but slowly they began to move. Tom picked up his old shoe and threw it straight at the boys. "Come on, move yourselves." he ranted. "You, Charlie, go and fetch Percilla from the big house. Henry, you get some wood and light the fire." ordered Tom as Charlie got up quickly and asked, "what about the baby dad?" "Put him at the bottom of the bed. Come on, move yourselves." Tom replied. Charlie then pushed back his hair, placed Jesse on the bed and left by the front door. Out in the yard the intense morning sun was just beginning to smash through the dawn's mist. Charlie squinted to find the gate, he stood for a moment, the gate came into focus he then quickly walked across the yard and out through the gate. He turned left quickly and set off down the lane, past the church and through Shalbourne towards the big house. The big house was actually the Manor House which was owned by Mr. and Mrs. Newman and lay about two miles the otherside of the village in a place called Six Acres. The Newman's had been kind to the family in all kinds of ways but mainly their kind act of offering Percilla, Charlie's older sister, a position as a scullery maid. The wages weren't a lot, but it brought in money for the family to live on, without it the family would have surely starved or even worse been forced to enter the workhouse.

Charlie arrived at the gates of the house and began to walk on the grass towards the house which could be seen, in the distance. Then suddenly there was a shout from behind a large tree, "hoi... you...! Get off my grass." The shout startled Charlie at first then he realized it was Bill the old gardener. Bill was a cheerful soul who often shared fruits from the trees with the local children. Bill walked towards Charlie and said, "oh, it's you young Charlie. What are you doing walking on my grass?" Charlie was quick to reply, "The sharp gravel on the drive hurts my feet." Bill looked down to see Charlie's feet, which were by now bleeding from his walk across the village and were to say the least, absolutely filthy. "Dear God lad! We'd better get those feet sorted out before you go up to the house." said Bill. Bill took Charlie's hand and led him towards the potting shed, which was conveniently hidden behind the orchards. The shed was like a gardener's paradise.

Bill sat Charlie on his potting bench and gave him the largest plum Charlie had ever seen, "here lad, eat this." Bill said as he began to bathe Charlie's feet with some cold water from an old watering can he kept under his bench. After a while, Charlie's feet stop hurting and Bill put some fine linen around the left foot which had a particularly bad cut on the underside. Bill said, "Now listen here young Charlie, it is important you look after your feet. Otherwise

you'll be crippled for life." Charlie looked at Bill in the eye and slightly annoyed, he said, "how can I do that when I only have one pair of shoes, which I'm only allowed to wear on Sunday for church." Looking around the shed Bill said, "arr... here we are, just the job." he pulled out an old dusty pair of old brown boots from behind two chipped flower pots; he blew off some of the dust. "Give those a clean with that cloth over there," Bill said pointing. Charlie turned around and there beside him on the edge of the bench was a damp linen cloth. Charlie wiped the boots and started to put them on, but he was interrupted by Bill, "wrong feet Charlie!" Bill laughed and said, "Here lad, let me." Bill changed the boots over to the correct feet and fastened them tight. "How's that then?" "Fine," replied Charlie, "A bit big, but fine. Can I really keep them? Are they really mine, Bill?" asked Charlie. "Well they're actually young Master James's, but he has plenty of others. I don't think he will miss the odd pair."

Bill turned and walked towards the door, opening it, he said, "best be getting on now Charlie. I take it you're looking for your Percilla." Charlie nodded and replied, "Yes." He then quickly jumped down off the potting bench and thanked Bill once more for the boots before starting off towards the house. Charlie hadn't gone far when Bill shouted after him, "Charlie!" Charlie turned around, "remember to use the back door at the house. Don't go through the front, will you?" Charlie waved and said longingly, "I know!" Bill watched as Charlie headed towards the house and laughed to himself to see such a little chap wearing such large boots.

When Charlie got back to the drive, he attacked it by jumping straight into the middle of the sharp gravel. It was fun to walk on the gravel kicking it from side to side, first with the left boot and then with the right. Finally, Charlie arrived at the house, it was tall, black and seemed to leer at Charlie the nearer he got. The house had three layers of very large windows. Each window was made from six panes of real glass. Charlie walked past the front door which consisted of two solid oak doors each having a very large brass door handle and knocker, these doors were at the top of six stone steps and had two very large urns at either side of them. Has Charlie continued to walk around the house he peered up and down the building looking through every window, sometimes he would catch a shadow of a person moving inside, at least there are people living in the house, Charlie thought to himself has he turned the last corner of the house, he could now see the back door of the house which was half hidden. This was because the kitchens were below the ground level, and you had to go down a couple of steps into a small porch, before entering the kitchens. Charlie stood in the porch at the back door of the house, the porch was filled with the smell of baked bread and fried bacon. Charlie's mouth began to water at these smells.

To the right of the back door was a vertical line of small windows. Charlie pressed his nose up against one of the windows and peered in. Inside he could see his sister busily helping a rather fat cook prepare breakfast for those upstairs. Just then the door opened. Charlie was hit by a combination of heat from the kitchen ovens and a loud voice, which asked, "Well boy, what do you want?" Charlie struggled to answer at first, but after composing himself, he said, "If you please sir. I've come to take our Percilla home, dad wants her." The butler, who was still holding the door handle, looked across at the cook and then in anger, said, "just like that!" he continued, "she can't possibly leave now, she has chores to do. The Newman's are entertaining this evening and there is still much to do." The cook looked across at Charlie, who was by now

stood just inside the kitchen door. She saw the desperation on Charlie's face and realized that there must be something seriously wrong. In a very low kindly voice the cook asked, "How's your mum Charlie? Has she had the baby yet?" Charlie was shocked that the cook even knew that his mother was having a baby and was stunned into silence. His silence caught the attention of Percilla, "Charlie!" she said, trying to get Charlie's attention. "Charlie, what has happened? Is something wrong?" Percilla knew there was and put down the coal scuttle. She walked towards Charlie. The tears began to slowly run down Charlie's face. Percilla began to shake Charlie by the arms and again said, "Charlie, tell me, tell me what has happened?" Charlie then let out an almighty scream, "She's dead! She's dead!" He then fell to his knees sobbing uncontrollably. "Who is dead Charlie, is it mother? Tell me," asked Percilla as she pulled Charlie to his feet. "Yes. I think she is," he stuttered whilst wiping his runny nose on a dirty jacket sleeve.

There was a long pause, which was eventually broken by a door on the otherside of the kitchen being rattled opened and in walked a well dressed lady. She spoke well and asked, "What an earth is the matter?" she looked straight at the cook who curtsied and replied. "It looks as though Percilla's mother has passed away in child birth last evening ma'am. The boy has come to fetch Percilla home." Mrs. Newman moved forward towards Charlie, who was by now being cradled in Percilla's arms and was still sniffling. She tapped Charlie on the shoulder and said, "Is this true young man?" Still with his head buried in Percilla's chest Charlie nodded slowly. Mrs. Newman then quickly spun around and headed back towards the door saying, "Come with me. William, get Thomas to bring the coach to the front door, immediately."

Charlie and Percilla unlocked themselves and followed Mrs. Newman, who was by now bounding through the house towards a mirrored dresser at the end of the entrance hall. She hurriedly grabbed her bonnet and placed it on her head frantically tying it very tightly under her chin. Charlie stood looking up at Mrs. Newman's reflection in the mirror and thought to himself what a very kind face Mrs. Newman had. The pair made eye contact and Mrs. Newman smiled at Charlie. However, before leaving the mirror Mrs. Newman swayed from side to side a little, stuck in her hat pin and winked cheekily at Charlie before turning towards the front door, "come children." Mrs. Newman announced as the trio walked through the door and down the steps to where the coach was waiting on the gravel drive in front of the house. Looking up Mrs. Newman asked Thomas if he knew where Percilla's father lived. Thomas nodded and Mrs. Newman mounted the coach followed closely by Percilla. Charlie was a bit apprehensive at first because he had never been in a coach before. "Come on Charlie, climb up." Percilla said as she offered him her hand.

Charlie climbed aboard and trying not to stand on Mrs. Newman's skirts, he manoeuvred into the seat opposite her. Mrs. Newman then gave two swift knocks on the roof of the coach and off it went. Charlie watched through the window as the outside world passed by so quickly, he had never seen anything like this before, it was truly amazing thought Charlie. The coach crunch its way down the gravel drive and out on to the muddy lane where the sound change to a sloshing squelching sound. Through the village, they travelled and then the coach came to a sudden stop, there was a silence, Charlie could hear the coach driver jumping down from his perch. The door open, Mrs. Newman was the first to get up and carefully step down out of the coach. She slowly walked through the gate and up the yard towards the front door of the cottage. Before she could knock the door flew open and there stood Mrs. Richardson with Jesse in her arms, "is Tom home?" asked Mrs. Newman. Mrs. Richardson curtsied and replied, "No ma'am, he's taken his wife's body to the church with the rector ma'am."

By now Charlie and Percilla had gotten down from the coach and were beginning to follow Mrs. Newman into the yard, but Percilla before entering the yard glanced down the lane towards the church, and in the distance, she could see her father walking back from the church. She started to run towards him; the closer she got to him the more of his pain, she could feel. By the time both met the pain was so intense that they were both in floods of tears and all they could do was to hug each other. They held the pose for some considerable time, but eventually, Tom put Percilla down very slowly and asked if she was alright. She replied, "Yes, I'm fine." They then both turned and started to walk back up the lane towards the cottage. As they walked Tom explained to Percilla that she would have to return home and begin to look after the younger children because he had to work in the fields and get the crops sown ready for the next season.

Percilla, on hearing this became very agitated at the prospect of becoming the family skivvy and said, "It's impossible for me to return home father. You all depended so highly on my wages and for me to return home now would mean we would all starve!" "Nevertheless," Tom replied. "You'll have to come home." "Why!" Percilla said frustratingly, "all that would do is make matters worse. There'd be an extra mouth to feed at home and no wages coming in. How does that make sense?" Percilla looked at Tom hoping he would see reason and allow her to remain at the manor house. She begged Tom to allow her to stay, but to no avail. The nearer they got to the cottage the worse the conversation got with both Percilla and Tom beginning to lose their tempers, eventually they reached the cottage gate, which was just as well because by this time the conversation was beginning to turn into an argument and would have probably resulted in both of them falling out.

They both pushed their way through the gate and up the yard, where they found Mrs. Newman engaged in gossip with Mrs. Richardson on the previous night's events. Tom coughed and removed his cap. Mrs. Newman turned around and said, "ah Tom, sorry to hear about Hannah." "Yes ma'am, it was very sudden and so unexpected. One minute she was here. The next she was gone." Tom replied. Just then Percilla started to weep. Mrs. Newman put her hand under Percilla's chin and slowly lifted her head, "now child, don't take on so. Come on, stiff upper lip. You've got other things to think about now." Before Percilla could answer, Tom butted in and said, "She's not happy ma'am, because I have asked her to return home to help with the children." Mrs. Newman looked at Percilla and then asked, "But Tom, how will you manage without Percilla's wages?" "It's going to be difficult, but what choices do I have?" Mrs. Newman thought for a while and then said, "I could take your oldest lad and use him as a stable lad, it doesn't pay much, but at least you'll have some money coming in." Mrs. Newman then hesitated, she looked at Percilla and whilst smiling said, "then Percilla could visit him on Sundays." she winked at Percilla, who smiled back in delight.

Just then the gate swung open and into the yard came a procession of people all of whom were carrying baskets of one size or another. The baskets contain food, there was bread, eggs and butter and some of the baskets even had potatoes in them. The last person to enter the yard carrying a small casket of ale under one arm and the largest leg of pork you could ever imagine on his other shoulder was Will, Tom's brother. Will wasn't a clever chap, but what he lacked in brains he made up with brawn. Will worked hard on the local pig farm which could be smelt if you were down wind of him. However, he was a cheerful chap and putting his arm around Tom, said cheerfully, "come on brother let's have a flagon of ale." There was a pause, and then Tom replied, "Too early for me Will, later perhaps." Tom then walked towards the gate, removed his cap and began to say good bye to Mrs. Newman, but before he could Mrs. Newman said, "Right Tom, I'll be going. Send the lad over first thing Monday morning." "Right ma'am," Tom stuttered as he helped Mrs. Newman step aboard the coach. She then let out a shout, "home Thomas!"

The coach sped off down the lane towards the village and by now the whole family had gathered outside the gate to wave the coach off. They were all still waving as the coach passed the church and disappeared out of sight. Percilla

then said, "Henry, you can stop waving now, Mrs. Newman can't see you anymore." Henry was quick to reply, "I'm not waving at her. I'm waving at those other people coming up the lane." Percilla place her hand above her eyes and peered directly down the lane, she saw what looked like the whole of Shalbourne village approaching the  cottage. As the people began to get closer and their faces began to be seen, Tom, recognize some of them, and said, "Its only family coming to pay their respects." He looked directly at Percilla and said, "Get inside and tidy around before they arrive love." Percilla started up the yard, removing her coat as she went. She then disappeared through the cottage door into the darkness of the cottage.

Tom, Charles and Henry all stood by the gate waiting to greet the family, who had not only come from Shalbourne, but the surrounding villages as well. Tom had always said to the children, "that they would never want for family whilst they lived in this area." Never a truer statement was made by Tom because he himself came from a family of six boys and four girls, who were all born, raised and lived in Shalbourne or the nearby villages of Ham, Inkpen or Buttermere. Except for Will all Tom's siblings had married and had families of their own hence the reason for the crowd now descending on the little cottage. As the crowd of family began to arrive, Tom began shaking hands and welcoming people. Charlie and Henry looked on in amazement, they had never realized that they had so much unknown family who lived locally and what surprised the boys even more was that quite a few of these unknown family members knew Charlie and Henry by their names. Eventually, the boys recognized a familiar face in among the crowd, it was Grandad Joseph. Both Charlie and Henry ran towards their Grandad and both were lifted off the ground and spun around, whilst doing this Grandad Joseph rubbed his unshaven chin against the boy's faces, which tickled and always made the boys laugh. Tom saw the boys run into the family crowd and wondered what they were up to. He followed them into the crowd and saw the boys receiving this traditional hello from his father. "Now then Tom," his father said as he bent over to put the boys down. He quickly stood back up and walked straight towards Tom. The pair hugged as the boys looked on. Whilst hugging his father, Tom looked over his shoulder and saw his younger brother, Joseph. Tom quickly pulled away from his father's hug, "what's he doing here?" Tom asked his father angrily. "Now don't start. He's only come to pay his last respects Tom." Tom took five paces back from his father and with his index finger, he started pointing at Joseph and said, "the last thing I need right now is him gloating." Both Charlie and Henry moved quickly through the gate and into the yard. They both knew that when their father started to point a finger it was definitely a sign that he was angry and it was advisable to move or get ready to duck.

Charlie ran up the yard towards the front door shouting, "Percilla, Percilla, come quickly!" but Percilla didn't answer. Charlie looked around frantically, he started searching all the faces that were by now crammed into the yard, but he couldn't see Percilla's face among them. Then, suddenly, a small gap appeared in the crowd, he could just see a group of women stood next to the front door. They were huddled around the old rocker. He pushed past two or three of the women and then Mrs. Richardson, who was stood at the front of the huddle and there in the middle of the huddle, rocking backwards and forwards, was Percilla. She was sat on the rocker with Jesse in her arms. All the women that were stood around Percilla were cooing and giving comments to Percilla about Jesse, who he looked like, whose nose he had and so on. Charlie couldn't understand why girls always had to do this, but they always did when they met babies, even when they met them in the church. Christenings were the worse, thought Charlie as he grabbed hold of Percilla's arm. "Come quickly, come quickly, Percilla," Charlie said frantically. "Oh what is it now Charlie?" Percilla asked as she rocked forward and stood up. "Its dad, he's going to start," Charlie replied. "Start what?" Percilla growled. Charlie then quickly said, "He's pointing at Grandad and Uncle Joseph." with the mere mention of pointing Percilla handed Jesse to Mrs. Richardson and set off down the yard at such a pace. She practically knocked four people over as she pushed her way through the crowd to the front gate.

She looked out through the gateway and there in the lane was her Uncle Joseph and her father rolling around in the mud and raining blows down on each other, her Grandad was desperately trying to pull them apart. Henry, who was peeping around the corner of the gate, excitedly said to Charlie, "it's started. Uncle Joseph and dad are fighting." This attracted the attention of other family members who started to stream out off the yard and into the lane. Percilla grabbed her father's arm and pulled him up from the mud whilst her Grandad pulled Joseph away from Tom in a vain attempt to stop the fight. However, Tom's reflexes were fully charged by now, and as he tried to elbow himself free of Percilla's grip the elbow hit Percilla in the eye. Percilla was stunned by this. All she saw was a yellow flash and then the pain. She screamed and held both hands over her eye, Tom panicked, he turned quickly and went to see if Percilla was hurt badly, she was by now leaning against the yard wall, but Joseph had broken free from his father's grip, he rushed at Tom and then struck Tom with a swift left hook to the jaw. Tom never reached Percilla. He quickly turned back to face Joseph, put up a guard and started to move to his left. Joseph was also on guard and moving towards Tom. Just then, Will came through the gateway and into the lane. "Come on chaps, let's all cool down." he said as there was a pause. Both fighting brothers looked at Will, then each other, and then went back to fighting. Will, having seen enough, grabbed both his brothers by the scruff of the neck and physically pulled them apart, he then threw both to the ground, Will spoke a little louder this time and said, "I said, pack it in!" Tom quickly got to his feet and snarled at Will, who was not intimidated by the expression. Joseph had ended up on his backside in a muddy puddle and wasn't pleased by Will's interference. Will angrily told Joseph to leave, and then he turned to his father and said, "You know Tom and Joseph don't get along. You know they've both hated each other since they were children, so why bring Joseph here?" "Seemed like a good idea at the time." his father replied, who was picking the mud from his face whiskers. Joseph then got up from the puddle, spat out some muddy blood and said to Tom, "I'll be back, this isn't over." He then turned, picked up his cap and started off down the lane. Suddenly, there was a rustling sound of dress silk from the crowd, a young lady pushed her way through the crowd and ran down the lane after Joseph; she linked his arm and they both promptly marched off with their heads in the air. Tom wiped away the mud from his face and said, "Ok, come on everybody, back inside, there's nothing else to see." he started to herd the family back inside the yard.

The last four people to enter the yard were Emma, Hannah's sister, her husband, Albert, Hannah's mother and younger brother, Richard. All of whom were both shocked and astounded to say the least at the events they had just witnessed in the lane. Hannah's mother walked straight towards Tom and slapped his face, "you're a disgrace, and you've brought shame on this day. Your wife not yet cold and what do I find you doing, brawling in the street!" She then lifted her nose in an arrogant way and dissolved back into the crowd followed by the rest of Hannah's family. Tom walked straight across the yard towards the door his face beginning to turn red on one side from the slap he'd received.

Arriving inside the cottage Tom poured some cold water from a bucket into a bowl. He removed his shirt and then began to wash his arms and face free from the mud of the lane. The water immediately turned brown, Tom felt for the towel, which was hung on a nail at the side of the bowl, eventually he grasped the towel, pulled it off the nail and began to wipe away the water from his face. Has he lowered the towel down across his face, he looked towards the door of the cottage and there in the doorway silhouetted against the bright daylight were his children, "are you alright dad?" asked Percilla. "Yes lass." Tom replied, nodding his head at the same time. "It's time to go." said Percilla. Tom opened a cupboard and there inside was a white shirt, the one he wore to church on Sundays. He took his best collar from the bottom of the cupboard and put them on with the only bootlace tie he had. He walked towards the children took his jacket and cap from the wooden hooks by the door and said, "Ok children, let's go." He then put his hands on the shoulders of the boys and turned both around at the same time, they were now all facing towards the outside of the cottage. The trio started to walk out of the cottage closely followed by Percilla, who was nursing Jesse in her arms.

Tom and the children walked down the yard and out through the gate into the lane, they turned towards the church and waited for the rest of the family to line up behind them. Eventually, everybody was ready and they started to walk slowly towards the church. Outside the church, there were more people from the villages awaiting the entourage. Tom and the children walked through these villagers, nodding at the ones they knew. At the door of the church, the vicar stood waiting in anticipation of greeting his parishioners who

 were by now following Tom's family up the path towards the church. Tom arrived in front of the vicar. The vicar shook Tom's hand and said, "Welcome Tom, you are most welcome and so are your children."

Everyone entered the church and took their places in the church. The rector closed the doors and the service began. The service ended with the makeshift coffin being carried out of the church and into the graveyard where Tom had dug the grave the evening before. Everyone stood around the grave as the coffin was slowly lowered and the vicar said the appropriate words. People queued to throw a hand full of soil down into the grave, once this was done everyone started to leave the church and make their way back up the lane towards the cottage. However, Percilla had decided not to attend the internment of her mother and had started back up the lane after the church service. This was partly due to her arms, which were beginning to ache with holding Jesse through a long church service.

Jesse also needed feeding and was beginning to wake up for his feed. Percilla had gone about half way up the lane when she was over taken by three of the mourners. They were walking at such a pace; it could only be described as scurrying. Then two more passed Percilla doing exactly the same stupid walk. As she got nearer the cottage the pace of the mourners passing her seemed to be getting quicker. By the time Percilla had reached the yard gate, mourners were passing her in full flight, in fact, they were running so fast that two of them nearly knocked Jesse clean out of her arms they all seemed so desperate to pass Percilla, who re-composed herself before entered the yard, she was then struck dumb by the sight she received, there were the mourners stuffing their faces with as much of the food as possible. It was now obvious to Percilla why the mourners had been so rude when passing her, everybody was in the same predicament has her own family; they were struggling to survive and were also starving.

Tom, Charlie and Henry came into the yard and started to eat before the food had been divulged by the hungry hoards from the villages. Charlie chomping on a potato said, "Percilla aren't you eating?" Percilla replied, "No, I have to see to Jesse first." and with that, she went into the cottage. Henry and Charlie, who had notice people putting food into their clothing, decided to hide some of the food at the back of the cottage for later, experience had taught the boys to get what you can when you can.

Eventually, people began to leave; they said their goodbyes and gave their condolences to Tom and the boys before leaving. The afternoon started to enter the evening and Tom was sat in his old rocker at the side of the cottage door pondering on the day's events as the last of the mourners left. Charlie and Henry were playing with their favourite stones in the yard and Percilla came out from the cottage and said, "they've all gone then." both boys answered together, "Yes!" and continued playing with their stones. Percilla looked at her father; she could see he was struggling with the pain of the day's fight. She lifted his head and said, "Does that hurt?" pointing to the fat lip which was still bleeding from a split at the back of the lip. Tom replied, "Yes... what about your eye?" "Not bad." replied Percilla. "It'll be a right shiner tomorrow though." Percilla pressed the eye lid delicately before saying; "I'll get you a damp cloth for your lip." she went inside and brought out Tom a damp cloth which he pressed against his lip.

Percilla sat down at the side of her father and place another damp cloth on her eye to ease the swelling. Both looked at each other holding clothes to their faces and broke out into fits of laughter. It didn't improve matters when they started to speak of the day's events, they both laughed even louder when Percilla tried to mention, through her laughter, how people had nearly knocked Jesse from her arms has they raced back from the church to get at the food and the thought of how some of them were walking, scurrying, made Percilla laugh even louder. Tom begged Percilla to stop, "don't make me laugh anymore, it's too painful." but they continued to laugh and talk until the dusk began to arrive.

Eventually though, there was a pause in the laughter and conversation. Tom stood up and announced, "well..." he paused, stretched and threw the damp cloth into the corner of the yard, before saying, "Mrs. Richardson said when Jesse was born last evening that it had been a long and hard time for both mother and baby. She forgot to mention that it was going to be an even longer and harder time today for the father of the baby. And after today's events, I don't think anybody could have known how hard it was going to be. What with Joseph and me fighting. People pushing and shoving to get at the food, and then both our injuries, you losing your job and Charlie getting his job, and that's not even mentioning our loss of your dear mother, what a day!" Percilla then said, "Well if this is Jesse's first day in this world. It can only get better, I hope!" There was then a scream from inside the cottage. Percilla and Tom looked at each other and laughed. Tom put his arm around Percilla's shoulder and said, "And it sounds like Jesse going to have the last word of the day as well." They both laughed and went inside the cottage to attend to Jesse. Both boys followed and the door swung closed.

Chapter Two: A smelly day at school.

Tom died a year after Hannah. Some said of a broken heart, it was more likely to have been malnutrition, which left him vulnerable to disease. The reason for his death seemed immaterial to the children when they realized what was to become of them. They had been orphaned and left at the mercy of a landlord whose only thoughts were of yield and profits. This retch of a landlord evicted the children from their little cottage, because he could see that the strips of land lay un-ploughed and therefore, profit would not be forthcoming. The eviction made the children turn their backs on the past. They left all their childhood memories of both parent's and family life sealed up in that little cottage. Their destinies now would lie elsewhere with other family relatives and the memories of that little cottage would only come from painful anniversaries.

Five years passed and another painful anniversary of Hannah's death came around. Every year that went by the anniversary seemed to take more out of Percilla and the children. Even though the memories of their parents were beginning to fade the anniversary always acted like a constant reminder of what they once had, the love of their parents and home, the small cottage. This year would prove to be no different and getting ready for the visit to the grave for the children, especially Percilla, was always going to be very difficult. "Come on Charlie, get ready." Percilla told Charlie, who was sat on a small three legged milking stool in the kitchen. She continued with a desperate tone in her voice, "where's Henry and Jesse?" "They're in the back yard," replied Charlie. Percilla walked towards the old wash bowl and jug which was laid on a wooden table in front of the kitchen window, she leant over the table and peered out through one of six panes of glass in the kitchen window, she rubbed the pane with her hand to remove some of the grime but there was no-one to be seen in the yard. "No they're not, go and find them and be quick about it," snapped Percilla. Charlie jumped to his feet, opened the kitchen door and walked across the backyard towards the gate which was hanging

only by one hinge. Arriving at the gate, Charlie held his hand at the side of his mouth and let out a long lingering shout. Henree... Jessee...." He waited for a moment but there was no reply.

Percilla started to fill the wash bowl with water from the jug but there wasn't enough water in the jug to fill the bowl. Percilla "sighed" and thought, fetch and carry, fetch and carry, that's all I seem to do nowadays. She then set off towards the kitchen door with the jug to get some more water from the well outside the backyard gate. Before she had reached the kitchen door Percilla was stopped by her Uncle Albert, who had come into the kitchen for something to eat. "Where is everybody?" he bellowed, whilst biting on a piece of stale bread which he had taken from the kitchen cupboard. Percilla cringed and said, "They won't be long Uncle Albert. Our Charlie's just gone to fetch them." He then slowly moved closer to Percilla, so close she could feel his warm breath on her ear. He then whispered very quietly, "how are you then my pretty?" Whilst doing this, he slowly moved the back of his hand up and down Percilla's arm. Percilla pulled back quickly but Albert moved forward just as quick maintaining the closeness. He again leant forward towards Percilla's ear and again whispered, "There's a price to pay for everything in life, and you owe me four years rent." Her Uncle Albert's voice changed to a more sinister tone, "and how are you going to pay your dear old Uncle Albert?" he asked.

There was a pause, which was broken by Percilla's Aunt Emma entering the kitchen, Percilla's Uncle Albert pulled back quickly. He smiled, and then winked at Percilla. Just then Charlie entered the kitchen followed closely by Henry, "where's Jesse?" asked Percilla. "Don't know!" came back the answer from both Charlie and Henry at the same time. Emma tutted and said out loud, "that child will be the death of us all, he's never where he should be!" Just then there was a shout from the front of the house, "anybody in?" Emma looked at Albert and said, "That'll be our Richard with the cart to take us to the churchyard. Go and tell him to come in Bert."

Albert turned, walked out of the kitchen and back through the parlour towards the front door. The front door was slightly open and through the gap Albert could see the small garden and the gravel path which led to the front gate. He pushed his head through the gap in the door and shouted to Richard, who was sat on a small cart just outside the front gate in the lane. "You had better tie her up and come in. Jesse's gone missing again." "What again?" replied Richard unsurprisingly as he jumped down from the cart. He then pulled the rains forward and over the horse's head and loosely tied them to the front gatepost. Richard then stretched for a moment, looked around, and hurriedly followed Albert back through the house into the kitchen where the rest of the family was stood waiting patiently. Richard greeted them one at a time with a nod of his head and a short, "morning, morning." He then saw Percilla across the kitchen, he removed  his cap quickly and smiled lovingly straight at her. Percilla blushed and reluctantly smiled back, but she instantly dropped her head when her Uncle Albert noticed the greeting.

There was a moment of silence which was broken by Emma saying, "Well we can't just stand here all day waiting for Jesse. Bert, you'll have to take us to the churchyard in the cart. Richard you go and look for Jesse and we will meet you at the churchyard later when you find him." Richard replaced his cap and left by the back door to start looking for Jesse. The rest of the family left by the front door and began to board the cart. Albert assisted the younger children by lifting them straight into the cart. He gave Emma his hand, which she used to pull herself up onto the cart, finally, he made a very special effort to assist Percilla to board the cart, his touches were delicate but all in the wrong places, it turned Percilla's stomach as she took her seat in the back of the cart. Albert walked around to the front of the cart, grabbed the rains and in one swift movement, he pulled them off the front gatepost and over the horse's head. He then climbed onto the front of the cart and viciously cracked the rains over the horses back whilst shouting, "Go on then!" to the horse. The horse began to lean forward and slowly the cart started to move towards the churchyard.

They hadn't gone far from the house when Percilla realized she had left her flowers back at the house. She had picked them herself that morning for her parent's grave and had set them in water by the back door. She shouted, "Stop!" Albert, pulling on the rains, turned and said angrily, "what's the matter now? We're never going to reach the graveyard at this rate." "I've left my flowers back at the house." squealed Percilla. Her Aunt Emma calmly looked at Percilla and said, "go and get them, you'll have to try and catch up with us later." Percilla jumped down from the cart and set off back down the lane toward the house.

It wasn't long before the small cart had disappeared from sight and Percilla found herself walking alone. She could hear, in the distance, a lowing cow and the sounds of the birds were beginning to become the dominant sound in Percilla's ears, this had a relaxing effect on Percilla, her thoughts began to turn to what might have been if her parents had lived longer and what would she have been doing if she'd have stayed at the big house working for Mrs. Newman, but upper most in her thought were how she was now going to cope with the unwanted attentions of her Uncle Albert. Percilla sighed and glanced up for a moment, in the distance, she could just make out the house coming into view. Then, suddenly, there was a loud shout. Percilla's heart missed a beat. The shout seemed to come from behind a grey stone wall which lined the whole lane, "and where are you going?" The voice said as Richard popped up from behind the wall. A startling Percilla took a step backward for a moment but then the moment lengthened, as she realized it was Richard, her heart started to beat faster, and she could feel her face beginning to get warm.

"Oh it's only you Richard." she said, hoping that he hadn't spotted her blushes. Percilla then lifted her head, pulled back a loose hair and hung it over her ear, before starting to walk towards the house, her pace quickened. Richard had noticed Percilla's blushes from behind the wall, but being the gentleman he was, he had decided not to mention them for fear of making matters worse. He laughed to himself has he cleared the wall with one almighty leap, to think that he could have such an effect on anyone, let alone Percilla. Richard landed with both feet together in the middle of the lane and then he set off after Percilla at the jog. When Richard came alongside Percilla, he grabbed her gently by the elbow which had the effect of turning Percilla towards him. He then said, "I asked you a question! Where are you going?" Percilla turned back towards the house and replied, "Not that it is any of your business Richard Crips, but I've left the flowers for mum and dad's grave back at the house." Percilla shook her elbow loose from Richard's grip and continued to walk towards the house. Richard put both his hands in his trouser pockets and started to walk alongside Percilla, the couple began to chat has they both walked towards the house, they found that they had a lot in common.

Eventually, they reached the front gate of the house. "You wait here while I go and get the flowers." Percilla said as she walked down the path and disappeared into the house through a poorly painted front door. Richard remained by the front gate and was feeling pretty impressed with himself, he began to consider what he should do next. After a while, he decided that he would ask Percilla's Uncle Albert if he could walk out with Percilla and what's more, he thought, I'll do it today. Richard's attention was then diverted by a loud bang. "Ready!" said Percilla as she slammed the front door and walked sprightly down the path towards Richard, she smiled at him. "Are you going to walk me back up the lane to the churchyard?" asked Percilla, hoping that Richard would oblige. "Only has far as the fork in the lane. Then I must go into the village to see if I can find Jesse." They both turned and started off back up the lane. They began to chat again, only this time it was about Jesse and the things that he got up to. However, it wasn't long before the conversation turned to the things they wanted for themselves, and by this time Richard had plucked up enough courage to ask Percilla to walk out with him. Percilla was secretly overjoyed but didn't show it when Richard asked, she just began to blush. "I'll take that has a yes then." Richard said as he pulled a long piece of hair off Percilla's blushing face. Percilla nodded in agreement and both were content with the deal. The contentment was short lived, with Richard continued to say, "of course I will have to see your Uncle Albert first to make sure he's alright about us walking out." The mood changed quickly and Percilla broke out into a panic, "no, no, no!" she screamed. "You can't do that!" Richard turned to Percilla horrified and puzzled by this sudden change of mood. He looked her straight in the eye and said, "It's only right and proper Percilla. Albert won't mind, he's a good chap. It's the decent thing to do."

The tears began to form below Percilla's reddening eyes, she begged Richard, "Please don't ask Uncle Albert that. I beg of you, please don't." By now the couple had reached the fork in the lane. "Why? What's wrong?" asked Richard again, with a puzzled expression on his face. "There's nothing wrong," snapped Percilla. "But if you ask him. I'll never speak or see you again." she threatened. Percilla then pulled her shoal over her head and stomped off down the left fork towards the graveyard. Richard was so stunned by the change in Percilla's feelings towards him, that all he could do was to stand there at the fork in the lane looking helpless and alone. He had never seen anyone's mood change so quickly and thought to himself. Perhaps that's what the lads in the pub meant when they said, "Women, who can understand them?" Richard watched as Percilla disappeared out of sight, she didn't even wave he thought. He turned and slowly started to walk down the right fork towards Shalbourne in search of Jesse.

Percilla arrived at the graveyard. She was tired and weary from her walk. Her Uncle Albert was sat on the cart outside the graveyard smoking his pipe. She smiled reluctantly at him, and then walked past the cart into the graveyard. Inside the graveyard Percilla could see that the usual crowd of family relatives, on her father's side, had gathered. And as usual they were all stood around chatting about the usual boring items such as the weather, crop yields and the price of bread. Percilla began to look for the boys and her Auntie Emma among the crowd of relatives, who by now had formed a curtain of black across the graveyard. There was no sign of them, so she began to search the faces of the crowd in more detail, hoping to see at least her Auntie Emma's face among them. However, as she searched, she started thinking to herself. This family is getting bigger by the year. Who are all these people? She paused... and then started to answer her own questions by pointing a finger at people in the crowd, saying to herself, "well. There is Uncle Will and his new wife, Sarah. And there's Uncle George and his wife, Sarah. Oh and there's Uncle Henry and his wife." Again she paused... a little longer this time. She then continued to say to herself angrily, "well, how am I supposed to remember all their names. They all have similar names or the same name! I know for a fact we have at least four Sarah's in the family now and if that wasn't bad enough there were another three babies born into the family this year, and one of them has been christened Sarah."

Percilla decided to make her way through the crowd towards her parent's grave, this proved to be easier said than done, everytime she tried to pass a family member, they would stop her and ask how she was doing.

This would then be followed by other questions of insignificance. Eventually, she found herself just kissing cheeks and curtseying her way through the crowd towards the grave. This again proved to be easier said than done for Percilla because the family members she knew, she could just kiss them without any embarrassment or the warm feeling of the red flush that usually accompanied it. However, other nameless faces in the family crowd, who were not so familiar to Percilla, she found it very embarrassing to kiss them and had more than one warm red flush whilst making her way through the crowd. Eventually, she arrived at the graveside to find her Aunt Emma, who had just finished laying her flowers on the grave. "Oh there you are Percilla my dear, you made it then." Aunt Emma said with a handkerchief under her nose. "Yes." Percilla replied as her normal colour returned. "Have you seen Richard or Jesse?" Aunt Emma went on to ask Percilla. "No!" Percilla replied sternly as she began to kneel so that she could lay her by now withered flowers alongside the others that were already decorating the grave. Percilla placed her flowers on the grave, she straightened them and then spread them apart a little, while doing this, she glanced up at the headstone, it had the names of her parents chiselled on it, she then wished for them to be alive and well again and thought to herself, that all her troubles would be over if they had been with her now, but as she stood up, she knew that this would never be. Percilla paused for a moment... she looked again at her parents' names and then she turned away from the grave.

Just then Percilla's Aunt Emma, sensing something was wrong, said sympathetically with her head to one side, "have you been crying my dear?" but Percilla was very quick to reply and said, "no Aunt Emma! It's the wind; it always makes my eye's water." There was a silence and then the pair split up. Emma walked back to the cart and sat with Uncle Albert, Percilla walked towards her Uncle Will, who greeted her with his usual grin and said, "Hello love. How are you keeping?" but before Percilla could answer, she began to fill up. Will could see that Percilla was upset, so he stepped forward and put his arms around her, he then hugged her tightly saying, "never mind lass, come and tell your Uncle Will all about it." He gently gave Percilla a kiss on her by now wet cheek. Although it did not stop Percilla from crying, it made her feel someone cared, and it seemed to help her hold back some of her tears. Percilla blew her nose and began talking to her Uncle Will about what had happened that morning with Richard, she told him most of the story, but decided whilst telling the story to leave out certain facts, for example, when Richard had said he was going to approach her Uncle Albert over walking out with her and how she had lost her temper, if she had told Will these facts of the story, he might have started to ask some awkward questions about why she wouldn't let Richard approach Albert. She dare not risk Will finding out the real reason. This would have led to a family feud and Percilla knew from experience that family feuds could last for years.

At the end of the story Will grabbed Percilla's hand, and started to rub it between his own hands gently. He gave Percilla a very large smile, the smile change to a grin and then he said out loud, "so it's a love problem! No problem, you've come to the right man!" Will's new wife Sarah, who was stood next to Percilla and had said nothing until now, "tutted," and said, "The right man, uh." Will continue to say out loudly, "ignore her; the first thing I must do is to have a quiet word in young Richard's ear. He's forgotten the most important thing about walking out with any lass." Percilla asked, "Oh! And what's that Uncle Will?" expecting to hear some ridiculous answer from her Uncle Will. "What's that? What's that?" said Will, with a very serious tone in his voice. "He's forgotten to ask me!" barked Will. Percilla looked puzzled by this answer and asked, "Whatever do you mean?" "I'm the head of this family since your father died. Richard must come to me, the oldest, and ask properly, if he wants to walk out with you." Percilla was absolutely delighted by this answer and looked towards the gate where her Uncle Albert and Auntie Emma were sat on the cart, she then said to Will, "what about Uncle Albert?" "Nothing to do with him, he's only a member of this family by marriage and that's a distant marriage. He's not blood kin like we are." snapped Will. Percilla sighed with relief inside and began thinking of Richard, while she was doing this, she noticed her Uncle Albert talking to someone in front of the cart. Percilla couldn't hear what was being said, but she could see her Uncle Albert's lips moving, he had also removed his pipe. As she stood there watching, her curiosity began to get the better of her. Desperate to find out who Uncle Albert was talking to Percilla started to move position slowly so that she could see more of the lane through the gateway. Firstly, the horse started to come into view, then a man's shoulder, she continued to move and then the man's back started to appear, eventually she could see the whole man who

was patting the horse and holding the rains at the head end. It was Richard! Percilla's heart nearly stopped, she panicked. She hurriedly said, "Must go Uncle Will." She then turned to Sarah and said, again hurriedly, "nice meeting you." Percilla curtsied, spun around quickly and set off towards the gate. Percilla dare not run in the graveyard, no-one ever ran in the graveyard, it was seen by all as disrespectful and frowned upon, so instead she used the fastest pace she dared without drawing attention to herself. Will and Sarah watched as Percilla made her way through the crowded graveyard quickly towards the gate, they were a little stunned at first by Percilla's hasty departure, but when they saw that Richard was at the gate, they both nodded to each other and said together, "love, it makes people do silly things." They then laughed, linked arms and set off for a walk around the graveyard.

Percilla made herself known to Richard, who had not seen her approaching, by walking through the gateway of the graveyard and out into the lane. Richard removed his cap hastily to acknowledge Percilla's presence, but didn't look at Percilla. Instead he continued talking to Albert and Emma, "I've searched all around Shalbourne and most of Ham and Jesse is nowhere to be seen. I've checked all the usual places where he goes or where I think he goes, but there's no sign of him." "He must be somewhere!" said Percilla, butting in. "Yes, but where?" Aunt Emma asked sternly. "The problem we've got is that there are too many places for one person to search." Richard said, looking up at Albert, who was by now beginning to feel the pain from the cart's wooden seat. "Yes and it'll be dark in a couple of hours." Albert replied as he jumped down from the cart, he continued, "we will have to get the family out to look for him." Percilla quickly interrupted again and said, "There's enough family here to set up a search." Emma looked at Percilla, who was by now calming down, realizing that Richard had not mentioned the walking out to her Uncle Albert. "Ok Percilla, you go and explain to them what's going on and bring them all here to the gate?" said Emma.

Ten minutes later the family was roughly gathered around the graveyard gates. Percilla's Aunt Emma began to take control and started to bark out instructions. "Get into pairs." she said, fluttering in among the family. "Percilla, since Richard works on the canal you and him go towards the canal." Richard and Percilla looked at each other and hesitated. This surprised Emma who asked, "What's wrong? What are you waiting for? Get started." Richard, after a moment of ear ache from Emma, nodded reluctantly and started off down the lane towards the canal, he did this without Percilla. "Be back in an hour." Emma shouted as Percilla started to walk down the lane after Richard. Eventually, she caught up with him and they both walked side by side, not saying a word to each other, they were so silent that they could still hear Percilla's Aunt Emma organizing the family into pairs, even though they had gone some considerable distance from the graveyard gates.

"Charlie, you go with your Uncle Will and check towards Rivar." "I can't Auntie Emma." Charlie replied. "I promised Mrs. Newman I would be back at work before four o'clock." "Ok, Henry, you go." she snapped.

Henry kicked a loose stone on the lane and said, "It's always me, never Charlie." "Never mind our Henry, we will call at my house for a drink, it's on the way." said Will, trying to cheer Henry up a little. "Remember to be back in a hour." repeated Emma as she began organizing the next pair of searchers. Will and Henry set off up the lane towards Rivar, Henry was a little reluctant at first, but then he remembered what his father use to say, "You would never want for family whilst living in Shalbourne." He never really understood what his father meant by this, but whilst Jesse had been missing, he could see how the family had rallied to help search for him. No-one in the family had refused to join the search, in fact, more family from Shalbourne and Ham had heard that Jesse was missing and had come to the graveyard to join in the search.

An hour passed and the searching pairs began to arrive back at the graveyard gates none of them had Jesse; furthermore, none of them had seen sight nor sound of the lad. Will and Henry were amongst one of the last pairs to arrive back and both could see how distraught with worry Emma and Albert had become. Their faces were grey and every wrinkle was poised to be highlighted the longer the worry went on. Emma looked at Will and said very faintly, "any luck?" Will just shook his head and slapped his thigh with his cap. He then sat down on the grass verge at the side of the lane and Henry joined him. "It looks like our Jesse as disappeared off the face of the planet." said Henry. Just then Percilla and Richard appeared in the lane, they were linking arms. "Anyway our Percilla's here now. She might have found him, that's if she's had time." Henry said, whilst nudging Will. They both grinned at each other and then layed back on the grass, both were chewing on a stem of grass.

"Gather round everybody." Emma said loudly from the top of the cart. Will and Henry lifted their tired bodies from the grass verge and slowly moved towards the cart. Others also moved towards the cart, slowly groaning with tiredness as they did so. "I know you're all tired of looking, but we must continue the search until we find Jesse." begged Emma. Emma's begging was cut short by a loud bang and a rowdy commotion coming from the schoolroom of the church. All heads turned quickly towards the door of the schoolroom, the door opened, then it slammed closed, then opened again and finally it slammed closed. Eventually, a small leg appeared, then an arm. Screams of, "get off me, get off me!" followed and could be heard for miles. Then, suddenly, from the darkness of the schoolroom, the vicar appeared. He had Jesse by the ear. The struggling pair cleared the schoolroom door, the vicar then saw the crowd stood by the graveyard gates and started to pull Jesse down the church path towards the crowd. There were murmurs from the crowd as they realized who the vicar was pulling by the ear. "Well at least he his alright." chirped up Will who then began to laugh. Emma and Albert were not amused by the sight of Jesse being pulled by the vicar, indeed they were so embarrassed both were seen to cringe. The vicar, with gritted teeth, arrived at the graveyard gates with Jesse, who was still twisting and struggling to get loose, said to Albert angrily, "is this yours?" "Yes." Albert replied, grabbing Jesse by his other ear. He instantly began to pull Jesse towards the cart saying angrily, "I'll sort you out when we get home young man." He then literally lifted Jesse into the cart by his ear. Jesse sat down in the back of the cart and started to rub both his ears, which were by now red and very painful. However, he still managed to give Henry, who was stood next to the back of the cart, a wide mischievous grin and a little childish wave. The crowd of by now discontented relatives, knowing that Jesse was safe, began to dissipate, and as they did so, some of them could be heard saying such things as: "What a waste of time." "He needs sorting out that lad." And, "He needs a damn good hiding that lad, wasting everybody's time and effort." On hearing this Jesse sank further down into the cart, thinking he'd better stay out of sight.

Just then, because he couldn't stand not knowing any longer, Henry jumped up onto the cart and said to Jesse keenly, "go on then, where have you been our Jesse?" "I went to school." Jesse replied, still rubbing his ears. "School, you're too young to go to school." said Henry, who was shocked by Jesse's answer. "I know that, so I sneaked in and sat at the back." Jesse said whilst grinning. "No-one wants to go to school!" said Henry. "It's horrible!" Both lads laughed and then Jesse said, "I wanted to see what it was like before I had to go to the school for good. I don't think I like it." "Well hard luck, you don't have a choice, you have to go!" Henry said. He continued, "Anyway, what didn't you like about it?" "The vicar, if you know what I mean!" Jesse said, pulling both his ears out from the side of his head. This brought fits of laughter from both lads. However, they were quickly silenced when their Uncle Albert climbed onto the cart and said, "You two, shut up!" Thinking that the vicar might hear them, the three of them sat there in the cart as quiet as mice, the only sound that could be heard was Albert puffing on his pipe.

Eventually, Aunt Emma could be heard saying to the vicar, "Yes vicar, yes. I'll definitely do that vicar. Good day vicar and thank you once again vicar." she then came to the back of the cart and glared at Jesse, her face was like thunder as Albert helped her up onto the cart. He then looked around to see where Percilla was, she was sat on the grass verge holding Richard's hand whilst talking lovingly to him, "Percilla!" Her head turned quickly towards Albert, "come on, we're leaving now." he snapped. Percilla was quick to her feet as if anger had overtaken her senses, but then, she took a deep breath and said calmly, "you lot go on. Richard is going to walk me back to the house." "No he's not! Get in the cart." growled Uncle Albert. Just then Emma butted in; she could see that Percilla needed to be alone with Richard. "Bert," Emma said sternly, "leave them alone, let Richard walk Percilla back to the house if he wants to." Albert turned towards Emma, his teeth grinding in anger, "their doing nothing wrong." Emma said calmly. This seemed to put

Albert at ease and he stopped grinding his teeth. She continued, "And anyway, I can't be bothered to listen to you arguing right now. I'm tired and want to get back." Emma then slyly winked at Percilla and smiled. Percilla smiled back and lipped a big, "thank you." Albert, who had begun grumbling to himself, turned back towards the horse and said, "Go on then." He then violently shook the rains and glared at Richard as the cart set off back towards the house.

"So you want to go to school?" Aunt Emma said, looking directly at Jesse in the back of the cart. "No, I only wanted to try it out, but now I've seen it, I've decided not to bother." Jesse replied, looking a little sheepish. Albert and Henry laughed. "Will you listen to him." said Albert as Emma's tone changed. "Listen here young Jesse, you're going to school, like it or not. The vicar said if you're so keen you can start next Monday." Jesse just shrugged his shoulders, which started Henry grinning. "I don't know what you're grinning at. You've to look after him." Emma said smugly as she pulled her shoal up over her shoulders to keep out the evening chill. Henry's grin disappeared almost instantly as he thought. I've to look after him, some hope! The cart then rattled its way down the lane towards the little house called home.

Dawn broke over the small village of Shalbourne on the Monday that was going to be Jesse's first day at school, the old cockerel crowed, which woke Henry. He opened his eyes slowly and looked towards Jesse, who should have been sleeping on the pillow next to him. Henry sat up quickly and realizing that Jesse wasn't there, he leapt from the bed, ran out of the bedroom and down the thin staircase which led to the back kitchen shouting, "Auntie Em, Auntie Em." "Whatever's the matter Henry?" Emma asked, whilst wiping her hands on her apron. "Jesse's gone!" replied Henry gasping for breath. There was then a giggle from the corner of the kitchen. Henry's head turned quickly towards the sound and there in the corner of the kitchen, sat at the old table, was Jesse eating a large boiled egg with an even larger chunk of bread in his hand. Jesse, showing the yoke of the egg on his teeth, grinned and gave a little wave. Emma began to laugh and said, "no, he hasn't gone, he's here having his breakfast." She placed both her hands on Henry's face and said sympathetically, "don't worry so much Henry, it'll be alright. Now go and get dressed, then come and get some breakfast before school." Henry turned and headed back up the stairs towards the bedroom. Emma looked at Jesse and said, "Now Jesse!" she paused and sat down at the table opposite Jesse, and looking into his eyes, she said, "try to behave yourself today at school and don't give Henry a hard time, please...." she smiled and tweaked Jesse's nose. He stood up and said very sternly, "so long as he doesn't try to boss me about things should be alright, and don't you worry about Henry Aunt Emma. I'll look after him." and with that, Jesse stomped out of the kitchen and into the backyard. Emma raising her eyes to the ceiling and in exasperation, thought to herself, that school won't know what has hit it when that child arrives.

Jesse, who was by now pondering in the backyard as to whether or not he should wait for Henry, eventually, he decided that he would, so he sat down on the old wooden bench under the kitchen window and waited quietly for

Henry to appear. Twenty minutes later, Henry appeared at the back door and asked, "Are you ready then?" Jesse, annoyed, replied, "Am I ready? Am I ready?" He got up from the bench and said harshly, "come on, cheeky sod. Am I ready?" Both boys left the backyard. Jesse was still shaking his head in disgust at Henry's comment as they walked around the house and out into the lane. They began walking up the lane towards the church schoolroom. As they walked Henry began explaining all the rules of the school to Jesse, which person to stay away from and how to address the teachers. On and on Henry droned, Jesse didn't say anything, instead he thought to himself let him have his moment. It wasn't long before Jesse's mind began to wonder and Henry's words became oblivious to Jesse, "right then!" Henry said as they arrived at the schoolroom door. "When we go in you must sit at the front with the kids of your own age." "What for?" asked Jesse. "Because the youngest kids sit at the front and every year, in summer, you move back a row until you reach the back." "What happens then?" "They throw you out." snapped Henry. This started Jesse thinking, he thought if he didn't like the school all he would have to do is move to the back row, and they would throw him out thereby solving the problem of going to school.

Jesse entered the schoolroom a little apprehensively at first. It wasn't that he was frightened by the schoolroom, because he'd attended Sunday school there since being old enough to walk. The appearance of the room had changed though, there were now rows of desks, each with a stool, instead of the semi-circle of just stools, which were used for Sunday school. The room had always had an unusual smell which Jesse liked. The smell was a mixture of old wood, chalk and floor wax. The moment Jesse smelt it; he was reassured and began to select a desk to sit at. He decided almost immediately that the one nearest the door would do him just fine, and he promptly sat down and began to study the other students in the class. He hadn't been sat down long when he was nudged in the middle of his back and a voice said rather rudely, "you... move!" and again he was promptly nudged, but this time further up his back. Jesse turned around to see this spotty red haired lad stood there. "This is my desk." he said, but unfortunately, he said it so loudly it attracted the attention of the teacher, who had just entered the schoolroom through the door from the church, opposite where Jesse was sat. "Earle White!" she said very sternly. "Please, sit down, now!" "I can't miss, he's sat at my desk." whimpered Earle. "Use one of the other desks then." the teacher ordered Earle, who began, very slyly, to use his knee to put pressure on Jesse's thigh.

Jesse was adamant by this stage that he wasn't going to move, so with a little push, he managed to push Earle's knee off his thigh. "Earle White, will you use another desk, please!" the teacher pleaded with him again, whilst putting her hands on her hips. The words had only just left her lips when there was an almighty, "Whack!" Earle went spinning past Jesse and ended up on the floor between the desks. He began to cry instantly and was holding his ear as if it was about to drop off. Jesse lowered his chin below his shoulders as a very loud voice bellowed, "Do as you are told boy!" It was the vicar. He looked straight at the teacher and bellowed, "discipline Miss Coleman, discipline!

That's what these children need." He continued, "A good side ditherer always does the trick." The vicar then walked promptly to the back of the room where he sat down at a very large well polished desk and began writing. Earle dragged himself up from between the desks, he wiped away his tears using his sleeve and whilst rubbing his ear looked at Jesse with daggers, if looks could kill, then Jesse would have been Earle's victim right there and then. Jesse, not wanting to cause any more trouble decided instead to return a rather nervous smile, which he hoped would pacify Earle, but Earle was having none of it and from behind his new desk, which was two desks along in the same row as Jesse's desk, he raised a very tightly clinched fist, and with white knuckles showing, he shook it threateningly at Jesse and said, "just you wait until playtime." He then sat down and silently carried on rubbing his ear.

The two desks between Jesse and Earle were soon filled up by two rather scruffy looking kids. Jesse nodded at them and then he got a whiff of something different in the schoolroom, he sniffed up again, but he couldn't quite put his finger on what it was, he then realized where the smell was emanating from, because it had entered the room and his nostrils at the same time, it was when the two scruffy kids had passed him to gain access to their desks, but again Jesse decided not to mention it for fear of causing more trouble, instead he thought to himself, I'll stop sniffing up as often, and I'll take deeper breaths that should do the trick. But after a while the smell became un-noticeable and the boy who was sat nearest to Jesse said, "Hello, I'm Henry and this is my sister, Ann." Jesse was just about to introduce himself to Henry when he was stopped by Henry's sister, Ann. "You don't need to tell us who you are. We already know who you are!" Jesse looked amazed and puzzled by this, "you're Jesse, our troublesome cousin. Our dad said we should keep well away from you. Our dad said your nothing but trouble." Jesse was horrified to think he was related to these two smelly scruffy kids and quickly said, "I'm not related to you. I've never seen you before." "Well!" said Ann, "take a good look around this schoolroom." Jesse rotated his head slowly all the way around the schoolroom, he could see children of all sizes and ages, including Henry, his brother, who was sat four rows back, he gave a little waved to which Jesse smiled. Jesse then turned his head back towards Ann and said rather indifferently, "ok, so what?" "How many of them do you know?" she asked. "One!" replied Jesse quickly, thinking he'd outwitted her. "Oh, only one," Ann said condescendingly. She then said, "Well, for your information we are all cousins of one sort or another." Jesse sat there in disbelieve, he looked at Henry, who was by now grinning and nodding his head in agreement with Ann. Just then Miss Coleman said, "Attention front row." All four of them turned their heads towards the front of the schoolroom and gave the teacher their full attention until playtime.

The morning seemed to pass quickly for Jesse, and before he knew it, playtime had arrived. Miss Coleman suddenly stood up and clapped her hands. Everybody in the schoolroom stopped what they were doing and looked directly at her, she then announced, "playtime children." Instantly the children started to put things away. Eventually, when everything was in its place and everyone was sat at their desks facing the front of the schoolroom,

Miss Coleman started to slowly look around the room, checking to see if everybody was ready. When she was satisfied, she said, "stand!" Everybody stood up and waited for the next instruction, which was given directly to Jesse, "lead on Jesse." Miss Coleman said as she pointed to the schoolroom door. Jesse turned and marched out through the door into the schoolyard followed by Henry, Ann and Earle, who suddenly made a dash at Jesse. It wasn't much of a schoolyard scrap, with Jesse throwing a few wild punches, which missed the target. Earle didn't fare much better, only having one punch received by Jesse. Because the fight had started so quickly and was just outside the schoolroom door, the rest of the children piled out of the schoolroom door and surrounded both fighters quickly. They then began chanting, "Fight, fight!" whilst clapping their hands. This caught the attention of Miss Coleman, who fought her way through the children. She grabbed both battling lads by the ears and dragged them back inside the schoolroom, where she stood them at opposite ends of the room facing the wall. They stayed that way for the rest of the day until home time.

The years passed and Jesse started to make his way to the back of the schoolroom. By the time he had arrived on the fourth row of the schoolroom, Earle White had become his arch enemy after the schoolyard scrap on that eventful first day. Jesse's cousins, Henry and Ann, on the other hand, had become his inseparable schoolroom pals, despite the smell. It didn't really bother Jesse, but one day Henry thought he owed Jesse an explanation for the smell and said, "Its our father's fault, he makes us clean out the cow sheds every morning before school, its part of our daily chores." After this explanation from Henry, Jesse never mentioned the smell again and because Henry and Ann were his best friend's no-one else in the school ever mentioned the smell either... until one hot summer's day.

For Jesse, the day started like any other, he got up, had breakfast, then waited for Henry and when he was ready, they both set off up the lane towards the church and the little schoolroom. On the lane, as usual, Henry started blabbing on about school and his friends, what they were doing and who was doing what and as usual it bored Jesse, so he just switched off and retreated into his own little world as he usually did. It wasn't long before they arrived at the fork in the lane, there was a low thick mist covering the right fork, which went towards Shalbourne. Henry gave Jesse a hard nudge. This had the effect of bringing Jesse back to reality quickly, "what's the matter with you?" asked Jesse, rubbing his arm where Henry had just nudged him. "I'm going down into Shalbourne," said Henry, who was already beginning to leave Jesse at the fork. "Why?" asked Jesse. "None of your business!" came back the replied from an irritable Henry, "I'll see you later at school." Henry then walked towards Shalbourne and waved to Jesse as he disappeared into the mist. Jesse shrugged his shoulders and continued to walk down the left fork towards school.

The sun came up and started to warm the back of Jesse's neck as he walked along the lane, after a while the warm feeling began to make Jesse feel quite lethargic. He hadn't gone far when he decided that he would sit down and take a small rest at the side of the road. He started looking around for a comfortable place to sit. The grass verge seemed quite tempting, thought Jesse; it had lush green grass and a particular nice slope from the lane up to the grey stone wall which ran all the way along the lane to the schoolyard. The only other place Jesse could find was a flat slab which was perched on top of the wall. He tried to pull himself up onto the slab but gave it up at the first attempt. It was just too much of an effort so early in the morning, Jesse thought. Instead, he decided on the grass verge. He promptly sat down on the grass verge with his feet in the lane and then slowly he layed back, as soon as his head touched the grass, he started to dream. After a while, he found himself beginning to sniff up, he thought to himself, that's a familiar smell. It reminded him of Henry and Ann, he hastily lifted his head off the grass and looked around thinking, perhaps it was Henry and Ann, who had sneaked up on him without him knowing. There was no sign of them, so he gently dropped his head back onto the grass, and continued with his dreaming. His dreaming didn't last long before it was again interrupted by the same horrible smell, this time Jesse sat bolt upright and said, bluffing, "ok! I know you are there, so you'd better show yourselves." Thinking this would frighten Henry and Ann into appearing. He waited for several silent moments, and then realized they weren't there after all and that the smell must be emanating from something else. Whatever it was, it must be very close by, thought Jesse. He continued to look around, still wondering where the smell was coming from. He started to sniff the air first to his right and then to his left, then to the front, and finally behind him, just then the stench hit Jesse and began filling his nostrils, "oh what a stink!" Jesse said out loud. There it was, the smell, it was behind him on the otherside of the wall.

Jesse jumped up from the grass verge immediately. Then, whilst rubbing the back of his trousers free from loose grass, he turned around and scrambled up the grass verge, arriving at the top of the verge, Jesse leant forward against the wall, and peered over the top, which he could just manage if he stood on his tip toes. There just behind the wall in the field was a steaming pile of cow muck and urine, which was fermenting in the warm morning sun. He stood there for a second thinking to himself how much the pile of cow muck smelt like Henry and Ann. This gave Jesse an idea and as everybody knows when Jesse got an idea, it generally meant trouble, not for Jesse, but usually some other poor sod who innocently got in the way. Jesse always seemed to be the one looking on and laughing. In a flash Jesse tore off a piece of his shirt sleeve, just a thin small strip, so if Auntie Emma asked, "why his shirt sleeve was torn?" he could always say, "he needed a handkerchief." She didn't mind if he tore his shirts for, "respectable items" such as handkerchiefs. He once cut his finger badly and needed a bandage. A bandage according to his Auntie Emma is also a, "respectable item". Jesse then climbed over the wall and into the field and whilst holding his nose, he walked up to the large pile of fermenting cow muck and dipped the small strip of his shirt sleeve into the wettest part of the pile. He did this several times making sure that the strip was completely covered with the smelliest cow muck and urine. He then climbed back over the wall, still clinching the smelly strip in his left hand tightly so that none of its smell would escape. Once back on the lane Jesse ran like the wind towards the schoolroom, he got there before anyone else.

The whole place was quiet, this suited Jesse's idea. He quietly walked towards the schoolroom door and then took a moment to catch his breath. He then slyly looked around, and began opening the door very slowly. He stopped when the gap was just wide enough for him to slide his head into the room. He looked around and saw that the room was empty. He then opened the door further and quickly slithered inside. Quickly, Jesse tip toed across to Earle White's desk and tucked the strip of smelly shirt sleeve, out of sight, under his desk.

Just then Jesse heard voices coming from the schoolroom door, the door shook a little and Jesse could see the shadows of the vicar and Miss Coleman on the frosted glass windows of the door. Jesse quickly got down between the desks and waited, he then noticed the door leading into the church was open and without hesitation, he was through it and into the church, he closed the door behind him and walked down the central isle of the church towards the main doors at the bottom end of the church. The doors were made of solid oak and had large brass handles located high in them. The brass handles were difficult to use and had to be gripped tightly in order to turn them. Jesse

reached up with his left hand to open the door, and as he did so the smell of cow muck returned quickly to his nostrils. He moved the hand rapidly to his nose and sniffed, the smell was horrendous. Jesse began to panic, realizing that if anyone else smelt the cow muck on him, he would be in serious trouble and his idea would back fire on him. He looked around to see if he could find anything, which would remove the stench from his hand. He then remembered the hand pump in the churchyard, "that'll do" he said to himself. He opened the door slightly and peered out in the direction of the hand pump and there, leant against the pump, was Earle,

"damn!" Jesse whispered to himself quietly. He closed the door quickly before Earle saw him. He stood there with his back pressed against the door, and then, right in front of him, the answer appeared, the font. Jesse looked at it and then gave a rather large grin as he removed the wooden lid.

Just then the school bell rang and everybody formed straight lines in the schoolyard. Miss Coleman, who was stood by the schoolroom door holding the bell in her hand, was looking piercingly at the lines to see if they were absolutely straights and that no-one, was talking. Some lines weren't straight enough, so she started marching up and down the lines pushing and pulling students into line. When she'd finished, she again looked carefully up and down the lines and decided that they were straight enough to be let into the schoolroom. She then, in a very high pitched voice, shouted, "Quiet!"

everybody froze and there were several silent moments, after which Miss Coleman gave the first line, which was nearest the door, the signal to enter the schoolroom. The lines began entering the schoolroom, each line tagging itself onto the last one. Jesse, who was by now, watching from just inside the church doors had decided to hang back and wait for Miss Coleman to go into the schoolroom. She did this after the second line had entered the schoolroom. Jesse then ran across the schoolyard and joined the back of the last line. He was still wiping the last of the font water off his hands on the back of his trousers as he entered the schoolroom, and with a final sniff of his hands, he took his stool on the end of the fourth row and looked towards the front of the class where Miss Coleman, was by now stood looking straight at him. She had a suspicious look on her face, which made Jesse feel guilty. He quickly lowered his head and looked towards Henry, who was sat next to him. This sheepish movement only served to confirm to Miss Coleman that Jesse had been up to something, she didn't know what, but thought, I'm going to keep my eye on that one today, she then laced her handkerchief with lavender.

The class began to settle down and the heat of the day began to make itself known. It wasn't warm, it was hot! And as the morning wore on the aroma in the schoolroom began to get particularly pungent due to the heat. Miss Coleman once more placed lavender in her handkerchief to camouflage the horrible smell which was circulating the schoolroom. Eventually, she couldn't stand the smell any longer and screeched, "My God! I can't stand this stench any longer." She opened the door and two small windows in the schoolroom to let some fresh air in. "It's those two miss, they stink!" said Earle, whilst grinning and looking at Jesse, but pointing in the direction of Henry and Ann. "That's it, I'm fed up with this smell everyday, so, all of you lot from the fourth row forward are going to have a wash, right now! Furthermore, from this day forwards, we are going to have washing sessions ever morning before school starts," said Miss Coleman, sniffing on her lavender filled handkerchief. Instantly, everyone turned their heads towards Henry and Ann and glared angrily at them. Henry glared back and then said to Ann, "Aren't we going to be the popular ones." Jesse, who was by now getting worried about Henry and Ann, tried to show a little solidarity by standing at the side of Henry, he then announced out loud, "it won't hurt any of you to have a wash!" "It's not healthy." Came back a furious reply from the middle of the room; Jesse looked around frantically to see if he could identify the replier, he suspected it had been Earle, but couldn't be sure. He then looked at Henry and said, "It doesn't seem to matter what I say or do, the rest of the school are going to blame you and Ann for causing them to have a wash every morning." He began to feel guilty about placing the smelly shirt sleeve under Earle's desk and was just about to come clean to Miss Coleman when Earle stood up and pointed straight at Henry and Ann and said, "Why do we all have to wash Miss? When it's quite obvious it's those two who are the problem, they stink!"

The statement received rapturous applause from the class, but annoyed Jesse. Earle could see the annoyance on Jesse's face and was just about to add insult to injury when Miss Coleman clapped her hands and shouted,

30

"Jesse, Earle, Henry and Ann follow me, please!" she then promptly walked towards the schoolroom door, but before opening it, she turned and said to the boys, "boys bring that old table." She pointed to an old table at the side of the schoolroom which was only used to stack chalk boards on. Miss Coleman then opened the schoolroom door and said, "Take it outside and put it at the side of the hand pump." She continued, "Ann, get the metal bowls from the back of the room, rows one, two and three outside in straight lines please." Together the rows stood up and in single file, they filed out of the schoolroom and into the mid-day sun which was by now beaming down on the schoolyard. The rows formed straight lines in the schoolyard, and not a single smile could be seen among the dirty little faces which were in these lines. Instead, the little faces were creased with worry about getting washed and catching, what their parents had always warned them against, "their death of cold!"

The sun was beginning to warm the children who were all stood in the schoolyard like a military band. Suddenly, they were all distracted by a clanking sound coming from the old table. It was Ann placing four metal bowls down on the old table. Each metal bowl seemed to make its own little note, which reverberated across the schoolyard as it was placed down firmly on the old table by Ann. She then filled them with water using a jug which was kept at the side of the hand pump. After she'd finished, she walked across the yard and joined the fourth line where Earle, Henry and Jesse were all stood silently waiting for more instructions from Miss Coleman. "Right, row four get washed!" Earle pushed Henry forward who intern pushed Jesse towards the old table, Ann tagged along at the back looking very uncomfortable with what was about to happen, "the rest of you lot form a queue behind Ann." Miss Coleman said, whilst looking towards Jesse, who had just finished washing his face, which consisted of a quick flick of the water from the bowl using both his hands. Earle followed him and did much the same thing. "Stop, come here you two!" Miss Coleman screamed across the yard. Jesse turned and wiping his face on his shirt, said, "What!" Earle laughed and both walked across to where Miss Coleman was stood with her hands on her hips. "Call that a wash!" she said angrily. This made both boys laugh again, which really annoyed Miss Coleman, she angrily grabbed them both quickly by the ear and led them back to the table. Pushing her way to the front of the queue, Miss Coleman said, "Take off your shirts and use the soap this time." Others in the queue began to remove their shirt quickly, fearing that they would be the next to have their ears tugged.

It was sometime before everybody in the class had finished washing to the standard expected by Miss Coleman, but eventually everybody began to enter the schoolroom where the lessons started in vain. The sun began beaming into the schoolroom through the opened windows and landing on Earle's desk, Jesse thought he'd seen a wisp of smoke come from under the desk but then dismissed it because he'd been looking directly at the sun which usually made him see funny things. Miss Coleman was busy writing on the blackboard, which ran along the front of the schoolroom, when she suddenly stopped, her head lifted up slightly, and she gave a little sniff. Jesse nudged Henry and pointed with his head towards Miss Coleman. Who was by now sniffing every corner of the room, eventually she stopped at Earle's desk and said, "You! I might have guessed. Get up!" "What?" asked Earle angrily as he got to his feet quickly, Miss Coleman leant forwards over the desk towards Earle and gave a long lingering sniff, "it's you who smells!" she said to Earle. Earle started to open his mouth to speak but was cut off by some rather sharp words from Miss Coleman. "Don't bother trying to blame other people!" she stomped towards the door, opened it and then turned to Earle and said loudly across the room, "outside! Ann, bring the scrubbing brush." Ann scurried to the cupboard and took out a very hard scrubbing brush which was used to scrub the schoolroom steps. She handed the brush to Miss Coleman, who followed Earle out into the schoolyard. The whole class rushed towards the windows eager to see what was going to happen. They all, some on tip toe, peeped over the window sills to see Earle and Miss Coleman walking towards the old table. At the table Miss Coleman took the scrubbing brush and began to rub soap onto it, "remove your shirt!" she said. "I'll get rid of the smell if it's the last thing I do!" she then started to scrub Earle vigorously with the brush. Earle screamed the moment the brush touched his freckled white skin, which turned redder with every sweep of the brush.

Jesse, realizing that everybody was looking the other way, took full advantage of the situation and removed the smelly shirt sleeve quickly from under Earle's desk; he then even managed to drop it out through the window where he had stood to watch Earle getting scrubbed. However, as Earle and Miss Coleman started to walk back towards the schoolroom, Jesse thought it would be better if he returned to his desk and not draw any unwanted attention to himself. He was just about to sit down when the door opened and everybody at the windows quickly returned to their desks, Earle entered the schoolroom first, he was bright red all over, in fact, you couldn't see where his face ended and his red hair started. This brought fits of laughter from the children, who were quickly silenced by Miss Coleman entering the schoolroom. She then walked to the front of the schoolroom, clapped her hands and said, "Home time children." Everybody rushed towards the door, all except Earle, who was sulking and still stinging from his scrub wash.

"See you tomorrow." Ann and Henry said to Jesse as they walked out through the school gates. Jesse returned a quick, "See ya." He then leant against the gates and watched as Ann and Henry walked away down the lane towards the fork. Suddenly, from behind Jesse, came, "are you ready?" it was Henry. Jesse spun around and replied, "Yes! And where did you get to this morning?" Henry didn't answer. Instead he just started walking towards home and said, "Come on." The journey home was quite uneventful. Neither boy said much to each other. Jesse did, however, show Henry the pile of cow muck, he'd used to soak the shirt sleeve in that morning, but Henry wasn't interested, his mind seemed to be elsewhere. The boys past the fork in the road and could just see their Auntie Emma's house, in the distance. As they began to approach the house they could see figures outside the house by the gate. "Is that our Charlie?" asked Jesse, walking a little faster. "It looks like him and that looks like our Percilla sat down on the step." Henry replied. "Something must be up." Jesse said, as they continued to walk even faster towards the house.

Eventually, Henry and Jesse arrived at the front gate of the house. They could see immediately that Percilla had been crying. "What's up our Charlie?" asked Henry, looking straight at Charlie, who was shaking his head. "Its Uncle Albert, he's dead!" replied Charlie. Jesse suddenly spoke up and said, "How did it happen? Were you there Percilla when it happened?" Percilla said nothing; she just kept staring into space. Jesse, because Percilla had not answered him, started to speak a little louder, "I'm talking to you!" he said leaning forward and nudged Percilla quite hard on her shoulder with the flat of his hand. This made Percilla jump up quickly, she screamed, "Yes! Yes! I was there. I was paying the bloody rent if you must know!" she then pushed her way through Henry and Charlie and sped off down the lane. Jesse looking very confused by Percilla's answer turned to Henry and Charlie and said, "What does she mean, paying the rent?" "Shut up our Jesse." They both replied together. There was a pause...

Chapter Three: Learning a Trade.

A couple of days later Percilla and Richard had decided to become engaged but decided to postpone the announcement following the un-timely death of her Uncle Albert, "Perhaps after the funeral," Percilla said to Richard, who just nodded in agreement. Meanwhile Aunt Emma had decided to call a family meeting in the front parlour, to discuss how the family was going to live. Apart from Charlie's half crown a week, Uncle Albert had been the only wage earner in the family, that's if you can call six shillings a week as a barge hand, a wage. The house also belonged to the canal company who Albert had worked for, so there was no rent to find. Everyone had gathered in the front parlour of the house, Aunt Emma stood up and began the meeting by saying, "Well I'm afraid we'll all have to work for our keep from this day forwards, including you Jesse, so there'll be no more schooling for you." Jesse smiled and gave a little cheer inside at the thought of never having to go to school again, he then asked enthusiastically, "What's to be done Aunt Emma?" Emma thought for a moment and then said, "There's nothing else for it, we'll all have to go to the Hiring Fair at Newbury and seek some sort of work." Jesse got more excited and quickly asked, "When can we go there then Aunt Emma? Can we go tomorrow?" Emma replied, "No, it all as to be arranged first. I need to speak to our Richard to find out when the next fair is and whether or not he can take us in the cart?"

There was a brief silence in the room and Emma took the moment to look around at each person in turn, instantaneously she could see that Henry was

the only person in the room that wasn't happy about going to the fair, "Henry!" Emma said sharply. Henry lifted his head slowly and gave Emma a false smile, before saying apprehensively, "Yes, Auntie Emma." "You don't need to come to the fair because you're going to have to replace Bert on the barges. That so we can continue living in this house. Neither do you Charlie, you're working. So neither of you has to worry about going to the fair, just keep sending the half crown a week Charlie." Charlie nodded and then grinned at Henry, which seemed to perk Henry up a bit. Just then there was a knock on the door, Emma walked slowly towards the door fearing what was on the otherside, she slowly opened the door. There on the front step stood two men in long greatcoats and top hats, both the greatcoats had, "NBP" and a number embossed in silver thread on their collars, "Hello ma'am, Newbury Borough Police, we've come about your husband's death." The first man said, whilst using a rather large knobbly stick to give Emma a salute to the brim of his hat. "You'd better come in then." Emma said rather nervously to both men. Everybody in the parlour instantly got up and without being asked, filed out into the kitchen. Percilla, being the last to leave, tried to reassure her auntie by saying, "Shall I stay Auntie Emma?" Emma replied, "No dear. I'll be alright. You take care of the boys."

The silence in the kitchen could have been cut with a knife as twitching ears tried to pick out the faint words of the conversation being held in the front parlour. The conversation went on for some considerable time, then, suddenly, there was a brief silence from the parlour, which was followed by the slamming of the front door as the officers left, everybody quickly rushed back into the parlour, where they found Emma sat in the large wooden arm chair, she was in floods of tears, "Whatever's the matter Auntie Emma?" Asked Charlie as he sat down opposite Emma, who slowly looked up and said from beneath her tears, which were by now beginning to drip off the end of her cheeks, "It would appear that your Uncle Albert didn't die of a heart attack, instead, they think he was poisoned." Gasps of astonishment came from around the room at this shock announcement. However, Jesse had noticed that Henry had gone exceptionally quiet again and hadn't gasped along with the others at the shock announcement. He then remembered how Henry had disappeared the day Uncle Albert had been found dead and thought to himself, I've just got to speak to our Henry on his own. He continued to watch Henry, who was by now sat on the arm of the chair with his arm around Emma's shoulder, "Never mind Auntie Emma." Henry said rather nervously. He then continued petting Emma for a moment before saying, "You've still got us." He paused for a moment, and then suspiciously asked, "Did the police say anything else about Uncle Albert's death?" "Yes, their coming back to interview everybody after the post-mortem has been completed. They said they will know more about how Bert died by then." Henry quickly became angry and said, "What, everybody, what the hell for?" But then, he suddenly realized that the others in the room were watching him and so quickly he changed the mood and quietly said, "Well I'm alright, I was with Jesse at school all day, wasn't I Jesse?" He looked straight at Jesse hoping to see some sign of agreement from Jesse, but Jesse was still deep in thought and just stood there doing and saying nothing. Henry repeated himself, only this time a lot louder, "Wasn't I Jesse!" the shout broke Jesse free from his thoughts, and he quickly replied, "Oh, yes our Henry, yes." He then pointed to the kitchen with his head and lipped, "You, now!" Both slowly headed towards the kitchen trying not to attract any more attention.

Henry entered the kitchen first and turned to greet Jesse with an abundance of words, "Just keep your mouth shut and everything will be alright." Henry said angrily, but quietly, so his Aunt Emma wouldn't hear, "What's going on?" Whispered Jesse, thinking by now that Henry had murdered Uncle Albert, "Never you mind just remember, if anyone asks I was with you at school all day, right!" Jesse nodded in agreement and they both returned to the parlour where Aunt Emma was saying, "At least we don't have to worry about paying for Bert's funeral. He was a member of the Burial Club. He must have accumulated quite a pretty penny by now." "You'll need it with the price of burials nowadays," said Charlie. "Who are you going to use?" asked Percilla. Emma began to become tearful again. She blew her nose and then replied, "The funeral directors in Shalbourne. I hear they're quite nice and reasonably priced." "What! Its £12 a throw there," said Charlie. However, seeing that his comment had upset his Auntie Emma even more, he continued quickly to try and correct the comment by saying, "But they do have a nice chapel of rest and the horse and coach are second to none." This brought a silence to the front parlour which was broken by Jesse saying, "Right, I'm off to bed."

Over the next few days not a lot happened around the house, Emma had spent most of her time grieving in the front parlour, where the curtains had been pulled on as a mark of respect and to let others know that the house was in mourning. Charlie had returned to the big house to continue working for the Newman's, although, he had been back twice to visit his Aunt Emma and on the second occasion the Newman's had sent flowers and their condolences with him. Jesse and Henry had spent most of their time mulling around in the backyard and were constantly being silenced by Percilla, and as usual, Jesse began to get bored with being told to do something quietly and not to make so much noise, so he decided that something must be done.

"This afternoon, I'm off," announced Jesse to Henry. "Off where?" Asked Henry as Jesse got up off the yard floor and started to pace up and down. "Anywhere is better than this." Jesse replied as he continued pacing. "Don't you start getting into trouble again," said Henry. He continued, "I know you when you're let loose." Jesse grinned; he stopped pacing and headed out of the yard gate. He walked around to the front of the house and into the lane. He was just about to set off up the lane, when a voice from the front garden said, "And where do you think you are going young man?" Jesse turned quickly and there in the front garden was Richard.

"Oh, it's about time you showed up, everybody has been waiting for you," said Jesse. "Been up to the smoke to do a little business, why have I missed anything?" Asked Richard, "I'll say," said Jesse, who was just about to tell Richard all about the events of the past week when the front door opened and out rushed Percilla. She ran straight towards Richard and jumped up into his arms, she gave Richard an enormous kiss on the lips and said, "It's terrible, they think Uncle Albert has been poisoned." "Who does?" Asked Richard quickly, "The police," Percilla replied as Richard began to put her down slowly onto the garden path. "What! Old Bert murdered, never." Richard removed his cap and sat down on the front door step. "Well I never," Richard said, shaking his head. He then looked up at Percilla and seeming very interested, asked, "Who do they think did it?" "They haven't said yet, but they're coming back to interview everybody in the family after the post-mortem." Percilla replied. Jesse then remembered about the Hiring Fair, and quickly blurted out, "When are you going to take us to the Hiring Fair?" "Hiring fair, what Hiring Fair?" Richard asked. Who was a bit bewildered and puzzled by Jesse's remark, "Oh, Auntie Emma wants you to take us all to a Hiring Fair to try and find some work," said Percilla, lifting Richard from the front step by his hand. "Come inside and Aunt Emma will explain everything," Percilla said excitedly.

It was dark inside the front parlour, very little could be seen with the curtains drawn. Emma, who was dressed in black, sat in her usual wooden arm chair which stood in the corner of the room. Percilla pushed Richard forward into the parlour where he stumbled over an old milking stool which Percilla usually sat on in the evenings, "Ouch, where are you Em?" He said squinting into the darkness of the room. "Over here," Emma replied. Percilla lit a candle which was stuck to the mantel piece with melted wax. The room instantly filled with light and Richard began to accustom his eyes to the yellow glow. "Oh, there you are." He said looking towards the corner of the room where Emma was sat bathed in the dull yellow light of the candle, which flickered in the draught from the empty fire place. Richards's eyes made contact with Emma's. She'd obviously been crying and was sat on the front edge of the chair with her handkerchief clinched tightly in her hands.

Richard walked straight across the parlour towards her. Emma stood up and they hugged each other tightly, "How are you?" He whispered softly in her ear as they hugged, "Oh, I'm alright, considering." Emma replied as she pushed Richard away from her. They both sat down, Richard then said, "Well this is a fine how you'd do." "I take it Percilla has told you what the police have said about Bert's death." "Yes, but I wouldn't worry too much about what they've said, it's just procedure," said Richard, trying to pacify Emma. He continued, "Anyway, what's this about the Hiring Fair?" "Oh, yes, I want you to drive us to the Hiring Fair next week on Martinmas," Emma said hesitantly. "Why? I could come and live here with you and Percilla. Then my wages will keep the family." Pleaded Richard, hoping that Emma would agree, but she didn't. Instead, she was quick to reply, "What a lockkeepers wage, that won't be enough to keep us all and you can't live here under the same roof as Percilla, it wouldn't be decent. What would people say? Anyway I still need a job to keep the boys when you and Percilla finally do get married." Richard rubbed his stubble put his cap back on and said, "Ok you win, I'll take you to the fair next week, but be warned, it's not what you think, there are a lot of rogues at these events and you don't always get what you want."

During the intervening week, the police had been back to say that the investigation into Albert's death was continuing. It was still hanging over the family on the morning of Martinmas. Richard had told Percilla, Jesse and Emma to be up early as Newbury was quite a distance, and they needed to set off early in order to get to the fair on time. This was no problem for Jesse, who was up at the crack of dawn. However, as usual Jesse became bored with waiting and his patients started to get the better of him, he decided to take a look outside, to see if he could see any sign of Richard coming down the lane. He stomped out through the front door, down the garden path and out through the gate into the lane. He then gazed longingly up the lane towards the fork. He hadn't been waiting long when he turned his head back towards the house, and shouted, "He's here now Aunt Emma." Jesse pointed up the lane at Richard, who had just come into view. Percilla hurriedly joined Jesse in the lane, and Emma shut the front door.

"Ready then," said Richard, jumping down from the cart and landing in front of Percilla. He then quickly gave Percilla a peck on the cheek and said, "All aboard then," and with that, Jesse, Percilla and Emma scrambled aboard the cart. Richard turned the cart around and was just about to head off back up the lane when the front door slammed and Henry came running down the garden path shouting, "Wait for me!" Richard pulled back on the rains and said, "I thought you weren't going to the fair." Emma butted in before Henry could answer, and said, "He's not!" Henry was stopped in his tracks by Emma's words and said, "Why can't I come?" "I need you to dig over the right side of the backyard and turn it into an allotment," ordered Emma. But seeing that Henry wasn't please by this order, she tried to appease him by saying, "We're going to need the extra food Henry." Henry nodded reluctantly and with his head down turned he walked slowly back up the path towards the front door, "See ya." He said, before disappearing back through the front door.

Richard cracked the rains and the cart set off down the lane on what was to be the first leg of the journey to Newbury. A silence came over the small cart as its occupants began to wonder about the fair, they all had different apprehensions about the fair, after all, none of them had ever attended a Hiring Fair before. Jesse broke the silence by saying to Richard, "What do we do at this fair then Richard?" "Well..." said Richard. "Basically everyone stands around chatting and wheeler dealing." Percilla then asked, "Yes but how do we get work from this fair?" Richard gave a sigh and took a sharp intake of breath before saying, "You lot will have to join the crowd and wait to be picked by a master." "Who are the masters?" Jesse asked. "Oh, you'll know the masters when you see one. They're the ones with the money and the posh clothes; you can't miss the masters," Richard said. He then asked the horse to trot on as time was passing and they had to arrive at the fair early enough to get picked for work. Richard also had a little surprise up his sleeve, which would take up sometime.

The little cart had gone about half way when Richard decided it was time for his little surprise, suddenly he announced loudly, "Here we are then, refreshments!" The announcement made Percilla jump. Richard laughed and then pulled out a basket from under the seat and with one hand, he held it aloft. At the same time, he pulled the cart to a halt, and jumped down off the cart with the basket still in his hand, happily he said, "Come on then you lot, breakfast." Richard headed for the nearest piece of green grass, everyone giggled and jumped down from the cart, they then followed Richard to the grass. Richard opened the basket to reveal slices of ham, some bread and a large jug of milk with some wooden beakers. As they sat there enjoying the treats of the basket the conversation soon came around once more to the Hiring Fair, "So, all we have to do then, is to stand there and wait for an offer of work." Percilla said to Richard, who was looking for a little reassurance, "Yes, but don't expect great money, the wages aren't too good for first timers," Richard replied.

38

This didn't seem to put anybody off, so Richard decided to tell them a little more about the fair, "You have to be very careful with these fairs." He hesitated, which gave time for the others to gather round and to come a little closer, "Whatever do you mean Richard?" asked Emma with a worried expression on her face. Richard thought a little longer and then said, "Well there's a strict regime which must be followed. You must let the regular servants go first. These people have been freed by their previous employers and have the right of the crowd. You will see them being freed by the Chief Constable." Richard stood up and continued to say, "All it means really is that the regulars get the first choice of any work." "How can we tell these regular servants?" Asked Percilla, "Oh that's easy, they all wear badges telling you what they are," said Richard. "Badges," everybody said together. "Yes, badges. Things like wisps of wool, which Sheppard's wear and whiplashes which Carter's wear. There all symbols of their jobs, you'll get use to it," said Richard. He then asked, "Has everyone finished? Because we have to get on," together Jesse and Emma replied, "Yes." They then got up from the grass, Percilla waited for Richard to extend her his hand, which he did. She then pulled herself up from the grass. They all walked back to the little cart and jumped aboard once more. Richard shouted to the horse, "Walk on then!"

And once more the cart started off along the lane towards Newbury on its final leg of the journey.

Arriving at the fair Richard pulled the cart over to the horse trough. He then tied up the horse whilst still allowing it to have a drink. After patting it on the neck he announced, "Well here we are then." He then dipped his neckerchief into the trough, wrung in out and tied it back around his neck. Emma stood up in the  cart and looked down the main street. All she could see was crowds of people who were filling the street from one end to the other, "My god, it's like a family occasion, there's that many people," said Emma whilst laughing. "Come on then, let's get in among it," said Richard, grabbing hold of Percilla's hand.

The four of them walked into the crowd and headed for the pub which was completely surrounded by people wearing very unusual clothing. Outside the pub, there was a desk; sat at the desk was a very stout man in a very posh black tunic. The tunic had two vertical rows of silver buttons and across the man's chest were medals, six in all, which shone brightly in the sunlight. At the back of the man were two other men who looked familiar to Jesse. He then realized that they were the officers investigating his Uncle Albert's death. Jesse tugged Richard's jacket and said, "Who's the fat posh guy sat at the desk?" Richard turned quickly and said, "Shhh... that's the chief constable Jesse. Everyone who wants work has to register with him." Jesse, Percilla and Emma stepped up to the desk.

"Come on then make your mark in the register and be quick about it," growled the chief constable. Jesse, Percilla and Emma hurriedly signed their names in a very large book that was laid flat on the desk, "That'll be 3d, a penny each," said the chief constable whilst looking at the book. "Oh, we can write, can we?" He said patronizingly. Jesse didn't retaliate; he just smiled politely and said, "Yes sir." He then cheekily gave the chief constable a salute, "Join that lot over there and wait to be picked," said the chief constable, grinning and pointing to a crowd of poor looking souls who were obviously very tired of waiting.

Jesse, Percilla and Emma started to walk towards the crowd when the chief constable said, "Wait a minute you lot." They all stopped and turned to look straight at the chief constable who was by now being whispered to by one of the other officers that had been stood behind him, "Madame, you are aware that there is an investigation going on into your husband's death?" The chief constable asked. Emma curtsied and replied, "Yes sir." After another whispered conversation with the officer, the chief constable said, "Then madam, you must let any master know that wants to employ you about the investigation. Do you understand madam?" Emma nodded and said, "Yes sir," she curtsied again and the chief constable then dismissed her with a flick of his hand. Emma didn't understand the hand signal and paused for a moment. The chief constable then patronizingly said, "Go on then madam; join the rest of them over there, quickly madam."

They had stood with the crowd for some considerable time when the chief constable stood up and said, "Right let's get started. Who's the first master?" A well dressed man appeared from the crowd and said, "I am sir." He then

 walked up to the desk and stood at the right side of the desk. "Call your first servant then," said the chief constable. The master then shouted the name of his servant and out from the crowd came another man dressed in a very fine smock, his shoes were very highly polished, on his right shoulder was a wisp of wool, the servant removed his top hat and stood to attention in front of the desk. The chief constable then asked the master a question. "Do you want to release this servant?" To which the master answered, "No sir," and with that, the master placed a penny on the desk. The servant in front of the desk smiled, nodded his head and then turned before walking back into the crowd whilst replacing his top hat. This went on for some considerable time with the master calling his servants in turn and each time when asked the question, he would answer, "No sir." Then he would place another penny on the table. Eventually, the master called a servant who was a tall, thin young lad, who wore no badge and wasn't especially that well turned out. The lad stood in front of the desk and the chief constable then asked the question. "Do you want to release this servant?" And this time the master said, "Yes sir." This time the master didn't move nor did he put down a penny on the desk, he just stood there whilst the young lad stepped forward and placed two old pennies of his own on the desk. The chief constable then gave the lad a piece of paper saying, "Here is your release certificate, don't lose it, you'll need it."

The lad nodded, picked up the certificate, and then sarcastically smiled at both the master and the chief constable. He didn't say anything; he just came and stood at the side of Jesse. "What's going on Richard?" Asked Jesse, who was looking a little worried, "It's alright Jesse, don't worry about it, everything is as it should be. The master by the desk over there has re-employed all his servants for another year, all except the lad stood next to you. He has been released by the master to find work elsewhere." Jesse was still a little bemused by what was going on and all sorts of questions began entering Jesse's head rapidly, the longer Jesse watched the goings on, the more questions entered his head.

The fair dragged on all morning with masters excepting and releasing servants. Jesse had managed after watching the process all morning to figure out what was going on, and he'd managed to answer most of the questions that had entered his head earlier. Richard, with a grin on his face, asked, "Do you understand it yet Jesse?" "Yes, I think so," Jesse replied, who was still looking a little puzzled. Jesse thought for a moment and then asked, "How long do the servants have to work for the master Richard?" "They work for a year then they come back here to be re-employed or released." Jesse thought for a moment longer before asking, "But what if you want to be released before next year?" Just then the lad who was stood at the side of Jesse said, "Aye lad, that's the catch. You can't leave! If you do, and they catch ya, they'll put ya in prison." Jesse was aghast by this and said, "Is that right Richard?" "Yes, I'm afraid so, but don't let that worry you. You'll be alright." The lad then spoke up again and said, "Sure, you'll be alright! But just remember, a year is a long time, when the bastards who you are working for make you work twelve to fifteen hours a day in the fields. And they'll put a flail to your back if they see you slacking. They do of course allow you to go to church on Sunday's, so don't worry lad, you'll be alright!" He stopped speaking for a moment and then, trying to reassure Jesse, said, "It can be alright though, if you get good food, it's not too bad." Jesse smiled uncomfortably and looked at Percilla, who pulled him in towards her skirts and said, "Don't worry I'll be with you."

Just then a well dressed master in a top hat and velvet jacket prodded Emma with a straight crook, "Are you four looking for work?" He asked. Jesse, Percilla and Emma all answered, "Yes!" Together, but Richard replied, "Not me, I work on the canal locks, I'm a lockkeeper. It's just these three." The master looked Jesse up and down and said, "Turn around and let me see ya feet lad." Jesse asked suspiciously, "What for?" Emma butted in and said, "Now Jesse, don't be rude and do as the gentleman as asked." Jesse turned around and lifted his feet up by bending each knee in turn so the master could see the souls of his feet. The master rubbed his chin and said out loud, "Umm... I don't know. You're a little skinny for hard work. However, I suppose if I get you well shod with a good pair of boots, you'll do."

The master then looked at Percilla and said, "You'll do for the milking and cheese making. Now...," he said whilst moving onto Emma. "Can you cook and keep house woman?" Emma curtsied and said, "Yes sir, but if you please sir, we must inform you that my husband has just passed away and the police are still investigating his death." There was a moment silence and the master removed a snuff box from his waist coat pocket, he patted a line of snuff onto his hand and with one almighty sniff, it disappeared up his nostrils, "I'm not so much bothered about your past madam, but as to your future." He hesitated and then said, "So long as you didn't do for the man and I can sleep safely in my bed at night, things should be alright." Emma smiled and then said, "What wages will you pay sir?" "Three shillings for the lad and seven shillings for you and the girl per week, have we a deal madam?" Emma looked at Richard, who shrugged his shoulders and said, "What choice do you have?" Emma turned and replied to the master, "Yes sir, we have a deal." The master opened his hand, spat on it and offered it to Emma, who reluctantly did the same and the deal was struck. Just then Jesse's eyes caught a flash of red hair in the crowd and thought I know that hair. He tried to see more of the person who kept disappearing in and out of the crowd but eventually the person disappeared, even when Jesse had stood on his tip toes, he still couldn't see who it was. He was just about to give up, thinking his eyes were playing tricks on him when he heard a familiar voice.

"Hello Jesse," said Earle. Jesse couldn't believe it, of all the places to bump into Earle White it had to be the Hiring Fair, "What are you doing here?" Earle asked whilst looking around. "I might ask you the same question?" Said Jesse, "Oh, I'm here with my father, he's looking for some new servants to hire. Oh, there he is," Earle said, pointing towards the master, who Emma had just struck the deal with. Just then the master turned around and said, "There you are Earle, where's Amos?" "He's in the pub dad." Earle replied. Jesse was absolutely dumbfounded when he realized that the master was Earle's father. I can't believe this. I'm not going to work at the Whites Farm, he thought to himself. "Come here Earle, I want you to meet our new servants," said the master. Earle stepped forward and his father proudly said, "This is Mrs. Emma Miller and her niece and nephew, Percilla and Jesse. My youngest son, Earle madam," the master then, with both hands on Earle's shoulders, pushed him forward towards Emma, who curtsied and said. "Pleased, I'm sure." Earle turned, looked at Jesse and started to laugh, "You, working for us, that'll be right," Earle said, pointing at Jesse. "No, I'm not working for you," Jesse replied quickly. Emma was taken aback by Jesse's answer and asked, "Do you know Earle, Jesse?" "Yes, we went to the church school together and I'm not working for him," Jesse said, whose bottom lip had appeared. He then folded his arms and turned his back on Emma, whilst he sulked.

Emma grabbed Jesse and said, "Don't be so ungrateful." She shook Jesse hard, his arms instantly unfolded as he stood up straight. He quickly turned to face Emma, who was looking towards the master, hoping he hadn't heard Jesse. Luckily, the Master was out of ear shot. The last thing Emma wanted was for the master to change his mind. She then grabbed Jesse and pulled him to one side. Emma quickly whispered in Jesse's ear, "Behave yourself, the deal as been struck and Master White has gone to pay the three pennies for us to the chief constable, once that has been done your working for a year, like it or not." Jesse glared at Emma and with gritted teeth again said, "No... I'm not working for the Whites." He then looked towards Earle, who was enjoying every moment of seeing Jesse squirm. So to prevent Earle enjoying

42

the moment further, Jesse decided to agree, if only to stop Earle grinning he thought, so Jesse nodded albeit reluctantly. Earle was overjoyed by this and shouted, "Yippee," whilst clapping his hands and jumping up and down.

Meanwhile Master White returned and brought his son Amos with him. Jesse didn't like the look of Amos, he was a tall dangly chap, with a square chin and his hair was also bright red like Earle's, although it was beginning to thin on top a little. Amos, who had just been pulled out of the pub, seemed to like the sound of his own voice, and Jesse could tell instantly that he wasn't going to get along with him. "Now then, what have we got here then?" Amos said brazenly, as he wiped away the slaver from his chin, he had obviously rushed his last pint of ale. "These are our new servants," said Master White, he continued, "Mrs. Miller, this is my eldest son, Amos. And what he says goes, his word is my word. He's a good supervisor and you'll find him fair." "Got that lad," Amos snarled, as he leant over Jesse.

Jesse could smell the beer on Amos's breath and pushed him away so he could once again breathe fresh air, "Yes, our Amos will look after you Jesse. Won't you Amos?" Master White said whilst grinning. "Of course I will, I'll look after them all," Amos replied. He then burped, nipped Percilla on the bum and winked at Emma, Richard was not amused by this and started to walk towards Amos, but Amos had already disappeared back into the crowd and was making his way back towards the pub. "He doesn't get many days off," said Master White, trying to excuse Amos's behaviour to Emma, who nodded nervously and then said. "It's time we were all getting back. Can we start a week Monday sir?" "Yes, no problem, we'll see you all then," said Master White, as he put his arm around Earle and said. "Come on lad, it's time we started back as well." With that, everybody disappeared into the crowd in different directions.

It was a bitterly cold November morning and the White's farm was a good hour's walk from Jesse's Aunt Emma's house. Emma, Percilla and Jesse all wrapped up warm and said goodbye to Henry at the garden gate, who set off in the direction of the canal whilst blowing into his cold hands. Jesse, Percilla and Emma walked the opposite direction towards White's farm, Emma kept looking back to see if Henry had disappeared out of sight as they walked. However, this slowed everybody down and Jesse became annoyed, "Come on Aunt Emma, we don't want to be late on our first day. Remember, we all agreed to meet Master White and Amos in the farm yard at seven o'clock sharp," Jesse said, whilst pulling Emma on by the elbow. All three began to pace a little faster and arrived at the farm a little before seven. Jesse could see just by looking around that there hadn't been much work done that morning.

"Morning, be with you in a minute," said Master White as he came out of the farmhouse whilst shutting the door behind him and pulling his braces over his elbows and onto his shoulders. "Now Jesse, we've got to plough the top field. It's been laid fallow for sometime, have you ever ploughed before?" Jesse thought for a moment and then said, "I used to watch the farmer by Aunt Emma's house plough but never tried it. I was probably too young at the time and didn't pay much attention to what was happening." "Never mind, I'll get

Amos to show you. He's still in bed now, a few too many last night," said the master, trying not to show his embarrassment at Amos being still in bed and not there to welcome the new arrivals. The master then looked at Emma and Percilla and said, "Girls, you two go up to the field where the cows are and fetch them back for milking. They should have finished eating the stubble by now," the master pointed up a steep dirt track which led to the field. "Jesse you come with me and I'll introduce you to Titan."

Jesse and Master White walked across the farmyard to a very large barn. The master opened the left door and there in a pen was the largest Shire horse Jesse had ever seen, he gasped. "Aye he's a big'en," said Master White, as he threw a collar over the animal's neck. "Eighteen hands high and weights nearly a ton, he's won prizes has our Titan. Just watch his feet!" Jesse instantly looked down at the horse's feet and said, "Why? They look alright to me!" The Master could see Jesse was completely perplexed by what he'd said and replied, whilst grinning. "Oh, there's nothing wrong with them. Just don't let him stand on yours with his." He then nudged Jesse and they both laughed as the master turned Titan and all three of them started off towards the fallowed field.

They'd walked past a couple of fields when the master suddenly said, "Here we are then, hold these." He handed Jesse the rains and began opening the gate to the field. Inside the field was a plough, it was gleaming and ready for use. "Well at least our Amos has brought the plough up for you. Come on lad bring him in," said the master. Jesse pulled the horse forward and around to what he thought was the front of the plough, "this end lad!" Jesse, feeling a bit

of a fool, turned Titan around and took him to the other end of the plough. He then realized that Titan was too far forward to be hooked up to the plough. "How do I get him to go backwards?" Jesse pulled on the rains but the horse just stood there staring at him. Jesse could have sworn the animal looked as if it was laughing at him. "Come here lad," the master said, taking the rains from Jesse. He then put four fingers on

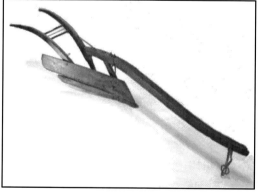

the nose of the horse and just pushed his head down and back. "He doesn't like that," the master told Jesse. Because the horse didn't like it, it started to move back without any trouble at all and with very little effort from the master.

It took a few minutes to get the plough ready for ploughing so Jesse took a seat on top of the wall, he was so engrossed watching the master get the plough ready he didn't notice Amos arriving. "What the hell are you doing?" Jesse looked around to see Amos stood right at the back of him. He had obviously just gotten out of bed, which side? Jesse was about to determine.

Amos clipped Jesse around the back of the head and said. "Leave it dad, we're paying this young bugger to do that, not sit on his backside watching." Jesse jumped down off the wall quickly and dusted his trousers off. He then waited for further instruction from either Amos or the Master. Amos grabbed the rains and said, "Come over here, eh, you." Jesse stood nearer, so he could see what was happening and said, "My names Jesse." "Oh, I… well watch." Amos started the horse and at the same time pushed the plough down into the earth, "See how it's done just keep it straight." Amos stopped the horse and said, "Here you are, it's all yours. Just keep the plough straight and level and the horse will do the rest, got it!" Jesse nodded reluctantly and took the rains from Amos; he then put them around his shoulders as Amos had done. Just then Amos noticed Jesse's feet and asked, "Have you no shoes lad?" Jesse replied, "No, never had any!" Just then Master White interrupted and said. "There's an old pair of our Earle's back at the house." "Okay dad, I'll fetch them up later," said Amos. He then looked at Jesse and said, "And you, get started on ploughing the first furrow, and for god sake lad. Keep it straight!" "No need for blasphemy our Amos," said the Master. A quiet, "sorry dad," came back from Amos, as he placed his hand over his mouth whilst grinning.

Jesse set off down the field, he didn't know if he was ploughing the field or the horse was, anyway he thought to himself at least we're going in the right direction. He then lifted his head to see how far the other end of the field was and to his surprise, he couldn't see the end of the field. By the time he eventually arrived at the end of the field his feet were beginning to bleed from the sharp stones being turned up by the plough. However, he was beginning to get the hang of it, or so he thought. He turned Titan at the end of the field and looked back up the furrow and thought to himself, that's not too bad, a little wonky in places perhaps, but not too bad for a first timer, he then closed one eye to see if it would improve the straightness of the furrow, "That won't make any difference," Earle said from behind the wall. "Call that straight and level, our Amos won't be pleased with that." "Earle White, I might have known you'd have something to say about it," said Jesse as he placed the rains once more onto his shoulders. Earle was just about to say something else when Jesse cut him off by saying, "Don't say another word. Get to school where you belong. Go on Titan." Jesse cracked the rains on Titans back and started off back up the field towards the gate. It seemed to take forever to reach the gate and Jesse's feet were getting worse with every step he took.

Eventually, Jesse could see the gate, and there sat on the top was Earle patiently waiting for Jesse to arrive. "Haven't you gone yet? I can't stand here talking all day with the likes of you. I've work to do, as you can see," Jesse said as he started to turn Titan. Earle replied, "Don't mind me, I'm sure." He then scratched the back of his neck, jumped down off the gate and set off for the schoolhouse. Jesse took a moment and walked out through the gate to see if he could see Amos bringing the shoes from the house. However, there was no-one to be seen between the house and him, he stared towards the house for sometime, but all he could see was the occasional glimpse of his Aunt Emma in the kitchen window, hopefully making breakfast, he thought.

Not wishing to appear lazy on his first day, Jesse decided he would continue ploughing. He looked down at his feet, and then he remembered he could tear pieces from his shirt, if it was for a good reason. He quickly tore off four pieces, two from each sleeve. He then bound them tightly around his feet and started to jump up and down, they tested alright, so Jesse pulled on the rains once more and again set off back down the field. He continued ploughing up and down the field for quite sometime. He couldn't quite remember if it was his eighth or ninth furrow he was ploughing, because by now he was concentrating more on his feet and the excruciating pain he was in, rather than counting the furrows. He had tried his best to ignore it, but it was slowly getting the better of him. He eventually turned Titan at the bottom of the field and was on his way back up the field towards the gate when he noticed Amos was waiting for him, hopefully with the shoes thought Jesse. Jesse eventually arrived at the gate and was feeling quite pleased with himself when Amos growled, "It's the worst ploughing I've ever seen lad. It's not level and do you call that straight?" He then pointed down a very wiggly furrow which Jesse had thought wasn't too bad.

"It's very difficult without shoes!" said Jesse, pointing to the blood stained rags wrapped around his feet. "I sent the shoes up with our Earle," said Amos, who was astonished to see that Jesse wasn't wearing them. "He never gave them to me," said Jesse who was beginning to sit down. "No, they're here behind the wall. He must have left them here for you." Amos threw the shoes towards Jesse and grinned. "Looks like our Earle's getting his own back on you lad, he told me he had a few old scores to settle with you." Angry and annoyed Jesse got up and grabbed the shoes. He began to put them on. The pain was excruciating as Jesse pushed on the shoes, but he didn't let Amos see that he was in pain, he just continued, with his back against the wall, to tie the shoes. Jesse did, however, think to himself, oh, he did, did he? Well I'll sort him out later. Amos watched as Jesse tied the shoes and said, "Well I'll leave you to it. Try and get the furrows next to each other, if you can and hold the plough level like I've shown you. Mind you, it's only for winter wheat, it's quite hardy stuff, it'll grow anywhere and in anything!"

Jesse nodded then stood up; he readied himself to start ploughing again. Amos watched for a moment then began to walk towards the farmhouse with a large grin on his face. The shoes were a little big, but at least Jesse's feet would be protected from the sharp stones. All day Jesse walked the plough up and down the field, the shoes began to rub at every step, each time Jesse took a step the shoes would rub a little more skin from his feet.

Eventually, dusk arrived and Jesse headed for the gate with Titan for the last time. Arriving at the gate Jesse unhooked Titan from the plough, all the time being acutely aware of what the master had said about Titan's feet, Jesse gave Titan a wide berth and more than a little bit of extra rain. The last thing I need right now, is for you to stand on my feet, thought Jesse, as he walked back down the track towards the farmhouse where Emma and Percilla were waiting. Jesse put Titan back in the barn and then joined Percilla and Emma for the journey home. All three, with weary and tired bodies, started the long trudge back to Aunt Emma's house, it had taken an hour that morning, and the evening's trudge had taken nearly two. This was partly due to Jesse having to keep stopping to rub his feet.

They arrived home to find the house in darkness and no sign of Henry. Percilla entered the house first and lit the candle on the mantel piece. Emma followed and Jesse hobbled in last. "Where's our Henry?" Jesse asked as he sat down in Aunt Emma's wooden arm chair. Emma replied, "It's unusual, I thought he'd be the first home, working nearer on the canal." Jesse then said, "He's probably gone down to Pewsey Wharf. There's always a queue coming back through Bruce Tunnel. Our Henry said that he's seen six barges waiting there to get through the tunnel. It's over 500 yards long. So I wouldn't worry. Anyway, what's for tea? I'm starving!" Emma and Percilla both replied together, "Kaile broth." "No, not cow fodder again," moaned Jesse who also had a disappointed look on his face. Percilla then verbally attacked Jesse saying, "You ungrateful little sod, you're lucky to get Kaile broth and it's good for you. Many

a child would be grateful for Kaile broth this time of the year." Jesse started gesturing with his mouth making a sound like a hen. He strutted up and down flapping his elbows whilst pushing his chin in and out. Percilla and Emma both laughed to see Jesse behaving like a chicken, but he quickly sat back down as his feet reminded him of his day's work, this made Emma and Percilla laugh even more.

"Come on fool, put your feet in here," Emma said, still smirking from Jesse's chicken imitation. She placed a tin bowl under Jesse's feet and began pouring warm water over them from the kettle which had been warmed on the hob. This made Jesse fall back into the chair. "Ahhh..." he said as the water flowed over his feet and began easing the pain. Emma then knelt down in front of Jesse and began to bathe his feet. She gently massaged each foot in turn, and then dried both feet together with a piece of old blanket. Jesse then put his feet down, one either side of the bowl. "Thanks, Auntie Emma," he said. Emma then gave Jesse's shins a nudge. This made Jesse automatically lift his feet, allowing Emma to push the bowl to one side. Jesse then placed his feet very gently back on the floor and Emma began binding them with strips of linen, which had been torn from the same blanket as the towel.

Eventually, Emma said, "There you go!" She clasped both of Jesse bandaged feet between her hands, "already for tomorrow, keep those bandages on tomorrow and the shoes won't be able to rub anymore skin off your feet." "Thanks again Aunt Emma," Jesse said as Emma began straining to get up from his feet. "I'm getting too old for this," Emma said as she slowly turned and walked towards the door with the bowl of now cold water clinched tightly between two hands. She opened the door and looked out. There was nothing to be seen beyond the garden gate but freezing pitch blackness. She paused for a moment, listened, but there was no sound of footsteps on the lane. Being disappointed, she threw the cold water onto the front garden, pulled her shawl over her shoulders, shuddered and returned to the parlour with the empty bowl. "Any sign?" Percilla asked as she returned from the kitchen precariously carrying a bowl of hot broth. Emma shook her head and said, "I can't see anything in that darkness out there, and its freezing." Percilla began to look worried, as she handed Jesse his broth.

The following morning Jesse turned over in bed. He half opened his eyes and looked straight across at Henry's un-disturbed bed. Jesse, still half asleep, then said to himself, "Perhaps our Henry's gone further than Pewsey Wharf? Maybe he's gone as far as Bristol? That'll take at least two days." He then went back to sleep and was awakened an hour later by the sound of voices coming from downstairs, he sat up in bed and anxiously opened his ears to listen. However, no matter how hard Jesse tried, he couldn't hear what was being said downstairs. Maybe it's our Henry getting told off by Auntie Emma, he thought. Then he made one of his decisions. I'll get nearer, so I can hear, he thought. Still in his night shirt, Jesse slowly crept across the bedroom and down the stair, making sure the boards didn't creek and hoping he would not disturb the voices who were talking.

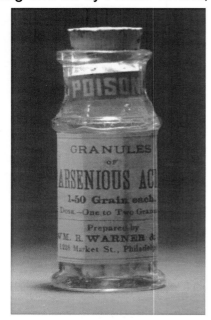

At the bottom of the stairs, he could hear his Auntie Emma's voice, but he didn't recognize the other two voices in the conversation, "Well madam. Henry as been arrested for the murder of your husband, he was arrested yesterday at his place of work. The post-mortem on your husband revealed that your husband was poisoned by arsenic. Inquiries have led us to believe that Henry was one of the persons involved. He was seen pinching the poison from the rat traps at the back of the shops in Shalbourne on the day your husband died," said a burly sergeant who was stood by the fire warming his backside. Stood at the side of the sergeant was a tall officer who continued to say, "We will of course need to speak to other family members about the day your husband died, including your brother, Richard. Do you know where he is?" Emma thought for a moment and then said, "He's probably at work on the locks at Caen Hill near Devizes, and that's where we should be, at work!" She then came to the bottom of the stairs and was just about to shout Jesse and Percilla when she realized, Jesse was already sat at the bottom of the stairs. Emma, who was startled for a moment said, "Go and get Percilla instead of giving me a fright sat there like that." Jesse laughed, turned and ran back up the stairs quickly, shouting, "Percilla, time to get up." He then went back into his own bedroom to get dressed.

The following few days dragged for Jesse as he continued to plough the field ready for the winter wheat. He had often, whilst ploughing the field, switched off and as usual entered his own little world of thought. He thought about Henry and how he was doing in jail, he thought about Richard and why the police wanted to see him. How could he be involved in the murder, when he told Jesse, he was away in London at the time of Albert's death? He'd also thought about Percilla, and what she had meant when she said. "Paying the bloody rent!" She nearly snapped his head off when he'd ask her about Albert's death that day on the front step. He was in the middle of all these thoughts when there was a sudden loud whack, the plough tried to jump out of the furrow, Jesse couldn't hold the plough, so he laid it down on to it side, whilst pulling Titan to a halt. He looked down at the plough. It appeared to be different somehow. Jesse scratched his head, stared down at the plough, and then he noticed that the plough blade was missing, he thought that's funny, where's the plough blade? He picked up the plough and moved it from side to side but couldn't see the blade anywhere. He was just about to give up looking, when a voice said, "Slacking again lad!" Jesse looked over his shoulder to see Amos approaching him quickly, "What's the matter now?" Amos asked angrily. "I can't find the plough blade," Jesse replied, a little half-heartedly. "Come here lad," Amos said, grabbing the plough out of Jesse's hands. He then pushed Jesse out of the way. Jesse thought this was rather rude of Amos but again remained silent. Amos then pushed the plough to one side and knelt down in the furrow where Jesse had just finished ploughing. He pushed his hands into the soil and pulled out a very bent blade. "You're supposed to plough around the boulders not through them." Amos cursed as he threw the blade at Jesse's feet. "That'll come out of your wages," Amos said as he stood up shaking his head. There was a moments silence and Amos picked up the blade and said, "Bring Titan and put him back in the barn. You're Aunt Emma and Percilla are waiting for you down at the house, you've all got to go to the police headquarters apparently."

Jesse walked back down the dirt track towards the farmhouse, his arms aching from ploughing and pulling Titan. Eventually, he arrived at the barn and put Titan in for the night making sure he had enough water and hay to last the night. He then closed the barn door and walked across the farmyard to the house. Jesse approached the door and knocked on it loudly. He then waited because he knew he wasn't allowed inside the house because of the mud from the fields on his shoes, which gets everywhere. A few seconds later his Aunt Emma answered the door and Jesse asked, "Are you ready then?" There was no reply from Emma. Jesse stared in through the doorway and could see Percilla sat with her long coat on waiting quietly on a small wooden chair, the door swung open to reveal his Aunt Emma pinning on her hat. Neither of them looked happy so Jesse tried to cheer them up a little by saying, "It's not that bad!" Suddenly, Percilla stood up and stomped quickly towards Jesse, "They've arrested Richard this morning," she screamed. No sooner were the words out of Percilla's mouth, when a constable appeared at the door of the parlour accompanied by Master White. "I'll expect them back tomorrow then, shall I?" "All being well sir," the officer replied, touching the rim of his top hat. "Come on then you lot," the officer said as he beckoned a path forward with his hand.

The group hadn't gone far, well in fact, they'd only just left the farmyard and were walking along the lane towards the police headquarters when Jesse suddenly said. "Why? Richard has got nothing to do with Uncle Albert's death. He was in London when Uncle Albert died, he told me so." "Nevertheless, they've arrested him this morning and we've got to go and answer some questions at the police headquarters, so stop moaning and let's get on," said Percilla.

The police headquarters were quite a distance and when the four of them arrived, they were pretty much exhausted by the walk. Emma suggested that the three of them should have a small break, to catch their breaths, before entering the police headquarters, she said, "It will help us to think before we answer any questions." The escorting officer agreed and said, "Okay, but not too long mind, the superintendent is waiting for you." He then pointed a bony finger at Emma and grinned. This had the instant effect of changing the worried expression on Emma's face to that of shear fear. The officer continued grinning has he removed his top hat and entered the police headquarters saying, "I'll let them know you are here." All three of them sat down at the side of the road in front of the police headquarters and said nothing, they waited in complete silence, each of them thinking about what was happening and what was about to happen.

After a while, Emma stood up and said, "Come on, let's get on with it. Let's get it over with and then we can all go home." She marched up the steps of the headquarters, the steps led to two swing doors. Emma pushed open one of the swing doors and walked into a small reception hall. At the far end of the reception hall stood a very tall, thin, black wooden desk, at the back of which stood a bulky little sergeant. On the desk, there was a very large opened ledger which the sergeant was peering into over his glasses. On one side of this reception hall, there was a sideboard, which was full of top hats and gloves. Jesse would have loved to have tried on a top hat, but decided to keep close to his Aunt Emma and Percilla, after all, he thought, I don't want to be arrested as well.

The sergeant lifted his head slowly, pushed his glasses up his nose and looked all three of them up and down, he then said, removing his glasses, "Sit over there!" He pointed to some wooden chairs on the opposite side of the room to the sideboard. He then turned and left by another set of swing doors, which were behind the desk. The silence was eerie and went on for sometime, Emma began tapping the chair arm with her finger nails and Jesse started to pace the reception hall floor whilst Percilla began reading all the notices, which were plastered around the walls of the reception hall.

Eventually, the sergeant returned, he didn't say anything; he just let the doors swing loosely behind him. This rattled the frosted glass as both doors thumped past each other. Eventually the door slowly swung closed and silent. The sergeant returned to the desk and once more an eerie silence overcame the little reception hall. After a few minutes, it seemed longer, a rather smart bearded officer appeared at the doors wearing a most unusual cap. His tunic was very long and black with a single vertical row of silver buttons running down the front of it. "This way madam," said the officer in a rather posh voice. He held open one of the swing doors and beckoned to Emma, who stood up  and walked towards the doors. At the same time Percilla and Jesse stood up and walked towards the doors. "Not you two," the bearded officer said, pointing at Percilla and Jesse, who quickly returned to their chairs. Emma continued towards the bearded officer, she curtsied and then walked straight past him and through the doors. Jesse, who was by now trying to see what was going on at the otherside of the door leant forward on his chair, he could see a long corridor at the otherside of the opened doors, but suddenly his view was terminated as the bearded officer let go of the door, and it swung shut.

The bearded officer quickly followed Emma down the corridor and said to Emma. "In here ma'am," pointing into a very small dimly lit room. Just inside the door of the room was stood the constable who had escorted Emma and the children to the headquarters. "Sit down please," said the bearded officer as he walked around the desk to the otherside. He then lifted his jacket and sat down with the jacket clear of his seat. Emma slowly sat down, composed herself and waited for the first question. "My name is Inspector Joseph Drewett. I am responsible for investigating the murder of your husband, Albert." He then opened a file, which had some different size papers inside it.

After rummaging amongst the papers for a moment, he asked Emma. "Was your husband unwell before he died?" But before Emma could answer another man entered the room. The Inspector stood up and said, "This is Superintendent Bennett, he oversees all inquiries taking place in and around Newbury." The superintendent nodded his head at Emma and pulled up a chair to sit down on, he then said, "Pray, continue Inspector Drewett."

The inspector cleared his throat and repeated the question. Emma thought for a moment, and then said, "Well he'd had headaches for sometime and was often very tired. However, he put that down to working hard on the barges. He'd also had the runs over the past few weeks and had been sick twice, he blamed me for that, saying, I was trying to poison him with my home made Kaile broth. However, it couldn't have been that, because we all had the Kaile broth. In fact, we had some last night. No-one has ever died from eating Kaile broth... have they?" There was a moment of silence followed by the inspector saying, "Quite, quite." The questions continued and Emma began to suspect that she was being observed by the superintendent. He hadn't said anything during the questioning. All he'd done was to sit there looking directly into

Emma's face, he'd watched every expression, sometimes he'd make a note in a little black book, which he'd pulled from an inside pocket of his jacket. Eventually, the inspector began asking questions about Albert's work and where he went during his work on the barges. "He went down as far as Pewsey Wharf quite regularly on the barges." Emma explained, "Anywhere else?" The inspectors asked, shrugging his shoulders, "Yes, he sometimes went down the canal as far as Bath, maybe Bristol, but very rare." Emma paused for a moment. Then enthusiastically she said, "Oh yes, recently Bert's company got a contract from Lord Pembroke's estate to deliver marble plinths for his new colonnade at Wilton House. Bert was so pleased that he'd actually met Lord Pembroke whilst delivering the plinths."

Emma suddenly stopped speaking as the superintendent quickly leant forward at the mention of Lord Pembroke's name and said, "Be careful madam whose name you involve in this affair." He then sat back and carried on observing. "What did the contract involved?" The inspector asked. "Bert's barge collected the marble plinths in London and took them to the bottom of Caen Hill Flight Locks, where they were loaded onto carts and taken to Wilton House at Salisbury," Emma replied. "How do you know this?" The inspector asked quickly, trying to catch Emma off guard. "How do I know? Bert did nothing else but moan about the weight of those bloody plinths. Day and night, he went on and on about them." The superintendent began to squirm on his chair and interrupted the proceedings by saying, "May I ask a question?" The inspector waved him on, he then turned and looked at Emma straight in the eye and said, "Did your husband ever meet your brother Richard on the canals during his work?" Emma smiled and said, "of course he did. Richard always had a cup of tea waiting for Bert at the locks. Everyday without fail, in fact, Bert used to say, it was a God send after travelling from London to the locks. He always looked forward to his cuppa tea at the lock with Richard." Emma paused, and then asked, "Why...?"

The inspector looked at the superintendent and said, "Well we believe that Richard was administering the arsenic to Albert in his tea at the locks. We have a number of witnesses who have seen Richard making the tea and have seen Richard and Albert sat drinking it at the side of the locks on various occasions." "Why would he do that?" Emma asked in disbelieve. "Richard won't say. We were hoping you might be able to shed some light on why?" "I've no idea." Emma replied. A silence came over the room, which was broken by the superintendent saying, "I think that'll be enough for now." Both the inspector and the superintendent began to get up, when Emma stopped them and asked, "What as Henry got to do with all this?" The inspector removed his cap, scratched his head and said, "Henry, we believe he was supplying Richard with the arsenic from various places, rat traps from farms and the like. Obviously, Henry wouldn't have look as suspicious as Richard hanging around Shalbourne where most of the arsenic was stolen from. However, we don't think Henry knew what Richard was using the arsenic for." Emma began to cry, her tears fell slowly at first, but then they began to stream as she removed a handkerchief from her skirt pocket, "Wait outside and we'll talk to Percilla next," said the inspector as he put his arm around Emma's shoulder. He then opened the door and walked Emma back up the corridor. He opened the swing doors and both Percilla and Jesse came to Emma's assistance, Emma struggled to reach the wooden chairs but with the assistance of Percilla and Jesse, she managed it, "You're next," said the inspector to Percilla.

Percilla let go of her Aunt Emma's hand quickly, she looked at Jesse and slowly moved towards the opened swing doors. The sergeant smiled reassuringly as Percilla passed the desk and through the swing doors to where the inspector was stood waiting in the corridor. "This way," he said as he started off down the corridor towards the small dimly lit room. Inside the room, the inspector sat down behind the desk and pointed a finger to the chair in front of the desk, "Sit there," he said. "This is Superintendent Bennett." "I'm the superintendent for the Newbury Borough. I oversee all crimes in the Newbury area," the superintendent said as he offered Percilla his hand. Percilla tried to shake hands, but she was shaking so much that she couldn't move her hand up and down. "Don't worry my dear you've done nothing wrong, just relax and answer our questions and everything will be alright," the superintendent said, trying to reassure Percilla. Percilla began to relax and started to answer the questions the best way she could. The questions started to become more intense and personnel, "How long have you lived with your auntie and uncle?" "Err… about…," Percilla didn't manage to answer the question before another question was blasted at her. "Do you like your Uncle Albert?" The room went silent. Percilla could feel herself beginning to blush. The mere mention of her Uncle Albert's name sent shivers down her spine. Both offices could see the reaction to the question and pursued it like a pair of grey hounds chasing a rabbit, "What sort of relationship did you have with your Uncle Albert?" Percilla just couldn't answer the question, instead, she clammed up and tears began to appear in her reddened eyes. The offices waited for a moment, so Percilla could compose herself, then the inspector said, "Percilla, please stand up." The superintendent looked at the inspector perplexed by this request, Percilla slowly stood up. "Open your coat please," the inspector said. Percilla began to sob even more as she slowly opened her coat to reveal a small bump in her stomach. "Are you pregnant?" The inspector asked Percilla softly, to which she replied, "Yes." Percilla collapsed into the chair, threw her arms onto the desk, she then laid her forehead on top of her arms and began to sob uncontrollably. "There's your motive," the inspector said loudly. "And I'll wager that Uncle Albert's the father." He continued to say feeling quite proud of his discovery. The superintendent turned to Percilla and asked, "Was your Uncle Albert the father of your child my dear." Percilla lifted her head slightly off of her arms and with tears still streaming down her red blotchy face; she looked up at the superintendent and slowly nodded her head. She then screamed in agony as her head returned to the top of her arms. The superintendent let Percilla weep for a moment longer. He then clicked his finger at the constable, who produced a white handkerchief, he then nudge Percilla who looked up and saw the handkerchief. She snatched the handkerchief from the constable and began wiping her eyes and nose, "Just a couple of more questions Percilla, then you can leave," said the superintendent.

There was a moment's silence. Then the superintendent asked, "Did you tell Richard about the baby and Uncle Albert?" Percilla was quick to answer, "Certainly not." Both officers gave each other a bemused look and as the inspector shrugged his shoulders he asked, "Are you quite sure Percilla. You never mentioned it to Richard!" Again Percilla denied telling Richard. "Does your Auntie Emma know about what's been going on?" Asked the superintendent, he looked straight at Percilla, watching her every reaction to the question. Percilla instantly sat up straight in the chair and screamed, "No, no, no, please don't tell my Auntie Em, she'll be heart broke." The superintendent looked at the inspector; they both got up and walked to the corner of the room, where they started to whisper to each other. On their return to the table, the inspector spoke in a more sensitive voice, "I'm sorry Percilla but your Auntie Emma will have to know sooner or later. I think its best that you tell her now." Percilla hesitated for a moment, and then reluctantly she nodded her head whilst blowing her nose. The inspector pulled out his pocket watch, checked the time and then turned to the constable, who had stood silently by the door throughout. "Fetch Mrs. Miller back down please." He said to the constable, who nodded his head and said, "Right away sir." The constable quickly opened the door and started off back up the corridor. On leaving the room, he'd left the door partially open, this enabled Percilla to hear every footstep as he walked back up the corridor, she heard the swing doors creak as the constable open them and then there was an incoherent mumbling, which was followed by the sound of two pairs of footsteps coming back down the corridor.

Eventually, the constable entered the room, followed by Emma. The noise of the swing doors could still be heard knocking against each other in the background as Emma sat down at the side of Percilla, the constable return to his position by the side of the room door. The swing doors eventually became silent and the constable closed the room door. The silence in the room could have been cut with a knife, it seemed to go on for an eternity, but eventually, Emma looked at Percilla, she knew instantly that there was something very seriously wrong. She waited for a moment, but then plucked up enough courage to ask Percilla, "What's wrong Percilla?" Percilla's head dropped quickly, her bottom lip began to quiver, and she began to weep. Percilla couldn't bring herself even to look at her Auntie Emma, let alone tell her what was wrong. All Percilla could do, was to keep repeating, "I'm sorry Aunt Em, I'm sorry Aunt Em." Emma shuffled around on her seat to face Percilla, she grabbed both of Percilla's hands and shook them a little, "Come on Percilla, what's wrong. You can tell me, whatever it is my dear." Percilla still couldn't bring herself to say what was wrong. She just sat there with her head bowed sobbing her heart out. This went on for sometime, but eventually, the inspector coughed, Percilla looked up at him, he then lipped to Percilla, "Go on." He nodded his head and winked to try and encourage Percilla to divulge what was wrong. Percilla nodded back to him, she gave a quick half smile and then sat straight up. She composed herself then wiped her nose again. The room went quiet and after taking a deep breath Percilla looked longingly at her Aunt Emma. She leant forward until her mouth was opposite Emma's ear; she then whispered the nasty secret that she had kept inside of her for five years, the secret that had ripped her life apart, and the secret that had ruined her relationship with Richard and now perhaps her relationship with her Aunt Emma.

Emma drew back quickly on hearing the secret, she glared at Percilla for a moment, and then Emma realized how hard the declaration of the secret must have been for Percilla. Emma's heart sank and then it melted. "Oh, my dear child, my dear, dear child," Emma pulled Percilla towards her and gave her a lingering kiss on the cheek. There was a tender moment as both hugged each other; it was interrupted by the superintendent saying, "Well we've enough evidence now to take the case forward." Emma and Percilla released their embrace quickly and turned to face the superintendent, "What do you mean?" Emma asked, "We now have enough evidence to charge Richard with the murder of your husband and Henry with accessory to murder." This had the effect of bringing both women to tears immediately, "Constable, can you show both ladies out," said the inspector as he lifted the file from the table. He then left with the superintendent close behind him.

"This way, if you please ladies," said the constable as he held out a hand to show the ladies out. Both Percilla and Emma held each other up as they walked back down the corridor towards the swing doors. They entered the reception hall where Jesse was sat waiting. Jesse stood up quickly and started to walk towards the swing doors. "About time too," he said as he started to walk through the doors. "Where are you going?" Jesse looked around to see the constable waving him back to his chair, "It's all over lad, and you won't be needed," the constable said. Jesse returned to his seat and said, "I never get to do anything." He crossed his arms in disgust and plonked himself down in the chair.

Just then the outside door opened and in walked Uncle Will closely followed by his wife, Sarah. Percilla instantly ran to Will, she threw her arms around him and said, "Oh, Uncle Will, it's been horrible." "Never mind lass, Uncle Will's here now." Emma looked at Will and asked, "How did you know we were here?" "I bumped into Amos White in The Plough; he told me you were here," replied Will. "I might have guessed he'd be in the pub," Emma said in disgust. Will then slowly pulled Percilla from around his neck and said, "You lot, outside. I've brought a cart to take you back home. I'll be out in a minute."

Sarah ushered Emma, Percilla and Jesse through the doors and down the front steps of the police station to the waiting cart. Will walked up to the desk and said, "What's happening Sergeant? I'm the head of the family and as you can imagine the rest of the family are also wondering what is happening?" The sergeant peered over his glasses at Will and said quietly, "I shouldn't really say." "But you will," said Will. The sergeant opened the swing door behind him and both men step through into the corridor. "In here," said the sergeant as he opened a small room door.

Fifteen minutes passed and Will came out of the small room shaking his head in disbelieve at what he had just heard. He walked back into the reception hall and out through the main entrance into the lane where everybody was sat in the cart waiting for him, "Come on Will, let's get the children home before they fall asleep," said Sarah. Will jumped up onto the cart and started the cart back towards Emma's house, he never said a word. The journey home was silent, no-one felt like talking and no-one did. Even when they arrived at the house no-one said anything, they just got down off the cart and walked straight into the house. Percilla lit the usual candle on the fire place in the parlour, Emma sighed as she sat down in the chair. Will entered the room and removed his cap before saying, whilst looking straight at Percilla, "Are you alright?" Percilla nodded her head and gave a false smile; she then said, "Yes, we'll be fine Uncle Will. Please just leave us." Will look towards Sarah, who had just entered the room with Jesse and said, "Ok love, we'll see you all later." He then used his head to direct Sarah towards the door. Jesse, who was stood by the front door, nodded his head to Will and Sarah as they left. He then closed the front door behind them.

Jesse walked towards Emma and said, "I'm hungry." "There's some bread and cheese in the kitchen and there might be a piece of turnip in the pantry if you're lucky," Emma replied, trying to pacify Jesse as he walked off into the kitchen. Jesse didn't have to think twice about what he was going to eat; he headed straight for the pantry and got the piece of turnip, that'll do me, he thought, as he crunched the first bite, "Right, I'm off to bed," Jesse shouted as he began to climb the stairs. "See you in the morning," he cried as he reached the top of the stairs. "Well at least someone in this house will sleep tonight," Percilla said to her Auntie Emma. "Yes, I don't think he realizes the full gravity of the situation, which is just as well perhaps," Emma replied. Percilla thought for a moment and then asked, "Why, what do you think will happen now?"

There was a long silence and Percilla sat down close to Emma. She then said, "They'll probably come up before the magistrate first; it's up to him what happens then." Percilla gently held Emma's hand and said, "What's going to happen to our Henry and your Richard?" Emma's eyes began to fill up. She then said, "I dare not think about what's going to happen to them both." Emma quickly pulled her hand away from Percilla and put both her hands together over her face, she screamed from beneath her hands, "Oh my god, they'll hang them both." Percilla instantly stood up; her expression was that of sheer horror. "No, no, they can't do that, we were going to get married," she cried. Emma stood up and grabbed Percilla, "Quiet, quiet, you'll wake Jesse." Percilla slowly sat back down realizing that she had lost the love of her life,

56

her precious Richard had gone. "We must be strong for Jesse," Emma said, handing Percilla some water. "Keep quiet about this in front of Jesse. He doesn't need to know. Now off to bed with you and I'll see you in the morning." The following morning life seemed much the same for Jesse. He got up as usual, started off to work with his Aunt Emma and Percilla as usual, so really nothing much had changed apart for the torrid silence, "What's the matter with you two this morning?" Jesse asked as the three of them walked along the lane towards Whites Farm. "Nothing's wrong with us," Percilla replied. "We don't always have to be talking to prove to you that everything is alright. Do we?" "Well if you two are worried about Henry and Richard, you're wasting your time because the constable said last night that it was all over and there was nothing I could do to help, so I reckon our Henry will be home tonight before us." Jesse then cheerfully skipped his way down the lane towards the farm.

Emma and Percilla laughed at Jesse's comments and said nothing to make him change his opinion of the situation. Emma said to Percilla, "Let him think that, if that's what he believes then he won't be hurt by what's going on." They eventually arrived at the farm to find Amos shouting and screaming at a very bent plough blade, "This is your fault, trying to plough through bloody stones." "I didn't do it on purpose," Jesse replied, kicking a stone across the farm yard floor. "Well we can't get another for three weeks and that field still as to be ploughed. Oh and by the way, it will cost you two and six out of your wages." "But I only get three shillings a week to start with," Jesse snapped. "Stop whingeing," Amos said as he threw a rather large hammer at Jesse, who managed to dodge the hammer quickly by doing a pretty smart side step.

However, Jesse didn't see the thick ear that was coming. In fact, he stepped right into it and got the full force of the slap around the side of his head. Jesse decided that he wasn't going to cry, instead he bit his tongue. This made his eye's water a little, but he quickly wiped them away before Amos saw them, "That should do it," Amos said, standing up straight. "Don't break it again, if you know what's good for you lad," Amos said pointing at Jesse.

Both lifted the plough together, but when Amos realized he had the heavy end, "You, ya little bugger, get hold of this end," he said, dropping his end of the plough and walking around to the lighter end. Jesse, who had not realized why Amos had wanted to swap ends dropped his end and walked to the heavy end. The moment Jesse picked the plough back up he could feel the difference. He didn't say anything, he just carried on has if nothing was wrong. He knew if he started to whinge it would give Amos another chance to give him another thick ear, he wasn't going to let that happen.

They started off up the track towards the field, Jesse in front and Amos pushing from behind. Amos used the plough like a prodding rod to speed Jesse along. The further up the track they went the faster Amos would prod Jesse. Jesse could hear Amos laughing, but he was determinate not to drop the plough, and as they got nearer the gate the prodding got worse, but Jesse became more determined, he even started to grit his teeth. Until eventually they arrived at the gate with Amos saying, "You're a gutsy little bugger, I'll give you that." He then threw down the plough and said, "Go get Titan and be quick about it. You can then get cracking in the field." Amos then carried on walking up the track towards the upper meadow. Jesse started off back down the track looking over his shoulder to make sure that Amos was still going in the opposite direction to him. He decided about halfway down the track that Amos was far enough away for him to sit on the wall and have a rest.

He quickly jumped up onto the wall and instantly pulled out his shirt from his trousers. He then examined his ribs where the plough had dug into him, whilst he was carrying it. He had a large red mark where the shaft had been resting. After giving the mark a rub, which seemed to ease the pain, Jesse looked towards the farmhouse and began tucking his shirt back into his trousers. Suddenly, Jesse had to look twice to make sure he wasn't seeing things. There, leaving the farmhouse, by the front door, was a policeman. Jesse jumped down quickly from the wall and started to run towards the house. Emma, who happened to be at the kitchen window of the farmhouse, could see Jesse coming down the track towards the house. She knew instinctively why Jesse was coming at such speed.

Emma walked out of the kitchen and into the hall. She quickly opened the front door and stepped out onto the garden path. This allowed Jesse to run straight towards her. "Slow down our Jesse," she said, grabbing Jesse by his arms. Jesse came to a sudden halt, "What did that policeman want Auntie Em?" Jesse blurted out trying to get his breath back. "Nothing for you to worry

about," Emma replied, trying to calm Jesse down. Percilla suddenly appeared from the kitchen and said, "He only wanted us to know that Henry and Richard had been before the magistrates this morning and that their case has been sent to the assizes at Newbury." Jesse pondered for a moment and then asked, "What are assizes?" "Oh, it's just a posher court. It's where a judge decides what happens," Emma told Jesse. Jesse sighed with relief. Emma saw the relief on his face and said, "I did tell you there was nothing to worry about. Now let's all get back to work before the master catches us."

Emma then returned to the kitchen with Percilla while Jesse fetched Titan from the barn and returned to the top field to continue with his ploughing. The rest of the day seemed uneventful for Jesse, as dusk began to appear over the end of the field; Jesse decided that this would be his last furrow. Arriving once more at the top of the field, Jesse laid down the plough, unhooked Titan and began walking him back to the barn, he made sure that Titan was bedded down for the night, and then he joined Percilla and Emma, who were waiting for him in the farmyard for the dreary trudge back home.

The trio were nearly home and dusk was nearly over. Jesse could just make out Auntie Emma's house through the nearly dark evening, when he saw the silhouette of a young man stood by the front gate. "There's our Henry," Jesse shouted at the top of his voice, "Told ya he'd be home before us, didn't I." Jesse started to run towards the dark silhouette, "Henry" he shouted, waving frantically at the silhouette. "Jesse, come back here!" Emma said, trying to grab hold of Jesse before he started running, but Jesse was too quick, he was gone. Emma and Percilla quickened their pace to try and catch up with Jesse. They both knew only too well that it couldn't possibly be Henry. As Jesse got nearer he began to realize that the silhouette wasn't Henry, but someone he'd never seen before. Jesse began to slow down; this gave Emma and Percilla a chance to catch him up. The silhouette had heard Jesse shouting and had turned to face, the by now out of breath trio. "Good evening," the man said whilst doffing his hat. "My name is Mr. Fredrick Page. I'm from the Kennet and Avon Canal Company." He paused for a moment and Emma said, "Oh, yes." Inviting him to say more, reluctantly Mr. Page continued. "I find myself in a somewhat difficult position, ma'am. Might I be addressing Mrs. Miller," Emma replied. "Yes, I'm Mrs. Miller." "Could I have a word with you in private please," said Mr. Page as he glared at Percilla and Jesse. "Come on Jesse, we'll put the broth on and slice some bread for tea." Percilla then pushed Jesse down the garden path by his shoulders.

Emma and Mr. Page continued to stand by the garden gate engrossed in deep conversation. Jesse, who had by now appeared at the window, was watching everything, but he couldn't see much in the darkness, disappointed, he returned to the kitchen. Anyway, he thought, I don't like that Mr. Page. This was partly because he'd asked Jesse to leave before he knew what he wanted. "I wonder what he wants." Jesse asked Percilla as she began cutting the bread on the kitchen table. "Don't be so nosey," Percilla replied. "He's probably brought our Henry's wages," Jesse said, taking a piece of bread off the kitchen table. "Sit down and eat your broth, we'll get to know soon enough," said Percilla. She then sat down to eat her own broth. They'd almost finished eating when the front door slammed, moments later Emma walked into the kitchen. She placed two piles of shilling coins on the table, she then stacked them neatly and said, "Well that's the last wagers we'll get from the canal company. Six shillings for Henry and six for Richard and what's more we've all to move out of this house." "What straight away?" Asked Percilla, who was shocked by Emma's news, "Apparently, because our Henry has not been to work, there giving someone else his job on the canal. Therefore, we have to move out of this house before the end of next week."

Emma began to cry and Percilla joined in, Jesse, just raised his eyes to the ceiling and said, "Oh, come on girls, it's not that bad." Percilla then got angry with Jesse and said, "It's as bad as it gets, you stupid little sod. Where are we going to live?" She then kicked out at Jesse, who had already sensed the change in Percilla's voice and was heading towards the bottom of the stairs in a bid to escape the kick. "I was only trying to help," Jesse screamed as he quickly climbed the stairs. A long silence came over Emma and Percilla as they both sat at the kitchen table, "Where are we going to go now Auntie Em?" Percilla asked as she placed a by now lukewarm bowl of broth on the table in front of Emma. "I was thinking of your Uncle Will and Aunt Sarah's place, they've got an extra room." "But that's miles away, it would take two hours to walk to the farm from there and that's if you're not tired," Percilla said, whilst handing Emma some bread. They were both sat there pondering what to do, when there was an almighty bang from upstairs. "What's he doing up there?" Percilla asked as she got up and walked to the bottom of the stairs. "Jesse, what are you doing?" she shouted. Just then, there was another almighty bang and then the sound of something being dragged across the bedroom floor. Emma got up quickly from the table and stomped past Percilla, who was just about to go up stairs to see what Jesse was up to, instead she found herself following Emma up the stairs. Arriving at the top of the stairs, they both looked into Jesse's bedroom and were amazed at what they saw. There, in the middle of a large mess was Jesse, he'd emptied out every drawer and his wardrobe of all his possessions and was busily sorting through them. "What on earth are you doing?" Emma asked, rather angrily, thinking that she would have to tidy it all up later. Jesse looked up and with his usual grin splashed across his face, he calmly said, "Packing!" He then continued with his sorting, whilst whistling his favourite hymn. Emma and Percilla looked at each other and began to laugh.

The next day all were up early as usual and arrived at work in plenty of time for Jesse to have a rare glass of fresh milk with Percilla in the farmhouse kitchen before he took Titan up into the field. "I'll finish that top field today with a bit of luck," Jesse said, feeling quite proud that he had nearly finished ploughing his first field. "You won't get it done sat there," Master White said as he entered the kitchen. Jesse jumped to his feet straight away and quickly left the kitchen by the back door. As Jesse entered the farmyard, he could see Amos coming down the track with the cows that were ready for milking. He quickly walked across the yard and entered the barn. Leaving the barn door slightly open, he watched through the gap, as Amos passed the barn with the cows and disappeared inside the milking shed. All clear thought Jesse as he began to lead Titan slowly up the track towards the top field, but there was a problem. Jesse got the feeling something wasn't quite right. He looked at Titan, patted his shoulder and said, "What's the matter lad?" Titan didn't respond he just stood there looking rather dejected. Jesse walked around him, but couldn't see anything visibly wrong. He pondered for a minute. Jesse knew something was wrong, and he knew from experience never to ignore his feelings about things like this. I'll fetch Amos, he thought.

Jesse tied Titan to the field gate and walked back down the track towards the milking shed. Half way down the track he met Earle. "Aren't you supposed to be finishing the top field?" Earle said as soon as he met Jesse. "I can't, there's something wrong with Titan," replied Jesse, who had a worried expression on his face. "He'll be alright, just crack the rains and push him on," Earle said, who began walking away. "No, I'm going to fetch Amos." "Oh, I wouldn't do that if I was you, he's having his breakfast and he doesn't like being interrupted when he's having his breakfast. Anyway, there's a big meeting going on in the kitchen, dads even there." The mere mention of a meeting sent Jesse's senses into overdrive. "Oh, what's it about?" Jesse asked Earle, pretending he wasn't really very interested. "I don't know but your Percilla and Aunt Emma were in on it too," Earle said, knowing that Jesse wouldn't be able to resist going to find Amos. "I think I'll still go and find Amos," Jesse said. "Suit yourself!" Earle replied, laughing to himself as he started off up the lane

60

towards school. Jesse walked down the rest of the track and across the farmyard towards the house. He crept around the house to the kitchen window, keeping low, so not to be seen by the people inside the house.

Arriving at the kitchen window, Jesse had to stand on his tip toes to see into the kitchen. He peered in through the window and there sure enough in the kitchen was his Aunt Emma and Percilla, who were both, sat on wooden kitchen chairs by the open fire. Master White was stood by the fire warming his posterior and looked to be thoroughly enjoying it. Jesse scanned the rest of the kitchen carefully. He eventually spotted Amos, who was sat at the table eating his breakfast. Jesse watched all of them for a few moments, but they were all so engrossed in conversation with one another, that none of them had even noticed Jesse watching them through the window. However, Jesse still couldn't hear what was being said inside, he knew they were talking, because he could see bits of food leaving Amos's mouth when he spoke.

Jesse then made one of his decisions. He would try to open the window slightly so he could hear what was going on. He placed his finger tips underneath the movable frame of the window and started to pull, carefully at first, then eventually with a little more force, it was no good, the frame wouldn't budge. Jesse tried again, only this time, he really put some effort into the pulling. Then suddenly the frame gave way, there was the sound of breaking glass and creaking wood as the whole frame came away into Jesse's hands. The sudden release of the window frame sent Jesse flying across the garden. Emma knew instantly who had just pulled out the window. "His nose will never rust," she said, heading towards the broken window. She poked her head out of the by now windowless frame and looked down, there in the garden was Jesse, laid flat on his back with a piece of the window frame in his hand. "I'm sorry Aunt Emma," he said as he stood up and dusted himself off. "What on earth were you doing?" Emma said angrily to Jesse, who replied, "I'm looking for Amos, there's something wrong with Titan."

Amos stood up quickly and marched to the window, "If you've damaged that horse lad, they'll be trouble." "I haven't touched him," Jesse replied instantly. Amos walked towards the backdoor, put on his jacket and cap, which were hung up at the side of the door and walked out into the yard, "Come on." He growled at Jesse, as they both set off back up the track towards Titan. Halfway up the track Amos bent down and picked something up, he began shaking his head, "What's the matter?" Asked Jesse, thinking he'd done something wrong, "Nothing!" Amos replied sharply. He then coughed and said, "Well it looks like you're going to be living here with us." Jesse was stopped in his tracks, "What! Live here, I can't believe that," he said as he continued walking up the track towards Titan. "Are you sure?" Jesse asked Amos, "Of course I'm bloody sure, we've just agreed a deal with your Aunt Emma. You lot work like slaves and we give you room and board. What a deal!" Amos said, with a large smile on his face.

Jesse couldn't believe he was going to have to live at Whites Farm and what's more, depend on the Whites for his food. How Aunt Emma and Percilla could have done such a deal without consulting him first, he thought. Jesse began walking once more up the track towards Titan. The deal was going around and around inside his little head and the nearer he got to Titan the more annoyed he became about the deal, until eventually, he arrived at the gate where Titan was waiting. Amos grabbed the rains and slowly began turning Titan towards the house, "Well are you going to have a look at him?" Jesse said rudely, expecting Amos to at least a look at Titan. Instead, he looked at Jesse and said, "No need lad. I found the problem half way down the track." Amos then threw an old horse shoe at Jesse, grinned and said, "Come on lad, you've a lot to learn yet."

All three of them walked back down the track towards the farmhouse. No-one said a word, but Jesse was definitely thinking about the deal that was done without his consent. They arrived back in the farmyard and Amos said, "I'll take Titan for his shoe putting back on. You get in the barn and clean it out, since that's where you're going to be sleeping, and oh, by the way, you're paying for the window." Jesse's laughed and thought to himself, since I don't get paid anymore, how are you going to do that, Amos? Amos began to pull Titan across the yard, Jesse, trying to stop Amos from moving, put his finger up and was just about to ask Amos more about the deal, when he thought twice about it, instead he decided he would speak to his Aunt Emma and Percilla about the deal on the way home that night. The afternoon dragged on for Jesse. But soon enough, Jesse found himself waiting in the farmyard for his Aunt Emma and Percilla. He had been considering what to say all afternoon. However, when Emma and Percilla came out of the house, he could only blurt out, "What have you done to me?" Emma and Percilla looked straight at Jesse and said together, "We haven't done anything to you." Jesse then said, "What's this deal then, if you haven't done anything to me." "Oh that!" Emma said as she put her arm around Jesse's shoulder. "Come on, let's go home and I'll explain," said Emma as they began walking back home. Emma began to explain their situation to Jesse and eventually finished by saying, "At least we won't have to walk back home like this everynight." Jesse thought about it for sometime whilst walking back home. Eventually, he decided, he had no option but to agree, he didn't like the deal, but thought it would only upset both his Aunt Emma and Percilla if he didn't agree, he couldn't do with them both crying again, he just couldn't cope with that he thought.

The week passed quickly and moving day came around. Jesse had finished his packing and was stood with Percilla at the gate waiting for Amos to arrive with Titan, who would be pulling the large cart used around the farm. Aunt Emma was inside the house busily polishing the little bits of furniture that she had, after all she didn't want the Whites to think she kept an untidy house. There wasn't a lot of furniture, and it wasn't of good quality, but what she had, she had kept nice and it all had memories of Uncle Albert written all over it. Suddenly, Percilla shouted, "Here's Amos now." She hurriedly went back inside to put on her coat and then returned with Emma, who was pinning on her hat. "Morning," Amos said whilst doffing his cap. He then jumped down off the cart and said, "Come on lad, let's get the stuff on board. We've work to do back at the farm." He slapped Jesse with his cap around the back of the head and walked up the garden path. Emma began pointing to the items of furniture she was taking with her, "Take that, leave that and don't forget that." She said as she busily wandered around the house. "Take your hands out of your pocket's lad and get a hold of the other end of this." Amos said to Jesse, who was getting fed up of Amos referring to him as, "lad" and said angrily, "My names Jesse, not lad!" Amos hesitated, looked at Jesse, and then said, in a rather posh voice, "Would his master like to bend his back and get hold of this wardrobe, please, pretty please." Jesse tutted and grabbed his end of the wardrobe.

They began to take it outside, but as they reached the front door their exit was blocked by a rather large gentleman, who said, "I'm looking for a Mrs. Emma Miller." "She's in the kitchen sir," Amos said, pushing Jesse and the wardrobe past the gentleman and out onto the garden path. "Who was that?" Percilla asked Jesse. "How would I know?" Jesse replied, struggling with his end of the wardrobe. Percilla walked quickly through into the kitchen, "Mrs. Miller, Mrs. Emma Miller?" Emma nodded, "I'm the Court Bailiff for Newbury. You have been summoned to appear at court next week to give evidence in the trial of, the state verse Crips." He then slid his hand into his inside pocket and took out a piece of folded paper, he held it out towards Emma, who took it from him and without more to do he fingered his top hat and said, "Good morning madam." He then turned and promptly left.

Emma began to wobble and Percilla could see she was going to pass out, so quickly, Percilla got hold of her by the arm and wrapped it around her shoulders to stop her from falling. She then managed to drag Emma to the small kitchen stool in the corner and sat her down. Being nosey, Jesse came rushing back into the kitchen to find out who the fat gentleman was. But when he saw his Aunt Emma, he was more concerned about her. "Are you all right Aunt Emma?" Jesse asked, kneeling down in front of her. "She'll be alright in a minute, come out of the way," Percilla said as she pushed past Jesse with some water. Jesse stood up as Amos came back into the kitchen. Amos wasn't happy and said, "Come on lad, let's get on." Jesse sensed some annoyance in Amos's voice, because Jesse had stopped helping him. "She'll be alright, go and give Amos a hand with the lifting." Percilla told Jesse, who had also sensed the annoyance in Amos's voice.

Jesse left the kitchen albeit reluctantly and began helping Amos pile the rest of the furniture onto the cart, "That's the last!" Amos said, pushing a small round table onto the back of the cart. The front door slammed and Percilla came down the garden path with the small kitchen stool in her hand, she put it on the cart and turned to look at the house for the last time. Whilst she was looking back, she could see her Aunt Emma standing at the closed front door, there was a weird silence for a moment, which was broken by Percilla gently saying, "Come on Auntie Em?" Emma turned slowly, blew her nose and then marched confidently down the path where she said, "Come on. Let's go!"

They all turned to face the cart; they then realized there was no room on the cart for them to sit, "Looks like you lot are walking." Amos said, laughing as he climbed up onto the cart. He then sat on Aunt Emma's wooden chair which he had conveniently placed at the front of the cart overlooking the horse, "Go on then Titan." Amos snapped the rains and the cart began to wobble down the lane towards the fork. It wasn't long before Amos and Titan had disappeared from sight, leaving Emma, Percilla and Jesse walking quietly along the lane. Jesse was walking on his own a little way behind Emma and Percilla. He was following the tracks being left by the cart; he'd invented a little game. He would put one foot in front of the other, making sure that the heel of his front foot always touched the toes of his other, and then he would see how fast he could walk like that without falling off the cart track. He did this for some considerable time, which made him fall further and further behind. Percilla had shouted to him twice, "Get a move on Jesse." But Jesse had ignored her and continued playing his game.

Eventually, he arrived at the fork in the road, he looked up to see if he could see his Aunt Emma and Percilla, but by now Emma and Percilla were nowhere to be seen. So... its back to the game, he thought, Jesse then looked down at his feet to start the game again when he realized the tracks had gone. He stopped suddenly and began to look around. He walked back retracing his steps. Eventually, he found the tracks again. They were going in the other direction towards Shalbourne. Funny, he thought, why are the cart tracks going the wrong way? He pondered for a moment, and then he heard Percilla shouting him again. Maybe Amos had some errands to do in Shalbourne, he thought, yes... that'll be it. Content with his own answer Jesse started to run towards the shouts of Percilla along the other fork.

It was an hour later when they arrived at the farmyard. Jesse went straight to the barn to get Titan, but he wasn't there. He turned and ran back to the farmhouse. When he got there Emma and Percilla were stood by the front door, "Where's Amos?" Jesse asked. "We don't know," Percilla replied awkwardly. All three of them stood there staring down the lane looking for the slightest movement. "Come on you lot, get some work done," said Master White as he came through the front door of the farmhouse. "We're waiting for Amos," Jesse replied. The master laughed and said, "Oh no you're not, it's our Amos's day off and he won't be back until late. So gets some work done. All of you!"

Evening came and still there was no sign of Amos. Jesse had spent most of the day cleaning the barn and making a little den at the back of the barn where he was going to sleep. Percilla came into the barn just as Jesse was finishing and said, "Teas ready." Jesse looked up and said smartly, "Don't you knock before entering a person's room?" "Sorry sir, I'm sure," Percilla replied. She then did a little curtsy and rested her index finger under her chin.

"Anyway, what did that chap want this morning?" Jesse asked, "Upsetting Aunt Emma like that." Jesse then put down the pitch fork he'd been using to spread hay around the barn with. "He was the bailiff," Percilla replied. "He'd brought Aunt Emma a summons to appear next week at the trial." Jesse was horrified, "Why! Aunt Emma's done nothing wrong." "No! Silly, she's only giving evidence at the trial, now come on, otherwise tea will get cold."

Both walked from the barn across the dark farmyard to the kitchen. They quickly sat down at the kitchen table and began to eat their teas, which was a very large hot potato, with melted butter and cheese mashed into it. All washed down with a flagon of milk, "Better than Kaile Broth?" Emma said to Jesse as he began tucking in. Not much more was said during the meal. The only sound to be heard was that of gulping and slurping as they all consumed their potatoes. Content with their fill, they all gathered around the open fire in the kitchen, they began talking in depth about the trial. In particular, what might happen to Henry and Richard if found guilty? Engrossed in the conversation the evening seemed to pass quickly, but eventually Emma stood up and said, "Enough talk, it's time for bed!" She walked across to the kitchen table, stretched across it and lowered the oil lamp. "Come on, we've all to be up early in the morning," looking at Jesse, who was still sipping the last of his milk from the flagon. Emma then lit a candle and handed it to Percilla, who began making her way upstairs to the front bedroom which she was going to share with Emma. Jesse said, "Goodnight," and left by the backdoor. He headed straight for his cosy little den at the back of the barn. Emma took a last look out of the window to see if she could see Amos, but there was still no sign of him, so she locked the backdoor and went to bed.

The next morning Jesse was awoken by the cockerel and the sound of horse hoofs stamping on the farmyard floor. He jumped up and looked out of the barn door, he did this so fast that he hadn't even given his eye's time to adjust to the bright morning sunlight. He squinted, put his hand over his eyebrow and looked across the yard towards the farmhouse. There he could just make out the cart, which was now empty. Titan, who wasn't even tied up, had obviously been standing in the yard for sometime because he was stomping, this usually meant that he was hungry. Jesse grabbed Titan's nose bag and walked across the yard. He could see his Aunt Emma coming out of the farmhouse, still in her nightdress, "Where's my furniture?" She asked Jesse as they both peered over the edge of the empty cart. "I don't know," Jesse replied, pulling down Titan's head, so he could put the nose bag on him. Jesse then patted Titan on his neck and said, "There you go boy." He then left Titan eating and walked back around the side of the cart to talk to his Aunt Emma.

Suddenly, there was a very faint groaning noise. Jesse said quickly, "Quiet Auntie Em." Both froze instantly. Jesse put his finger over his lips and pointed over the wall. The noise started again, this time a little louder. Jesse peered over the wall and there, laid flat out in the garden, was Amos, still drunk from the previous day's drinking. Jesse looked towards his Aunt Emma and lipped the word, "Amos." She lipped back, "where?" Jesse pointed over the wall and into the garden. Emma was absolutely furious. She instantly rolled up her sleeves and went back into the house. A couple of minutes later she reappeared at the door with a large bucket of cold water. Whoosh, the full bucket of water went straight over Amos. He sat up straight instantly, wiped his eye and said, "What the hell!" "Where's my furniture?" Emma screamed at Amos, who was still a little dazed and groaned, "What furniture?" "My furniture," Emma screamed, "Oh that furniture! Sold and drunk madam," Amos said, falling back over. Jesse, who was by this stage in fits of laughter, laughed even more when his Auntie Emma said, "I'll give you what furniture." She then stomped inside for some more water.

Earle appeared at the door and said, "What's going on?" Jesse said, "Come here quick." But he wasn't quick enough. Emma barged past him, knocking Earle flying. Again there was a massive whooshing sound as the water went over Amos. This time Amos stood up and the mood changed quickly, he was furious and said, "Enough women, enough." He lifted his hand to fetch Emma a slap, but was brought to a sudden halt by a deep voice saying, "Our Amos!" Amos looked around and there up in the bedroom window was Master White, "Give Mrs. Miller the money you got for her furniture." "There's nothing left. I supped it all last night." Amos replied, whilst wringing his shirt tails out. Emma looked up at Master White and said, "You knew he was going to sell my furniture, didn't you?" "Where did you think we could keep it madam?" Master White said in disgust whilst shutting the window. Amos walked out of the garden and told Jesse to put Titan away, which Jesse did before giving him an extra ration of carrots.

Everybody calmed down and things began to return to normal, Master White compensated Aunt Emma for her furniture, although she always maintained it was worth more than he gave her. Jesse and Amos went to plant winter wheat in the top field, "Like this lad, make sure it drops into the furrows." Amos said whilst broadcasting the seed down the field, "Here you try." Jesse set off with the seed bag around his neck broadcasting the seed, "That's it lad. Keep going until the whole field is done." Amos said holding his head. He then disappeared down the track towards the farmhouse. Jesse spent all morning broadcasting seed in the field, and at last he reached the end of the field. A good job he thought, he then sat down on the wall for a well deserved rest.

He looked back up the field and thought there seems to be a lot of birds in the field today, he never gave it another thought as his stomach was saying it was dinner time, so he set off back towards the house, hoping Auntie Emma had something good for dinner. He was just entering the yard when Amos shouted from the barn, "Where are you going?" "For my dinner," answered Jesse. "No you're not, you haven't got time. You've got to harrow that winter wheat before the birds eat the lot. The whole field has to be done today, so go get Titan and go back up to the top field. I'll meet you there." Jesse turned and walked back to the barn. He collected Titan and started off up the track towards the top field with him.

Arriving at the top field Amos was nowhere to be seen, so Jesse sat on the gate and waited, his stomach rumbled. Eventually, quarter of an hour later, Amos arrived and said, "Here you are lad a farm worker's lunch." He lobbed a white turnip at Jesse, who began crunching on it straight away. At the side of the gate, up against the wall, was laid a rectangular frame which was partly covered by overgrown grass and weeds. Amos started pulling out hands full of grass and weeds from around the frame. In time enough grass and weeds had been removed to allow Amos to finally tug the frame free from the grass and weeds, "Here you are then lad," Amos said as he threw the frame down onto the ploughed field. Jesse then noticed the frame was covered in spikes and thought to himself that looks dangerous, "Don't worry lad, it's upside down, the spikes go down into the soil." Amos flicked the frame over and then fastened it to Titan, "Now, put your weight on the frame by standing here. Then all you have to do is drive Titan down the field slowly pulling, both you and the

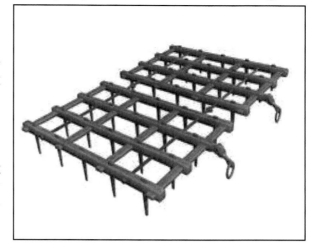

frame along, got it!" Jesse nodded and stood on the frame in the position Amos had said. He then cracked the rains and said, "Go on then," to Titan, who set off down the field.

Jesse, however, didn't follow. Instead he went flat on his back as his feet were pulled from under him by the frame. Amos began laughing as he walked back down the track towards the farmhouse. "That's the bit you've to practice. It's all to do with balance lad." Jesse jumped back up and quickly ran after Titan, "Woo Titan, woo." Jesse said, grabbing the rains which were being dragged along the ground. Again Jesse stood on the frame once more, but this time he leant back a little and bent his knees more, "Right!" He said, gripping the rains, "Go on Titan." This time he was ready and managed to go the length of the field, a little wobbly, but nevertheless, he did it. However, arriving at the bottom of the field Titan suddenly turned left, Jesse and the frame did not, the frame hit the wall and so did Jesse. Titan carried on back up the field, the frame, which was making a terrible clanging noise, followed him. Jesse, who by now had a gashed head and numerous grazers, didn't know whether to run after the frame, rub his head or grab the rains and pull Titan to a halt. He eventually managed to get up and decided to limp after Titan, "Woo Titan, woo," he said, pulling Titan to a halt. Titan stopped, Jesse then collapsed in a heap on top of the frame.

After a short rest Jesse began to rub the wounds he had sustained. However, in the chaos, Jesse hadn't noticed the sound of laughter coming from the otherside of the wall. He got up and stomped towards the laughter, his angry face peered over the wall to discover Earle and Amos in fits of laughter at the otherside of the wall. Earle, trying not to laugh, pointed at Jesse and said, "That's the funniest thing I've ever seen. It's was even better than when I did it." "Oh, and that's another thing you've to practice... turning!" Amos said, looking at Earle. This made them both begin to laugh again, this time even louder, they both couldn't stop laughing. Even when they turned, linked arms around each other's shoulders and walked back down the track towards the farmyard. Jesse, who was furious, could still hear them laughing, in the distance, ten minutes later.

Determined not to be beat Jesse mounted the frame once more and set off back up the field towards the gate. It wasn't long before Jesse got the hang of turning and riding the frame up and down the field, in fact, Jesse began to enjoy riding the frame. He thought it was better than walking up and down the field, although by the end of the day his legs were beginning to ache from the constant pressure of the frame. It was dark and had been for sometime when Jesse arrived at the barn to put Titan away for the night. He was so exhausted he didn't even have the energy to walk the distance to the farmhouse for his tea. Instead, he limped his way to the back of the barn; put his head down on the pile of straw he called a pillow, and was just about to close his eyes, when he sensed he wasn't alone.

Quickly, Jesse sat up and spun around, thinking it might be Earle up to his tricks again. Jesse peered through the darkness of the barn towards the door, which was now partially open. This put Jesse on his guard immediately, and he started to strain his eyes. He could just make out Titan, who was by now calmly eating his hay. Jesse slowly peered around the barn, fist clinched, if that's Earle come to annoy me, he thought, I'll give him what for. However, then Jesse saw some movement, the silhouette was coming towards him. He recognized the silhouette straight away and began to relax his clinched fist, "Jesse, Jesse." The silhouette whispered, "Over here Auntie Em." "I've brought you a plate of food. I thought you might be hungry." Emma said as she struggled through the darkness towards the sound of Jesse's voice.

Jesse was grateful his Aunt Emma had brought him some food. "Thanks Aunt Em, you're a gooden," Jesse said to Emma as she sat down beside him in his homemade bedroom. Jesse began tucking into a very large egg and ham sandwich and some water as Emma looked around the place where Jesse lived. "Not much of a bedroom," Emma said to Jesse. "It'll do me." Not wishing his Aunt Emma to be worried about him. "How are you coping?" Jesse asked, trying to change the subject. "I'm okay," Emma replied quickly. There was a long pause and then Jesse said, "Percilla?" Again Emma paused and looked at Jesse, she then thought, there's no point in lying to Jesse anymore and said, "Percilla, she's struggling today. She's received her summons to appear at court next week, this morning. She went to pieces when the bailiff handed it to her." "Poor Percilla," Jesse said, shaking his head. He then came to one of his decisions, "Tell her not to worry. I'll be with her when she goes to court!" Emma pondered for a moment and said, "I'm sorry Jesse, but you can't come to court. Master White won't let you go." Jesse was outraged; he jumped up quickly and began screaming at his Aunt Emma, "What, why not? He can't stop me from going. I'm going and that's all there is to it."

Jesse then sat back down in a huff, "Calm down Jesse," Emma said. "Master White needs you to be here working. Anyway if you haven't been summoned then there's no reason for you to be there." Emma paused and with two fingers, she lifted Jesse's chin up, and said, "Come on, cheer up. It'll all soon be over." Jesse nodded reluctantly and said, "Okay Aunt Emma. I'll stop here and work." Emma stood up with the empty plate and turned. She was just about to leave, when she noticed that Jesse had prepared two beds. She pointed to the second bed and jokingly asked. "Expecting company?" Jesse was quick to reply, "That's for our Henry when he comes home. He'll need to sleep somewhere!" Emma's heart sunk, a tear came to her eye, she tried to say goodnight, but the words simply wouldn't come. So she quietly walked out of the barn and across the yard to the house. After Jesse had heard the house door slam, he layed down and went to sleep.

Chapter 4: Trial, Retribution and Child Birth.

Jesse woke up as usual to the sound of the cockerel crowing; he stretched, and then walked out of the barn into the morning sunlight. To wake himself up properly, he took a quick swill in the horse trough. Just then the cockerel jumped up onto the edge of the trough. Jesse looked at the bird and said, "You, ya bugger, I'll have you yet, one of these mornings." He then threw the mucky piece of cloth he was using to wipe his face with at the cockerel. The cockerel squawked and fluttered across the yard, where it joined the other hens. Jesse followed it and reckoned to kick out at the cockerel.

He missed wildly and continued to walk across the farmyard towards the house for his breakfast. The kitchen was quiet as Jesse entered by the backdoor. The only sound to be heard was the sound of the log fire crackling in the kitchen hearth. Jesse strolled across to the table and sat down. After a moment's wait... he heard the sound of footsteps on the stairs. A moment longer and Percilla entered the kitchen, closely followed by Emma and Earle, not a word was said. Jesse, struggling with all this silence, decided he'd had enough and reluctantly announced out loud, "Well today's the day then!" Jesse was going to say more, but was quickly stopped by both Emma and Percilla, who both turned and frowned angrily at him, "We don't need reminding," Emma snarled as she poured some hot water from the kettle into an old chipped teapot. "What do you want for your breakfast?" Emma snapped at Jesse, "What is there?" He asked sheepishly, "There's some gammon that Master brought in yesterday after he'd killed two pigs." "That'll do me, with an egg," Jesse replied, rubbing his hands in expectation.

Emma put a large frying pan on the hob and moved it into the fire. She then slapped a large piece of gammon down onto the middle of the pan, instantly it began to crackle and spit. The smell of the gammon filled the kitchen, Jesse's mouth began to water, he looked across at Percilla, who hadn't spoken at all that morning and said, "Why don't you have some gammon our Percilla? It'll put you on a good footing for the rest of the day." Percilla looked across at Jesse, her face was gray, she said nothing as she began to gip. She quickly put her hand up to her mouth and started off towards the door. As she flew past Jesse little droplets of liquid began to spurt out between Percilla's fingers. She managed to reach the backdoor before lunging out into the garden where she began to be sick behind a water barrel.

Jesse, realizing that something was wrong, stood up quickly and followed Percilla outside. Emma wasn't far behind him, "come out of the way Jesse." Emma said, trying to pull Jesse back from peering over the barrel. "What's the matter our Percilla?" Jesse asked, showing concern. Percilla began to stand upright once more. She wiped her mouth with her cardigan sleeve. Emma handed Percilla a cloth and said, "Don't use your sleeve." Percilla nodded and wiped her chin clean with the cloth whilst placing one hand on her stomach. Jesse, feeling frustrated by this time, "Sighed," and asked again. "What's the matter?" Emma became annoyed, "Nothings the matter!" She growled at Jesse, who was by now nearly smothering Percilla. "She must be unwell," he said. "No, it's quite normal." Emma told Jesse as she pushed him away from Percilla, "But she's just been sick. Has she eaten something?" Jesse asked, again looking very concerned for Percilla.

Percilla leant over and began to be sick again, "No you twit, she hasn't eaten anything." Earle chirped up, as he leant against the frame of the backdoor. "Isn't it obvious? She's like our cows. She is going to have a baby!" Jesse looked at Earle, who had a large grin on his face, and said, "No, she's not!" "Suit yourself!" Earle said. He turned and started to walk back into the kitchen. Jesse made a run at Earle, but was stopped by Emma, who grabbed him by his shirt collar and said, "No you don't, that's the last thing we need today." She then threw Jesse down the path and out into the farmyard, saying, "Go on. Get on with your work." Jesse, who was wiping his nose with his sleeve, angrily asked, "What about my breakfast?" "I'll bring it to you, now go," Emma replied, pointing towards the barn. Jesse began to walk away, when a voice from behind him, said, "I see you're still up to your tricks our Jesse."

Jesse looked around quickly to see Charlie stood there, "Charlie, what are you doing here?" Asked Jesse, surprised to see Charlie. Emma quickly began shaking her head at Charlie, who then hesitated to answer Jesse's question. Jesse noticed that Charlie was looking past him. So he quickly looked over his shoulder to see Emma. Who tried to stop shaking her head, but Jesse had seen the remnants of her shaking and said, "What's going on?" Charlie replied, "Nothing! I was just passing, so I thought I'd call to see how you were all doing." Jesse turned his head back to face Charlie and said, "Passing, why where are you going?" Charlie began to try and make up a destination when Emma quickly said, "He's going to the church to visit your mum's grave." "Yes, that's it. I'm going to the graveyard." Jesse was suspicious and a short silence followed while he thought about Charlie's answer, "If anyone is interested. There's a burning smell in here," Earle said, shouting from the kitchen. Emma then said to Jesse, "Your breakfast." She dashed back into the kitchen followed by Charlie, who had his arm around Percilla. He sat her down at the kitchen table and began talking to her.

Jesse, who had been left on his own in the farmyard, sighed and started off across the yard towards the barn. He then changed direction and walked up the track towards the top field, he had been ordered by Amos to repair the fence to stop the cows getting into the field. The fence was interwoven brushwood. Jesse began weaving the new brushwood into any holes which he thought cows might be able to get through. It wasn't long before his hands began to bleed because the brushwood was tough and sharp and weaving it wasn't easy either. On occasions the brushwood would stab Jesse, he wasn't bothered by this because his mind was elsewhere. Jesse was more concerned by what was happening back at the house.

All sorts of questions were entering his mind as usual. What did Charlie really want? Was Percilla really going to have a baby? The more he thought about the morning's events the more questions entered his mind. Eventually, he was brought back to reality by his Aunt Emma saying, "Here's your breakfast." She was gasping for breath, "It's quite a trek up here, isn't it?" Jesse, who was still not convinced that Charlie had come to visit because he was passing, said, "Why's our Charlie going to mum's grave today? It's not the anniversary!" Emma looked at Jesse and said, "Okay Jesse, you win!" She sat down on the grass and handed Jesse his breakfast on a plate, "Eat!" She said. Jesse began to eat and Emma put her arm around him, "If you must know," she said quietly. "He's here to tell us that Mrs. Newman is going to let us use her coach to take us all to the court. Percilla can't walk all that way to Newbury in her condition." With his mouth full, Jesse asked, "Is our Charlie going to the trial then?" Emma thought for a moment and then replied, "Yes, he's going to support Percilla. She needs him to be there, can't you see that?" There was a silence as Jesse thought about it. He chomped on another piece of gammon and said, "Well I suppose so, but I still don't see why I can't come!" Emma sympathetically looked at Jesse and said, "Let's not go over that again. Master White needs you here and that's all there is to it." Emma got up off the grass and pulled some loose grass from her skirt, she then discarded it gracefully. Jesse handed her the empty plate and said nothing, he went back to working on the fence. Emma walked back down the track towards the house still worrying about Jesse.

Arriving back at the house, Emma entered the kitchen to find Percilla and Charlie still talking, "Come on you two, we still have work to do." Percilla looked in amazement at her Aunt and said, "What work do I have to do?" "You have to salt down the rest of those pigs that Master White killed yesterday. They're in the barn hung up. There are two lambs there as well. You might as well do them all before we go. Charlie, you tell Mrs. Newman, we will be pleased to accept her offer of the coach and make sure you thank her for me." Charlie stood up, gave Percilla a large kiss on her cheek and said, "I'll see you later." He winked at her and left the kitchen saying, "See you later Auntie Em." Emma mumbled an, "Emm...." and continued cooking breakfast for Master White and Amos, who she could hear moving about upstairs.

Jesse had completed most of the fence when he looked down the track and saw Amos making his way up the track towards him. What does he want now? Jesse thought to himself as he pulled another piece of brushwood into position. Amos arrived, spat out a piece of fat and then looked down the fence and said, "That's no bloody good, this piece here needs a post." Amos shook the fence, and it wobbled, "Go get one from behind the barn." Jesse was just about to start off back down the track, when Amos said, "Hurry up lad, we haven't got all day." He then kicked out at Jesse, who moved quickly to evade the kick. It took Jesse sometime to get the post and carry it back up the track to the top field, where he found Amos and Earle sat enjoying the morning sun. "Oh, you're here. We were just about to send out a search party for you," Earle said, nudging Amos. They both started to laugh at what seemed to Jesse a poor joke. Jesse sat down to get his breath back, "Hey, you haven't time to sit down lad. Get on with it." Jesse jumped up and grabbed the post. He dragged it towards the fence and then stood it up and said, "What now?" Earle laughed and said, "What now? Now, you need a spade."

Jesse looked around and said, "Where do we keep them?" He'd no sooner said it, when he realized it would be back down the track to the barn, "Have a guess?" Amos said, sucking on a piece of grass. He then leant back to enjoy more of the sun and pulled his cap down over his eyes before saying, "Go on then. Go get it." Earle, who was laughing, said, "I can't stand this any longer. I'm off to school." He turned and walked off up the track towards the church whilst Amos just sat there enjoying the sun.

It took most of the morning to finish the fence, then Amos said, "Come on lad, I'll show you how to use a flail. We've corn to thrash in the barn." Amos set off back down the track towards the barn leaving Jesse to bring the spade and the loose pieces of brushwood leftover from the fence repairs.

"Where have you been?" Amos said sarcastically as Jesse entered the barn. Jesse just shrugged his shoulders and threw the spade into the corner of the

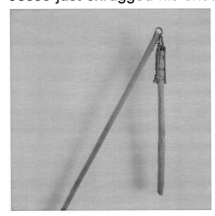

barn, "Open both doors and let some light in." Amos told Jesse, as he swept a square piece of barn floor directly inside the doors, "Right lad, first you get the corn and spread it on the floor like so." Amos scattered the corn evenly over the square he had just swept, "Now, when you've done that. You get your flail and hit the corn like so." Amos swung the flail over his head and whacked it down on the corn, "Keep doing that, and you will see the husk begin to separate from the corn. This pile on the floor needs flailing at least three times, so you move

around in a circle flailing as you go and when you've been around three times. Well I'll be back to show you how to separate the husks from the corn, but I must answer a called of nature right now."

Amos handed Jesse the flail and then set off towards the farmhouse in rather a hurry. Jesse began flailing, moving round as he swung the flail, he'd completed three revolutions of the corn and because the flailing had caused a lot of dust, which by now had reached the back of Jesse's throat, he decided to have a break. He began coughing, which forced him to the front of the barn, he walked out of the dust and into the yard, quickly he took a drink from the horse trough and then began to look around to see if he could see Amos. Just then Mrs. Newman's coach rattled into the yard, the driver spun it around in the yard and parked it in front of the farmhouse gate. The horses were restless whilst waiting.

But eventually Percilla and Emma appeared at the front door and began walking down the garden path. Charlie, who was in the coach, jumped down and ran up the garden path to meet Percilla and Emma, he kissed them both on the cheek and escorted them to the coach door. He then gave them assistance into the coach before boarding the coach himself. The coach door slammed shut, just then Jesse notice that there were no footmen on the coach. He looked around once more to see if he could see Amos. Amos was nowhere to be seen. Time for one of my decisions thought Jesse. He decided quickly that he would go to the trial after all. So he quickly ran to the back of the coach and jumped up onto the footman's ledge making sure no-one had seen him. There was a moment but at last the coach set off, Jesse hung on tight, he then looked back at the farmhouse just in time to see Amos, who was just coming around the corner of the house. Amos, seeing Jesse sat on the back of the coach, started to run and shout after the coach, he waved his fist at Jesse but Jesse just waved back and thought, hard luck mate, you're too late.

The coach rattled on through dale and village until eventually it arrived at a very busy place, Jesse had never seen so many people, shops and pubs. Everyone seemed so busy that they didn't even have time to notice Jesse at the back of the coach. Eventually, the coach stopped in front of a very large

 elaborate building with pillars, there were men wearing black gowns and grey curly wigs busily going in and out of the building. Jesse jumped down off the coach and quickly ran down an alley. The alley ran down the side of the building. Jesse was very careful not to be seen. Halfway down the alley there was a door, Jesse slowly began to twist the handle, he opened the door slightly, but suddenly he heard voices, quickly he closed the door and stood at the side of it trying to look inconspicuous. The door opened and a boy of about the same age as Jesse appeared. He looked at Jesse and said in a well spoken voice, "You there!" Jesse looked at the boy and said, "Yes." "What are you doing here? This is the judge's entrance and not for the likes of you." Jesse didn't like the boy's attitude and quickly snapped, "Why are you a judge?" "No but my father is, so move on," the boy replied. "Or I'll fetch the court officer, and he'll move you on," the boy said, pointing the way out of the alley to Jesse. Jesse not wishing to attract any attention said, "Oh, please don't do that. I need to see a court case being held here today." The boy's ears pricked up at the mere mention of a court case, "Which case is that?" He asked. Jesse began to explain to the boy all that had happened and how he'd gotten there and how important it was that he didn't get seen by his Aunt Emma, Percilla or Charlie, "My names Harry, Harry Pips," he said, holding out his hand. Jesse looked down at the hand and then quickly replied, "Oh, Jesse." Jesse shook Harry's hand tightly.

Harry then produced a piece of chocolate from his jacket pocket, which he snapped in half, he then gave half to Jesse whilst popping the other half into his own mouth, "Well I suppose you want to go in and see the case." Harry said, whilst dribbling chocolate from the side of his mouth. "Yes please!" Jesse answered keenly. Harry pointed towards the door with his head, he pulled up his trousers by the belt and said, "If we're quiet and I mean really quiet, not a word mind. I know a place where we can go and see your court case." Harry opened the door and enticed Jesse to follow him, "This way," He said. Both boys crept quietly down a long corridor. The corridor was full of half frosted glass doors, it seemed endless, but eventually they reached the end where there was a flight of stairs. Jesse and Harry climbed the first flight of stairs, then another flight then another and so on until they were both out of breath from the climb.

At the top of the last flight of stairs there was a small frosted glass door, similar to those in the corridor. Harry opened it and said, "We can see everything from here." They both entered and Harry sat down on a very large red velvet armchair, "Well! What do you think?" Jesse looked around and said, "Very nice, but how can we see anything from up here?" Harry stood up and walked across to a panel on the wall, he slid the panel back slowly to reveal the whole courtroom below, "There you go," he said proudly. "You can see the whole courtroom from up here and what's more no-one can see you. If you don't open the panel fully, my father uses this room sometimes to observe other cases that he has an interest in."

Jesse looked down on the courtroom through the opened panel and thought, this is great. I can see everything from here. Just then someone entered the courtroom. Jesse quickly ducked back and closed the panel. Harry laughed and said, "Don't worry; they can't see you up here. Anyway they never look up." He slowly opened the panel making a gap of about two inches, this was just enough to observe the courtroom without being discovered. He then looked down through the gap into the courtroom. "It's only the clerk of the court getting things ready," Harry told Jesse, who was by now stood a very safe distance back from the opened panel. Just then there was a knock on the frosted glass door. Jesse looked at Harry horrified thinking that they had been discovered.

However, Harry simply said, "Enter!" The door open slowly and a man entered, he was dressed in a black suit with a grey tie. The man paused for a little in the doorway, not quite entering the room, he then coughed, "Oh, it's you, Master Harry." The man said, as he removed his hand from covering his mouth, "Yes Mellor's, would you bring us some tea and some of your delicious crumpets, please." Mellor's looked Jesse up and down, coughed again and said, "Very well Master Harry." He then reversed out of the room closing the door behind him.

Jesse reluctantly walked back across the room towards the panel. He then leant forward and peered through the open gap that Harry had left. Jesse could see that the courtroom was beginning to fill up with people, some had wigs on and some didn't. His attention was distracted for a moment as Mellor's came back into the room with a large tray in his hands, "Your tea and crumpets, Master Harry." Mellor's placed the tray down on a small table which was sat between two armchairs, "Will there be anything else Master Harry?" "No not just now Mellor's." Mellor's again looked at Jesse, only this time he glared at him over his half rimmed glasses, which Jesse ignored and walked over to the small table. After sitting in one of the armchairs, Jesse said, "These smell good, what do you call them again?" Harry laughed, and began to finger the crumpets, "Crumpets, crumpets Jesse." Harry replied, taking a very large bite of his first one. Jesse waited for a moment then reluctantly took a bite. Harry watched Jesse's face as he chewed on his very first crumpet, he chewed slowly at first, then a little faster but when the butter hit Jesse's taste buds, he couldn't get enough. Jesse gobbled his way through four crumpets to Harry's one in a matter of a few minutes. Harry had never seen anyone eat so quickly, "Slow down Jesse, you'll give yourself indigestion!" Harry said to Jesse as he grabbed at the last crumpet on the plate.

"It's a nice room you've got here," Jesse said to Harry as they both laid back into the armchairs. "It's not, if you've to spend all day sat here waiting," Harry replied. Jesse was puzzled by what Harry had said and asked, "Don't you work then?" "No, I'm away at boarding school most of the time. I just sit here when I'm on holiday from the school. It's still better than being at school!" Jesse eagerly nodded in agreement and thought to himself anything's better than school, remembering his own school days. A sudden silence came over the boys as they both sat there thinking about their school days, it was broken by the words, "All, rise."

Harry jumped up and said, "Here's my father now." Jesse was startled for a moment and quickly jumped up himself, thinking Harry's father had entered the room. Instead when he turned around he saw Harry peering through the gap in the panel, "Come and have a look Jesse," Harry said, waving Jesse towards him. Jesse walked across to the panel and put his head at the side of Harry's so they both could see through the gap, both using one eye. "That's my father in the red gown and the white wig sat at the front," Harry said proudly. Jesse said, "Oh yes, I can see him." He then began looking around the courtroom to see if he recognized anybody, but it was difficult using only one eye. Eventually, Harry said, "Well once you've seen one case, you've seen them all." He then went and sat back down in his armchair giving Jesse a two eyed view of the courtroom. "Bring up the prisoners," the judge said loudly to two very smart police officers, who were stood to attention at the front of the court.

The officers immediately disappeared down some stairs behind a box, which had two chairs evenly placed in it. There was a moment's silence and then the whole courtroom was filled by the sound of metal door's clanging and the rattle of chains. The whole court seemed to lean forward in anticipation as two decrepit looking figures in chains began to climb the stairs. Jesse was dismayed and appalled at what he saw when the figures reached the top of the stairs. The figures began to hobble towards the chairs assisted by the officers, whose job it was to make sure that the figures didn't trip up over their own chains. Jesse looked again at the figures, which were filthy and their clothes were in tatters. He stared in disbelieve and thought, these figures can't be our Henry and Richard, it can't be them.

Jesse tried in vain to identify the figures. However, after some considerable time he still had not recognized any identifiable features of the two figures. There was a murmur from the courtroom as both men sat down. The judge banged a wooden mallet on his desk and asked for silence, he then shuffled in his seat and looked towards the box where the men were sat, "Stand up!" He growled. Both figures immediately stood up and at that moment Jesse recognized them both, it was definitely Richard and Henry. Jesse was so upset at recognizing Richard and Henry that he had to look away for a moment. Jesse held back the tears but one got away from him, and he quickly wiped it away with his dirty shirt sleeve. Meanwhile, Harry who had been watching Jesse from the luxury of the armchair said, "What's up Jesse?" Jesse looked across at Harry with tear filled eyes and said, "Oh, nothing." He then wiped his nose with his sleeve. Harry got up and walked towards the panel. He peered over Jesse's head and through the gap in the panel and said, "Is that your brother down there?"

Jesse hesitated for a moment and said, "I think so, it's hard to tell. They both look so filthy and scruffy." Harry seeing that Jesse was upset tried to pacify him by saying, "Oh that's how most of the prisoners appear." He took another look through the gap and said, "In fact, they look better than most, considering that they've been in Reading Prison for a month or more." Harry walked back to the armchair and said, "It'll soon be lunch time. I fancy some beef pudding, what about you?" Jesse didn't answer straight away; he was too interested in what was happening in the courtroom below. He just said, "Whatever," and continued to watch the case, which dragged on the rest of the morning. Everybody, who was anybody, stood up in a smaller box and said their piece about the case. The judge then whispered to a gentleman in front of him who shouted, "All, Rise." And everybody in the court stood up whilst the judge left, "Come on Jesse, get your lunch." Jesse turned towards the two armchairs and

there on the table in between the chairs was a plate of beef pudding covered in gravy. Jesse said, "Oh, I couldn't, you've done enough for me today." Harry pointed to the pudding and said, "It will only be thrown away if you don't eat it." He continued to eat his own pudding and the gravy began to run down his chin, he quickly caught it with a napkin before it fell off the end of his chin. Jesse sat down and began to tuck into the beef pudding, this is delicious he thought.

"What time does the court start again?"

Asked Jesse, as he sat back in the chair feeling bloated by the meal. "Oh it won't be long," Harry replied. He then stacked the plates on top of each other and sat back in his chair, "Why don't you move the chair nearer the gap, then you can watch what's going on whilst you are sat down," Harry suggested to Jesse. "Good idea," Jesse replied, and he started to pull the chair across to the gap. He then sat down and got himself comfortable ready for the case to start again. It wasn't long before the case re-started and his Aunt Emma was first to be called. Jesse could hear her name echoing down the corridors to where she was sat. It took a while, but eventually his Aunt Emma came down the main isle of the court and stood in the small box. As soon as she saw Henry and Richard, she began to cry, they both put their heads down and Jesse thought he saw tears dropping from Henry's face.

People in the court started asking his Aunt Emma questions, most of them seemed pointless to Jesse, he began to get bored with the proceedings. Eventually, Emma was told to sit down and the superintendent was sent for, again it took a little time for the superintendent to walk down the aisle to the box, but eventually he got there and climbed up into the box. His questions seemed to be the same as Emma's, which began to bore Jesse and his eyes began to get heavy as the beef pudding took hold of him. He looked across at Harry and saw that he was sound asleep in the other armchair. Why not Jesse thought, he slowly laid back into the armchair, opened the gap a little more and snuggled down to have a nap. He thought if anything of importance took place, he would hear it.

Some hours later Jesse was awakened by Mellor's shaking him and saying, "Sir, young sir, wake up sir." Jesse began to wake up, slowly at first and then he remembered where he was, he jumped up quickly and said, "The court case, what's happened?" He looked through the gap and the courtroom was in complete darkness, "Where is everybody?" "The case finished some twenty minutes ago sir. Master Harry has left with his father some minutes ago." Jesse was panicking, "What happened in the case? Do you know?" Mellor looked at Jesse and said, "Were you related to the people on trial sir?" "Yes, yes, tell me what has happened." Mellor's, who knew the results of the trial and knew that they weren't good, sat Jesse down in the armchair and pulled

the other armchair up close, both sat on the edge of their chairs facing each other. Mellor's then said, "Its not good news young sir." Jesse began to cry, "The youngest of the men on trial has been transported. I think they called him Henry."

Jesse stopped crying for a moment and said, "Henry, yes Henry! He's my brother. They're not going to hang him then?" "No sir, he's been transported." Jesse smiled and sat back in the chair, "That's good news," Jesse said, with a smile on his face. "Is it sir? Are you aware of what transportation is?" The smile instantly disappeared from Jesse's face. He replied, "No not really. Tell me, tell me what it is, is it bad?" "Your brother is going on a ship to the otherside of the world, and he won't be coming back. Well I've never heard of anybody coming back. They never come back from there," Mellor's said, staring down at the floor. "At least he's alive!" Jesse said, with a sense of relief in his voice. He then sat forward in the chair and reluctantly asked, "Now tell me, what about Richard? The other man on trial." "Arr... the older gentleman, the news of Richard I'm afraid is the worst possible. Unfortunately, he is going to be hung for murder. Was he a relative sir?" Jesse looked up and said, "No, not really, he was going to marry my sister." Jesse began shaking his head and said, "Poor Richard." Mellor's replied, "quite."

Jesse then suddenly realized that Percilla, Charlie and his Aunt Emma must have started back towards home. He stood up quickly and said, "The coach! I have to go." Jesse turned towards the door and set off running, at the same time he said, "Thank you, oh... and thank you for the food." He then ran back down the steps and up the corridor to the side door. He pushed open the door and walked out into the alley. It was dark and very lonely in the alley, so he headed straight towards the front of the building. Jesse began frantically looking around for the coach. He searched down most of the streets around the court building, but to no avail.

Eventually, he arrived back in front of the court building and sat down on the pavement, he started to think about what he was going to do, "Did you find the coach?" Jesse spun his head around to see Mellor's stood there. "No! They've gone back without me, I'm afraid," replied Jesse who was feeling quite sorry for himself. Mellor's then asked quietly, "Where do you live? Is it far?" Jesse looked up at him and shrieked, "Is it far, is it far? I don't even know which way to go, never mind how far it is!"

There was a moment silence and Mellor's sat down at the side of Jesse on the pavement, before saying, "You're in quite a predicament then." Jesse slowly nodded his head in agreement with Mellor's and asked, "Do you know which way Shalbourne is?" Mellor's laughed, "Shalbourne!" He laughed again and said, "I'm from Inkpen, do you know where Inkpen is?" Jesse jumped up quickly and said, "Yes! It's the next village; we share the common with farmers from Inkpen." Mellor's stood up and said, "Come with me." He started to walk towards the pub, which was across the otherside of the road from the court. Jesse stood up and followed. He wondered where they were going. About halfway across Mellor's turned to Jesse and said sternly, "Wait here! I'll be back in a moment." He then disappeared through an archway at the side of the pub.

Jesse turned around and put his back against the pub wall. It wasn't long before Jesse began to notice the people going in and out of the pub. Busy place thought Jesse; he was just about to look up the side of the pub to see if there was any sign of Mellor's when there was an almighty bang and two men burst out through the doors of the pub. Neither man touched the pavement; they both flew through the air and landed in the road. Jesse was startled and moved quickly around the corner of the building, he glanced back around the corner to see what was happening. The men were rolling around in the road being cheered and goaded on by a mob, which had followed them out of the pub. Some of the men in the mob started to join in the fight. Jesse couldn't believe his eyes as the women began to join in as well.

One woman pulled another woman into the road by her hair, whilst screaming what can only be described as verbal abuse at her. The fight seemed to cover the whole road and everybody in the pub had become involved, Jesse even saw passers-by becoming involved. It wasn't long before the sound of whistles and pounding feet could be heard as the Newbury Police began to arrive. The police waded into the mob and started to grab people by their arms, at the same time they were pushing other fighting couples apart.

Just then a black box cart arrived being driven by the tallest policemen Jesse had ever seen. The policeman jumped down from the front of the cart and grabbed the first person he came across. The victim, a young lad who was kicking and punching out at anybody or anything, was dragged by the policemen to the back of the cart and thrown un-ceremonially into the back of it. He then began to look around for his next victim, Jesse pulled back, not wishing to be the next victim. After the police had thrown two or three people into the back of the cart, the mob began to realize that their numbers were beginning to deplete, this gave them the signal for a mass exodus. They all began to disperse quickly. People began making a run for it before they were arrested themselves.

Two pushed their way past Jesse and disappeared through the archway at the side of the pub. Suddenly, it all went quiet. Jesse slowly peered around the corner to see what was going on. Everybody had gone, the only remnants left to say that there'd ever been a fight was an old flat cap in the gutter and the police box cart making its way slowly down the road. Jesse came from around the corner and watched as the cart turned the corner at the bottom of the road, "Are you ready then?" A voice said from behind Jesse, he turned to see Mellor's sat there on a beautiful black stallion. "Come on then," Mellor's said, offering Jesse a hand up onto the horse. Jesse accepted the hand reluctantly and was pulled up onto the back of the horse.

"What a nice quiet evening," Mellor's said as he spurred the horse on with his knees. Jesse grinned to himself and replied, "Yes, very quiet!" The horse moved off with a jerk, forcing Jesse to grab hold of Mellor's by the waist, "Not so tight young sir," Mellor's said, pulling Jesse's arms from around his waist. Jesse quickly returned the arms saying, "It was an awfully long way down from where he was sat." Mellor's laughed and the pair began to make their way through the town at a nice steady trot. It wasn't long before Jesse became more confident about riding on the back of the horse and decided to ease the pressure on Mellor's waist, after all he thought it's better than walking.

Jesse had switched off and entered his own little world, he could hear Mellor's saying something, but it was all a blur. Just then the horse began to speed up and Jesse instantly applied the pressure again around Mellor's waist, "What's going on?" Jesse asked, bobbing up and down and trying to hang on, "Nothing! But we've got to get a move on otherwise we'll never get home," Mellor's replied. Jesse hung on for dear life as the horse sped across the countryside towards home. Eventually, the horse began to slow down, and then it stopped at a crossroad, "Now young sir, Shalbourne is about ten miles in that direction. Just stay on this road and you won't get lost." Mellor's grabbed Jesse's arm and lowered him to the ground, "I'm sorry I can't take you any further, but my wife and children are waiting for me at home, and I'm already late."

Jesse knew his way from the crossroads, so he wasn't too bothered about being left there. He simple lifted his hand up towards Mellor's and said, "Thank you, thank you for everything." Mellor's leant forward towards Jesse and shook his hand. He then kicked the horse with his heels and set off. Jesse stood there for a moment and watched Mellor's disappear into the darkness. He then turned and began walking in the direction Mellor's had told him to. It wasn't long before Jesse began to realize how dark it had become. In fact, he was finding it very difficult to see his way. He was beginning to feel very vulnerable and alone in the darkness. Jesse's mind began to work overtime, what if I'm attacked by foxes? What if I get murdered? No-one would ever find me out here. Then, suddenly the moon appeared from behind the clouds, it lit up the whole countryside. Jesse was amazed, it was as if the Lord God himself was lighting up Jesse's way home.

A good five hours later a very weary Jesse could see Whites Farm, in the distance. There was no light coming from the farmhouse and all seemed quiet as Jesse entered the farmyard, he quietly walked across the yard towards the barn. Arriving at the barn door, Jesse paused for a moment and listened, he could hear the very faint sound of someone singing inside the barn. Jesse froze and slowly began to open the barn door, but as soon as Jesse touched the door it let out a creek, the sound travelled for miles on the silent winds of the night. The singing suddenly stopped and a voice from inside the barn said, "Is that you ya little bastard?"

The barn door swung opened quickly catching the wind and Jesse off guard. It knocked him clean off his feet. The door hadn't hurt Jesse, and he quickly jumped back up onto his feet, he then recomposed himself and looked towards the barn doorway. There, with the candle light flickering at the back of him, stood Amos, he was holding a flail in one hand and a jug of ale in the other. Staggering forward Amos wiped the drool from his mouth with his shirt sleeve and said, "Get in here ya little sod." Jesse impudently replied, "Not bloody likely!" Amos took another swig from the jug and staggered forward. Jesse started to move back quickly. Amos then took another two staggering steps towards Jesse, but at this point the ale got the better of him, he tripped up over his own feet and knocked himself out on the corner of the horse trough. Jesse walked slowly towards Amos, hoping that he hadn't killed himself on the horse trough, but Jesse need not have worried, because as he approached, Amos turned over and began snoring. This stopped Jesse in his tracks for a moment, but then he realized that Amos was only sleeping. He continued cautiously to walk past Amos towards his own bed at the back of the barn, but before closing the barn door Jesse turned toward Amos and gave him a real hard kick on his shin. This made Amos move a little, but it didn't wake him. Jesse went to bed feeling very satisfied.

The next morning Jesse peeked out through the gap between the barn doors to see if Amos was still lying in front of the horse trough, he wasn't, so Jesse used it as an excuse to go back to bed and have an extra half hour of blissful thoughts and dreams. Has he laid there on his bed of straw his thought soon turned to Henry and whether or not he would ever see his brother again. "Jesse, Jesse. Are you there?" Percilla said, entering the barn. Jesse jumped up suddenly and said, "Over here Percilla." She walked towards Jesse and handed him a sandwich made from a large piece of gammon between two thickly cut slices of bread, "Here, Auntie Em sent you this and said you must stay out of sight this morning. Amos is after your guts!" Jesse grinned and said, "I'll bet he is." He then took a large bite of the sandwich, not really caring about what Amos wanted, "I suppose you know all about what happened at the trial yesterday," Percilla asked Jesse as he continued to consume the sandwich. "Yes, I was just wondering about our Henry and whether or not we will ever see him again." Percilla suddenly held her stomach and said, "I must sit down." Jesse quickly moved some tools from in front of an old chest and said, "Here, sit on this. You're not going to be sick are you?" Percilla, still holding her stomach, hitched herself up onto the top of the chest and snapped, "No, I'm not going to be sick." She smiled nervously at Jesse and said, "That's better." She then shuffled further back onto the chest and said, "Of course we'll see our Henry again. We've been granted a final visit before he gets transported. It's the last chance to see him before he goes."

Jesse's eyes lit up at the thought of seeing Henry again, but this happiness was short lived as he remembered his Aunt Emma's words when he wanted to go to court. "Master White won't let me go," he said, looking at Percilla, hoping that she would reassure him. "You don't know that," She replied. "Yes I do, he hates me!" Jesse turned and thumped the side of the barn. At that moment, a dark shadow appeared at the barn door and said, "There you are." He pointed at Percilla, "You outside!" It was Amos. Percilla quickly shuffled her way down off the chest and headed towards the door. Amos picked up a flail and closed the door behind Percilla. He then slowly turned to face Jesse and said, "Now lad! It's just thee and me."

Percilla, realizing what was going to happen next, set off towards the farmhouse kitchen shouting, "Auntie Em, Auntie Em." However, Emma was busy in the kitchen giving Master White his breakfast and was oblivious to what was going on. This soon changed when Percilla came bursting into the kitchen, saying, "Amos has caught our Jesse, and they're both locked in the barn." Instantly, Emma wiped her hands on her apron, grabbed her shoal and was heading for the backdoor when Master White shouted, "Stop!" Emma froze and looked at Master White. Percilla moved closer to Emma, "Both of you sit down! It's time that lad was taught a lesson and our Amos is the man to do it, so sit, both of you!" Emma and Percilla both slowly walked towards the table and sat down, a silence came over the kitchen. The only sound that could be heard was Master White cutting his gammon, the scraping of a knife on a plate made Percilla cringe.

Eventually, Emma stood up, took off her shoal and walked silently across to the peg where she hung it up. Master White put his knife and fork down on his plate and burped. He picked up his tankard, swigged off the last of his milk and then pulled his watch from his waist coat pocket, he was just about to announce the time to everyone when Amos came barging into the kitchen. He was livid, he threw the flail down onto the table and said, "The little bastards off again." Emma and Percilla looked at each other in astonishment, Master White said, "Less of the swearing our Amos. What do you mean, he's off again?" Amos took a deep breath and said, "The little bugger had made a small trap door at the back of the barn so he could escape through it, but I couldn't. He was off like a little jack rabbit." Emma and Percilla looked at each other again and burst out into fits of laughter. This only served to irritate Amos even more; he banged his fist down on the kitchen table and said, "When I do catch him, he'll know about it!"

Jesse managed to stay out of Amos's way for a couple of days and had arranged with Percilla to leave him food behind the barn under a flat stone. On the third day Jesse felt at ease, knowing that it was Amos's day off, he'd spent most of the day threshing the corn and had become hungry. It must be teatime Jesse thought, he wandered around to the back of the barn and there sure enough under the stone was a pie with a small tankard of milk. He was just about to bend down to pick up the pie when he felt a red hot stinging pain at the back of his head, "Gotcha!" A voice said. Jesse's hands automatically lifted to rub the back of his head, he looked around, wondering what had caused the pain, but before he realized what was happening, Amos was down on him, raining blows to both Jesse's face and body. Jesse immediately curled up into a ball and began screaming. Amos, not being able to reach Jesse's face with his fist, began to kick Jesse in the ribs. After four or five vicious kicks, Amos said, "There, ya little sod. That'll teach ya." He then turned and walked away leaving Jesse still curled up in a ball. Jesse stayed curled up in agony for sometime, but as darkness began to fall and the rain drizzled down the back of his neck, he slowly uncurled himself. Every movement was agony, the blood from his nose and mouth had dried on his face and neck. Jesse tried to stand up straight but was unable to. Instead he hobbled back around the barn to the horse trough.

He started to wipe away some of the blood from his face and neck using the usual mucky cloth, which was hung over the end of the trough. Every touch of the wet cloth made Jesse wince, especially around his left eye, which seemed to be getting bigger by the minutes. The pain of using the cloth proved to be too much for Jesse, so he decided to get the pain over in one go by ducking his whole face into the trough. He took a deep breath and plunge his head into the trough, it stung like hell, but Jesse gritted his teeth and hung under the water for a few moments longer.

The ducking was interrupted by Percilla pulling him up by his hair, "What on earth are you doing now?" She said getting soaked from Jesse, who shook his head the moment it was clear of the water. Percilla jumped back and was about to give Jesse a piece of her mind for soaking her when she noticed the excruciating expression of pain on Jesse's face. Jesse began to sob and Percilla stepped forward and hugged Jesse saying, "Amos!" Jesse nodded and they both hobbled into the barn out of the evening's heavy drizzle which was slowly turning to rain, "I'll fetch Auntie Em, she'll know what to do." Percilla headed off quickly towards the farmhouse, all Jesse could do was to lay flat on the corn he'd threshed earlier. A couple of minutes later Percilla arrived with Emma close behind. Master White had come out of the house but had thought it wise to wait in the yard.

Emma and Percilla helped Jesse up off the corn and walked him toward his bed of straw at the back of the barn. Whilst laying Jesse down on his bed, Emma asked, "Where's the pain Jesse?" Jesse grinned and replied, "Everywhere!" Emma was not amused by Jesse's answer and said, "This is not the time for your nonsense, now. Where's the pain?" Jesse pointed to his ribs and then spat out some blood. Emma on seeing the blood looked at Percilla and said, "Percilla, go and tell Master White, we need a doctor." Percilla ran back into the yard where Master White was waiting patiently. He looked at his watch and said very nonchalantly, "Is he alright?" To which

Percilla replied, "No, he's bloody not. He needs a doctor and fast." Master White put away his watch and walked across to the barn, "Madam, are you sure the lad needs a doctor? They're very expensive."

Emma looked up and said angrily, "See for yourself, he's nearly killed the lad. Do you want to see Amos hang?" The Master began to stammer, "O...f ...cous...e of course not." "Then get the doctor, quick!" Master White began to untie Titan. He fumbled at the rains but eventually managed to undo them. After a struggle to mount Titan, he set off towards the village. Jesse began to cough. "Fetch some water Percilla," Percilla didn't answer. Emma looked up and said, "Percilla!" Percilla again didn't answer; she just stood at the barn door crying, "Is he going to die Aunt Emma?" Percilla asked, wiping her nose with a rather dirty looking handkerchief, "Not if I can help it, now go and get some water!" Percilla went around behind the barn where she had left the pie and milk for Jesse earlier that day. Quickly, she picked up the tankard which was still full of milk and tossed it away, she then walked briskly back around the barn to the horse trough.

Percilla skimmed the scum off the top of the trough and quickly dunked the tankard into the trough allowing some cool clean water to enter the tankard. She turned and headed towards the barn, Percilla was just about to enter the barn when the door flung open and out staggered Amos with a jar of ale in his hand. He wiped his mouth free from drool and said to Percilla, "There's nothing wrong with him. He's putting it on, the little bastard!" He then angrily slapped Percilla across the face with the back of his hand before pushing his way past her. Percilla went flying back towards the horse trough and the tankard went the other direction and landed on the yard floor spilling its contents, "Drunken bastard!" Percilla said to herself, getting up from the yard floor and dusting herself down. She quickly looked around to see where Amos had gone, there was no sign of him, so she refilled the tankard and took it inside the barn. Emma nearly bit Percilla's head off when she eventually returned, "You took your time! Where have you been?" Emma snapped. "Amos treated me to one of his delights." Answered Percilla, she pointed to the red mark which had appeared down the right side of her face.

The evening drizzle had turned to a down pour when a knock came on the barn door, "Anybody in?" A voice said from outside the barn. Percilla walked to the door and stared out into a dark rainy night, she flinched as the rain began to hit her face. "Come on lass, let us in," said Master White, who was stood in front of the barn door with Titan and the doctor. All three were absolutely soaked to the skin, "Where's the patient?" The doctor asked as he pushed his way past Percilla. Percilla didn't say anything she just pointed to where Jesse was laid. The doctor marched promptly towards Jesse and knelt down beside him. Emma stood up and stepped back to give the doctor better access to Jesse. She then noticed an unusually fusty smell coming from the doctor. Perhaps it's the rain she thought; she quickly placed her handkerchief over her nose and gave it a little sniff. Percilla and the Master joined Emma, they all stood and watched as the doctor examined Jesse, the doctor prodded and poked at Jesse.

Eventually, the doctor stood up an announced, "Broken ribs! That's the problem." He looked at Master White and said, "The lad will have to rest for at least a month, he can't work in this condition. He must lie still for at least a month." "What! He's got chores to do." "Well I'm sorry, but he can't work. Furthermore, he needs to be kept warm, so we'll have to move him into the house." Master White quickly replied, "Impossible, there's no room in the house." The doctor became angry at this point and said sternly, "You'll just have to make room! If you leave him out here he'll catch his death, pneumonia." Emma and Percilla both gasped and looked straight at Master White, who realized he better make room in the house or he'd be in deep trouble. He thought for a moment, and then slowly, but reluctantly said, "I suppose he could have our Earle's room for a month. Earle can sleep out here, it won't hurt him." Everybody nodded in agreement and then began deciding the best way to move Jesse into the house without causing him more pain.

The doctor began binding Jesse's ribs tightly with some long bandages, "There you go, change the bandages every week, and you should be fine." He said, looking up at Emma, who nodded. "I can hardly breathe," moaned Jesse, who was gasping for breath. "That's normal," the doctor replied, he continued, "Don't worry. Just lie still." Master White sneezed and said, "Shuffle onto this board, and we will lift you across the yard to the house." He placed a piece of an old board, that he'd used to block a hole with at the side of the barn, at the side of Jesse, who then shuffled his way across the floor onto the board, "Right everybody get hold of a corner." Master White said, bending down to pick his corner up. "Just a minute," Emma said, grabbing a grey horse blanket, which was hung over a nearby partition. "This will keep the rain off you," she said, throwing it over Jesse, who grinned as it hit his chin and began to tickle.

The four of them walked in unison toward the farmhouse across a rainy windswept yard carrying Jesse on the board. They struggled to get through the garden gate and the backdoor with Jesse on the board and because of this, they decided that it would be easier for Jesse to try and walk up the stairs. It was simple, there just wasn't enough room for all of them and the board to get up the stairs, so Jesse took a deep breath and swung his legs around ready to get off the board, he paused for a moment letting his legs dangle over the side of the board. He eventually gritted his teeth, placed his feet on the floor and stood up whilst holding his ribs and trying desperately to breathe at the same time. "What's the matter with him?" Asked Earle, who had just sat at the table and watched them struggle through the backdoor with Jesse. "Never you mind our Earle, just come and give a hand to get him upstairs."

"Upstairs! Why where's he going?" asked Earle, getting hold of Jesse's arm, "Your bedroom!" Master White replied, wiping the rain from his forehead with his hand. He then flicked the water off his hand and quickly returned it to his nose as he began to sneeze again, "Bless you!" Emma and Percilla said together. Master White pulled out a red dirty handkerchief from his pocket and began blowing into it. Earle, thinking he was going to have to share the bedroom with Jesse, quickly dropped Jesse's arm and shouted, "I'm not sharing with him!" Jesse squealed as his arm dropped rapidly down to his side, "Careful Earle! That's right you're not sharing. You're moving into the barn." Replied Master White, who then got hold of Jesse's arm, wrapped it around his own shoulder and started off up the stairs with him. This left Earle speechless at the bottom of the stairs. He just stood there with his mouth open in disbelieve at what he'd just heard. Percilla saw the expression on Earle's face and said, "Close your mouth Earle." She pushed his mouth closed using the tips of two fingers under his chin. She then started off up the stairs after the Master and Emma, with the doctor following closely.

It wasn't long before Jesse was tucked up in Earle's bed and the doctor was taking his pulse. "Everything seems normal," said the doctor, putting away his stethoscope and pulling out the pillar from behind Jesse's head. "You won't need this," he said, handing it to Emma, who placed it on the wooden chair in the corner of the room. The doctor continued talking to Emma about what should be done to aid Jesse's quick recovery, "Remember madam, the lad must lie absolutely still, in order for the ribs to mend properly." Emma smiled at the doctor and nodded her head. She then thought to herself. What, our Jesse stay still, some hope! The doctor then turned to Master White and was just about to say something when Master White interrupted him by saying, "Right then!" The Master quickly man handled the doctor out through the bedroom door and down the stairs to the kitchen. As both men stood by the backdoor, the doctor, who had attended many farm lads' injuries, said, "By law I should report the lad's injuries to the police." There was a moment's hesitation, "No need for all that nonsense," said Master White, rummaging through his waistcoat pocket for coins. "Here, this should take care of your bill," said the Master. He then grabbed the doctor's hand and thrust two coins into his palm, whilst looked around quickly, checking to see if anybody was watching. He then slowly began to curl up the doctor's fingers, enclosing the coins within; he sneakily winked at the doctor. Who quickly opened his hand, looked down and saw an agreeable amount of money. "But, since he's being well cared for, I think things will be fine," he said, nodding his head and pulling up his collar before entering the darkness of the rainy night.

Jesse laid there for over a week just staring up at the ceiling. Sometimes, to amuse himself; he would squint at the cracked plaster in the ceiling, this made faces appear in the plaster, but after a while, even Jesse became bored with this. Another week went by and Jesse had tried his best to lay there contented, but as usual he got bored. This particular morning had been like the previous seven, boring, boring, boring! So after dinner, Jesse felt slightly better and had begun closing first one eye, then the other, to see if he could spot any more faces in the ceiling, he was just beginning to get bored again, when there was a knock on the bedroom door, "Anybody in?" A voice said.

Instantly, Jesse knew it was Charlie and said, "Come in ya fool," "Not dead yet then?" Charlie said, peeping around the edge of the door. Charlie grabbed the small wooden chair from the corner of the room and plonked it down at the side of the bed, "Now then, how ya doing our Jesse?" Charlie asked, looking at the marks on Jesse's face, "I'll live," replied Jesse. There was then an awkward silence which was broken by Charlie saying, "That's good news about our Henry, isn't it?" Jesse quickly asked, "What news?" "The visit," Charlie replied. Jesse looked at Charlie and miserably said, "Oh, that!" This answer startled Charlie, who asked, "What do you mean? Oh that? I thought you'd be happy about seeing our Henry." "How can I go looking like this?" Jesse moaned, whilst lifting his hands up, which was very painful. "It's not for another month. You should be well by then," said Charlie, who could see that Jesse was still unhappy about not been able to see Henry, so he continued to say, "We're all going, including you!" Jesse, who was by now filling up, said, "Promise!" Charlie nodded his head and got hold of Jesse's hand.

Just then Charlie remembered the sweets he'd brought for Jesse, "Oh, before I forget. I've brought you something." Charlie quickly dipped his hand into his inside jacket pocket and said, "Here you are." He handed Jesse a small brown paper bag. Jesse sat up a little and Charlie pushed a pillow under Jesse's head, "What are they?" Jesse asked, squinting into the bag. Charlie, who by now had a large grin on his face, said out loud, "Boillies! Hard as rock, boillies,  they last forever." Jesse put his thumb and fore finger into the bag and took out what looked like a very round stripy coloured stone. After smelling it, Jesse said, "Well what do I do with it now?" Charlie started to laugh and said, "You suck it fool!" Jesse reluctantly put, what he thought was a stone into his mouth, he began to suck, a smile began to appear on Jesse's face, he'd never tasted such a sweet smelling thing before and said, "These are great!" To Charlie, who stood up and said, "I've got to go." Charlie put the chair back in the corner and saluted Jesse, who returned the salute. Charlie grinned and then left closing the door behind him. Jesse just laid back and snuggled down into the pillow with a boillie bump protruding from his cheek. Jesse sucked on the sweets for the next two days, but eventually they ran out and the boredom returned. The only enjoyment he had was sneaking over to the window and waving at Earle, who was doing all of Jesse's chores until he had recovered. Earle had complained about Jesse to the Master and Amos, saying Jesse was, "Putting it on." But nothing had come of his complaining.

A month had passed and Jesse was still laid there as usual staring at the ceiling. He closed both eyes and began thinking about what he was going to do that day to amuse himself he'd also gotten fed up with winding Earle up from the window. However, his thinking was abruptly interrupted when Emma entered the bedroom carrying a bowl of hot water, closely followed by Percilla carrying some towels, "Come on you, up!" Emma snapped at Jesse, who instantly sat up in bed, and asked, "What's going on?" "You're having a wash!" Percilla replied, rolling up her sleeves as she began rubbing the soap onto a wet cloth that had been laid in the bottom of the bowl. Emma pulled Jesse's nightshirt quickly over his head and said, "Arms up!" She then began to unwind the bandage from Jesse's ribs. "Time this was changed," she said, walking out of the bedroom with the dirty bandage. Percilla set about washing Jesse's back, she rubbed it gently in a circular motion, before lifting his arm and washing his armpit as she made her way around to the front. Suddenly, Jesse realized that Percilla was washing his front, he quickly grabbed the cloth, and pushed Percilla's hand away, saying in a superior voice, "I can do that bit myself, thank you," "shy are we?" Percilla asked, laughing at the expression on Jesse's face.

Just then Emma came back into the bedroom holding a clean bandage, which she had just ripped from an old underskirt she was going to throw away. "Good job I kept that old underskirt," she said, putting the bandage down on the bed and taking the wet cloth from Jesse. She dipped the cloth back into the bowl and rubbed some more soap on to it before continuing to wash around Jesse's other armpit. Meanwhile Percilla had begun drying Jesse's back with the towel. Everybody was busy rubbing and scrubbing, when a voice from the bedroom door said, "Looks to me like you are ready to get back to it." Everybody suddenly stopped what they were doing and instantly looked in the direction of the voice, "Aye, you heard me; it's back to work for you my lad." Amos then turned and went back down the stairs towards the kitchen.

"Right, that'll do ya," Emma said to Jesse. She handed Percilla the wet cloth who tossed it into the bowl. "Come on now, get dressed. We're all going to see our Henry before he leaves," said Emma. Jesse was up and out of the bed like a shot, "Great, what time do we leave?" He asked, tucking his shirt into his trousers. "After breakfast," Emma replied. "What about Richard, will he be there?" The room suddenly fell silent and Jesse realized he'd said something wrong, "What, what? What did I say?" Percilla looked at Emma, then at Jesse and then ran out of the room crying. Emma followed saying to Jesse, "You and your big mouth!" Exasperated, she then said, "Richard was hung three days ago!" Jesse's head dropped quickly, he sat down and slowly began putting on his shoes before walking towards the bedroom door where he stood for a moment and listened. He could hear his Aunt Emma trying to comfort Percilla in the next room. Jesse waited and eventually his Aunt Emma came out of the bedroom, closing the door quietly behind her, "I'm sorry." Jesse said, in a very quiet voice. Emma smiled gently at him and said, "You weren't to know." Both quietly crept down the stairs for breakfast.

Jesse joined Earle, who was already sat at the kitchen table waiting patiently for Emma to get him some breakfast ready. Emma glanced at Earle and walked across to the fire, she poured out two steaming bowls of porridge from a large pan which had been simmering on the hob. She then poured a little fresh cream onto the porridge. The cream ran around the inside edge of the bowl and then disappeared down into the porridge, "Here, get this down you. It's nice and lumpy, just how you like it." Emma said to Jesse and Earle, who were by now drooling in anticipation of the porridge.

Both started gobbling the porridge as soon as the bowls hit the table in front of them. Percilla then entered the kitchen. Both eyes were still red from crying. Jesse stopped eating and stood up; he walked slowly towards Percilla, put his arms around her and said, "I'm sorry our Percilla." He hugged Percilla for quite a while, but eventually they separated and Percilla said, "I'm alright." She gave Jesse a small delicate kiss on his cheek and reluctantly smiled at him. Jesse returned to the table where he continued gobbling his porridge. Percilla sat down opposite Earle, who had almost finished his porridge, "That was very tasty." Earle said, wiping his mouth with the back of his hand. Just then Charlie popped his head around the backdoor and said, "Is everybody ready then?"

Jesse and Percilla got up from the table leaving Earle sat there wondering what was going on, "Where are you lot going now?" Earle asked, thinking that Jesse was going to help him with the chores before he had to go to school. "Mind your own business," replied Jesse, closing the door behind him. Emma

picked up her shawl and a large hand basket which she had packed with food for the journey. It also contained some parting gifts for Henry and before leaving the kitchen Emma looked at Earle and said, "See ya later Earle." Earle grunted in reply and Emma walked towards the door. She was just about to open the door when it opened from the outside and in came Master White. He sneezed twice and then looked directly at Emma, "You're off then," he said, with a blocked up nose.

Emma nodded and sheepishly stepped past him saying, "Bless you! You should be in bed with that cold master." The master coughed into his handkerchief whilst nodding his head.

Emma walked out of the back garden into the farmyard where Mrs. Newman's coach was stood waiting for her. She looked up and there, next to the driver, was Jesse. The driver jumped down and took Emma's basket from her, "What are you doing up there?" Emma asked Jesse, thinking about his broken ribs. "Charlie said I could sit up here if I wanted to," replied Jesse, looking full of mischief. Emma, still unsure, looked at the driver and said, "Is that alright with you Thomas?" Thomas laughed and said, "Aye... ma'am, but I'll bet he changes his mind when it rains."

The coach set off and Jesse loved the breeze hitting him full in the face, it was so fresh that it made his eye's water, but that didn't bother him. The coach passed through Shalbourne and out onto the main highway. Jesse didn't recognize the road or where the coach was taking him, so he turned to Thomas and said, "How long before we reach Reading Prison then Thomas?" Thomas cracked the whip over the horses head and replied, "Were not going to Reading Prison. Henry's not there anymore lad, he's been transferred." Jesse paused for a moment and was just about to ask, when Thomas said, "Before you ask, he's been transferred to Woolwich, partly because Reading Prison is too overcrowded." Jesse pondered for a moment longer and then said, "I hope Woolwich Prison is better than Reading Prison!" Thomas didn't answer, he just continued cracking the whip over the horses.

The coach had travelled for about six hours when it turned into an inn yard and by now Jesse was beginning to feel the cold. Thomas shouted to everybody, "Thirty minute break whilst the horses are changed." Jesse jumped down and opened the small coach door. Emma stepped down from the coach and turned to help Percilla down. They both quickly pushed past Jesse saying, "Get out of the way Jesse!" They were in that much of a rush that they nearly trampled Jesse, "What's the matter with those two?" Jesse asked Charlie, who just laughed and said, "They need the toilet. Percilla is pregnant, remember?" Jesse just shrugged his shoulders and opened the basket which was tied to the back of the coach. He grabbed a small pie for both him and Charlie, "Here," he said handing Charlie his pie. They both then sat among some barrels, which were piled in the yard and began eating their pies. After a moment Emma and Percilla returned and saw that Charlie and Jesse had started eating without them, "Couldn't you two wait?" Emma said, looking inside the basket. She then turned to Charlie and said, "Charlie. Go and get a tankard of ale from the inn keeper." She handed Charlie some coins and a tankard which she pulled from the basket.

Jesse had finished eating his pie and was sat watching Percilla and Emma eat theirs, when Charlie returned with the ale, "Here you are, real ale!" Charlie announced, taking a good long swig from the tankard. The tankard then passed to Jesse, who just did the same as Charlie, but Jesse, who had not tasted strong ale before was shocked by the taste and it made him stop drinking quickly. Jesse began coughing and choking on the bitter taste as soon as it hit the back of his throat. He quickly handed the tankard back to Charlie, who passed it to Percilla whilst grinning. Charlie began patting Jesse on the back saying, "That's it lad, cough it up!" Jesse eventually stopped coughing and said, "Gosh! That was strong." He then went to a nearby trough and took a long drink of fresh cold water.

When Jesse returned, Thomas had joined the group and was taking a drink from the tankard. Emma handed Jesse a sandwich and then gave one to Thomas, "Come on everybody, we must get on." Thomas said, opening the coach door. Jesse quickly jumped inside the coach and said with a full mouth of sandwich, "I bag's this seat." Emma looked at Percilla and said, "That didn't last long." Jesse was puzzled by what Emma had said and asked, "What didn't last long?" "Our peace and quiet," Emma replied, climbing on board the coach whilst pinching Jesse's cheek. Charlie and Percilla followed and began spreading out the travel blanket across everybody's knees as they sat down. The coach pulled out of the inn yard and set off once more towards Woolwich. Jesse had prattled on for sometime before the warmth of the blanket began to make him feel tired. A sudden silence came over the coach as Jesse fell asleep and the coach ambled onwards towards Woolwich.

Some hours later the coach rattled into the streets of Woolwich, it began making its way through the narrow dimly lit cobbled streets towards the docks. The streets were lined with small houses, each had a candle lit window and smoke coming from a chimney. The coach rattled on, the sound of the wheels echoed loudly around the cobbled streets and began to wake Jesse. Jesse slowly sniffed the air, he could smell fish. Fish he thought, the coach then came to a sudden halt and Jesse sat up. He leant out of the coach window and looked up to see a pair of huge black wrought iron gates with the name Woolwich Dockyard written in gold on an arch which hung above the gates,

"Thomas! Thomas!" Jesse shouted. Thomas jumped down from his seat and said, "What's the matter with you now?" "This isn't the prison!" Jesse snapped. "You've brought us to the wrong place, this is the dockyard!" Thomas took a deep breath and replied, "The prison is over there." He then pointed to a very large ship, in the distance, which was painted black and white and seemed to have clothes hung from poles, which were sticking out from holes in the side of the vessel.

Jesse stepped down from the coach and looked towards the ship. There was a line of men entering the ship in single file, they were all dressed in the same clothes, cotton striped jackets and trousers with a rather unusual hat pulled down over their ears. The ship itself was lit by lamps, which could be seen swinging in the nights wind. Using the light from these lamps Jesse could just make out the name of the ship, which was written across the back of the ship in gold letters. Jesse began to spell out the name, "W...A...RR...I...O...R..., Warrior!" He then asked, "Is our Henry's on that ship?" Charlie chirped up from behind Jesse and said sympathetically, "I'm afraid so, it's called The Great Warrior Hulk. It's a left over warship being used as a prison because places like Reading Prison are so overcrowded. There are other ships up and down the river doing the same thing." "Come on then," Jesse said, with giddy excitement. "Let's go and see our Henry!" He began to walk towards the ship, "Come here young man, its way past our bedtimes and anyway we can't see Henry

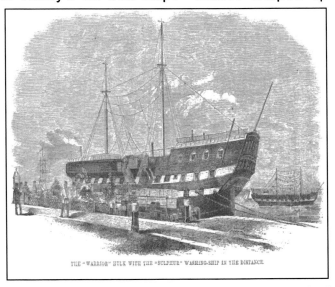
THE "WARRIOR" HULK WITH THE "SULPHUR" WASHING-SHIP IN THE DISTANCE.

until tomorrow, its way too late tonight." Emma said, as she grabbed hold of Jesse and pulled him back into her skirts. Just then, to get Emma's attention, Thomas coughed into his hand and said, "The rooms are ready ma'am, if you'll follow me." He then pointed with the flat of his hand towards the door of an inn across the street.

All four of them followed Thomas across the lamp lit street towards the inn. Percilla read out the name of the inn, "The Old Sheer Hulk. An appropriate name I suppose for around here," she said, still following Thomas, who then turned to Emma and said. "The inn keeper is expecting you ma'am, he'll show you to your rooms." Emma nodded and thanked Thomas, who then returned to the coach. Emma Percilla and Charlie began to enter the inn, but Jesse, being his usual nosey self, looked back to see where Thomas had gone and ended up walking straight into the closed door of the inn. Thomas, who was by now leading the coach back across the street by the lead horse said, "I'd watch where I was going if I was you." Jesse nodded in agreement whilst rubbing his nose at the same time, "Don't worry it hasn't dropped off, you'll be alright," said Thomas, laughing as he walked the coach and horses up the side of the inn towards the stables.

The next morning Jesse was awoken by Charlie's snoring and a very peculiar clonking sound, which seemed to be coming from outside in the street. Jesse jumped up on the bed and looked out through a small half opened window. However, the window was so dirty that he couldn't see much so he decided to open the window fully and lean out. Below in the street there were men dressed in very dirty clothes, all of them were wearing flat caps. At first there were only a few, but it wasn't long before their numbers began to swell as more men came out of the small houses which lined the street. Some of the men stood by their house doors for a few moments before joining the procession which was heading straight through the dockyard gates, which were by now open. The clonking sound got louder the more men that joined the procession, Jesse then realized it was the men's clogs on the cobbled street that was making the clonking sound.

Eventually, the sound got so bad that it woke Charlie. Jesse was just about to shut the window when a dreadful waling noise started. The noise went on for about ten seconds, which seemed longer. Jesse held his hands over his ears as Charlie pulled the window shut, "What's going on our Jesse?" asked Charlie, wiping the sleep from his eyes and yawning. Jesse paused for a moment and said, "Looks like everybody's going to work. It seems to be a very noisy business going to work around here." They both laughed. With the window shut the sounds from outside were instantly depleted and Jesse put down his arms and released his ears. Jesse then turned to Charlie and said, "What's for breakfast?" "How should I know what's for breakfast," replied Charlie as he gave Jesse a hard stare. Just then there was a knock on the door and Emma appeared with some cold porridge in two bowls. "Here's your breakfast. I'm sorry but there was no cream to soak it in." She then turned and went back into her room she was sharing with Percilla.

It wasn't long before all had had their breakfasts and were stood waiting for Jesse outside the inn, "Where his he now?" Emma asked Charlie, who replied, "He was right behind me, but then; when I turned around to see where he was, he was gone!" Emma put down the basket which contained the parting gifts for Henry and shouted, "Jesse! Come on." There was no reply from inside the inn, which annoyed Emma; she tutted and stomped back inside the inn to see where Jesse was. Emma hadn't been gone long, maybe a minute, when Jesse came walking down the side of the inn with Thomas, "Right, come on then let's get started!" He said rubbing his hands with excitement. No-one answered. Percilla and Charlie just glared at Jesse, who asked, "What, what's wrong now?" "Aunt Emma's gone back inside looking for you," Percilla growled at Jesse whilst pulling at his jacket to straighten its shoulders. "I went out the backdoor to get Thomas," replied Jesse. Emma return from her search looking very annoyed that she hadn't found Jesse, but when she saw him stood waiting for her with the others, the annoyance became more of a sense of relief, "Oh, you're here! Come on, we're going to be late." Emma said, breathing a sigh of relief and looking at Percilla, who just looked skyward with her eyes.

The small party walked across the street and entered the dockyard through the large gates. They followed the same route that the workers in their clogs had done hours earlier. They hadn't walked far when the street began to fork, at the fork; there was a sign that read Warrior, the sign pointed down the left fork in the general direction of the ship, which Thomas had pointed out the night before. The other arm of the sign pointed down the right fork and read, <u>DOCKS ONLY</u> in big bold letters, which had also been underlined. Jesse looked down the right fork, and in the distance, he could see people pushing things and pulling things on carts, there were boxes and barrels stacked high on the quayside beside ships. There were people carrying sacks on their shoulders, and women, who seemed to be just stood at tables, "A regular hive of activity isn't it?" Jesse said to Charlie, who replied, "Aye... it's all happening over there." Pointing towards the docks; "Looks like hard graft to me." Percilla said to both. They both nodded in agreement and said together, "Aye and for very little pay. I'll wager." The three of them laughed and then continued to follow Emma and Thomas down the left fork.

They'd nearly arrived at the quay when they saw what Jesse thought was a policeman, but it turned out to be a prison guard. The guard was sat in a small pillar box at the side of the street, in front of the box was a barrier to prevent anybody from going any further along the street. Emma handed the basket she'd been carrying to Charlie and said, "Here, hold this for a moment." She then lifted her coat and pulled out a light brown letter with some writing on it from her skirt pocket. She promptly handed it to the guard who took the letter into the box and placed it on a little shelf, he then removed a piece of paper, which was hung on the wall of the box and began to run his finger down it. He suddenly stopped about half way down the paper, looked up and shouted, "Hey you!" He pointed at Jesse, who had already ducked under the barrier and was ready to walk on. Jesse looked back at the guard and said, "What!" "Get back on this side of the barrier," the guard snapped. Jesse instantly came back around the barrier and stood quietly between Charlie and his Aunt Emma. "Alright madam," the guard said, handing Emma her letter back. He then looked at the basket Charlie was holding and said, "What's that?" Before Charlie could answer Emma butted in and said, "There gifts for our Henry to take with him on his journey." The guard grabbed the basket from Charlie and said, "Not allowed! This is a prison not a Sunday school picnic!" He then, inconsiderately, threw the basket into the bottom of the pillar box and said, "You can collect it on your way out."

Emma was absolutely distraught by the thought of Henry leaving without the things she had wrapped so tenderly for him. Not to mention the fact that she'd brought them all the way from home. If looks could have killed, then that guard would have been dead there and then on the spot, thought Jesse as he began to comfort his Aunt Emma. The guard lifted the barrier and said very rudely, "Stay together and don't talk to the prisoners, unless you are told to do so. Don't touch the prisoners or pass them anything. Do you all understand?" Everybody nodded and said very faintly, "Yes sir." The guard then shouted, "I didn't hear you!" All of them stood up straight and said again, only this time louder, "Yes sir!"

Arriving at the quay, which was down several steps from the street and was stuck out into the river, they could see the ship. Jesse hadn't realized that the ship was anchored out in the middle of the river and that the five of them would have to be rowed out to the ship, it wasn't far, but it was far enough if you couldn't swim, thought Jesse. Stood at the top of the steps to the quay were two men, one old with a hump on his back and the other young with a large blotchy red face. They were both dressed in cotton velvet waist coats. The oldest of the men asked, "Are you going to visit the Warrior ma'am?" He then doffed his cap, as Emma replied, "Yes." "That'll be a penny each then ma'am," said the man, leaving his cap in front of him to receive the pennies. "What!" Cried Emma, "A penny each," Emma was livid. The old man tried to calm Emma down by saying, "We do bring you back as well ma'am, at no extra charge!" Emma looked at the man and then, grudgingly, took some pennies from her skirt pockets; she tossed them into his cap, "Here, and don't come again!" Emma snarled. The old man took the pennies out of his cap quickly and fingered his eyebrow. He then plonked the cap back on his head, "This way," the old man said, leading them to a rowing boat which was tied to the end of the quay.

After he'd helped Emma and Percilla into the boat, he then held the boat steady whilst Jesse, Charlie and Thomas got into the boat by their own efforts. He then walked to a wooden post and untied the boat before sitting on the middle seat of the boat. He drew the ores from off the floor of the quay, and placed one on either side of him. He then began to row. The journey across to the ship didn't last long, which was just as well because the old man had become tiresome and did nothing else but moan about how the rowing gave his back some jip.

Arriving at the ship they were greeted by another guard who helped them out of the rowing boat and onto a makeshift platform which seemed very unsafe to Jesse. As Jesse stood up on the platform he sniffed up, "What on earth is that smell?" He asked looking at Charlie, who was beginning to receive the scent himself. Charlie instantly put his sleeve across his nose and began to gip. Emma reached for her handkerchief and quickly stuck it under her nose, but the aroma of the ship took its heaviest toll on Percilla, who was instantly sick over the side of the platform. The old man began to row away saying, "It takes a while to get use to the smell, but you'll be alright in a couple of minutes." He then cackled and continued to shout from the boat, "Watch out for the bombs!" He'd no sooner said the words when there was an almighty splat as a bomb hit the platform, just missing Jesse. He jumped to one side saying, "What the hell was that?" "It's those mucky sods up there, throwing their sewage out of the portholes." The guard said, reaching for a brown stained mop, which was leant up against the side of the ship. The guard dipped the mop in the river and with one swoop; he pushed the remains of the bomb into the river. Flipping the mop over the guard then removed the stain from the platform which had been left by the bomb. After leaning the mop back against the ship, he turned to Emma and said, "Up the steps and through the door at the far end of the deck."

Emma started up the steps with everybody following in single file. They snaked their way across the deck towards the door where there was another guard stood. He politely asked Emma, who was at the front of the line, "Who have you come to see?" Emma handed the guard her letter, he spent a couple of minutes studying the letter before saying, "Wait in here and I'll fetch him to see you." The guard opened the door and showed them all into the room beyond. The room was long and the boards creaked when they were stood on. Tables lined the right side of the room and the only light in the room came from square barred windows, which ran down the left hand side of the room. Charlie and Jesse sat down at the first table whilst Emma and Percilla paced up and down the boards of the room.

Just then an iron gate at the far end of the room clanged closed as a young boy entered the room carrying a bucket of water, the water looked dirty and greyish in colour. He began using a ladle to fill the cups, which were set out on the tables. When he reached Jesse and Charlie, Jesse pulled back to allow the boy to fill the cups which were on the table where he was sat. The boy  didn't say anything he just smiled at Jesse. However, his smile was noticed by the guard, who had just entered the room with Henry, "You! Outside," the guard said to the boy. The boy cowered and ran sideways out of the door leaving his water bucket at the side of Jesse's feet.

Emma ran straight to Henry and flung her arms around his neck, kissing his face a couple of times. Percilla then reluctantly gave Henry a small peck on his cheek saying faintly, "Hello our Henry." Jesse and Charlie got up and shook hands with Henry, who looked across towards the table, he saw the cups of water set out on the tables and walked straight across to one. He took a drink from the cup. Jesse and Charlie were horrified that Henry had drunk such dirty water. Henry saw their facial expressions and said, "What's the matter with you two? You drink when and where you can in here." He returned the empty cup to the table and sat down. Everybody gathered round the table to talk to Henry including Thomas, who was introduced to Henry by Percilla. Thomas, who had stayed in the background for obvious reasons, said, "Hello Henry, how are you doing?" He then sat down at the end of the table. Henry thanked Thomas for bringing the family to see him and replied, "I'm alright. Please thank Mrs. Newman for lending the coach." Thomas nodded, as Henry began talking to Charlie and Jesse, who had just sat down on what felt like slightly damp benches.

The talking went on for about two hours and eventually ended with Jesse asking the question. This was the question everybody had been evading and putting off for fear of up-setting Henry. However, this still didn't stop Jesse from asking it, "Well then, when do you leave?" Jesse looked straight at Henry, who paused for a moment and then looked around the room at all the faces that were obviously waiting for him to answer, "I'm to be put aboard the

Isabella in about three weeks. She's bound for a place called Tasmania sometime in May," explained Henry, who was beginning to fill up. "Is Tasmania far from here?" Asked Jesse who seemed to think it would be a fine adventure going to distant parts on a ship. Henry, who was by now holding back the tears said, "They say it's so far away from here that nobody ever returns from there." There was then a sudden uncomfortable silence, no-one knew exactly what to say, everybody just sat there staring aimlessly into space. The silence was eventually broken by a guard entering the room and saying, "Right then folks, it's time to leave."

Emma and Percilla got up and began hugging Henry. Emma began to cry and so did Percilla. Charlie and Thomas held back for a moment and then walked towards Henry. They nodded at Henry and gave him a small hug whilst shaking his hand. Jesse was the last to stand up and was already crying as he walked across the room towards Henry. When he reached Henry, Jesse put both his hands around Henry and began to hug him. Henry, who was by now beginning to cry himself, returned the hug. The pair continued hugging for a few moments, but then, just before they released, Henry whispered quietly, whilst holding back the tears, "Don't worry our Jesse, I will return. I will come home, someday!" Henry then quickly released Jesse, winked a wet red eye at

him and quickly walked quietly back out of the door. That was the last time they saw Henry.

The guard said, "Right you lot, outside please, quickly, their coming back for dinner." The guard herded the five of them out of the room and out onto the deck. "Wait over there," the guard said sternly pointing to an area of decking at the side of the ship which overlooked the shore and the quay.

Jesse looked over the side of the ship towards the quay where he could see the prisoners coming back towards the ship. Jesse then turned to look at the guard and asked, "Where have they been?" "They've been working in the arsenal which is just down the street," the guard replied. Charlie came and stood at the side of Jesse; he peered towards the quay and said, "Gosh... I didn't realize there were that many prisoners living on this ship." The guard laughed and said, "Yes, there are about 1600 souls on this smelly wreck of a ship."

They all stood and watched as the prisoners marched down the quay in single file towards the rowing boats which were waiting to bring them back to the ship. The first lot of prisoners piled onto the first two rowing boats which then began to make their way back across the water towards the ship. It was surprising that the rowing boats hadn't sunk they were so overloaded with prisoners thought Jesse. It wasn't long before the first batches of prisoners arrived at the ship and were being marched across the deck towards the dining room, "Right, you lot down the steps and onto the rowing boat." Emma glared at the guard who then hesitated and coughed before saying, "Please." "I should think so, good manners cost nothing," Emma said, setting off down the steps with the others in close pursuit.

A few minutes later Jesse found himself sat in a silent rowing boat making its way back to the quay. The old man rowing began moaning again, "I don't know what they do on that ship." He said, "But no-one ever speaks on the journey back. It's a complete mystery to me." Percilla glared at the old man and said angrily, "Shut up, you stupid little man." They all disembarked from the rowing boat as quickly as possible, and began pushing their way through the prisoners who were desperately trying to get aboard the same small rowing boat. Jesse shouted, "Give us a minute to get off!" As two prisoners pushed past him, "Hurry up then!" The first prisoner replied. The second prisoner, who felt it was necessary to explain their rudeness, said, "Its first come, first served. And the last man aboard ship doesn't get any dinner." He then scrambled aboard the rowing boat whilst Emma tried in vain to pass the rest of the prisoners, "Coming through, coming through!" Emma shouted, pushing her way through the prisoners towards the street. Everybody followed the same pathway opened up by Emma.

At last they all managed to get off the quay and back onto the street which led back to the pillar box, Emma collected her basket and then told Thomas to run on ahead and get the coach ready to leave, which he did. It took sometime, but eventually, they all reached the gates of the dockyards. At the gates, everybody turned and looked back at the ship for the last time, the ship that Henry called home. Jesse then said, "Well he smelt a bit, but really, he didn't look too bad, considering." Everybody agreed and Emma said, "Come on, let's get back home." She turned and stepped aboard the coach, which had just arrived in front of the dockyard gates. Jesse said, "I'm going on top." He scrambled up the side of the coach and sat next to Thomas, who looked down to see that everybody was on board. Satisfied that everybody was, he cracked the whip and said, "Go on then lads," to the horses. Jesse looked back and watched the great ship disappear from sight, but just before it did, he said quietly to himself, "See ya our Henry. I do hope you'll come home, someday."

The coach made its way back towards the small villagers of Berkshire, up and down dale they travelled, across barren landscapes, until eventually Jesse could see a familiar light in the upstairs window of the Whites Farmhouse. The coach pulled into the farmyard and did a complete turning circle so it would be facing the right direction to go straight back out when its occupants had alighted. Jesse was the first to get down from the coach followed by Emma and Percilla, who shut the coach door. They both turned around to say goodbye to Charlie, who had stayed aboard the coach.

Charlie leant out of the coach window and gave Emma and Percilla a kiss on their cheeks, "Where's he gone now?" Charlie asked, looking around for Jesse. "I'm here; you're not going to give me a kiss on the cheek, are you?" Asked Jesse, who was stood on the coach step at the otherside and was by now leaning into the coach through the open coach window. Charlie slid across the seat to the otherside of the coach, "Now listen! Our Jesse, seriously now," Charlie said, wagging a finger at Jesse. He then continued to say, "You've got to stay out of trouble. You're the man now, you've got to look after Aunt Emma and Percilla, things being the way they are, with Percilla being pregnant and all." Jesse nodded his head eagerly and said, "Sure thing our Charlie. I'll look after them!" Jesse then quickly jumped down from the coach step. "See ya," he said, before disappearing inside the farmhouse leaving Charlie shaking his head and grinning inside the coach.

Inside the farmhouse, the atmosphere hit Jesse like one of Amos's thick ears. It's very quiet in here, thought Jesse. Jesse's eyes slowly scanned around the kitchen, which seemed to have a quiet serenity about it. Jesse's eyes stopped scanning as they reached Emma and Percilla, who had just come in the door behind him. They too instantly felt that something was wrong and quickly fell silent. Emma looked across at Earle, who was sat at a candle lit table and said, "Earle! What's the matter?" They all moved slowly towards Earle, it was then that they noticed Earle had been crying, he replied, "Its dad, he died an hour ago, pneumonia." Earle began to cry again, "Where's Amos?" Emma asked, whilst taking off her coat. Jesse sat down at the table and Earle wiped his nose before replying, "He's upstairs with dad." Earle began staring at Jesse. This constant stare made Jesse feel very uncomfortable, so he decided he would be better off out of the way. Jesse yawned, did a false stretch and said, "I'm off to bed." He began to stand up but Emma quickly snapped at Jesse and said, "Sit down! Show some respect lad."

Jesse quickly plonked himself back down at the table and Earle continued to stare at him. Emma told Percilla to boil some milk, and then she quietly made her way upstairs, she paused for a moment at the top of the stairs, corrected her skirts and then slowly opened the door to the master's bedroom. There, laid out on the bed, was Master White. The room was lit by two candles, one on each side of the bed. Amos, who was sat quietly on a chair at the side of the bed, turned his head slowly. When he saw it was Emma, who'd entered the room, he said, "Oh, your back." Emma replied quietly, "Yes, do you need anything?" "No, just leave me. I'll be alright. You'll be tired from your journey, just leave me and go to bed." Emma curtsied and reversed out of the room slowly. Just then there was a loud crash from the kitchen followed by Percilla screaming. Emma rushed down the stairs quickly, so quickly, in fact, that she stepped down two steps at a time to reach the kitchen quicker. She told Percilla to stop screaming and then saw why Percilla was screaming. Jesse and Earle had each other in a death grip and were rolling around the kitchen floor raining blows down on each other. Emma bent down and grabbed both battling lads by their ears. She quickly pulled both of them up from the floor saying, "You two should be ashamed of yourselves, fighting, and the master not yet cold in his bed upstairs." "He started it!" Growled Jesse wiping blood from his lip, "You killed my dad!" Earle screamed, while still trying to hit out at Jesse with wildly flinging arms.

Emma, who was still holding both lads by the ear, dragged them both to the table and sat them down, where she eventually released their ears, "Now then, what's this about Jesse killing the master?" Emma asked Earle, who was still snarling at Jesse. Earle replied through gritted teeth, "Dad caught pneumonia going out on that rainy night for him a doctor, it's his fault. He's always causing trouble." Jesse was quick to reply, saying, "It wasn't my fault I needed a doctor in the first place. It was your bloody Amos who'd caused the trouble." Earle stood up and was just about to say something else when he was interrupted by Emma, who screamed, "Enough!" She banged her fist down on the table and said, "I want no more of this nonsense. Both of you go to bed." There was a moment silence followed by Emma screaming, "Now!" Earle quickly moved and made his way upstairs, but Jesse before leaving looked at Emma and said, "I suppose I'm back in the barn." Emma just nodded her head and sat down, her lip began to quiver, and she put one hand up to her forehead, "Here, this will help you to calm down." Percilla said, handing Emma a cup of warm milk. Emma said, "Thank you." She then raised the cup to her lips. Still shaking, she took a sip from the cup. Percilla sat down opposite Emma, and they talked late into the night, eventually Emma said, "Come on, I've calmed down now. It's time we were in bed." Percilla lifted the candle from the table and led the way up the stairs to the bedroom.

Next morning Emma was up first, she hadn't slept well but had still to prepare breakfast for Amos, Earle and Jesse before they started work. She dressed and then went to check the master's bedroom to see where Amos was. The master's bedroom door was opened so Emma walked straight in, she noticed that the candles had burnt themselves out and that there was no sign of Amos, so she began to leave, but just before she did, she looked towards the master, shame, she thought. She then leant over the master's body and pulled up the linen bed sheets gently over his face. "There that's better," Emma said to herself, before leaving and shutting the door behind her. She thought Amos might have gone to bed, so quietly, she went to check Amos's bedroom, she quickly, but quietly walked along the landing to where Amos's bedroom was. Before entering the room, Emma knocked gently on the door and waited for a moment, nothing happened. She knocked again and then slowly began to open the door. The room was in darkness, except for a small beam of morning sun light, which was coming into the room through a small gap in the curtains. This beam of light helped Emma to see that Amos's bed hadn't been slept in. She reversed slowly back out of the room and closed the door, she then went downstairs to prepare breakfast.

Entering the kitchen all seemed quiet. Emma walked towards the fire and placed some kindling in the middle of some cinders, which were still hot from the night before, she turned and was suddenly startled by the shape of Amos's sat bent over the kitchen table. At the side of Amos's head, on the table was a half empty whisky jug and an empty flagon of ale. Emma realizing it was Amos began to rattle and bang things to try and wake him up. Eventually, he stirred. Amos slowly lifted his head off the table and grabbed the whiskey jug. Amos took a good long swig and then turned to Emma and said, "Where is he?" "Who?" replied Emma, knowing exactly who Amos meant, "You know who I mean," Amos said, staggering towards Emma.

Emma pushed Amos back away from her and said, "I don't know who you mean." "That little bastard you call a nephew." Amos said, with the slaver running down his chin. He took another swig from the jug, wiped his chin and then tried to give Emma a kiss. He grabbed her around the waist and pulled her in close towards him. Emma turned her head and began trying to struggle free but Amos was too strong, he held her tightly whilst kissing her neck. Emma eventually managed to free one hand and slapped Amos hard across the face. Just then Percilla entered the kitchen saying, "What's going on?" Amos released his grip on Emma instantly and tried to stand up straight. Emma straightened her apron and adjusted her hair. Amos, who took another swig from the jug, said, "Nothing is going on, nothing at all." He grinned, burped and staggered out of the kitchen through the backdoor. Emma glanced through the kitchen window to see where Amos had gone. She then said, "Percilla, quickly." Percilla looked towards Emma, "Go and tell Jesse that Amos is drunk and looking for him. Go out of the front door, quickly Percilla, quickly." Percilla left by the front door and ran quickly around the side of the house and across the yard to the barn. She quietly called for Jesse, who replied, "Over here." Percilla quickly walked towards Jesse, who was quietly grooming Titan. Percilla hastily explained to Jesse that Amos was drunk and looking for him and that he should keep out of sight for a couple of days, but Jesse just continued to groom Titan using long strokes of the brush. After a moment's thought, Jesse made one of his decisions and said to Percilla, "No! I'm not hiding from him again, if he wants me, I'm here." Just then the barn door flew open and there, with a back drop of morning sun light stood the silhouette of Amos, "Ah! There you are; ya little sod." Amos took another swig from the jug and staggered forward towards Jesse. Percilla panicked and ran around the inside of the barn to escape Amos. "I'll fetch Auntie Emma," she screamed, disappearing out through the barn door.

It wasn't long before Percilla and Emma were running across the farmyard towards the barn fully expecting to see Jesse half beaten to death by Amos, but as they entered the barn, the place seemed very quiet. Emma and Percilla came to a sudden stop. They looked around to see Jesse, who was still calmly brushing Titan, "Where's Amos?" Emma asked Jesse. "He's over there," Jesse replied, pointing to a dark area at the back of the barn. Emma and Percilla slowly walked to the area and there in among some old tools, laid on the floor, face down, was Amos, he appeared to be a sleep. Emma walked very cautiously towards Amos. She turned him over and began inspecting him. On closer examination of Amos, he appeared to have a large bump to his head. Emma turned to Jesse and asked, "What happened?" Jesse continued brushing Titan and said calmly, "Oh, he walked into that low beam above you." Emma stood up and looked at the beam. She looked back down at Amos and then tried to gauge the height of Amos against the height of the low beam. "Emm… very suspicious," Emma said to herself. She then turned to Jesse and asked, "Are you sure that's what happened?" "Yep…." Jesse said, walking Titan out of the barn towards the horse trough. "Leave him there, let him sleep it off. He'll be alright," Jesse said to Emma, who nodded and went back to the farmhouse with Percilla. They entered the house at the exact same time that Earle was leaving for school, "Seen our Amos this morning?" He enquired. Emma and Percilla both answered together, "No!" Earle looked at them both suspiciously, hesitated and then set off to school.

100

A week later Master White was buried with all the trimmings and local people said, "How grand his funeral had been and that it was a credit to Amos," who had arranged the whole event. After the funeral things on the farm began to return to normal. Amos took his rightful place as the new master and the months began to roll by.

At the same time, Percilla began to swell and Jesse on the odd occasion would poke fun at her, as she wobbled around the farm, doing her chores. That was until one cold dark night when Jesse was awoken by Emma, "Jesse, Jesse, wake up!" Jesse jumped up quickly ready to defend himself, but then, he realized it was his Aunt Emma and not Amos. Jesse quickly asked "What's wrong?" He lowered his clinched fists as Emma replied, "It's our Percilla, and she needs the doctor. Go into Shalbourne and fetch him, quickly." Emma then rushed back to the farmhouse whilst Jesse pulled Titan out of his stall and clambered up onto his back. Before leaving Jesse looked towards the farmhouse, he could see his Aunt Emma up in the bedroom running backwards and forwards frantically. "Go on then," Jesse said to Titan, spurring him on with his heels.

The road was dark and very twisty in places, a little spooky thought Jesse, which made him push Titan on even faster. Titan began to trot and the sound of his hooves could be heard for miles as they entered the village. They past the small houses and shops which lined the main street of the village but none of them had any light coming from them. Eventually, they arrived at the thatched cottage which belonged to the doctor. Jesse hammered on the door until a light appeared in the upstairs window. The window open and out popped the doctor's head. "What is it now?" He scowled. Not wishing to be disturbed at that time of the night. "Please sir," Jesse said, trying to show some patience. But underneath, he had a burning desire to get back to the farm quickly, "It's our Percilla, she needs you, quickly sir." "Is that the lass at Whites Farm?" The doctor asked. "Yes sir." Jesse replied quickly. The doctor thought for a moment and then said, "Alright boy, you ride on ahead and I'll

follow." Jesse remounted Titan quickly and was just about to set off when the doctor stopped him by saying. "Have you a cart at the farm we can use?" Jesse was puzzled by this request and answered the doctor, saying, "Yes!" "Good," said the doctor, who then pulled the window shut.

Jesse rode back to the farm as quickly as Titan could take him. As soon as he arrived in the farmyard, he tied up Titan. He then rushed into the house, straight through the kitchen and up the stairs to Percilla's bedroom. Where he stopped at the door and knocked. There was a moment's pause followed by footsteps and then the latch being lifted as Emma answered the door. "He's on his way." Jesse said, trying to regain his breath. "Alright, well done," Emma said pushing Jesse back from the door. "Is she alright?" Jesse asked, trying to look over Emma's shoulder into the bedroom. "This is woman's business Jesse, so off with you. Go downstairs and wait for the doctor."

Jesse slowly turned and walked back down the stairs into the kitchen, he sat at the table. While sitting there staring at the hob, where pans of water were boiling, Jesse began wondering to himself. I wonder why they need so much hot water he thought and what's more, what do they do with all that hot water? It's a mystery to me! Just then there was a knock on the door. Jesse quickly got up and opened the door to find the doctor stood there rummaging through his black bag. Jesse said, "Upstairs!" He pointed to the bottom of the stairs. "Right boy," said the doctor, pushing his way past Jesse as he made his way across the kitchen towards the bottom of the stairs. However, before climbing the stairs, he turned to Jesse and said, "That cart I asked you for. Get it ready now!" Jesse looked at the doctor in amazement and said, "What, now!" "That's right, now!" Replied the doctor, he then went upstairs.

Jesse walked back outside into the cold night air, which stung his face. He quickly, untied Titan, from where he had left him and walked back across to the barn. Jesse pulled down Titan's harness from the stall shelf and began to fasten Titan into it. After fastening Titan to the cart which was kept at the side of the barn next to the large cart they used for hay making. Jesse started off back across the yard towards the farmhouse, pulling Titan and the cart behind him. The yard would have been in total darkness if it hadn't been for the light coming from Percilla's bedroom, which was suddenly extinguished when Jesse was about half way across the yard, leaving him in complete darkness. That's funny he thought, what's going on now? Just then the darkness disappeared as the farmhouse door open and there stood Percilla being propped up on both sides by Aunt Emma and the doctor. Jesse ran forward to take the place of Emma, who was just about to drop her side. "Get her into the cart, quickly," said the doctor, who was by now literally dragging Percilla down the garden path towards the cart. Jesse helped Percilla aboard the back of the cart where she laid down flat. Emma put a pillow underneath Percilla's head and covered her with a horse blanket. The doctor then clambered aboard and knelt down at the side of Percilla, Jesse helped Emma onto the front of the cart. He then walked around the front of Titan and climbed aboard the cart on the otherside.

It wasn't long before Jesse decided he wanted some answers and a little way down the road Jesse looked at his Aunt Emma and said, "It might help if I knew where we were going." Emma, who was obviously annoyed about something, said, "Anywhere, it doesn't seem to matter where, anywhere but here." The doctor then said, "Go towards Ham, she can have her baby there." "That's miles away. It's in another parish," said Jesse, looking bemused by what was happening. "That's the general idea," Emma snapped. "What is?" Jesse said to Emma, still bemused by what was going on. "That is!" Emma replied. Jesse, who was by now losing his patience pulled Titan to a halt and snarled. "What the hell's going on? I'm not going any further until I know exactly what's going on?" Exasperated Emma said, "The doctor here won't deliver our Percilla's little Bastard. Well not in our parish, because it has no father." Jesse was shocked by this and said, "What difference does it make

102

where the child is born? "Well it would appear that any child which has no father or means of support becomes the responsibility of the parish where that child is born, if the child becomes destitute. Our parish apparently doesn't want that responsibility and has instructed the doctor not to deliver any bastards within the parish boundaries. Consequently, we have to go to another parish and deliver the baby there. The baby then becomes the responsibility of that parish and not ours, got it!" Jesse was stunned and for the first time in his life he didn't know what to say, he just shook his head. Emma shrugged her shoulders and said. "It's all to do with money as usual." The doctor then banged on the side of the cart and said, "Can we get on now? Please...." Jesse cracked the rains on Titan's back and said, "Go on then lad. Ham it is."

They'd travelled some miles that night and dawn was just beginning to arrive when the cart arrived in the quiet parish of Ham. The only sound to be heard was Titan's hooves as he ploddered along. Jesse turned to his Aunt Emma and said, "It's gone awfully quiet back there, are they alright?" But before Emma could answer Jesse spotted the signpost and said, rather proud of himself for getting them there. "Look, we're coming up to the signpost saying we're in Ham." Jesse, trying to get the attention of the doctor so Percilla could have her baby said, "Doctor, doctor," but there was no reply. "Is he asleep?" asked Jesse. Emma turned and looked down into the back of the cart. She nodded her head at Jesse, who said, "Bloody marvellous, he brings us halfway across Berkshire and then goes to sleep on us. I'll pull in over here."

Jesse swung the cart into the gateway of a field and jumped down, he then proceeded to walk around the cart to the back. At the back of the cart Jesse paused for a moment, looked at the sleeping doctor, who looked very comfortable under the blanket he'd pinched off of Percilla. Jesse shook his head and then grabbed the doctor's leg, which was hanging limply over the back of the cart. Jesse shook the leg and the doctor slowly began to wake up. By this time Jesse had glanced across at Percilla, he noticed that she wasn't moving. On further inspection, he could see that Percilla had turned grey, and her lips were blue. Jesse knew instantly, his heart sunk as he felt Percilla's ice cold hands. Emma was just about to say something when Jesse stopped her and said, "It's too late Auntie Em, she's gone, she's bloody gone Auntie Em." Emma looked over the rim of the cart and saw the condition of Percilla, she broke down. She instantly fell to her knees and began screaming, this shook the doctor and suddenly he was wide awake. "What's wrong?" The doctor stammered. Jesse leant forward into the cart and pointed to Percilla. "That's what's wrong! Get out, get out you idiot!" Jesse screamed, whilst literally pulling the doctor out of the cart. Jesse then grabbed the doctor's bag and flung it towards the gate, saying under his breath. "Useless, useless bloody idiot," he then walked towards his Aunt Emma and picked her up off of her knees. He pulled her close into him and tried to comfort her, but by now Emma was hysterical.

It took sometime for Jesse to calm Emma down, but eventually, he managed it. Well, enough to get her back up onto the cart. Emma then turned to Jesse and said very softly, "Come on Jesse, take us home." Her chin sank onto her chest and the tears began to flow. Jesse covered Percilla with the horse blanket, looked across at the doctor, who was by now stood by the gate shivering, and said, "You, ya fool. You can make your own way back." Jesse then clambered up onto the cart, spun it around quickly, and headed off back down the road towards home, leaving the doctor stood by the gate still shivering and stranded.

Chapter 5: Marriage, First Love and the Poacher.

Percilla was buried with her parents in the graveyard at Shalbourne. The death certificate said she'd died in childbirth but both Emma and Jesse knew the real reasons. The doctor also knew the real reasons for Percilla's death and because of this, he always gave Jesse and Emma a wide berth when he saw them out and about. Sometimes, just for the fun of it, Jesse would go out of his way to accidentally bump into the doctor, this embarrassed the hell out of the good doctor, but Jesse thought of it as getting his own back for Percilla.

It took a good three years for Emma to get over the death of Percilla; she always blamed herself for allowing the doctor to move Percilla. Jesse had also found the three year period very difficult, not just dealing with Percilla's death, but also having to deal with his Aunt Emma's mood swings. He always had to take care what he said and how he said it, the slightest thing would set Emma off in floods of tears, and sometimes, even the mere mentioning of Percilla's name was enough to bring on the tears.

As for Amos, the three years had made him meaner and more argumentative, his drinking had got worse and his treatment of Jesse was harsh to say the least. Although on the up side of things, when Amos was sober, he taught Jesse well. Which was just as well because by the time Jesse was sixteen he was basically running the farm on his own, with very little help from either, Amos, who seemed to be constantly sleeping it off, or Earle, who only worked if he thought Amos was sober and checking on him.

However, all of this came to an end one brightly sun drenched morning in June. That morning, Jesse was up as usual with the cock crow. He opened the barn doors wide enough to let the morning sunlight strike the back of the barn. He then began to wash, which consisted of his usual quick flick of cold water from the horse trough followed by a quick wipe around with his sweaty neckerchief. Jesse would then dip his neckerchief back into the trough, ring it out and tie it back around his rope ridden neck.

Once that was done he decided that he would sit at the side of the trough and enjoy some of the morning sun before breakfast. As he sat there Jesse thought how peaceful it was to enjoy the morning sun with his eyes closed, if he listened carefully, he could hear the birds singing in the nearby trees and the hens in the yard, who were clucking gently. His thoughts began to drift as his face warmed. He began thinking of family, firstly, of Henry and where he might be right now and then of Charlie, and how he was doing working for the Newman's, and lastly, Percilla and how he missed her. It then dawned on Jesse that he was the only one left on the farm that was in his family. That's if you don't count Aunt Emma but she's not real family, not close family thought Jesse. He then picked himself up from the ground, dusted off the back of his trousers and headed towards the house for his breakfast. On his way towards the house he saw Amos coming towards him, "Morning lad, how's things?" Amos said in a very polite voice. Jesse was stunned for a moment. Amos didn't usually speak to him so politely. As Amos got closer Jesse noticed that he'd been washed, he'd even had a shave and if Jesse wasn't mistaken Amos was wearing new clothes. Jesse stopped for a moment and stared at Amos, who was grinning from ear to ear. Amos seemed to glide past Jesse, as though he was walking on air, at that moment Jesse got a whiff of an unusual fragrance. He sniffed up and thought he could smell roses. Jesse dismissed the thought instantly, thinking the morning sun had gone to his head, but as he watched Amos disappear across the yard towards the barn, he thought, what the hell's the matter with him? Amos entered the barn and began to whistle, the whistle then turned to a humming noise. Jesse definitely knew that something was wrong and that Amos was up to something. What he was up to Jesse didn't quite know, but he thought, I'd best be on my guard for the next few days, just in case.

Jesse entered the kitchen and there seemed to be an air of difference about the place. There were flowers from the meadow on the table and his Aunt Emma was busily cooking breakfast. "Morning love," she said, swirling a duster over the Welsh Dresser, "Breakfast won't be long." Jesse sat down at the table facing Earle. They both looked at each other and then together they both shrugged their shoulders. Jesse leant across the table and whispered to Earle, "What's going on?" Earle whispered back, "Don't ask me. I couldn't get any sense out of our Amos this morning either. He seemed to be day dreaming and the smell." He began waving his hand in front of his nose. Just then they both quickly became quiet as Emma placed two plates on the table, "Here's your breakfast, nice soft eggs and a piece of bacon," she said. Jesse tore some bread from a loaf which was sat in the middle of the table next to the flowers and began dipping it into the eggs. Emma continued flirting around the kitchen doing her usual chores, and then suddenly she announced, "Right, I'm off." Emma grabbed her shawl and started to pin on her hat. Jesse asked, "Off where?" "None of your business!" replied Emma, picking up a very large square basket which was sat on a stool by the backdoor. Emma then checked her hat in the mirror before turning to Earle and Jesse. "You two, don't forget to wash those dishes when you've finished." She then left slamming the door behind her.

A sudden silence descended on the kitchen as both lads sat there eating their breakfasts. It was broken by Jesse, who jumped up and ran upstairs. He headed straight for the window in Earle's bedroom. Jesse pulled back the curtains slowly and stood back, carefully he peeked out through the window being careful not to be seen. He could see his Aunt Emma making her way up the track towards the top field. She kept glancing back towards the farmhouse, as if she was checking to see if anyone was watching her. Jesse stepped back thinking she'd seen him, but after a moment he realized she hadn't and continued to watch her. He watched quietly as Emma stopped by the top field's gate, again she looked back towards the farmhouse which caused Jesse to step back a little more.

It wasn't long before Amos appeared on the track with Titan, who was pulling the small cart. It was the same cart Percilla had died in. Amos stopped by the gate and jumped down off the cart. He was greeted by Emma, who gave him a long lingering kiss. Jesse was absolutely startled by this and said to himself "Well I never!" Just then Earle came into the bedroom and asked, "What are you up to now?" "It's not what I'm up to you should be worried about," replied Jesse, pointing towards the window with his head. Earle pulled back the other curtain just in time to see Amos kissing Emma for the second time, only this time he had Emma bent over backwards whilst he kissed her, "Is that what I think it is?" Earle surprisingly asked Jesse, who just nodded his head and said, "Yep, it is!" After Amos had finished kissing Emma, he helped her up on to the cart; he then heaved the basket into the back of the cart and climbed aboard himself. Jesse and Earle could do nothing but watch in amazement as the couple rode off arm in arm into the distance.

Emma and Amos were missing all day, and both lads had to make do with a piece of old cheese and the rest of the bread left over from breakfast. It did for both dinner and tea. At tea Jesse said, "Wait until I see my Aunt Emma. I won't half give her a piece of my mind, kissing Amos like that." "Aye... and I'm going to do the same with our Amos. After all I don't want to become a relative of yours or your family." Jesse just tutted and left the kitchen by the backdoor. He walked out into a warm dry summers evening where the swallows were diving low over the farmyard collecting flies. Jesse dipped his head in the horse trough. He then shook it vigorously free from water as he stood back up. After rubbing his hair, Jesse layed in his usual place overlooking the farmyard, he closed his eyes and began drifting off into a light snooze. He'd laid there for about an hour when he was awoken by the sound of Titan's hooves clattering into the yard. Slowly, Jesse opened one eye and looked down the yard to see Amos leading Titan towards him and the trough. "Here lad, put him away," Amos said, letting go of the rains. Titan began drinking from the trough and Jesse stood up, he patted Titan gently on the neck and then asked Amos where his Aunt Emma was. Amos instantly flew into a rage and said angrily, "How should I know where your bloody precious Aunt Emma is?" He fetched Jesse a quick smack around the head and said, "Get on with putting Titan away and less of your lip lad." Amos stomped off towards the farmhouse leaving Jesse rubbing the back of his head and swearing under his breath.

Jesse unhooked Titan from the cart and took him into the barn, he placed Titan's harness on the shelf and began brushing him down, whilst brushing him down, Jesse glanced out of the barn towards the track. There on the track was Emma making her way back down the track towards the farmhouse, she was still carrying the large basket she had taken out with her earlier that day. Jesse threw down the horse brush and walked to the barn door. He leant on the door for a moment and waited for Emma to enter the yard. Just as he was about to go and talk to Emma, he glanced towards the farmhouse. There, stood at the backdoor, was Amos. Jesse slowly moved back inside the barn and started to close the door. He didn't close it completely. He left a gap, just large enough to see through. Jesse watched through the gap as Emma arrived at the backdoor of the farmhouse, Amos leant forward and took the basket from her, he then held open the door for Emma, who entered the house. Before Amos followed her in, he looked towards the barn to see if anyone was watching, satisfied that no-one was, he turned and shut the door behind him. Jesse, who was still not happy about what was going on, and what he had seen that day, returned to his den at the back of the barn, he laid down and began chewing on a horse carrot, his mind was doing overtime, thinking about what he had seen that day, it was sometime before he dropped off to sleep.

The following morning Jesse was awoken by Amos, who said, "Get up ya lazy bugger, it's gone six, and we've corn to harvest." Jesse stirred and rubbed his eyes. Amos lifted the sickles and scythes down off their hooks and shouted, "Come on lad, make a move!" He then kicked Jesse in the back, which made him squirm a little. However, it did hasten Jesse out of his bed, "Start sharpening these scythes," Amos said quickly. "And have them done before I get back with the help." He ordered, as he un-ceremonially dumped a pile of scythes at the side of Jesse's feet, who was by now rubbing his back and saying, "What about my breakfast?" To which Amos replied, "Stop bellyaching. Here, they'll do ya." He then threw a couple of horse carrots at Jesse's feet. Jesse looked down at the carrots for a moment and then kicked them to the otherside of the barn saying, "No thanks!" "Suit yourself." Amos said, leaving the barn on Titan.

Jesse watched as Amos trotted off towards Shalbourne. He took down the sharpening stone from its hook and walked outside. Jesse sat on the edge of the trough and began sharpening the scythes. He'd sharpen scythes before and had always prided himself on how sharp he could make them using just the stone and a little water from the trough. Once, he'd even cut himself testing one of them for sharpness, it was that sharp. Jesse began using long strokes of the stone down the scythe blade, occasionally dipping the stone into the trough. He then remembered that he needed to speak to his Aunt Emma about the previous day's events. Jesse dropped the scythe onto the floor, shoved the sharpening stone into his pocket and set off towards the house, thinking he might even get some breakfast, if he was lucky.

However, as he entered the back garden Earle came out of the house and said, "I wouldn't bother. She's not saying anything about yesterday. I've already tried to find out about it. All she will say is that she went shopping and that's it!" Jesse continued past Earle saying, "She'll tell me, I'm family. Anyway I want my breakfast!" Earle held out a tatty looking sandwich and said, "She sent you this." Jesse looked at the sandwich and quickly snatched it from Earle's grip leaving part of it in Earle's hand. Jesse threw his part of the sandwich on the garden and tried to open the backdoor, but it was locked. Jesse thumped the door and shouted, "You'll have to talk to me sooner or later." He then angrily turned and walked back to the trough with Earle, where they both began sharpening the scythes in silence. After most of the scythes had been sharpened, Earle began straightening the sickles and checking to see if the handles were on tight enough. He then broke the silence, by saying, "It should be a good year, this year." Jesse didn't answer, he just nodded his head. Just then Earle stopped what he was doing and said, "Listen! Can you hear singing?" Jesse, who was still annoyed, said, "This is not Sunday School." "No! Listen," Earle said, putting his hand in front of Jesse's face.

They both stood quietly for a moment and sure enough, in the distance, the sound of singing could be heard. "It can't be the church, that's too far away to be heard," said Jesse, standing up at the side of Earle. Both lads walked across the farmyard and up the track towards the top field. When they arrived at the top of the track they could see, in the distance, Amos, who was riding Titan at the front of a procession of grubby looking people. Earle said, "Look over there, it's our Amos. Who does he think he is, Napoleon?" Jesse laughed and said, "Aye... and we all know what happened to him!" The singing got louder as the procession got nearer. "I don't recognize the songs, do you?" Earle asked Jesse, who replied, "Maybe there not locals." Earle nodded his head as both lads made their way back to the trough and the job in hand.

It wasn't long before the procession arrived in the farmyard and Amos jumped down off Titan and led him into the barn. The procession began to disperse around the farmyard, some women and children sat down, some men began talking in groups and others made their way towards the trough where Jesse and Earle, were finishing off sharpening the last of the scythes. Jesse and Earle watched as the strangers drank from the trough and dipped their neckerchiefs into the cool water, they then wrung them out before returning them to their necks. As they were doing this the men could be heard talking to one another, Jesse and Earle couldn't understand a word the men were saying. Jesse looked at Earle, who looked back with a confused expression on his face. He then laughed and shrugged his shoulders, just then Amos came out of the barn. He noticed the look on Earle's face and said, "Don't worry lad, their Irish, aren't you?" Amos slowly put his arm around a scruffy, thin gaunt looking man who was wearing an unusual wide brimmed hat and smiled. The man replied by saying, in a very strong Irish accent, "To be sure sir, to be sure, here for the summer sir, all the way from the emerald isle sir."

There was a moments silence and then Amos said, "Come on then, let's get started." He picked up a scythe and headed towards the cornfield where the long corn awaited. Jesse hurriedly started to hand out the scythe to each man in turn. They then followed Amos towards the cornfield. It wasn't long before every man had a scythe and the women and children had begun queuing to collect their sickles. Jesse waited for a moment before handing out the sickles. This was to allow the men to get in front with the cutting. Whilst Jesse was waiting, he began to examine the line of women and children; some of the women were hardened veterans of seasonal farming work and were very use to the hard work involved, this could be seen in every windswept wrinkle on their faces. The children, on the other hand, weren't schooled and were only wearing homemade clothing, which was of a very poor quality. Jesse felt sorry for some of the children, who didn't even have shoes, he remembered the days when he didn't have shoes and how blistered and painful his feet use to get. Twenty minutes passed and the women were getting restless so Jesse started to give out the first of the sickles.

Each woman in turn stretched out her hand to receive a sickle from Jesse, who by now had begun noticing the condition of the women's hands; they were bruised and full of blisters. In places the skin was missing, caused by the work, no doubt, thought Jesse as he continued handing out sickles. He'd nearly finished handing the sickles when he noticed a soft hand among the harden ones. This made Jesse lookup for a moment to see who the owner was.

Suddenly, the sounds around Jesse became faint as though in the background, he wiggled a finger in his ear to correct it, but to no avail. People who were moving began to slow to a stop. In fact, the whole world around Jesse seemed to slow down as he caught a glimpse of the most attractive pair of green eyes he'd ever seen. The moment the pair made eye contact, they both began to blush. Jesse could feel his face getting hotter by the minute. However, his cut off from reality and his blushing gaze were soon interrupted by Earle. Who had been stood trying to get Jesse's attention by nudging him and screaming at him, "Come on, our Amos will be waiting for us." But Jesse didn't answer Earle, who was by now becoming irritated by Jesse's gormless expression and said. "Have ya gone deaf or something?" Earle waited for an answer, but again Jesse didn't answer, he just continued staring wilfully into the girl's eyes. Jesse slowly handed the girl a sickle, she smiled at him and said, "Thank you." "You're welcome," Jesse replied, who continued to stare at the girl. As the girl left Jesse sighed, he then turned to Earle and said, "Yes!" "Yes what!" Earle screamed. Jesse suddenly shook himself and said angrily, "Will you come on, were going to get flailed by Amos if we're not careful." "Me, me come on," Earle said, amazed by Jesse's comment. "You've got a cheek, it wasn't me wasting time looking like a love struck cow, was it?" Earle then picked up a scythe, put it over his shoulder and waited for Jesse, who began picking up the rest of the spare scythes and sickles, "I don't know what you mean I'm sure." Jesse replied struggling to carry the spare tools. "Here, get a hold of some of these and make yourself useful for a change," said Jesse, dropping a couple of sickles on the ground. Earle picked them up and both lads made their way to the cornfield.

Jesse and Earle lined the spare tools up against the dry wall at the side of the gate, which was open. Earle began looking around to see where Amos was, Jesse, on the other hand, had other things on his mind. He was looking for the girl with the soft hands, just then he spotted her and waved, she waved back and received a quick slap about the back of the head for doing so by an older woman who was stood at the back of her. The woman glared at Jesse, who quickly put his hand down and reckoned on he'd done nothing wrong, "Right then you two." Amos said to Jesse and Earle, rubbing his hands, but before Amos could say anything else Jesse said, "Oh! I've forgotten the sharpening stone." He then disappeared quickly through the opened gate and back down the track towards the trough where he'd left the stone. "What's the matter with him?" Amos asked Earle, who just shrugged his shoulders and said nothing.

As Jesse entered the farmyard, he could see his Aunt Emma busily laying out food for the help, she had placed a board on top of the trough and was busy laying out all kinds of delights, there were pies, potatoes, bread and cheese, even cream to pour on some cold porridge, which was sat in a large pan at the pump end of the trough. Jesse walked slowly towards Emma, he was just about to ask her about the previous day's events, when she said quickly. "Don't you start today our Jesse, I haven't got time for your questions today Jesse." Jesse stopped and sensed that it wasn't the right time to ask Emma about Amos and her. So he changed what he was going to say. "But I was only going to say 'that you've done us proud' Aunt Em." Emma put her hands on her hips and said, "Emm...." Jesse quickly grabbed a potato, bent over to pick up the sharpening stone and said, "I'll see you later then." Emma nodded and Jesse walked slowly back to the cornfield where Amos was organizing the help into teams of five.

"Ah! There you are, right Jesse, you keep an eye on the scythemen at the corn line. Make sure they bend and cut the corn as far down as possible." Jesse, who couldn't be bothered, looked at Amos and said, "What difference does that make? We only want the corn at the top." Amos quickly became angry and fetched Jesse a thick ear. He started to rant at Jesse, "Do as you are told for once. We need as much straw as possible, you fool!" Jesse rubbed his ear and stomped off to the corn line where the scythemen were busy cutting the corn. He hitched himself up onto the wall and began watching the men work. It wasn't long before Amos came across and said, "Here, use this to check the height of the stubble." He handed Jesse a stick with a notched cut in it, "Don't let the stubble get above that notch." Amos said. Jesse took the stick from Amos and nodded his head; he then continued to sit on the wall, watching the scythemen. Amos became exasperated, he pulled Jesse off the wall and threw him towards the stubble saying angrily, "Get using the stick then." Jesse quickly began measuring the stubble and Amos returned to the back of the group, where he started to give Earle instructions, "Right Earle, you're in charge of the gatherers and the binders. I'll watch the stookers and rakers at the back. Make sure they bind the bundles tight. Otherwise, they will fall apart when we take them to the barn, got it!" Earle nodded his head and then Amos handed Earle a stick, similar to the one he'd given Jesse. He then whispered something in Earle's ears and Earle nodded in agreement.

Jesse had been measuring the stubble all morning and was becoming bored with doing it. And to make matters worse Earle was also beginning to get on Jesse's nerves with his constant reminding, "It's getting longer again!" Meaning, that the corn was being cut too short and that Jesse wasn't checking it correctly, he was just about to give Earle a piece of his mind, when he noticed the girl with the soft hands gathering up corn quite close to where he was sat. Jesse smiled as the girl noticed him watching her. She bent down to gather another bundle of corn and in doing so revealed a very large amount of cleavage beneath a low cut blouse. Jesse froze and stared, he couldn't wait for her to gather up the next bundle of corn, so he could have another look. Jesse even shifted his position on top of the wall to get a better view. After a while, Jesse found that he could predict when and where she was going to bend down to pick up the next bundle, he even had the scythemen cut in a certain direction, so he could see more of the girl's cleavage as she gathered up the corn. He played the game for the rest of the morning and by the time Aunt Emma had called everybody to eat Jesse had become completely infatuated by the girl's cleavage.

Everybody hurriedly walked back to the trough and began eating the food that Emma had prepared. Jesse and Earle quickly lifted a potato each from the board and then Jesse tucked some cheese and a chunk of bread inside his shirt. Earle grabbed a small jug of milk, and then joined Jesse, who had sat down to eat under a wall some distance from the main group of helpers. Just as Jesse was biting into his potato Earle nudge him and pointed with his head towards the girl, who was approaching them, she smiled nervously and then said, "Canisitwithyoutoeat!" But neither Earle nor Jesse could understand what she had said. They both just looked at each other and then Jesse said slowly, "You'll have to slow down when you talk. We can't understand you when you talk so quickly." The girl took a deep breath, and then infuriated, she said slowly, "can I sit with you to eat?" Both lads nodded and then moved apart to allow the girl to sit between them, "I'm Jesse and he's Earle." Jesse said, chomping on his potato. The girl replied abruptly, "Megan!" Jesse handed her a piece of bread and they sat there in the midday sun enjoying the food.

After about ten minutes Amos shouted, "Come on then you lot, back to work!" Everyone slowly began to stand up. They used the same speed to return to the cornfield. Once at the cornfield Jesse took up his position at the corn line, he measured the stubble and said, "Right, carry on!" The scythemen nodded, put on their hats to protect them from the midday sun and started to cut the corn using long sweeps of their scythes, to help speed things up, some of the women began using their sickles to cut alongside the men. Other women and the girls began raking it clear of the cutters whilst the binders were quick to collect bundles and began binding them into sheaths, the minute the sheaths appeared the stooker's built stooks with them, "Ten to a stook mind, otherwise the corn won't dry properly." Amos shouted to the old men, who began building the stooks.

The dust from all this activity could be seen floating in the afternoon sun, the work was hot and sticky, not to mention back breaking and thirsty. Amos drove the helpers on hard, not easing up for a minute, anyone caught slacking was given a roasting from Amos's sharp tongue. It was late into the afternoon before Amos shouted, "Break!" The scythemen dropped their scythes instantly they heard the shout and said, "He's a hard task master this one." They then went towards the gate where Emma was stood with a bucket and some bread. Each helper took a drink of water from the bucket using a large ladle, and then accepted a small piece of bread from Emma, who was busily cutting the pieces from a loaf she was balancing on top of the wall. Jesse took his piece of bread and didn't say anything to Emma. Instead he looked around to see where Megan was, she was sat in the middle of the stooks chewing her bread. Jesse walked across and sat beside her, he didn't say anything at first he just sat there watching his Aunt Emma giving out the last of the bread.

"They're not happy," Megan said, looking over her shoulder at Jesse. "Who isn't? Jesse asked. Megan sighed, and then said, "The men folk. Your Amos he's working them too hard. There's sure to be trouble!" Jesse stood up and quickly corrected Megan by saying, "He's not my Amos and don't think it's got anything to do with me. I work for Amos just like the rest of you!" Megan looked up at Jesse and realized she'd made a mistake, "I'm sorry, but I thought you were part of his family." "No! My family is either dead or elsewhere. I'm on my own on this lousy bloody farm," Jesse said angrily. There was then more than a few moments of silence followed by Jesse plonking himself back down at the side of Megan. He bit into his bread and began chewing slowly. Whilst chewing, Jesse began to look around. Firstly, he looked down the field at the stooks and thought to himself how beautiful they looked as they glowed like gold in the sun drenched field. He then turned and looked across towards the gate, where he could see Amos and his Aunt Emma laughing and joking. This infuriated Jesse, especially when their hands touched gently as he took the last of the bread from her.

The afternoon seemed to drag on forever but eventually evening came, and the helpers began to tire. The sound of happy laughter and singing that they had set off with that morning had disappeared and all they wanted now was to go home. The dust in the field had become thicker than ever, it danced in the evening sunlight making some of the helpers cough and splutter. Jesse had used a piece of his sleeve to cover his mouth, this stopped some of the dust from entering, but eventually, even he began coughing. "That'll do us for today," shouted Amos as darkness could be seen coming over the horizon at the bottom of the field. "That'll do us, that'll do us. I'll bring some bloody candles tomorrow," said one of the scythemen sarcastically, who was not happy about how long they had worked. On hearing this Megan said, "Calm down da, you know it will only cause trouble."

Megan grabbed her dad's elbow and began leading him back to the farmyard, Jesse and Earle followed with the main group of helpers, they could hear the discontent among the helpers and decided it might be safer to hang back. Eventually, Amos caught up to them and said, "What's the matter with you two?" Jesse turned to Amos and replied, "There's going to be trouble, there not happy!" Amos just tutted and said, "That lot, they'd never be happy, even if you paid them five bob a day for two hours work, they still wouldn't be happy! They're always moaning! They just don't like hard work, that's their trouble!" Earle and Jesse started to speak together, but Jesse stopped and allowed Earle to continue what he was saying, "Whatever made you pick this lot? I mean, Irish! Besides not being able to understand a word they're saying, they seem a bit rough." "Aye... and if they start trouble, they'll take some stopping!" Jesse added, looking worried. "Oh! I'm touched, you two concerned about me," said Amos grinning at Jesse, who replied. "I'm not bothered about you. It was Aunt Emma I was thinking about." Amos stopped suddenly, thought for a moment and then said, "Look lads, I didn't have any choice. These Irish people were all I could get. The local lads and lasses are either already working on other farms, or they've left for the big cities." Jesse's ears pricked up at the mention of 'big cities' and said, "Why, what's in the big cities?" Amos didn't answer Jesse as the trio entered the farmyard. Instead he said, "Hi love," to Emma, who was waiting by the backdoor for them.

The next morning Jesse had been told to fetch the cows for milking, so first thing, he was up early and could be found herding the cows back down the track towards the milking shed. On his way down the track Jesse noticed a small procession coming towards the farm from the opposite direction. He stopped for a moment and took a good look, "Humm...." He said to himself, thinking that the procession looked a lot smaller than the previous day's procession, which Amos had led looking like Napoleon. He continued down the track with the cows and as he entered the farmyard with the cows, the procession entered from the otherside. He continued across the farmyard and left the cows outside the milking shed ready for Aunt Emma, who had taken charge of the milking and cheese making since Percilla's death.

Jesse walked slowly across the farmyard to where the procession had stopped, he then said chirpily, "Morning!" But the people in the procession didn't answer they just slowly looked up at Jesse and leered at him. Jesse shrugged his shoulders and thought to himself, please yourselves. He then sat down and put his back against the garden wall. Whilst Jesse sat there he noticed that the people didn't seem very happy, they all seemed very tired as well. Maybe Amos did work them too hard the previous day, thought Jesse as the farmyard fell quiet. It went so quiet that Jesse could hear the swallows in the barn chirping away merrily. Just then a lonely brown pheasant quickly ran across the yard startling everybody. Well at least that got everybody smiling thought Jesse. Just then a voice from the procession said, "What are we doing today?" Jesse searched the procession to see who had asked the question, it turned out to be a tall skinny woman with a hunch on her back, "I don't know yet." Jesse replied, pulling up a piece of grass to chew on. "Where's the gaffer?" The woman enquired, "Oh, he'll be along in a minute," Jesse replied, looking nervously towards the backdoor of the farmhouse. As time passed the tired looking people in the procession began to sit down, some began to lie down and close their eyes.

Jesse stood up and walked towards the backdoor, he was just about to open it when Earle appeared from the otherside, "Where's Amos?" Jesse angrily asked Earle, who hesitated to answer. Eventually, Earle spoke up and said, "He's indisposed and can't make it this morning. So come on, it's up to us to take care of things." Earle then slammed the backdoor and walked down the path towards the gate, leaving Jesse stood there shaking his head. Jesse hesitated to move at first and thought about going inside to have words with Amos. However, he decided against this and walked down the path saying under his breath, "Indisposed! Hung over more like." Earle could see Jesse wasn't happy and tried to cheer him up by saying, "Don't worry Jesse, Amos has told me exactly what he wants us to do. Let's just get all this lot up to the field and get them started on the corn." Jesse grinned and then said, whilst pointing to the people, "What lot's this then? You mean this lot here!" Earle looked at the tired procession of people, who were by now spread over the grass, half of them were hard asleep and the other half were sat going to sleep. Earle couldn't believe his eyes, "Where is everybody?" He asked.

Megan was the first to stand up; she walked across to Earle and angrily said, "They're not coming because Amos worked them too hard. They've gone to another farm where the food and breaks are better and they don't have to work as long." Megan then pulled out her tongue and sat back down. Earle, who was startled, hesitated for a moment; he looked at the motley group of people and said, "They'll have to do! Come on you lot, let's get started." Earle began pushing and pulling sleepy bodies until everybody was awake and walking along the track towards the cornfield. Arriving at the cornfield Earle began putting people into teams. He then turned to Jesse and said, "You need to take two women into the next field and turn the hay that our Amos cut last week. He wants it to dry quickly, there's some pitch forks by the wall." Jesse didn't hesitate he immediately selected Megan and said, "I'll only need her!" Megan, who was quick to oblige, grabbed a pitchfork from the wall and said, "Ready when you are," to Jesse, who was by now beaming all over his face at the prospect of spending the whole day with Megan alone. Earle, who saw Jesse's face just looked skyward and said, "Not you as well!" "Don't know what you mean!" Jesse said, tripping up over a sheath and falling head long into the pitchforks, which were propped against the wall.

After picking himself up, Megan and Jesse climbed over the dividing wall into the next field and began turning the hay. It wasn't long before Jesse suggested that they have a break by the far wall, Megan nodded and both went and sat down by the wall. Jesse began telling Megan about how he'd ended up at the farm, the death of his parents and Percilla. After which Megan told Jesse her story, about her home back in Ireland and the reasons why she had come to England to work. The conversation went on for sometime, both found each other's company warming, they both found it easy to talk to one another and on occasions found that they had things in common. However, the conversation was cut short by the arrival of Amos, who had spotted them sat down from the otherside of the field. "I don't know! The minute my backs turned, you lot skive off," he shouted across the field. Jesse and Megan were quick to their feet and began turning the hay using the pitchforks. Amos continued on into the cornfield where he began speeding things up straight away. "Come on you lot, get a move on. We haven't got all day!" Amos growled at the scythemen. It seemed to speed them up until Amos turned his back to talk to Earle, "Where is everybody?" "This is it, the rest have gone elsewhere to work. Apparently, you're too hard a taskmaster for them," Earle replied, raking the next sheath of corn. Amos began stacking the sheath into stooks and said, "They'll be back, mark my words, they'll be back!"

The corn cutting and hay turning went on all week. Many a stook had been built but then came Sunday, the day of rest. Jesse was up early and had prepared the small cart ready for church. He entered the kitchen and said, "Carts ready." Emma came down the stairs and began putting on her best hat using a very long hat pin to tie it down. She then shouted, "Amos! Are you ready?" "Alright, alright, I'm ready!" Amos said; coming down the stairs dressed in a bowler hat and the poorest fitting striped suit Jesse had ever seen. Both Jesse and Earle started to grin at each other, "What's the matter with you two?" Amos asked, trying his best to fasten the shirt collar to his shirt. "Nothing," Earle replied, who started to make his way towards the backdoor whilst trying not to laugh. Jesse quickly followed and the moment the pair met outside they became one and fell about laughing whilst hugging each other. Amos then kicked the door closed whilst Emma sorted out his collar and tie. Jesse and Earle jumped up onto the back of the cart, still laughing but trying their best to control the laughter.

However, when Amos appeared at the backdoor dressed in his so called Sunday best. The laughter from the back of the cart got worse, but then, it suddenly went quiet, "What's that?" Jesse asked Earle, who had a puzzled expression on his face. There was a funny squeaking noise, squeak, squeak and again squeak. Both lads sat up and looked over the rim of the cart towards the door where the sound was coming from. The sound suddenly stopped and so did Amos. "These new shoes are a bit squeaky love," Amos said to Emma. He then continued to walk towards the cart, squeak, squeak, every step a squeak. Jesse and Earle went into fits of laughter and fell back into the cart. Amos, who was by now becoming annoyed, glared into the cart and said bluntly, "Shut up! Or I'll fetch the pair of you a smack around the ear." This didn't help the situation it just served to make matters worse. As the tears of laughter began to run down Jesse's face, Emma, who was beginning to grin herself, walked down the path and was helped aboard the cart by Amos, he then clambered aboard himself.

Jesse and Earle began to settle down and only the occasional chuckle could be heard from the back of the cart, which was accompanied by the shaking of the head. Jesse sighed and was wiping away the tears using his sleeve, when Amos pressed the brake pedal of the cart, squeeeak went the shoe. This immediately sent Jesse and Earle once more into fits of laughter. They tried their best to calm down, but everytime Amos pressed the break, the noise would reverberate around the cart starting the laughter off all over again and by the time the cart had reached the church Jesse's sides were aching from laughing. This annoyed Emma, who jumped down from the cart the moment it stopped and stomped around to the back. She grabbed Jesse and hauled him from the back of the cart, "Round here!" Emma screamed, pulling Jesse to one side. "Enough now Jesse, just remember where you are." Jesse nodded his head and said, "Tell him then," pointing towards Earle who was still trying

to stop laughing. Emma gave Earle a frosty glare, which brought the laughter under control very quickly.

Before going any further, Emma looked both lads over, she straightened Jesse's jacket and dusted the back of Earle's trousers with the palm of her hand, she then said, "You'll do, come on." They all turned towards the church and marched quietly up the path towards  the church's front door where the vicar was waiting to receive his parishioners. Earle and Jesse were still trying their best not to laugh and on approaching the door had still got wide grins on their faces. The vicar took hold of Emma's hand and asked where Amos was. Emma replied, "He's just tying up the horse and cart." The vicar then looked at Jesse and Earle and commented, "How nice it was to see such happy parishioners entering the church." This even brought a smile to Emma's face and Jesse thought he'd even seen her holding back the laughter. "Thank you vicar," Emma said politely as she pulled back her hand and quickly walked down the aisle with Jesse and Earle following.

They took seats in their usual pew and Emma began looking around to see where Amos was. Jesse noticed that Emma was becoming more anxious the longer Amos took. Then, to everybody's surprise, Amos appeared in the isle at the otherside of the pew and not a squeak was to be heard. As he arrived at the end of the pew, he looked up at Emma, who had a puzzled look on her face. He then, with a very wide grin on his face, held up the shoes and pointed to them. He had taken them off before entering the church. Emma smiled politely and nodded in agreement at what he had done. Amos then walked sideways along the pew to join Emma, he sat down, took hold of Emma's hand lovingly, laid it on his thigh and placed his own hand carefully on top of it.

The church filled up quite quickly and the vicar closed the door, he then took up his usual position at the front of the congregation. This was the point when Jesse usually turned off but for some reason he didn't. The service dragged on for nearly an hour and Jesse as usual was becoming bored with the usual riggers of the service, at one point during the sermon he nearly fell asleep, but Earle had nudged him back to life. Jesse was ever so pleased when he heard the vicar eventually say, "And finally." Jesse began to stand up but was quickly interrupted by Emma saying abruptly, "Jesse sit down!"

The vicar then finished off his sentence by saying, "The Banns." Emma and Amos stood up and walked down to the front of the church, they were accompanied by other couple's who lined up along the front of the church. The vicar then read something from a book and began calling out the couple's names, this included Amos and Emma's names. Jesse quickly turned to Earle and said, "What's going on?" Earle grinned and said, "Looks like our Amos as popped the question." "What question?" Jesse asked Earle. Who replied in a squeaking childish voice, "Will you marry me?" There was a moments silence and then Jesse said, "She can't, she can't do this to me." Earle quickly said, "Well if you got any objections, now's the time to say." Jesse quickly jumped up and ran to the front screaming, "No! No, she can't marry him, I won't let her!" This sudden outburst got the attention of everybody in the church. The church suddenly fell silent as Jesse reached the front. The vicar screamed, "Stop!" Jesse came to an abrupt halt right in front of the vicar, who looked down at Jesse and said with a different tone in his voice, "Now child, who is it you are objecting to?" Jesse quickly pointed to his Aunt Emma, who turned to the vicar and said, "Take no notice of him sir, he's only kidding," she then frowned at Jesse, who took a step backwards.

The vicar could see that Jesse wasn't happy and said politely to Emma, "Now, now, he has the right to be heard." The vicar turned to Jesse and said. "Now child, it's a very serious matter objecting to a marriage. What are your reasons for objecting?" Jesse blurted out, "She's my Auntie." This made the whole congregation laugh and some people began to shout, "Sit down ya fool." The vicar raised his hand and the congregation fell silent once more, "I'm sorry but that's not a good enough reason to stop the banns being read. Have you anymore reasons?" Asked the vicar; Jesse thought for a moment and then quickly said, "She's been married before!" The vicar looked at Emma, who replied, "My first husband is dead sir." She curtsied and the vicar looked back at Jesse and again said, "The reason is again not valid and cannot stop the banns being read." Jesse began to cry and the vicar said, "Return to your seat, please."

Jesse turned and ran as fast as he could up the aisle and out of the church, slamming the door behind him. Amos could see that the whole event had upset Emma, and he whispered in her ear, "Don't worry, I'll have a word with him." Emma nodded, as she blew her nose on a clean handkerchief that she had tucked up her sleeve. The vicar read the banns and the service quickly ended, no-one mentioned the incident to Amos or Emma as they were leaving the church, partly because most of them knew Jesse and the character that he was. They did, however, receive comments like, "You'll have to sort that young one out Amos." To which Amos would smile and nod his head in agreement at the person saying it. Amos helped Emma and Earle back onto the cart, and then looked around for Jesse, "I'll just have a quick walk around to see if I can see him," Amos said. "I wouldn't bother," Earle chirped up, wanting to get back for his dinner. Amos waved Earle off and walked back around the church.

At the back of the church Amos paused for a moment, he removed his bowler hat and wiped the rim with the end of his tie. He looked down the graveyard towards the stones, he wasn't sure at first, but thought he could see a pile of clothes on the floor next to a grave. He replaced his hat and slowly walked nearer the clothes, as he got closer he realized the clothes were on a grave and weren't clothes at all, it was Jesse lying in a heap on his parent's grave crying his eyes out. "Now then," Amos said sympathetically. This made Jesse sit up quickly. Jesse wiped his nose with his sleeve and said abruptly, "What do you want?" Amos replied, "I want to marry your Aunt Emma, can't you see that?" There was a moments silence and then Amos said, "Do you really hate me that much lad? Surely you can give me a chance of making your Aunt Emma happy." Jesse shook his head and said, "No! She's my Aunt Emma, not yours!" Amos looked back towards the cart and could see Emma coming up the path towards him. Amos signalled her to wait by using a hand gesture; he then looked back at Jesse and said, "Can't you see that all this is upsetting your Aunt Emma?" Jesse didn't answer Amos, he just began to cry in silence and the big tears slowly streamed down his face, eventually dropped off his cheeks into his lap. "Look at her," Amos said, pointing back to where Emma was stood wiping her eyes with a handkerchief. Jesse stood up and looked at his Aunt Emma. He paused for a moment. Jesse knew the moment he made eye contact with Emma that he was causing her pain, real pain, and Jesse couldn't bear the thought of hurting his Aunt Emma. He ran towards her screaming, "I'm sorry, I'm sorry Aunt Em." Her open arms received him and as she hugged him, she gently said, "I know, I know Jesse." Amos walked back towards the hugging pair, he walked slowly to give them time to talk but as he got closer, he said, "Come on let's get back."

The following weeks were very busy for everyone on the farm and Amos had found some more help, they were Irish like the help they already had, but everybody seemed to get on with each other and more importantly the crops were being harvested, which pleased Amos when he was around. And finally, that large field of corn was all cut, the sheaths had been made and the stooks were drying in the field which meant that Jesse and the help could take five minutes rest before starting on the next large field of corn. Jesse handed out the water whilst Earle handed out the bread. Everybody was sat on top of the wall taking a well earned rest when Jesse spotted Amos in the field, "What's he up to now?" Jesse asked Earle, "No idea," Earle replied.

They both watched as Amos flittered from one stook to another, he seemed to be bending over each stook, for some reason. Eventually, Amos got closer to where the boys were sat, and they could see that Amos was dipping his arm deep inside each stook, "What ya doing our Amos?" Earle asked. Amos stopped for a moment and said, "Checking to see if the stooks are completely dry." Earle thought for a moment and then arrogantly said, "They should be near enough by now. They've had enough sun." Amos, sticking his arm into another stook angrily said, "No lad, near enough is not good enough, these things catch fire if they're not really dry. All the moister has to be gone before we can stack them. The carters will be here tomorrow, so we have to make sure that there dry today." And with that, Amos continued with his checking. Jesse, who was stood close by and had heard what Amos had said, said, "How can these things catch fire?" Jesse shook a stook which released a small cloud of dust, "I don't know, but our Amos knows what he's doing and if he says that they can catch fire, then they can catch fire," Earle replied.

The following morning Jesse hooked up Titan to the large cart and began walking him and the cart up to the cornfield. When he arrived at the field, the help was already there waiting for Amos and the day's instructions. Jesse looked among the help for the one he couldn't stop thinking about, and there, sure enough, stood by the wall, was Megan. Jesse tied Titan to the gate and walked briskly across to Megan, "Morning! And how are you this fine morning?" Jesse asked, sitting down at the side of Megan, who returned a smile that lit up the whole field. She then replied quietly, "Morning you." She smiled again but this time straight at Jesse. Megan moved closer to Jesse and began speaking quietly in a pleasant Irish accent, "I missed you this weekend," she said, before planting a sweet delicate kiss right on Jesse's lips. Jesse instantly began to blush and stood up, "Not here! People will see." Megan laughed and said, "Who's bothered? I'm not!" She then stood up and breezed past Jesse in a flirting manor before disappearing into the crowd of helpers saying, "Later lover." Jesse just smiled nervously and returned to Titan by the gate where Earle had arrived with two other large carts, "These are the carters who are going to move the straw. So get this lot loading the sheaths onto the carts," Earle told Jesse, in a demanding voice. Earle then turned to the carters and said, "Come on lads, get these carts into the field quickly."

The help moved away from the gate as the carts rattle through into the field. Everybody grabbed pitchforks and began throwing the sheaths up onto the carts. It wasn't long before the carts became full, "Right, what do we do now?" Jesse asked, looking around for Amos. Amos was nowhere to be seen and Jesse's eyes slowly stopped at Earle, "Where is he?" Jesse angrily asked.

 Earle, at first, tried to ignore the question, but Jesse was having none of it, he quickly walked across to Earle, who had his back to him and spun him around, "Well! Where is he?" Jesse asked again, only this time right in Earle's face. Earle began to stammer, "He's not well Jesse, honest! He's in bed, he's ill Jesse." Jesse pushed Earle to the ground and said, "Liar! He's been sucking on a jug again. I'm getting sick of this carry on." Earle quickly picked himself up and said, "It's not my fault Jesse. What are you picking on me for?" Jesse didn't answer Earle. Instead he turned around and set off back towards the farmhouse.

Jesse vigorously pushed open the backdoor which startled Emma, "What do you want now?" Emma asked Jesse as she turned her head quickly away from him. Jesse paused for a moment then dismissed the action and thought no more of it until he made inquiries as to where Amos was, again Emma shied away from Jesse and began saying, "Oh! He's not well. He'll be out later, when he's feeling better." Emma said this with her back to Jesse and not once did she make eye contact with him. Instantly, Jesse knew something was wrong, so he sat down at the table and said, "Well I'm here now, so I might as well have some breakfast." Emma walked towards the fire and said, "Oh no you don't, you eat when the rest of them eat. So get out there and help Earle bring those crops in." Jesse stood up and was just about to stomp out of the kitchen in disgust when he noticed Emma using her handkerchief to dry a wet eye. He walked towards her but once again she shied away. The nearer Jesse got the further away she went, "Go on then, get out there and help Earle!" Emma shrieked whilst still moving backwards.

Nevertheless, Jesse had become suspicious and quickly lunged at her. He quickly grabbed Emma's arm with one hand and with the other he slowly pulled Emma's face around towards him by the chin to reveal a large black bruise running the length of her face. Emma flinched, "Don't! Don't our Jesse! Please don't!" Emma said, as she began to cry, "Who's done that, as if I need to ask?" Jesse said pointing to the side of Emma's face she had tried to conceal from him, "It's nothing!" Emma said, trying to calm Jesse down, who was by now absolutely furious. "It's nothing! I don't call that nothing, just look at your face. It's badly bruised and you have a small cut just under your ear, and that eye. Well... it's going to be a real beauty by tomorrow. Where is he? I'll kill him!" Jesse said, making a dash for the bottom of the stairs. Emma quickly grabbed Jesse by his collar and said, "It was an accident Jesse, he didn't mean it." She pulled Jesse back from the stairs and said, "Please, leave

120

it Jesse and go back to the field." Jesse paused for a moment and then turned to Emma saying, "And you want to marry a drunken bastard like that!" Jesse broke away from Emma and walked towards the door shaking his head. Emma followed Jesse down the path and out into the farmyard, she quickly overtook Jesse and blocked his way by standing in front of him.

Emma walked backwards and tried to stop Jesse by pushing his shoulders, "He's a really nice person Jesse, if you give him a chance. Can't you try and get along with him." Jesse stopped and shook his head. This annoyed Emma intensely, and in a fit of anger, she slapped Jesse across the face saying, "You un-grateful little sod. You'd have starved if it hadn't been for Amos." Jesse didn't say anything; he didn't even rub his face as it turned red and began to sting. Exasperated, Emma threw her arms up in disgust and stomped off towards the milking shed where the cows were waiting.

Jesse walked back towards the cornfield, he began thinking, and it wasn't long before he was deep in thought, he realized that the only person left on the farm, which he thought he could depend on and trust, had gone. He felt betrayed by his Aunt Emma. I certainly won't be able to trust her any longer, Jesse thought. She was obviously going to side with Amos, especially if any arguments broke out, he thought. The slap on the face had taught him that.

Jesse walked on further, he eventually did rub his face where a red mark had appeared, but just before entering the cornfield, he had a final thought. And from this day forwards I had better watch what I say and do in front of Aunt Emma. Just then a familiar quiet Irish voice said, "Oh there you are." Jesse looked up to see Megan staring down at him from the top of a cart of sheaths, "We thought we'd lost you for the day, slipping off like that," Megan said, sliding down off the cart. Earle pitched a couple more sheaths up onto the top of the cart and said to the Carter, who was an old man with a beard, "Right, this one's ready. Take it into the hayfield next door, you two, go with the cart and unload it." Jesse glared at Earle and said, "Don't tell me what to do. I know what to do!"

The old Carter adjusted his hat, cracked the rains and started off towards the gate. Jesse and Megan followed. Eventually, Jesse and Megan arrived with the Carter in the hayfield. They began unloading it straight away, if you could call it unloading. It was more like just throwing the sheaths from the top of the cart and allowing them to land anywhere and anyhow, upside down, on their sides, it didn't seem to matter to the young couple, who just kept smiling and laughing at each other as they threw off the next sheath in a completely different way than the last one. Jesse would kick one, and then Megan would use her hip to flip one off the cart.

"Don't just throw them anywhere!" Growled Amos who had just entered the hayfield by the top gate, looking like death warmed up, "The sheaths need to be stack like bricks so the hay can go on top. Come down here and I'll show you how to make a rain proof haystack," Amos said, pointing at Jesse and Megan, who quickly jumped down to join Amos. Amos began gathering up some of the sheaths, he then arranged them like bricks, "Make sure you lay the sheaths with a slight slope so the rain runs off." Amos said to Jesse, who was watching with great interest as Amos very carefully laid the foundations of a haystack.

Amos then turned to the old Carter and said, "You! Pick up the rest of the sheaths and hand them to me." The old Carter began collecting the sheaths and dragging them towards Amos, who was busy laying them frantically. Then, suddenly, Amos stopped, held his forehead and said, "Right Jesse, you do the stacking." He then pointed at the old Carter and Megan and said, "Whilst you and her unload them and pass them to Jesse. Work as a team and the job will get done faster." Amos then stood up, leant back and rubbed the back of his neck saying; "Whilst I go and get the hair of the dog!" He set off back towards the farmhouse leaving Jesse wondering what the hell he was talking about.

It took a while, but eventually, Jesse got the hang of building haystacks. The day was long and Jesse, Megan and the old carter had built between them three fine haystacks, even Amos had said how good they were, which surprised Jesse because Amos never said anything good about what Jesse did. They'd just finished the third haystack when the old carter said, "That's enough for me. I'm off." He quickly headed through the gate and back down the track with his cart. This left Jesse and Megan alone for the first time; they both slid down from the top of the third haystack and ended up on a bed of hay, which surrounded the stack. They both laid there for several minutes watching a single cloud make its way across the light blue summer sky before Jesse said, "See that cloud." Megan replied, "Yes! It looks a little lonely on its own." There was a moment's silence as Jesse slowly clasped Megan's hand with his, "It's just like me, all alone!" "You're not alone, you've got me." Megan replied, as she turned towards Jesse and gave him the sweetest kiss of his life, so sweet, it made his toes curl. Jesse enjoyed it so much that he returned the favour only to be pushed away by Megan, who said, "What's your rush? A kiss has to be relished slowly, like cooking a good Irish stew. Not rushed and drooled over." Jesse instantly wiped his lips with his sleeve and then looked at Megan in anticipation of their next kiss, but suddenly from the direction of the gate her name was called.

Megan quickly jumped up and went to the end of the stack, being careful not to be seen, she said, "It's my da!" To Jesse who quickly pulled Megan back from the end of the stack. He put his hand over her mouth and whispered into her ear, "Quiet." He then kissed her ear gently before rolling over to the other end of the stack and squinting slowly around the end of it to see if he could see Megan's father. Sure enough by the gate was Megan's father looking across the field for Megan. Megan began to giggle as she tried to pull Jesse back towards her but Jesse fought off her pulls with his hands. Jesse watched as Megan's father put up his hand to the side of his mouth and again shouted, "Megan!" He waited for a reply, he listened intensely, but no reply came. Slowly, he turned and walked away. Jesse turned to Megan and said, "He's gone!" Megan replied, "Good!" She then grabbed Jesse and pulled him onto her. They began kissing and cuddling under the stack which resembled a fresh baked loaf of bread as it sat there in the field under the warm golden evening sun. However, it wasn't long before the evening sun was replaced by dusk and then darkness, but the young couple didn't care, as time was the last thing on their minds. His first passionate time seemed to pass quickly for Jesse. It was cut short by Amos and flame carrying Irishmen who were annoyed that they'd spent the last two hours of darkness searching for Megan.

Luckily, Jesse had heard the mob arriving at the gate of the hayfield. This had given both of them, time to stand up and correct their clothing. Jesse smiled at Megan who pulled out a piece of hay from her dress. She then gave him a final kiss before appearing to the mob. "There she is!" Said a small Irishman who lifted his torch to reveal Megan to the rest of the mob; Megan covered her eyes from the light with her arm and said. "I must have nodded off da, I'm sorry." She then slowly walked towards her father who heaved a sigh of relief. Amos wasn't so convinced at Megan's explanation and walked suspiciously towards the stack, he lifted his torch as he walked around the back of the stack, nothing could be seen. Everybody seemed content that Megan had been found safe and well and began walking back to the farmyard where Amos said, "Goodnight."

However, Amos was still not convinced by Megan's story and decided he would pay Jesse a visit in the barn. He walked across to the barn and opened the door quietly by lifting it slightly so the hinges didn't squeak. The barn lit up as Amos entered with his torch, he walked to the back of the barn where he found Jesse who had a blanket wrapped around him. On seeing the light, Jesse lifted his head from his pillow and turned to face Amos. Squinting and reckoning on to be still half asleep, Jesse asked, "What's up?" Amos looked at him and then said suspiciously, "Nothing, just checking you're alright." Jesse turned away from the flame's light, pulled out a piece of hay from his vest and said, "Of course I'm alright! Why shouldn't I be?" Amos left the barn, dipped his torch in the trough and was just about to walk back to the farmhouse, when he could have sworn, he'd heard giggling. He listened intently but the whole farm seemed to have gone quiet, he shook his head, thought no more about it and walked back to the farmhouse where Emma was waiting for him.

The following Sunday was the big day, all banns had been read and the happy couple were going to tie the knot. Jesse and Earle were up early and had started their daily chores to allow them to attend the ceremony which was going to be held in the church at eleven o'clock prompt. Even Amos was up and about early helping Emma who had spent most of Saturday cooking and baking things for the small reception planned to be held outside the farmhouse after the ceremony, provided the weather held off of course. The weather that day wasn't perfect, but it wasn't bad either, it was a warm grey day with plenty of clouds blotting out the sun and if the rain held off it would be a near perfect day for holding a reception outdoor's. Jesse and Earle had finished their chores and were stood by the horse trough discussing what relation to each other they would be after the ceremony. Jesse had stopped the conversation dead by saying, "I've enough cousins on my father's side already without adding anymore. Especially one's I don't like!" He then disappeared into the barn and re-appeared sometime later with Titan. Jesse pulled Titan slowly to the trough and allowed him to take a drink, whilst he attached the small cart.

Eventually, everybody and everything was ready for the big day. Earle and Amos had already set off for the church. Jesse had mounted the cart and brought it around to the farmhouse garden gate, where he waited patiently for Emma, the blushing bride, to appear. Titan began picking at the grass by the gate whilst Jesse was forced into day dreaming by the wait. The farmyard was quiet and the fields were empty as Jesse's mind began to wonder, his thoughts began to turn to Megan, as he looked up the track towards the cornfield. Then suddenly, at the top of the track, he caught a glimpse of what Jesse thought was a man. He'd no sooner seen the man and he was gone. The man vanished into a sun beam which had appeared as the sun came from behind a cloud, "Come on Jesse or we'll be late." Emma said, waking Jesse from his day dreaming. "Did you see that?" Jesse asked Emma who was by now sat at the side of Jesse on the cart. "See what?" Emma asked, looking puzzled at Jesse who quickly tried to cover up what he'd said by saying, "Oh... nothing!" He then cracked the rains and said, "Go on Titan, walk on." Titan began pulling the cart out of the farmyard and up the track towards the top field.

As the cart arrived at the top of the track, where the man had appeared earlier to Jesse, Jesse began slowing the cart down. Suddenly, and startling Emma at the same time, Jesse stood up, and whilst still holding onto the rains, he began looking across the fields; there was nothing to be seen. "Jesse, what are you doing?" Emma asked, whilst elbowing Jesse in the leg, hoping it would shock him out of his gazing around, "Nothing!" Snapped Jesse, "Well come on then, were going to be late!" Emma said, urging Jesse to speed up the cart. "Alright, alright, I was just checking something," said Jesse as he sat back down in the cart whilst having a last look over his shoulder. Just at that moment Jesse caught another glimpse of a dark shadow entering a clump of trees at the far end of the cornfield, "There! Over there!" He screamed at Emma, who quickly turned to see nothing. "What! What am I looking for?" Emma asked, looking confused. Jesse, who was by now stood up again in the cart and pointing towards the trees, "Over there, did you see him?" Jesse looked down at Emma whose face said, "See what!" Jesse, realizing that Emma hadn't seen anything, slowly sat back down and disappointed, he gave Titan a quick crack of the rains and said, "Go on then, go on, walk on."

Arriving at the church Jesse soon forgot about the man when he saw the beautiful smiling face of Megan looking up at him. It was the best thing he'd seen all day. She and some of the help had turned up at the church including Megan's father for the ceremony. Jesse jumped down from the cart smiled at

Megan then walked around to the otherside of the cart where Emma was waiting for him to help her down from the cart. Jesse held up his hand to Emma, who grabbed it tightly, she then climbed down without letting go of the hand. Emma's grip changed from Jesse's hand to his elbow, she tugged at the elbow and Jesse allowed her to link arms. Both straighten their clothing and checked one another's hair before starting off towards the church. Their way was blocked by Megan who said directly to Jesse, "Got a kiss for ya sweetheart then my lad?" Jesse began blushing and said, "I'll see you after the ceremony." This was not the answer Megan wanted to hear, and she immediately stomped off showing her displeasure at Jesse's answer, "She's trouble! You'd be better off stopping away from that one." Emma told Jesse, as they both entered the church.

Just inside the church door the verger stopped them both and said, "Wait here!" He then opened the inner door and gave a signal to the organist who began playing the Wedding March. "Slowly then," the verger said as he opened both inner doors. The congregation stood up as Jesse marched Emma down the aisle to where Amos and Earle were waiting anxiously.

The service was over quickly and before Jesse knew where he was he found himself driving the lead cart of a small procession of carts back towards the farm. The happy couple spent the journey in the back of the cart, kissing loudly, and by the time the cart arrived back at the farm this kissing was beginning to make Jesse feel sick. He pulled up outside the farmhouse and let Amos and Emma get out of the cart before he led Titan and the cart across the farmyard towards the trough, where he tied him up and took off his harness. As other carts began arriving in the farmyard, Emma started to bring

out the food from the house on large trays. Amos set about getting the barrels of ale ready by braying in the taps, he then, using a small tankard took a sample, which he swigged off in one swift movement, "That's good stuff!" Amos said, wiping the froth from his lips with the back of his hand. It wasn't long before everybody started eating and drinking and there was much merriment and dancing until late in the afternoon.

As the afternoon changed into evening and the drinking went on and on, Jesse noticed that Megan's father and some of the Irish help seemed to be drinking more than everybody else. The merriment began to change and there seem to be a lot of whispering going on. Amos too had had his fill of ale but was continuing to drink and slaver over any young thing he could find, much to the annoyance of everyone, including Emma, who was clearing away the remnants of the food.

Eventually, Amos arrived at Megan who was sat on the wall by the farmhouse gate, "Now then, here's a pretty little thing," Amos said, slopping ale over Megan who pulled back as Amos threatened to kiss her. Jesse seeing this was quick to re-act. He began to move quickly towards Megan, but unfortunately, so was Megan's father and a couple of stout Irish lads. Amos, who was by now becoming very irritated by Megan's refusal continued to taunt her by saying, "Oh! I'm not good enough for the likes of you!" He said, "You prefer the likes of that little brat, Jesse! Don't you? You're his bit of stuff, aren't you?" Amos took another swig from his tankard. He then burped and lifted Megan's chin up so he could see her eyes. "Go on then, go to that little brat. See if I care!" Amos growled as he threw Megan across the farmyard floor. Suddenly, Amos found himself being thrown across the farmyard floor. Only he landed awkwardly and squirmed as he hit the ground. Before he could recover from this Megan's father and the stout Irish lads were raining blows down on Amos and saying things like, "Drive us like slaves would ya," and "We'll teach ya to respect ya workers, ya bastard!" And with that, they continued to punch Amos. Jesse grabbed Megan and began pulling her away from the fight. Just then Earle came thundering past Jesse, he was kicking and punching out at everything in sight, "Come on Jesse get in! Help our Amos!" Earle screamed, as he started to help Amos, who was by now getting up from the ground and giving back some of what he had just received. Jesse looked at the fight and then made one of his decisions. Why should I? He thought. He turned away, put his arm around Megan and walked her slowly back towards the barn. Just before they entered the barn Jesse looked back and could see his Aunt Emma trying to break up the fight, which was much bigger by now, as other relatives and Irish helpers had joined in.

Megan and Jesse entered the barn and sat just inside the open barn door watching from the shadows as the fight went on. "My da's going to feel it tomorrow," said Megan, "Yes! I think they'll all be sorry in the morning." Jesse replied, pulling out two large pieces of pie from his jacket pocket. He handed one of them to Megan. The couple sat there talking about the usual things that young couples talk about when they're alone. However, the conversation eventually, got around to when Megan would be leaving. Jesse held Megan's hand and asked reluctantly, "When are you going home then?" Megan thought for a moment and said, "As soon as the harvest is in. Why?" "Oh, nothing, I was just wondering," Jesse replied, as he took another bite of his pie. The fight went on for sometime, but eventually everybody was punched out and began leaving.

Megan's father walked towards the barn and said angrily, "Come on Megan, we're leaving and we're not coming back!" Jesse was horrified at the thought of not seeing Megan again and turned to look straight at Megan, who said, "Don't worry Jesse. I'll come back tomorrow and if not tomorrow, then as soon as I can. You'll wait for me, won't you?" She then managed to look straight at Jesse for some sign of acknowledgement, whilst struggling with her father's firm grip on her wrist. Jesse nodded his head and then watched helplessly as Megan's father dragged her away down the track, her voice began to fade into the distance and all Jesse could do was to stand there watching from the barn door as they both began to disappear over the top of the track. However, just before Megan disappeared, she managed to blow a kiss towards Jesse and with that she disappeared from sight.

The next morning Jesse found himself sat alone in a fireless kitchen, he waited and waited. But eventually, he decided that no-one was coming and began loading his pockets with some of the leftover food from the reception. Once his pockets were full he left the kitchen, slamming the backdoor behind him, thinking the noise might wake up the occupants. He paused outside the door to see if it had worked but there was no sound of any movement, not a sound. Jesse tutted to himself and walked across the yard and out onto the track. Moments later Jesse had arrived at the next cornfield that needed cutting and by now the warmth of the morning sun and the trek had made Jesse feel quite lethargic, so he decided to take a rest and have his breakfast. Jesse thought a spot against the wall facing the sun would be nice and the ideal spot to have his breakfast. He sat down in the soft corn and laid his back against the wall. He hadn't been sat there long when he was startled by a high pitch squealing noise. What on an earth is that? Thought Jesse, nearly choking on a frazzled sausage, Jesse quickly jumped to his feet and looked

around to see where the noise was coming from. It was coming from the otherside of the wall. Jesse quickly jumped up onto the wall and was just in time to see a dark grey rabbit in the last throws of its death dance, it made Jesse shudder and to stop himself being sick he spat out the last piece of sausage he was chewing.

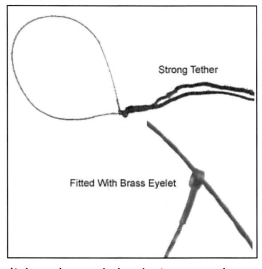

The poor creature had been snared by a piece of string, which had been tithed to a stake. The stake had then been firmly pushed into the ground. Jesse jumped down from the wall and examined the noose around the rabbit's neck closely, he then thought... poachers... Amos won't be pleased, he hates poachers. Jesse quickly jumped back over the wall and continued with his breakfast, after which he sat there in the warm morning sunshine letting it digest. Whilst sitting there Jesse decided that he would hide the rabbit and say nothing to Amos about the poacher. It would be far less fuss, he thought, as he closed his eyes and slid down the wall. After about an hour Jesse began wondering where everybody was, none of the Irish help had turned up and when he looked back down the track towards the farmhouse it all seemed very quiet. He waited for a further half an hour and then decided something must be done, so he set off back down the track towards the house. On entering the kitchen he looked towards the table where Earle was sat nursing a fat lip with a piece of wet cloth. "That's a nice one," Jesse said, sitting down at the table across from Earle who said nothing and turned away from Jesse. "Oh it's like that, is it?" Jesse said, standing up again. There was a moments silence and then Jesse turned and walked back towards the backdoor. But before leaving, he said, "If anybody around here is interested there are still crops to get in and there's no help to do it with." He then looked across at Earle, who was sat motionless and silent, still holding the cloth against his lip. Jesse tutted and left by the backdoor, he slowly walked across the yard towards the barn and his den. After looking at his bed for a moment, he decided to take a nap, he didn't usually take naps during the day but seen as nobody else seemed interested in work, and he couldn't do it all himself, he thought... why not?

The next day Jesse was sat on the horse trough waiting, his legs dangling over the side, he sat there most of the morning waiting for Megan, but she never came, neither did the Irish help. After sometime Jesse shrugged his shoulders and assumed that she must have gone back home to Ireland or was working for someone else, either way he'd gotten bored with waiting and began doing some of his overdue chores.

It was three days before the badly bruised Amos and Earle turned up for work and there was still no sign of the help. It took almost three months for the three of them to get in the rest of the crops. Jesse had never been worked as hard by Amos and was determined to decline the offer of work at the next Hiring Fair, which seemed to come around very quickly. However, Jesse had forgotten that it wouldn't be him answering the Chief Constable's question. It would be Amos and as you would expect with Jesse being unpaid, when Amos was asked the question, "Did he want to release Jesse?" The answer from Amos was a definite, "No!" Jesse tried to object but the Chief Constable did nothing but growl at Jesse and told him to shut up and not to interrupt the proceedings.

Two years passed and so did the ridiculous unfair proceedings at the Hiring Fair, each year Jesse would object and each year he would be told the same thing, 'shut up and stop interrupting the proceedings,' followed by Amos answering, "No!" And then paying the fee of a penny for Jesse's labour. After the third Hiring Fair, Amos had again paid the penny and Jesse found himself back in the barn among the farm tools and hay. Early the next morning Jesse was laid in his bed looking up at the barn rafters thinking that he would never be able to escape the farm and the treacherous grip of Amos. In desperation Jesse even contemplated making a run for it, anything is better than this, he thought. However, this thought was interrupted by a voice shouting from outside the barn, "Jesse, Jesse are you there?" Jesse immediately recognized the voice, it was Amos, he jumped up quickly and walked to the barn door, he opened it slowly.

Outside in the yard stood Amos with his shotgun broken over his arm, "Come on were going to catch that bloody poacher," Amos said, loading a couple of shells into the shotgun. "I haven't seen him around for sometime," Jesse said reluctantly, staring down at Amos's gun, "He's still here, I know he's still here. Over the last couple of years this chap as robbed us of chickens, rabbits and I'm almost sure that this year he's taken a couple of sheep, so this morning, I'm going to have him!" Both set off towards the small forest which encroached onto the farm at the otherside of the cornfield. Amos sat down by the cornfield's gate and then turned to Jesse and said, "Right, you go around the otherside of the forest and flush him out towards me." Jesse looked down at the gun and said, "What! Are you mad?" "Don't worry, I won't hit you. I'm a good shot," Amos said, tapping his gun barrel gently.

Jesse reluctantly set off around the back of the forest. He nervously looked back towards Amos, who beckoned him on into the trees by waving. It was dark inside the small forest and Jesse found the darkness very uncomfortable and disturbing. In among the trees you could hear nothing, it was an eerie silence. Jesse picked up two sticks and began tapping them together, this helped put Jesse at ease, and he felt more comfortable doing it, thinking that if anyone was in there, they'd hear the sound and be off before he got too close to them. The last thing Jesse wanted was a confrontation with some desperate poacher. No sooner had he started tapping the sticks together when he heard a rustling sound and then the sound of running footsteps, he stared hard into the darkness and could just make out the image of a man running from a make shift shelter about ten yards in front of him. The man was fast and disappeared quickly into the darkness of the forest, a couple of seconds later Jesse heard the sound of Amos's shotgun. Two shots rang out and then the forest returned to its eerie silence.

Jesse continued to tap the sticks together and walked nearer the make shift shelter. When he got to the shelter, it turned out to be a small settlement. Someone was obviously living there. He looked around and could see a small bed inside a really poorly constructed wooden shelter, there was a small fire mounted on several flat stones. The fire had a spit with newly skinned rabbit on it, the skin lay nearby. The spit itself had been constructed from twigs off the forest floor, "Another of our rabbits, no doubt." Amos said as he approached Jesse. "Did you get him?" Jesse asked Amos, who was by now destroying the make shift shelter. "No! But the buggers not going to live here anymore, I'll make sure of that!" Amos said, as he continued standing on parts of the shelter. He did this until every stick of the shelter had been broken or snapped in half, all that was left, when he'd finished, was a pile of broken twigs. The final degradation of the little settlement came when Amos urinated on the fire and the half cooked rabbit, he grinned at Jesse whilst doing this, "There! That'll do us." Amos said, fastening up his flies. He then turned to Jesse and said, "Come on lad. Let's get back." Both Amos and Jesse set off back towards the farm, Amos loaded his gun as they walked; he then placed it broken over his arm. "Just in case," he said to Jesse as they walked back out of the forest and headed for the track across the cornfield.

They entered the farmyard and Amos said to Jesse, "Get the small cart ready, you can take me into Shalbourne after dinner." Jesse nodded and went to fetch Titan from the barn. About an hour later Jesse was sat outside the house waiting for Amos to finish his dinner, Titan seemed a bit nervous, for some reason, and Jesse was trying to calm him down by talking to him, "Woo Titan, steady boy." Jesse gently pulled back on the rains. Just then Amos appeared, "Stop pulling on the rain's lad." He walked down the side of Titan checking the harness and patting him gently. "Far too tight lad, far too tight," Amos growled. He then began slackening the harness and started to mumble to himself.

After he'd finished Amos slowly walked to the front of Titan and began examining Titan's mouth. Just then a shot rang out, it bounced off the wall just at the back of Amos, quickly Jesse jumped down from the cart and Amos ran and hid behind Titan, "Where is he Jesse?" Amos asked. Jesse angrily replied, "How the bloody hell would I know?" They both slowly lifted their heads above the cart and stared up the track. There at the top of the track was the poacher; he waved his fist at them before turning and disappearing from sight. "Come on, let's get him!" Amos said lifting Jesse into the cart. He quickly retrieved his gun from behind the garden gate and slung it into the back of the cart. Amos was absolutely furious; he jumped up onto the cart and cracked the whip over Titan's back, shouting, "Go on boy!" The cart sped off up the track at a deadly pace towards where the poacher had been stood. Jesse was forced to cling onto the cart for dear life, thinking it was going to tip over at any minute. However, it didn't and when they got to where the poacher had been stood, he'd disappeared into thin air.

Amos quickly jumped down from the cart and retrieved his gun from the back of the cart. He quickly straightened it and set off running across the cornfield. At the otherside of the field Jesse watched as Amos let go two more shots from the top of the dry stone wall. Amos then paused for a moment whilst staring into the forest; he eventually turned and jumped back down off the wall. After walking back across the cornfield towards Jesse, Amos said, "Got the little bugger that time." He shrugged his shoulders and climbed back aboard the cart feeling quite proud of his shooting. He threw his gun into the back of the cart and said, "Come on then lad, I've earned that drink!" Jesse pushed Titan on towards Shalbourne where he pulled up outside The Plough Inn and allowed Titan to take a drink from the trough. Amos jumped down from the cart and told Jesse sternly, "Don't wait for me lad, go straight back.

Oh! And look after my gun for me." Jesse nodded his head and Amos disappeared inside the pub. Whilst Jesse was sat there waiting for Titan to finish his drink, he noticed a crowd of people gathered in the village square. I wonder what's going on over there, thought Jesse; he continued to watch closely from the top of the cart.

In the middle of the crowd were two men sat on a cart, a very posh cart, posh because any cart that had lamps was seen by the locals as been posh. The men looked very debonair in their bowler hats and tweed jackets. All of a sudden, one of the men stood up in the cart and began speaking and waving his hands about. Jesse couldn't quite hear what the man was saying and Jesse being Jesse; well, he just had to get closer. He jumped down from the cart and tied Titan to a nearby post.

After pausing for a moment, he pulled up his trousers, tucked in his shirt and began to make his way towards the crowd. As Jesse walked towards the crowd he had past some men who were walking away from the crowd, they were all carrying pieces of yellow card. Some of the men could be heard saying things like, "Why not? There's nothing around here but starvation!" and "Well I'm definitely going at five bob a week!" Jesse walked into the crowd which was by now beginning to dissipate a little, this didn't put Jesse off, he continued towards the men and their posh cart.

Eventually, Jesse found himself at the front of a small crowd of people who were stood just in front of the posh cart, "What about you young sir?" One of the men said to Jesse. Jesse looked around thinking the man meant someone else, "Yes you! You look fit enough for a hard day's work! Do you fancy it then?" Jesse, realizing the man meant him said, "Fancy what?" The man replied quickly, "Why a job lad, up north!" Jesse hesitated and didn't know what to say. The man jumped down off the cart and grabbed Jesse's elbow, "Come here lad, let me explain." The man pulled Jesse to one side, slightly away from the crowd, "Now then lad! My partner and I represent a large mill owner up north; he's looking for young strong lads like you to work for him in his mill." The man hesitated and then continued to say, "Are you interested lad?" Jesse was speechless and just shrugged his shoulders. The man saw that Jesse might be interested so he continued trying to persuade Jesse to agree, "It pays five bob a week and a place to stay," the man said. Jesse's eyes lit up at the thought of five bob a week and a place to stay, "I don't know," Jesse said reluctantly. "How much are you earning a week now?" The man asked Jesse, who immediately became embarrassed to repiy and said quietly, "Nothing, just board." The man quickly dipped his hand into his inside pocket and pulled out some cards, "Here lad! What you waiting for? There's money to be had!" He then handed Jesse two of the yellow cards. "That's your ticket for the canal trip up north," the man said, pointing to the first of the cards. "And the other you must give the mill manager when you get there. It guarantees you a job, got it!" Jesse nodded and started to walk away whilst still staring down at the two pieces of card. He hadn't gone far when the man shouted after him saying, "The cards are only valid for six months after that there are no guarantees!" Jesse turned back to face the man and nodded. The man returned a two finger salute to his bowler hat and jumped back up into his posh cart.

All the way home Jesse thought about the proposition, he had so many questions about leaving, he didn't know what to do, so he decided that he would sleep on it and think about it the following morning. However, sleeping on it wasn't as easy as Jesse had thought. Jesse laid there in his bed for hours, tossing and turning and when he eventually did get off to sleep, it was only a very light sleep. It was one of those times when you think you are asleep, but you're not, you're aware of every little movement around you. Jesse could even hear Titan breathing across the otherside of the barn. It was the early hours of the morning when Jesse was disturbed by what he thought were footsteps inside the barn and a cold draught as if the barn door had been opened and closed. He didn't move at first and dismissed both as nonsense. Thinking to himself, there's no-one there, he turned over and tried to carry on sleeping. Just at that moment Jesse got a feeling, it was a very cold uneasy feeling. That he wasn't alone in the barn, this put Jesse's sensors on full alert. And just when he thought he was nodding off again, he heard a gentle rustling of straw, this woke Jesse immediately and made him sit bolt upright in his bed.

Jesse adjusted his eyes to the darkness of the barn and then began looking around slowly. He slowly began turning his head, scanning every nook and cranny of the barn, but then his head stopped and his heart nearly did the same thing as he spotted what he thought was the shadow of a man in the dark recesses of the barn, "I know you're there, whoever you are?" Jesse said nervously. He stood up and got ready to have a go, when suddenly, a voice from the darkness, said, "Hello our Jesse, still up to your tricks I see." The man stepped out of the darkness to reveal himself.

Chapter 6: The Poacher and the Way Northward.

The voice from the shadows seemed very familiar. It seemed to have a caring friendliness about it. However, Jesse still couldn't identify the black shadow now facing him and was still unsure about approaching the man. Still on his guard and keeping one eye on the man, Jesse walked sideways across the barn towards the barn doors. Using one hand Jesse slowly pushed the doors open which allowed the white moonlight of the night to flood into the barn. Again Jesse adjusted his sight and stared back into the barn to where the man was stood. However, then, suddenly, the man slouched forward and groaned as he fumbled to his knees. Jesse quickly ran towards the man and managed to catch him before he fell completely forwards onto his face. "Thanks our Jesse," the man said, putting his arm around Jesse's shoulder for support. This action brought Jesse's eye's to within twelve inches of the man's face and the words, 'our Jesse' had made Jesse's head spin so quickly to look at the man's face, he nearly head butted the man.

Jesse was then suddenly stopped in his stride at what he saw. The shock made him instantly throw the man to the barn floor. The man landed on his back face up and yelped as he hit the floor. Jesse then screamed, "Henry! Henry, is it really you?" "Shhh..." the man replied, placing the palm of his hand over Jesse's mouth. There was a long silence as both brothers looked at each other in the eye, then Henry said, "Yes, but it nearly wasn't, thanks to your mate with the shotgun." He sat up and pointed down to his blood stained trouser leg. Immediately, Jesse knelt down and began to examine the leg, "Nasty!" He said as he turned to look at Henry's face, which was by now showing the agony and the pain of being shot. Jesse, still stunned by Henry's appearance, continued to say, "It's bleeding rather badly." Jesse then grinned and shook his head, "I still can't believe it's you, our Henry, back home." "It soon won't be if we don't stop that bleeding," Henry said, tugging at his

trouser leg. Jesse quickly jumped up and said, "There are some old strips of material at the back of the barn, we use it for binding the sheaths." "Go and fetch some Jesse, quickly!" Henry said, as he began picking out the buck shot from his leg.

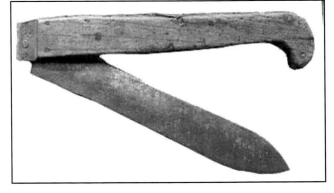

Jesse returned quickly with a handful of strips, "Here you go," he said, throwing the strips on to the floor at the side of Henry, who was still picking out the buck shot. "Have you got a knife?" Henry asked Jesse who was by now so enthralled watching Henry pull out the buck shot from his leg that nothing else existed. "Jesse!" Henry said in exasperation. "Have you got a knife?" Jesse looked at Henry's face, which was still full of agony, and said, "No! Not here, but there's a Folding Gully in the house," "Go and get it. I need to get the rest of this shot out of my leg, it's in too deep to reach with my fingers."

Jesse crept quietly across the farmyard then up the garden path towards the kitchen. As he walked across the kitchen towards the knife drawer, the only sound he could hear was that of his own heart pounding quickly in the darkness. He paused for a moment, took a deep breath and was just about to open the knife drawer when a voice from behind him said, "And what are you up to?" Jesse quickly pulled his hand back from the knife drawer and spun around to see Earle sat at the bottom of the stairs, "Earle! You sod, you gave me such a fright," Jesse said, holding his chest with one hand. Earle stood up and said, "And what are you up to?" Jesse thought for a moment and then said, "Oh, I can't sleep so I came to see if there was any food going spare." Earle looked at Jesse very suspiciously and then said, "There's some bread and cheese on the table, if you want it." He then began to climb the stairs saying, "Goodnight ya sod." Jesse waited until Earle had reached the top of the stairs and had disappeared from sight. He then quickly opened the knife drawer, took out the gully and before leaving grabbed the bread and cheese from the table.

Back in the barn Henry had lit a lamp to help him to remove the shot, but he was still struggling to remove the really deep shot from his leg and the pain was getting unbearable. When he saw Jesse approaching with the gully, he smiled and said, "Well done our Jesse." Quickly Henry opened the blade from its wooden sheath and began gouging out the pieces of shot, every piece deeper and more painful than the last one. Eventually, he stopped and said, "Right, it's your turn now our Jesse, you've got to pull out the last few pieces of shot for me." Jesse was horrified and said, "I'm not doing it. I might kill you!" "Don't be stupid, you won't kill me!" Snapped Henry, who then paused for a moment and looked firstly at his leg and then at Jesse. He sighed and said assertively, "Listen our Jesse, I can't do it. I'll probably pass out with the pain. You've got to help me here Jesse." Henry handed Jesse the gully and said, "When you've finished removing the shot, wrap some strips around my leg tightly to stop the bleeding." Henry looked again at Jesse, hoping he would see some sign of agreement but Jesse just sat there shaking his head, "If you don't get the shot out, I will surely bleed to death or even worse die of blood poisoning," Henry said.

Jesse, after a moment reluctantly leant forward over the leg. "Which holes are the pieces in?" Jesse asked as he began examining the holed riddled leg. Henry pointed to two holes and said, "There are two pieces of shot in those holes. You must get them out, right Jesse!" Jesse nodded half-heartedly and began digging. Henry placed a piece of rolled up strip into his mouth and began biting down on it. The first piece of shot wasn't too bad. It came out without much trouble. However, the second piece was well into the leg and to make matters worse Jesse had to wiggle the gully blade to retrieve the shot. Henry stiffened at the first wiggle of the gully blade. He then passed out as Jesse gouged deep into his leg for the shot. Eventually, after several wiggles, Jesse managed to remove a large piece of shot from the hole which began bleeding profusely, the blood was thick and dark red, it oozed from the hole and down the side of Henry's leg.

Quickly, without panicking, Jesse folded some strips of material into a thick square and placed them over the hole. After which he began wrapping the leg tightly with the rest of the strips. After several blood sodden layers, the bleeding began to stop and Jesse began to ease back thinking he'd done a good job considering he didn't know what he was doing. Jesse made Henry comfortable by propping his head up with some clean straw. He threw Henry's old overcoat over him to keep him warm and then laid down himself. Whilst lying there, looking up at the barn ceiling, Jesse suddenly realized that if Amos or Earle should enter the barn in the morning, they would see Henry straight away. Jesse got up from the floor and looked around for something to hide Henry with, the only thing that was available was some old fence post piled in the corner of the barn. Jesse began moving the pile of posts to the back of the barn leaving enough space between the pile of post and the barn wall for Henry to lie in. Once the posts were in position, he then had the task of dragging Henry into the space. Henry wasn't that heavy but moving him without starting his leg bleeding again was difficult, and it took Jesse quite sometime to get Henry hidden behind the pile of posts. Eventually, Henry was hidden at the back of the posts and Jesse finished off the hiding place by placing the bread and cheese, he'd gotten from the kitchen, just inside the entrance, he then piled lots of straw up against the entrance. When he'd finished Jesse stood back and admired his work, just then he was overcome with tiredness and decided to go to bed. Wearily, Jesse headed back to his bed in the den where he laid down. There was no time for thought. As soon as Jesse's head hit the straw pillow, he was asleep.

The following morning Jesse was awoken by the farmyard cockerel, which on a normal day would have annoyed Jesse, but on this particular day he was grateful to have been awakened before Amos or Earle. On hearing the first crow from the cockerel Jesse was up and heading towards the pile of posts. He quickly removed the straw from around the entrance to the hiding place and looked in to see how Henry was. To his delight Henry was sat up with a big grin on his face enjoying the bread and cheese. "We need to change these strips our Jesse," Henry said, with a mouth full of bread as he began pulling off the blood stained strips from his leg. Jesse quickly fetched some more strips from the back of the barn and handed them to Henry. There was a moments silence whilst Henry began changing the strips. It was broken by Henry saying, "I suppose you want to know what happened to me!" Jesse, who by now could barely contain himself, blurted out quickly, "Yes! Oh yes please, do tell. I can't wait to..." but just as Jesse was about to complete his sentence by saying, "hear" he was interrupted and his keenness to find out what had happened to Henry was cut short by a voice from outside the barn.

Both Jesse and Henry looked at each other and then froze. They listened for a moment and then Jesse said, "Quick! Lay down! I'll be back later!" Jesse quickly covered the entrance with the straw and walked to his den. He then walked from his den towards the barn doors. He did this to make it look as though he was coming from the den and not any other part of the barn, which was just as well because just at that moment, Amos came into the barn. He instantly began screaming abuse at Jesse and whilst ranting said, "Come on ya lazy sod we've got work to do." He then kicked out at Jesse, who was quick to dodge the kick. Amos turned and was just about to leave when he noticed the fence posts had gone. "Where have those fence posts gone to?" He asked Jesse who quickly replied, "I've been tidying the place up a bit." Amos gave Jesse a frowned stare which made Jesse feel uncomfortable. However, Jesse was determined not to let his face slip so he continued to answer Amos wearing his best innocent look. "I have to live in here, don't I? Can't I clean up once in a while?" Jesse said. He then pointed to the post at the back of the barn and said, "Your precious posts are over there, out of my way." Amos looked at the post, nodded his head and snapped, "Come on!"

The day dragged for Jesse, all he could think about was Henry and what had happened to him. By dusk Jesse's head was spinning with a thousand and one questions he wanted answers to. Eventually, the day did come to an end and as usual Amos and Jesse entered the farmyard very tired and ready for tea. They usually headed straight for the kitchen, where the sweet smell of roast pork was emanating from. However, on this occasion Jesse began to split from Amos and began to make his way towards the barn, "Where are you going? Don't you want any tea? It smells like pork," Amos said to Jesse, who was by now half way across the farmyard. Jesse turned and looked back towards Amos and said, "Just going to wash the sweat off in the trough. I won't be long." Amos continued on into the kitchen and was greeted by Emma, who gave him a small peck on the cheek. He then walked past Emma and joined Earle, who was already sat at the table, "Where's Jesse?" Emma asked, looking out through the backdoor into the farmyard. Amos began tucking into his tea and said, "He's gone to get washed," "Washed!" Emma said surprisingly. "He's never bothered before, wonder why now?" she asked as she closed the door, "Earle instantly replied, "He's up to something. You mark my words, he's up to something!"

Emma sat down at the side of Amos and began asking him how his day had been. It wasn't long before Jesse entered the kitchen looking cleaner than when Amos had left him. He walked across to the table and was just about to sit down at the side of Earle when Earle jumped up and shouted, "Right! I'm glad you're all here. I have a surprise, wait here!" He said as he quickly dashed up the stairs. Jesse plonked himself down at the table and said wearily, "What now?" Jesse began eating his tea which was by now beginning to go cold. Everyone could hear Earle upstairs banging and clattering about in his bedroom. Occasionally the sound of footsteps could be heard on the kitchen ceiling as Earle strutted about the bedroom.

However, it wasn't long before the whole place fell silent, Emma looked at Jesse and then at Amos, she then asked, "What's going on?" Amos just shrugged his shoulders and said, "I'm dammed if I know." All three of them sat at the table looking puzzled at one another. Eventually, the silence was broken by the sound of Earle's footsteps on the ceiling. They all looked up at the ceiling and followed the sound of each step across the ceiling towards the stairs. All eyes then turned towards the bottom of the stairs as Earle began his descent, not much could be seen at first, but as Earle arrived at the bottom of the stairs and walked out into the candle light of the kitchen, Jesse nearly choked at what he saw. Earle was dressed in a police constable's uniform, "Well.... What do you think?" He said, feeling rather pleased with himself, he then did a quick twirl for everybody and grinned. Amos began to laugh and pointed at Earle, "You a copper!" He said; slamming both his fist down on the table, his head followed as he continued to laugh uncontrollably. Jesse, after coughing up a piece of pork that nearly choked him, sat at the table with Emma in amazement and said nothing. "Well I've joined, and that's all there is to it!" Earle said who was by now becoming very irritated and annoyed at Amos, who was still laughing at him. Eventually, as things began to calm down Emma stood up and said, "Well I think it's very honourable that Earle wants to be a policeman and protect us all from harm." "Thank you Emma. I'm glad someone thinks I'm doing the right thing," Earle said, turning to look at Jesse, hoping that Jesse would side with his Aunt Emma. However, Earle was disappointed as Jesse just continued eating his tea and said nothing.

Amos began teasing Earle as he strutted up and down the kitchen in his new uniform saying, "How great it was going to be to catch criminals." Eventually, Amos was told by Emma to stop teasing Earle and that he should be

encouraging the lad instead of teasing him. Amos's attitude then suddenly changed, "Yes you're right. I should be encouraging him to be a copper. Well he's not a very good farmer, right Jesse!" Amos then nudged Jesse, who nodded his head in agreement and they both then burst into fits of laughter. Earle didn't pay Jesse and Amos much attention because he knew that Emma would eventually talk them around. So suddenly Earle announced that to keep Emma safe on the farm, he would personally, "Hunt down the poacher the very next day and have him locked up for poaching." Emma smiled, but Jesse didn't and Amos then said, "Oh! I don't think we need to worry about that little problem anymore. My good shooting abilities took care of him, didn't they Jesse?" Jesse looked at Amos and said reluctantly, "Oh... I... you certainly took care of him, Amos!" Jesse then stood up, kissed his Aunt Emma goodnight and left. Jesse entered the barn and quickly removed the straw from the entrance to the hideaway, he whispered quietly, "Henry, Henry are you there?" "Yes Jesse, I'm here. Have you brought me something to eat? I'm starving," asked Henry. Jesse shook his head and said, "You'll have to wait until everybody's gone to bed. I'll nip back into the kitchen and get you something then. Anyway your strips need changing." Jesse started to change Henry's strips once again and said, "It's drying out quite nicely, you should be alright. There's no sign of it turning nasty." "Good!" Replied Henry as he made himself comfortable by packing some more straw under his leg. Jesse sat down at the end of the hideaway and began warning Henry that they would have to be especially careful now that Earle had joined the police force. Henry nodded in agreement and then Jesse prepared himself to hear Henry's story by pulling in both his legs and sitting cross legged.

"Right now, what happened?" Jesse asked Henry, who began by saying, "You had just left the ship after your visit. I watched as you were all rowed back to the shore. I even waved but none of you looked back. After that I was ordered by the officer to go back to my deck and get ready for tea. Tea! That's a joke. Anyway, I arrived back on my gun deck, the deck where I slept, to find a group of men whispering in the corner of the deck. The place went silent when they saw me. I didn't say anything. I found keeping myself, to myself, was easier in a place like that. I just walked past them and went to my hammock. They weren't a happy bunch, and as I laid there I could hear them planning something, at that time, I didn't know what.

Anyway, a couple of days passed and everything seemed to be normal. If normal's the usual floggings, where men's backs would be stripped clean of skin using the cat. And if that wasn't enough to kill a man, they would then throw you into the hold, not many men came back from there. Full of rats and rancid water, men went crazy in there. Conditions aboard ship weren't good, in fact, they were downright dreadful and a lot of the men weren't happy about their lot. Some of the men would complain daily to the officers about everything, the food, the sleeping arrangements not to mention the creepy crawlies, and things like flees and nits which bit the hell out of you.

The last straw came on a cold frosty morning. The men from my gun deck were on the top deck taking their daily walk, whilst doing this you weren't allowed to stop or talk to anybody, you just walked up and down the deck. Sometimes for hours on end or until the next deck of prisoners came up for their walk. However, on this particular morning, two men from our deck had stopped walking and were looking over the side of the ship towards the pier, "Look at this lot coming!" The first prisoner, said, pointing towards the pier. At first I couldn't see what he was pointing at and just as I got close enough to the two prisoners to see, an officer appeared and gave them both a good whack with his truncheon. "Get walking!" The officer screamed at them. The first prisoner scurried away but the second prisoner, a chap named Tom Moore, risked getting another whack with the truncheon, when he calmly asked the officer, "Where's that lot going?" He pointed to a long line of men who were stood on the pier.

The officer got really mad and gave Tom a right beating, "None of your bloody business!" He screamed at Tom. The officer then turned and looked at me. I put my head down and carried on walking." Jesse altered his position and then asked Henry, "Why? Would he have beaten you up as well?" Henry scratched his leg, adjusted it slightly and said, "Oh yes, some of those officers loved nothing better than to whack you with their truncheons. Anyway, it turns out that these men were prisoners from another hulk which was moored further down the river and it had sunk. They were coming aboard to join us on our already overcrowded hulk. I knew the second prisoner, Tom Moore, he was a mean piece of work and I knew there was going to be trouble, as soon as we went back down to our gun deck.

138

We all arrived back on our gun deck together. I went straight back to my hammock, Tom Moore, on the other hand gathered up his usual cronies and again they began planning. Whatever it was they were planning, nothing more happened that day until early evening when some of the prisoners from the sunken hulk were allocated to our gun deck. They were a rowdy bunch and some of them were Irish, who didn't like being ordered around by the officers. They got along well with Tom Moore and his mates. It wasn't long before all decks, not just my deck, began to fill up with hammocks. On my deck, the hammocks actually touched each other and men began elbowing one another to gain more space during the night, this led to terrible fights amongst the men." Henry then stopped talking. There was a moment silence as he looked across at Jesse, whose eyes were beginning to get heavy. "Jesse, don't go to sleep," Henry said, kicking Jesse with his good leg. Jesse, who was half asleep, immediately jumped up, he got up so fast that he bumped his head on the roof of the hideouts.

This woke Jesse up quickly and whilst rubbing his head said, "I'll go and get you some food from the kitchen, and then I'm off to bed. You can tell me the rest of the story tomorrow." Jesse sped off towards the kitchen still rubbing his head and returned some minutes later with some mutton on a plate and a half eaten loaf of bread, "What! Nothing to drink," Henry asked, whilst grinning at Jesse. "Cheeky bugger, I'll get you some water from the trough," said Jesse waving a small tankard at Henry. Jesse gave Henry his water and then covered up the entrance with the usual straw and just in case Amos came snooping. He piled a couple of fence posts in front of the straw to make it look more convincing as a pile of posts.

The next morning Jesse wandered into the kitchen, he found his Aunt Emma and Amos sat at the table holding hands and talking. However, the talking came to an abrupt halt the moment Jesse appeared. Jesse didn't say anything he just sat down at the table and waited patiently for his breakfast. He could only assume that the talking must have been about him, why else would it have ended so quickly? This abruptness to stop talking had brought an awkward silence into the kitchen, which was broken by Jesse asking, "What's the matter with you two?" He looked directly at Emma, who was by now pouring him a bowl of porridge from a large pan, "Nothing's the matter with us," Amos replied pretending to give Jesse a clip around the back of the head. He then turned to Emma and said, "Go on then, ask him!" Jesse continued to look at Emma and said, "Ask me what?" There was again an awkward silence and still Emma said nothing. Amos was infuriated at Emma's silence. He got up and stormed out of the kitchen saying, "You bloody sort it out then. I'll see you later!"

The door slammed as Amos closed it behind him. Emma then brought Jesse his bowl of porridge and placed it on the table in front of him, "Careful, it's hot!" She said placing a spoon at the side of the bowl. She then sat down opposite Jesse. Emma sighed and was just about to say something to Jesse when she was interrupted by Earle, who had appeared at the bottom of the stairs, "Right then. I'm off to earn a crust," he said fastening on his belt and slipping his truncheon into his pocket. "How do I look then?" He spun around and then popped on his helmet. Jesse looked him up and down and then said, "Like a pra...." But before he could finish his sentence, Emma said quickly, "That'll do Jesse." She turned to Earle and said, "Very grand lad. I'm sure you're going to do well," Earle smiled and thanked Emma.

Just then there was a knock on the door. Earle quickly went and opened the door. "Won't be two minutes sarg," he said. Emma handed Earle a brown bag and said, "Good luck!" She then held open the door. The beefy sergeant gave Emma a frown and said, "Luck ma'am. Luck as got nothing to do with it, but don't you worry ma'am, we'll find that poacher. And you'll be able to sleep safe in your bed at night again." He then raised his finger to the brim of his helmet. Emma smiled and nodded her head, she then closed the door. She watched through the small kitchen window for a while as Earle and the sergeant walked up the track and disappeared into the field at the top.

She then turned and sat back down at the table, "Now then Jesse. What have you been up to?" Emma asked Jesse who was just about to open his mouth when Emma stopped him by pressing her index finger on his lips. "And before you start, none of your tales, right!" Jesse nodded his head and snapped, "Nothing, honest. I haven't been up to anything, honest!" Emma waited for a moment and looked Jesse straight in the eye, "Are you sure?" She asked seriously. Jesse nodded his head and then Emma said, "So then where's my mutton gone that I cooked yesterday. Furthermore, there's some bread missing, it was on that cutting board, right there!" Emma pointed to an empty board sat in the middle of the table. Jesse thought for a moment and then said, "I got hungry during the night. The empty plate is in the barn. I'll go and fetch it." Jesse got up and was just about to set off back to the barn when Emma screamed, "Stop! Sit down!" Jesse sat back down at the table and looked at Emma, who sighed and said, "Jesse, there was enough mutton on that plate to feed all of us for tea, and that's not counting the bread. Did you eat it all?" Jesse quickly replied, "Yes! I'll fetch the empty plate back to prove it." There was a moments silence then Emma said, exasperated, "Ok, ok, fetch the plate back but remember, no more midnight feast after this. We haven't enough food to go around let alone allowing you to pinch it at night." Jesse nodded his head and went to fetch the plate from the barn. As Jesse entered the barn he realized that he had a problem, no more midnight feast meant that Henry wouldn't have anything to eat. How was he going to get Henry something to eat without the other's knowing he thought?

On his way back to the kitchen with the empty plate Jesse came up with the only solution he could think of... he would have to eat his evening meal in the barn, and then he could share it with Henry, if he received any sandwiches or vegetables such as turnips or potatoes for his lunch from Aunt Emma, he could save some of them for Henry. Jesse entered the kitchen feeling quite proud of himself for solving, what he thought was a difficult problem. He then gave Emma the plate before proudly announcing, "That from this moment onwards, I will eat my evening meal alone in the barn." "Oh no you won't!" replied Emma. "You'll eat them at the table like everybody else. Otherwise you won't get any, got it!" She then firmly prodded Jesse in the chest. Jesse knew that Emma meant what she said and that it wasn't worth arguing with her, so he reluctantly nodded and left to join Amos in the fields.

As usual, Amos worked Jesse all day until dusk and they both arrived back in the kitchen tired but ready to eat. Earle was already sat at the table waiting patiently for them, "About time too," Earle said as both Amos and Jesse sat down. Emma began serving the meal and after placing them on the table everybody began tucking in. The four of them sat there eating and talking about the day's events, and as you might expect, it wasn't long before the conversation got around to the poacher, "Well did you catch the poacher?" Amos asked Earle, who was quick to say, "No! But we did find a trail of blood on the otherside of the wood." Amos, who made everybody jump by suddenly slamming his fist down on the table, said, "Yes! I knew it. I knew I'd hit the bugger." He then nudged Jesse with his elbow and said, "Didn't I say Jesse, didn't I!" Jesse, who was by now rubbing his arm, said. "Alright, alright, don't get carried away."

Earle continued to explain how the sergeant and him had spent the day following the trail of blood and had lost it at the back of the barn. As soon as Earle mentioned the barn it sent a shiver down Jesse's spine. Jesse became very worried about what Earle was going to say next, he knew from experience that Earle would suggest a search of the barn. However, before he could suggest the idea, Amos butted in and said arrogantly, "I don't think you need worry about that poacher. I've taken care of him, haven't I Jesse?" Jesse agreed with Amos by nodding his head and saying sternly, "Aye... Amos, you took care of that one." Amos's ego hit the ceiling when Jesse agreed with him. He started to strut up and down the kitchen still ranting how he'd shot the poacher. Relieved that Earle had not been able to suggest a search of the barn Jesse began to get ready to leave the table. However, Jesse's troubles were still not over, just as he began to rise from the table he glanced across at his Aunt Emma, who must have noticed the worried look on his face when Earle had mentioned the barn. Instantly, she caught Jesse's glance in a glare, she was obviously not convinced by Jesse's pretence and siding with Amos. She continued to glare at Jesse until he broke eye contact with her by leaving the table.

Jesse opened the backdoor and stepped out into the black cold night air. He hadn't walked far across the farmyard when a voice from the kitchen door shouted him back. He turned to see his Aunt Emma coming down the garden path towards him. She grabbed Jesse by the loose material of his Jacket shoulders and said, "Jesse! I don't know what's going on but you're up to something. I know you and I can tell when you're up to something. I'm warning you Jesse, Amos won't tolerate much more of your antics." Jesse pulled back quickly releasing himself from Emma's grip, he wiped his nose with his sleeve and then said, with anger in his voice, "Good! Then I'll be rid of this place. Let him throw me off, see if I care!" Emma was shocked by Jesse's reaction and was going to say something else but Jesse quickly turned away from her. Not giving her a chance to say anything else, he stomped back towards the barn totally ignoring Emma shouts of, "Jesse, I'm talking to you. Jesse.... Ok, then have it your way, see if I care!"

Jesse was fuming as he entered the barn. Still fuming he walked straight to his den and slammed himself down onto his bed. He laid there for a few moments trying to calm down when a voice from the back of the barn whispered quietly, "Jesse, Jesse, is that you?" Jesse replied, "Yes it's me, I'm still here, regrettably." He stood up and walked towards the hideout. Jesse began removing the straw from the entrance to the hideout, and as soon as he had removed the straw from the entrance Henry said, "I'm starving, have you got any food?" Jesse looked at Henry and hesitated. He shook his head and then said, "We've got a few problems to sort out our Henry." Henry could see that Jesse wasn't happy and said, "Had a bad day our Jesse?" Jesse nodded, and then he sat down beside Henry in the hideout.

The two lads sat there for a moment and Jesse composed himself whilst Henry got comfortable by re-adjusting his leg, then Jesse began explaining the night's events to Henry. After he'd finished, Henry thought for a moment and then said, "Food is our biggest problem. I can't survive on fresh air and whilst I'm laid up with this leg, I can't go poaching for food. Besides that it's too risky now with Earle and that sergeant on my trail. Perhaps we should come clean to Aunt Emma she'll give me some food until I'm up and about again, she's not a bad lass really." Jesse was appalled at what Henry had suggested and quickly replied, "Out of the question! She'd tell Amos straight away, she's not like she use to be when you knew her. She's changed, especially after she married that sod." "Oh, she's married to him. I didn't know that. That puts a different light on the matter."

Both Henry and Jesse sat there for about ten minutes thinking about what to do, and then Henry said, rubbing his growth ridden chin, "There's only one thing for it, you'll have to go poaching. It won't hurt you and nobody will suspect you." Jesse looked straight at Henry and said, "What do I know about poaching?" "Don't worry it's easy, I don't mean catching meat. I mean nicking things from places like fields and orchards, an apple here, and a plum there, no-one will miss them. In the fields there are carrots, turnips not to mention potatoes. That's our answer, living off the land." Henry said, clicking his fingers and pointing at Jesse. Jesse couldn't think of anything else and reluctantly had to agree with Henry by nodding his head. After a moment Jesse sat down and said, "Anyway, to the rest of your story." Henry scratched his head and said, "Oh, I... where was I?" Jesse replied, "The men were having terrible fights because the hammocks were hung too close together." "Yes that's right. Conditions became unbearable and the stench was getting so bad that you could hardly breathe on the gun decks. It was the cabbage soup, they used to feed us. It gave you wind and diarrhoea.

A couple of weeks after the new prisoners had arrived from the sunken hulk. Tom Moore and two of his cronies' noticed that, not just the cabbage soup had been reduced, but all the food rations had been reduced and when they asked a young inexperienced guard, who had the brightest red hair I'd ever seen, the reason why. His answer wasn't what Tom Moore and his cronies wanted to hear. The guard told Tom that the reason was the 'new prisoners' who had to share the ship's quota of food, and from now on, everybody, would be on half rations until the new prisoners leave.

142

The guard laughed as he told Tom the reason. You don't laugh at a man like Tom Moore. Well, not if you want to stay in one piece. I knew straight away there was going to be trouble, so I left the gun deck quickly and went up on deck for my exercise. As I left the gun deck, I could hear Tom Moore saying, 'Come on men, are we going to stand for this?' There was a lot of crashing noises and men began shouting, which I might add hasten my departure. I got on deck and reckoned on to be walking up and down. Suddenly, a lot of prisoners came rushing up from the gun decks. Tom Moore was leading them. The prisoners rushed the officers that were on deck. Some of the prisoners had truncheons which they'd pinched from the officers below decks. They bludgeoned the officers on deck to death. It wasn't a pretty sight, I can tell you, blood all over the place. After all the officers had been taken care of, their bodies were un-ceremonially thrown overboard. I watched as the bodies floated off down the Thames, the body of the young red haired officer was among them, shame; he was only a young lad.

Tom Moore was in his element, having full control of the hulk, but it wasn't to last. A detachment of Royal Marines saw to that!" Jesse interrupted Henry by asking, "What are Royal Marines?" Henry laughed and said, "Oh, they're the best soldiers this country has to offer. Those lads didn't take any prisoners nor did they mess about, they were straight in, bayonets and swords at the ready and in the middle of the night. I only survived because I followed this old lad through a gun port into the Thames. The old lad drowned, after being shot in the leg by a marine from the ship's deck. I tried to hold on to him but I couldn't. I had all on trying to keep myself a float.

However, after a long swim I managed to pull myself out of the river on the opposite bank. I looked back towards the hulk and saw the warrior on fire. I could see men jumping from the ship, some of them were on fire. I sat there on the bank of the river in the middle of the night, dripping wet, watching, as the Warrior slowly sank.

Eventually, the cold water of Mother Thames extinguished the flames and I was plunged into darkness. But by this time a crowd of on lookers had gathered, so I made myself scarce. There's really not much more to tell. I stole some clothes from a washing line and made my way back here. After that I lived off the land for a couple of years, the rest you know." "Why didn't you show yourself before now?" Jesse asked Henry, who hesitated for a moment, he then looked Jesse in the eye and said, "I was a wanted man Jesse. People in and around Shalbourne knew me and what I'd done. How could I show myself? I didn't even know who you were living with, did I?" Jesse thought for a moment and then accepted Henry's explanation by nodding his head. He then asked, "Are you still wanted?" Henry's voice changed to a whisper, "Well, a lot of men drowned that night and their bodies were never found they just floated off down the Thames never to be seen again. I think the authorities will have put me down as missing, presumed drowned and so long as it stops that way, I should be alright. However, I still can't show myself around here. Just in case somebody recognizes me and tells the authorities or Earle." Jesse agreed and then said, "I'm off to bed." He got up from the floor and walked back to his den, "Cover me up then," said Henry. Jesse tutted and returned to cover the entrance to the hideout.

Over the next few weeks Jesse found it hard to feed Henry and his leg seemed to be taking forever to mend. However, Jesse decided that he would make Henry a walking stick. This might hurry him along and get him up and about again he thought. It took a while, but eventually, Jesse found a stick of birch in the small wood nearly the right shape and size for the job. He spent sometime chipping and shaving the stick to shape using the gully. Once the stick was ready Jesse held it up and admired his handy work. That'll do he thought and decided that he would give Henry the stick that very evening along with a half eaten piece of gammon he'd managed to save from his lunch. Jesse had worked all day alongside of Amos, and the end came extremely slowly as usual, tea wasn't much better that evening with Earle prattling on about what he'd done in the police that day, and who he could have arrested, if he had wanted to. Eventually, Jesse slowly rose from the table and wearily bid everybody a goodnight. He wearily headed back towards the barn, and as he past the trough, Jesse quickly bent down and picked up the stick, which he'd hidden underneath the trough along with the gammon earlier that day.

Jesse entered the barn and instantly, without thinking, began to remove the straw from the hideouts entrance. Suddenly, at that moment, Jesse was interrupted by Emma, who had followed him across the yard and into the barn unnoticed, "What are you doing?" Emma asked Jesse, who was startled for a moment. He quickly composed himself and then said, "Oh, it's you Aunt Emma; you gave me such a fright." Jesse quickly turned to face Emma whilst trying to conceal the stick behind his back. He then quickly dropped the gammon onto the barn floor where it disappeared instantly beneath the straw which covered the floor. Emma began looking around the barn. She then said, whilst slowly walking towards Jesse's bed. "What are you doing over there?" Jesse, who had to think quickly, snapped, "Rats!" He then lifted the stick from behind his back and waved it in the air.

Jesse quickly walked towards Emma thinking that if he stayed in front of the hideout Emma might walk towards him and discover the hideout. Jesse threw the stick towards the corner of the barn and then asked Emma. "Why? What do you want?" Confidently, he layed down on his bed and put his hands behind his head. He then waited for Emma to answer, "Oh, I came to see if you were alright. You seemed a little quiet at tea this evening." She touched Jesse's forehead with the back of her hand and then said, "I hope you're not coming down with something." Jesse, was quick to reply, and said irritably, "No, I'm ok, just a little tired. Anyway who can get a word in edgeways with Earle going on like he did." Emma smiled and then said, "Ok, if you're sure

144

you're alright. I'll go… goodnight." Emma walked back towards the door and left.

Jesse waited for a moment, and then he quickly jumped up and ran to the door. Slowly, Jesse looked around the edge of the barn door and watched as Emma returned to the farmhouse where Amos was stood in the doorway waiting for her. As soon as the farmhouse door closed and Jesse thought it was safe, he walked over to the front of the hideout and began searching for the gammon, "What are you looking for?" A voice said from inside the hideout, "I brought you a piece of gammon but I had to drop it around here." Jesse said, patting the straw as he tried to locate the gammon, "I know and very tasty it was indeed," said Henry whilst grinning and patting his stomach. "Is that all you've got me our Jesse?" Henry asked, looking very disappointed that there wasn't more food, "I'm afraid so," Jesse replied. He then thought for a moment and said, "Oh, I did get you something else." Jesse quickly walked across to the corner of the barn where he'd thrown the stick and picked it up, "Here, this is for you!" Jesse said, blowing the stick to remove some loose straw from the shaft, he handed it to Henry. "That'll get you going again," said Jesse, eager for Henry to give it a try. Henry hobbled to his feet and said, "Come on then, let's give it a try." Jesse put Henry's right arm over his shoulders whilst Henry used the stick with his left hand. However, the moment Henry put his weight on to his bad leg an agonizing pain shot up his leg from toe to hip. The pain was so bad and instant that Henry let out a horrendous scream, which echoed around the barn and across the yard. Jesse was surprised no-one in the house had heard the scream. Henry quickly pulled his arm back from around Jesse's shoulders and sat back down. He paused for a moment to get his breath back and then after a moment began to hobble back into the hideout on his bum, he turned to Jesse and said, "I'm obviously not ready for that! Not just yet!" Jesse, who was extremely disappointed, began shaking his head, "What are we going to do? We can't carry on like this. Emma nearly caught us tonight," said Jesse as he began to fill up. Henry, realizing Jesse was upset, tried to appease him by shaking his knee and saying to him quietly, "It'll be alright our Jesse. I just need to practice. I'll try again tomorrow."

A silence descended on the small hideout and neither lad felt like talking. They sat there for quite a while, but eventually Henry broke the silence by saying, "Come on our Jesse. Perk up, I'll have another go tomorrow." Jesse nodded his head, wiped his nose with his sleeve and then said, with a serious expression on his face, "We still need to decide what we're going to do when you do get better. We can't stay here; you'll get caught, especially with Earle snooping about the place." Henry nodded in agreement and after a moment's thought said, "Aye… I've been giving that some thought. Like you say, we can't stay here. I'm told there's plenty of work up north." As soon as Henry mentioned, 'north' Jesse got up and ran to his den. "Won't be a moment," he said. Henry watched as Jesse rustled around for a couple of minutes in an old tin box which he kept at the side of his bed. Eventually, Jesse said, "Yes!" He held up the two yellow cards that he had been given by the two mill agents in the square at Shalbourne.

Jesse showed Henry the cards and eagerly said, "These cards guarantee us passage and jobs up north if we want them." Henry looked at the cards and said, "Go on then, read them out. You were always better at reading than I was." Henry handed the cards back to Jesse, who tilted them towards the lamp light, so he could see the writing. Jesse then coughed to clear his throat and said, "Henry Wheatley's and Sons, Butt End Mills, Chadwick Folds Lane, Mirfield, Yorkshire... that's up north." Henry answered, "I know, I know. What else does it say?" Jesse repositioned himself and then continued to read the card, "Promises to pay the bearer of this

> *Henry Wheatley's and Sons Ltd.*
> *Butt End Mills,*
> *Chadwick Folds Lane,*
> *❧ Mirfield, Yorkshire. ❧*
>
> *Promises to pay the bearer of this card passage by canal to Mirfield from anywhere in England.*

card passage by canal to Mirfield from anywhere in England and since we are in England. That means us!" Jesse smiled and felt quite proud of himself for reading out the card; he then shuffled the two cards and began to read out the second card, "It's the same company and the address is the same," he said. "The only difference is that the card promises to give the bearer of the card, a job!" Henry scratched his head and asked, "What sort of job?" Jesse replied, "I don't know but it pays five bob a week. The mill agent said so." Henry, who was a little cynical, said, "I don't know, it seems a bit too good to be true." Jesse became angry at this point and began shouting at Henry, "What other choices have we got? At least up north no-one will know who you are and you will be able to walk around without the fear of being caught and locked up." Henry thought for a moment and said, "You're right! Up north it is then, when I can walk again." Henry then layed down and Jesse said, "Goodnight." Both lads went to sleep that night with a lot of things on their minds.

The weeks seemed to pass slowly and Jesse was getting a bit worried because the cards were only valued for six months, after that, they were worthless. Then one night, Jesse entered the barn to find Henry stood up. "Look, no hands!" He said as he walked across the barn. Jesse was delighted but annoyed at Henry for being out of the hideout, he quickly snapped, "What are you doing? What if I'd have been Amos? You didn't know who I was before I entered the barn. You should stay in the hideout until I open the entrance. We don't want you getting caught at this stage." Henry's face changed, he picked up the walking stick and went back inside the hideout without saying anything else. Jesse sat down in his usual place at the front of the hideout. Henry then broke his silence by saying, "I thought you'd be pleased. It was meant to be a surprise." Jesse smiled at Henry and said, "Yes I know what it was meant to be but it could have cost us dearly. What if I'd been Amos?" Henry agreed and promised Jesse he wouldn't leave the hideout again. Jesse smiled at Henry and threw a handful of straw at him. "I am pleased you're getting better though," he said. "But when do you think we'll be able to leave?" Henry who was by now stretched out inside the hideout and exhausted from his little jaunt, said, "Not so fast our Jesse. I'm walking, but I still need the stick to walk any distance. However, I reckon we should plan to leave next week. I should be strong enough by then." Jesse

146

gave a small cheer and punched the air, "At last! I'll be rid of this hell hole of a farm," he said elatedly.

Over the next few days Jesse began secretly collecting things that he thought might come in useful for the journey, a knife and fork from the kitchen, a bowl, a cup and some clothes from Earle's bedroom which he thought would fit Henry. However, the most important item on Jesse's mind was food and there was very little of that to be had. He'd tried his best to save more from the packed lunches that Emma gave him, but to no avail, hunger usually forced both Henry and Jesse to finish the food off the same evening in the barn. "There's only one thing for it." Jesse said out loud, whilst finishing off a piece of very tough ham. "We'll have to pinch the lot the night before we go." Puzzled, Henry looked across at Jesse and said, "Pinch what before we go?" "The food," said Jesse. He continued, "Aunt Emma always cooks the meat the night before we eat it. She lays out the bread and the sliced meat on the kitchen table the night before, she hasn't got time in the morning with all her chores, milking and the like." Jesse shook an old dark green blanket and laid it flat on the barn floor, he placed all the items he had taken into the middle of the blanket and said, "There, that'll be easier to carry." He then grabbed the four corners and tied the blanket into a small bundle. "Well I'm ready for off," he exclaimed whilst pushing a stick through the bundle. Henry laughed and said, "You're keen aren't you?" "I sure am! When are we going?" Henry, not wishing to upset Jesse or prolong his agony any longer said, "Tonight!" Jesse's head spun quickly towards Henry, "Great! I can't wait," Jesse said excitedly. He then smiled at Henry and sat down. Henry began exercising his leg by walking up and down the barn, "How does it feel? Do you think you'll be alright?" Asked Jesse, trying to show concern, but secretly, deep down inside, Jesse was hoping that Henry was alright and that they could begin their way northward as soon as possible. "Oh I'll be alright. I'll still need the stick for a while but I'll be alright," replied Henry, sitting down at the side of Jesse.

Henry and Jesse sat there for sometime talking about their childhoods; their parents and how they missed the little cottage by the church, but eventually Henry got up and walked towards the barn door. He opened it and looked out into the darkness, "Well...." He said stretching. "This is as good a time as any," he said, beckoning Jesse to the door. "Go and get the food from the kitchen and we'll be off!" Henry told Jesse, pushing him out into the darkness. Jesse immediately sped off quickly towards the kitchen and without hesitation; he grabbed the bread, meat and some apples from the table. He didn't waste any time, he just piled it all up onto a plate and headed back towards the barn where Henry was still waiting at the door. "That was quick," said Henry, helping Jesse into the barn with the food. Jesse opened the little green bundle and poured the food into the blanket. Henry grabbed an apple and said, "Right then, let's go!" Jesse retrieved Earle's clothes from the bundle and threw them at Henry, "Not before you get changed, you stink!" Jesse said, waving his hand in front of his nose. Henry smelt himself and said, "I thought that was you, working with pigs, cows and that." Both lads laughed and Henry got changed. It wasn't long before Jesse and Henry were briskly walking up the track towards the top field. Both were in high spirits and looking forward to the journey. At the top of the track Jesse pulled Henry back by his elbow and said, "Hang on a minute." He turned slowly and looked back towards the farmhouse. Jesse stood there for a moment staring aimlessly back at the farmhouse as dawn began to arrive. He heard the cockerel crowing and straight away he thought to himself, I never did sort that bird out. Henry put his arm around Jesse's shoulders and said, "Second thoughts our Jesse?" Jesse sniffed up and said, "No, not really. I was just wondering if I should have said goodbye to Aunt Emma, she has done so much for me."

Just then, Jesse thought he saw the upstairs curtains move. In fact, he was so sure, that he lifted his hand and began waving frantically, "Who are you waving to?" Henry asked, looking towards the house. Jesse realizing no-one was there slowly stopped waving and put his hand down, "No-one," he said sadly. "Come on then, let's get moving!" Henry said, striding out. Jesse shrugged his shoulders, took a last look at the farmhouse and whispered under his breath, "goodbye farm goodbye all." He then turned and ran to catch up with Henry, "Now then, which way to the canal?" Henry asked.

148

Chapter 7: The Canal, Work and Fraud.

Dawn had made its presence felt by scattering the morning dew in and around the wide open spaces of Berkshire. Henry and Jesse had walked and talked their way towards Shalbourne. They'd had a couple of rest bites to ease the pain in Henry's leg. The stick that Jesse had made had come in very handy, it had kept Henry going over the difficult parts of the track.

Arriving on the outskirts of Shalbourne the rain began to pour and the smell of wet straw began to drift across the fields towards Henry and Jesse, who had decided to take shelter in an old derelict farmhouse. "At least it's dry in here," said Henry, as he slowly began to slide down the wall whilst keeping his bad leg straight. Eventually, Henry's bum hit the floor, and he sighed as he placed his back against the wall. Jesse pulled a small wooden door closed, which roughly filled the hole in the wall, it was rotten and beginning to fall apart, but it kept out some of the wind and rain. Jesse joined Henry up against the wall. He slowly untied the little green bundle and pulled out two reasonably sized pieces of meat, he slapped the first piece of meat onto a slice of bread and handed it to Henry saying out loud,

"Breakfast!" He then started to prepare the other piece of meat for himself. It wasn't long before Jesse had taken a large bite from his bread and meat and was beginning to tie the bundle back up.

The room went quiet for a moment as both lads devoured their breakfasts. "It's a bit dry," said Henry, struggling to chew the last mouthful of bread and meat. "Would sir like a glass of wine with his breakfast?" Jesse asked in a very high pitched posh voice. Henry began to laugh and said, "Ya silly sod!" He pushed Jesse sideward's using his shoulder and Jesse pretended to slide down the wall until his head was laid on the floor. Henry then wiped his mouth with the back of his hand and said to Jesse. "Well, where are we heading?" Jesse sat back up again and took another bite of his bread and meat before answering, "North!" "I know that stupid! I meant, where do we go from here?" Jesse stood up and leant out through a hole in the wall where the window frame was supposed to be. "Over there, towards Bagshot," he said, pointing to a small village in the distance. Henry stood up and joined Jesse at the hole; he looked towards the village and said, "Looks calm enough." "All the same, we're going to stay to the fields until we get to Hungerford, that's where the canal is. It'll be safer!" Jesse replied.

The rain didn't ease up and three hours later Jesse had become bored, he tried to occupy himself by throwing stones at some wood pigeons who were nesting in the rafters, but eventually, boredom drove him to say, "Come on let's go!" He grabbed the little green bundle and threw it over his shoulder. Henry clambered to his feet and said, "What about the rain?" "I think it's in for the day. No point in hanging around here all day. We can only get wet once!" And with that, Jesse opened the rotten door and walked out into the rain. Reluctantly, Henry followed but not before he placed a rather thick strip of material over his head and made sure it was tucked completely into his coat collar. Hoping the rain would ease off, the lads kept south of Bagshot staying well away from the village and any farm dwellings they came across. However, the rain got worse and in a vain attempt to stay dry, Henry pulled up his coat collar until it covered his ears. "Jesse, we've got to get out of this rain, we'll catch our deaths," moaned Henry, with the rain running off the end of his nose. Jesse didn't answer at first, he just kept walking, but eventually, after some thought and time, Jesse angrily answered, "Stop whingeing and keep walking, it won't be long before we will be able to see Hungerford, the canal's there!"

After a good two hour trudge across muddy fields and climbing over dry stone walls the rain began to ease. Henry looked up into the sky and then removed the strip of material from his head. He wrung it out and then wiped his face and neck with it. "I'm glad that's over," he said. Just then the clouds allowed the sun to break through. Sun beams struck the fields in front of them and the day didn't seem quiet as miserable. Even Jesse managed to smile at Henry as he suddenly pointed down the valley towards a small town in the distance, "Look! There's Hungerford, we're nearly there, at last!" Jesse said excitedly as Henry lifted his head and looked towards the town. There was a moments silence and then Henry, with a worried look on his face, began to bombard Jesse with a succession of questions. "What about me? I can't go into the town. What if someone notices me?" Jesse laughed and said, "Stop, stop with the questions." He placed his hand over Henry's mouth and said, "Don't worry our Henry I've already thought about that. I'll go in first and find out where we go to travel on the canal."

Jesse walked into Hungerford leaving Henry hidden behind a wall at a small tee junction just outside the town. There wasn't much to see in Hungerford,

just a small High Street lined with small quaint shops. The shops didn't seem to be very busy and there weren't many people about. This enabled Jesse to walk down the street basically un-noticed.

At the end of the High Street Jesse walked between two houses, which were painted black and white, their red tiled roofs shone in the afternoon sun. At the back of the houses Jesse entered another world, it was the canal, and it was alive with activity. Jesse had never seen so many people busily working in one place before and to gain a better view of what was going on, he decided to walk up onto a bridge, which was small and made of red brick, the bridge spanned the canal. At the centre of the bridge, which was the highest point on the bridge, Jesse stopped and leant on a small wall which lined the bridge on both sides. He looked down onto a small wharf which was just in front of the bridge, he watched in amazement as cranes swung backwards and forwards loading crates onto barges.

Once loaded, horses would pull the barges away from the wharf allowing other barges to pull up to the wharf. The place was amok with barges moving backwards and forwards along the canal as each barge joined the queue to be loaded or in some cases to be unloaded. The wharf itself was lined by official looking buildings and sheds. Jesse stood there for a while watching all the activity, but then decided that this would be the best place to ask about the barges that went northwards. He straightened his hair and polished his shoes, using the back of his trouser legs, before walking down onto the wharf. The first building on the wharf had two large doors with a company name written on them. It read in large white letters J. Wooldridge and Sons, Builders. Jesse slowly pushed open one of the doors, not right open, but just enough to quickly glance inside, "What do you want?" A voice said loudly from a small office just inside the doors. Jesse pushed open the door completely and walked towards the office. Instantly, a scrawny little man came out of the office to meet Jesse. Jesse quickly removed his cap and took out the yellow cards from his jacket pocket, he then said politely to the man, whilst pointing at the cards, "Excuse me sir, I wonder if you could help me?" The man didn't answer, he instantly began to bundle Jesse back out through the open door, "You can't come in here lad, its private property," said the man. After the man stopped pushing the pair found themselves back outside the large doors in among some crates. The man then took hold of Jesse by the elbow and said, "Now then lad, what do you want?" Jesse straightened his clothing and then again, asked the man politely, "Sir, can you tell me where I can find the barges that are going up north?" Instantly the man began to laugh, "There are no barges here that go northwards lad. They can't do that from here!" The man continued to laugh, which annoyed Jesse so much so that his face began to change colour, this only served to make the man laugh even louder and longer.

Eventually, the man sat down on a large crate and began to compose himself before saying, "I'm sorry lad, but you see the old Kennet and Avon only goes from east to west. So the barges can only travel from east to west or vice versa." The man then stood up and began to use his right hand to show Jesse the difference between north and south and east and west. The gesture reminder Jesse of the old priest back home who used a similar gesture when he blessed you, the man continued to do this for a few moments and then he said politely, "Got it lad, east to west. Isn't that right Bert?" Jesse looked over his shoulder to see a grubby un-shaven man approaching, "Aye… that's right Bill, east to west or west to east." Bert then looked Jesse up and down and asked, "Why lad, where ya going?" Jesse, who was by now reluctant to say anything, said, "Well… I thought I could go up north using these cards. They promise the bearer, that's me! Passage up north on the canal," Bert looked at the cards and said, "Oh, you've got some of those bloody cards. I've seen those before, there a scam lad!" Jesse looked puzzled and said, "What do you mean?" Bert rubbed his chin and paused for a moment, he then said sympathetically, "You'd better sit down lad." Bert sat on a crate and took out a piece of bread from an old bag which was laid on the floor.

He then invited Jesse to sit down on a crate with a hand gesture. Jesse sighed and plonked himself down dreading the worst. Bert could see Jesse wasn't pleased and said, "Right lad! First off, are you alright?" Jesse lifted his head and nodded reluctantly, Bert then began to explain, "Those scam cards you have there are full of promise. People turn up here all the time thinking that they're going to get a free ride on the canal to wherever. The truth of the matter is, there not worth a light." Bert then took a bite from the bread and began to chew. He stood up and walked up and down for a moment. "You see lad, it's like this..." said Bert as he began pointing the piece of bread at Jesse.

"When people arrive here with those bloody stupid cards, it's already too late. The cards have already done their nasty business. Most people with those cards have already burnt their bridges by the time they get here, either by telling their lords and masters to shove their job where the sun doesn't shine or by running away without getting the proper release papers from the chief constable, which are you?" Jesse, not wishing Bert to know his business, quickly replied. "Neither!" Bert paused for a moment and then said, "Oh, you'll be alright then. You'll be able to go back home then, won't you?" Jesse squirmed for a moment and then said faintly, "Not exactly." Bert offered Jesse the remainder of the bread and Bill appeared from the double doors with three mugs of tea on a tray saying, "Here you go then. Get this down ya; it'll make you feel better." He placed the tea down on a crate.

All three men sat there for about half an hour, sipping tea in among the crates and discussing what Jesse should do next. Bert took a swig of his tea and said, "If you are still serious about going up north, then you need to get onto the Oxford Canal. That canal goes up north." Bert took another swig of his tea whilst Jesse thought for a moment before asking, "And how do I get there?" There was a long silence and Bill began to tap his finger nails on a crate. Bert looked at Bill and the silence continued. Suddenly, they both said

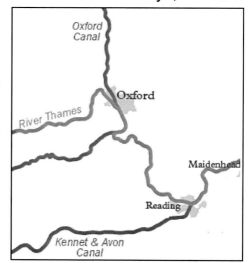

together, "George Hams!" "That's it." said Bert, slapping his leg with his cap. "George needs help with Unity. It's the perfect solution." Eagerly Jesse asked, "Who's George Hams?" Bill stood up and threw the last of his tea onto the floor before saying, "George works on the barge Unity with his son Tom. However, Tom is ill at the moment and is held up in the lock keeper's house at Marsh Lock which is just down the canal about a quarter of a mile. George has been stuck there all week waiting for his son to recover. That's not going to happen. You could perhaps help George take Unity up to London." Jesse jumped up quickly and shouted, "But I don't want to go to London. I want to go up north!" Bert quickly grabbed Jesse and said, "Calm down lad, calm down. You will only have to go as far as Reading because George has family there who can help him the rest of the way to London." Jesse sat back down and took a deep breath. Bert then said, "When you get to Reading George will point you in the right direction, north! Reading is where the Kennet and Avon Canal meets Old Mother Thames. The Thames goes northward to Oxford and meets up with the Oxford Canal at Oxford. Jesse looked down at the scam cards and shook his head. Bill then said, "What have you got to lose lad?" This encouraged Jesse to agree, so he nodded his head and put the scam cards back in his inside jacket pocket. "Yes, you're right. I've got nothing to lose," Jesse replied. "Come on then lad, I've got to go up to Marsh Lock to do some maintenance on the lock gates. I'll introduce you to George," said Bert as he smiled and put his arm around Jesse's shoulders.

It wasn't long before Jesse and Bert were walking back along the canal towpath towards Marsh Lock. Bert had brought along his bag of tools which he carried over his shoulder. As they walked Jesse started to bombard Bert with all kinds of questions about the canal. The questions came so fast and furious, Bert wasn't even given time to answer a question before Jesse fired the next question at him. Eventually, Bert had to stop Jesse, "Woe lad, woe, you're burning my ear off. I don't know the answers to all your questions; you need to ask George. He knows all about the canal, he's worked on it for long enough. You'll like George, he's a nice chap and he'll be able to give you all the answers you need. Speak of the devil." Just then a tall skinny man appeared from beneath a barge hatch. He jumped down onto the towpath. Jesse noticed the man's fingers as he rolled up a rope which was laid on the towpath. They were long and scrawny as if they were made for rolling up rope. He did it with such ease. The man wore a cloth cap with the peek at the back, which he turned to the front the moment Bert and Jesse approached, "Now then George, what you up to?" Asked Bert as he approached George, George looked up and continued rolling up the rope, before saying, with a sad tone in his voice, "Not a lot! I can't do anything with my lad laid up." Bert smiled and hoping to cheer George up, he said, "I've got just the thing you need." He then pointed at Jesse. George turned and laughed, "What him?" He said, throwing the rolled up rope onto the barge. "And what does he know about canal work? He's a farmer's lad." Jesse was quick to defend himself by saying, "Is that your horse over there on the towpath." George replied, "What of it." "Well, I know more about horses than you'll ever know," Jesse replied. Bert let out a loud laugh and then said, "I can see you two are going to get along just fine. So I'll leave you two to get to know one another. I've got work to do." He then headed off towards the lock gates, "Ok lad, fetch the horse, if you can put his harness on lad, then you might have yourself a job lad!" The word 'lad' reminded Jesse of Amos, "My names Jesse, not lad!" Jesse quickly snapped as he started to walk towards the horse.

It wasn't long before Jesse had untied the horse and had brought him back down the towpath to the barge. Jesse quickly pulled the harness off the back of the barge and fastened it onto the horse, this suitably impressed George,

"Well done Jesse, you've obviously dealt with horses before. Now all you've got to do his steer him down that towpath until we reach Reading. After that my nephew James will take over from you." "Do I get the job then?" Jesse asked. George replied, "I suppose so, it pays a tanner a day and one meal a day which might be hot or cold, ok!" Jesse nodded his head and began to lead the horse down the towpath using a piece of string, he'd attached to the horse's bit.

They hadn't gone far, when Jesse realized that the horse didn't really need him to steer, so he just continued to walk alongside the horse whilst hanging onto the piece of string looking as though he was actually steering, but actually, he'd drifted off as usual into his own little world of thought. He began thinking about his Aunt Emma, Amos and Earle, and what they were all doing at that moment in time, and if they'd miss him or not. Oh… and how glad he was that they hadn't found Henry… Oh my god Henry! Jesse had forgotten all about Henry, who was still waiting at the tee junction on the road just outside Hungerford. Jesse stopped suddenly and so did the horse. However, the barge didn't, it just carried on sailing past the both of them. The towrope slackened and then began to re-tension as the barge passed. "What are you doing?" Screamed George from the back of the barge, as the horse started to back up and the towrope quickly became taut. The front end of the barge began to turn as the towrope pulled it into the near bank, the back end of the barge quickly drifted around and banged into another barge moored on the far bank. There was a series of large bangs and the barge began to list.

George, who had hung onto the tiller arm to stop himself from falling overboard was absolutely livid and began screaming at Jesse the moment he managed to shakily stand up. The owners of the moored barge came out of their hutch and began screaming at George. This directed George's attentions away from Jesse for a moment, however, it wasn't to last, George knew the owners of the moored barge and their screams turned to laughter as they realized it was George and his new lad. All parties checked their barges for damage, which was quite minimal, a scratch of paint here a small dint there.

George threw a line across the canal to Jesse and then tied it to the back of Unity, "Right Jesse!" He said. "Tie that towrope from the horse to the rope ring on the towpath. Now pull this rope very slowly towards you. And for God sake, be careful," said George, hanging onto the teller arm. Slowly, as Jesse began to pull, the barge began to straighten up and both George and the barge began to drift nearer to Jesse's side of the canal. Eventually, the barge was moored and George jumped clear of the barge. He then asked Jesse, "What the hell happened? You can't just stop like that! You have to slow down gently." Jesse scratched his head and said, "I'm sorry, but I just remembered something important." George tutted and looked down at Unity, "She's listing pretty badly, the loads shifted," he said. He then looked back at Jesse and said, "What did you remember that was so important, it nearly caused a disaster?" Jesse began to blush and said, "Well... I have a brother. He's back in Hungerford waiting for me. He's supposed to be coming with me up north." There was a silence and then George said, "I'm sorry Jesse, but I can't afford two lads wages. I'm sorry lad." Jesse's heart sank, and then he said, "What if you just paid me and my brother worked for nothing?" The silence returned, George then rubbed his chin before reluctantly saying, "Tell you what lad. I can't afford two wages but I could provide food for you both. It won't be a lot, but it's my best offer. And let's face it! If you're not here to help me, I'm stuck again!" Jesse nudged George's arm gently using his fist, smiled and excitedly said, "Thanks George! We won't let you down, I promise!" Jesse turned and started to run back up the towpath towards Hungerford. George shouted after him, "Don't be long, we've this load to put right before we can move." Jesse carried on running and shouted back, "Ok George! I won't be long."

Jesse ran back along the towpath for about two hundred yards and then realized it would be quicker to go overland to fetch Henry. He clambered over a dry stone wall which ran parallel to the towpath and began to cross a field which still had the corn stubble in it. About half way across Jesse had a feeling that he wasn't alone, he stopped and slowly looked around. He was right; there in the corner of the field was the largest black bull Jesse had ever seen, its horns were long and twisted to a point in front of its head. Jesse slowly continued to walk across the field hoping that the bull hadn't seen him, but as he got closer to the wall at the otherside of the field, he began to hear the sound of heavy hooves coming towards him. Jesse glanced around to see the bull coming at him at full charge, its head was down, and it was in full flight heading right for him. Jesse started to run, he managed to get to the wall and get at least one leg over the wall, but he wasn't quite quick enough, his other leg was still on the same side as the bull. The bull gave its head a quick flick and Jesse's leg went flying through the air along with quite a bit of the stone wall. Jesse landed on his backside in the middle of a small road at the otherside of the wall being bombarded by pieces of stone from the wall.

Instantly, Jesse curled up into a ball and put his hands over his head to protect himself from the falling stone. Eventually, the stones stopped falling and the only sound that could be heard was that of the bull snorting as it glared over the wall at Jesse, who slowly began to uncurl. Jesse looked up at the bull and said, "Arr... ya bugger!" Jesse suddenly stopped talking as he felt a pain in his leg. He looked down to see a blood stain beginning to appear on his thigh, "Will you stop messing about?" Henry said as he came up from behind the wall at the otherside of the road, "Where the hell have you been? I've been stuck here for hours." Henry screamed at Jesse whilst throwing the little green bundle over the wall. Jesse quickly stood up and limped across to the bundle. Henry eased his bum up onto the top of the wall and then pulled his bad leg over the wall before stepping down into the road very carefully, "That bloody bull nearly had me!" Jesse bleated out as he opened the bundle. "It looks as though it as." Henry said, pointing to Jesse's thigh where his trousers were by now deep red with blood. Jesse dropped his trousers to reveal a long gash. Henry knelt down and looked at the gash closely, "It's nothing. It's just a graze. Arr… the bull was only playing with you," he said grinning whilst using a strip of material to wipe away some of the blood. Jesse bound the leg with some of the strips and then said, "We've got to go. George is waiting for us." Jesse pulled up his trousers and Henry asked, "Who is George?" Jesse started off down the road and said, "Come on. I'll tell you all about it as we walk."

It was about an hour later when Jesse and Henry arrived at the barge, both were limping and Jesse's thigh had a little blood showing. George looked at the pair of them limping along the towpath and laughed, "What have I taken on here?" He said. Jesse, who was trying to stand up straight, said, "This is my brother Henry." George approached, looked at Henry's leg and then said, "You didn't tell me your brother was an invalid. And what the hell happened to you?" Jesse looked down at his thigh and said, "Oh… its nothing. I had a little argument with a bull and Henry's not an invalid. He's just recovering from a shooting accident, aren't you Henry?" Jesse gave Henry a nudge, and he began stuttering, eventually, he managed to say, "Oh yes! My own stupid fault, I dropped the thing and bang, a leg full of shot!" Henry smiled nervously as George looked both up and down. He then said, shaking his head, "I must be mad, employing invalids. But what choice do I have?" He turned back towards Unity and said, "Well… come on then, don't just stand there! Let's get this load sorted before it gets dark."

"What ya carrying skipper?" Henry asked as he stepped aboard Unity. "Deal boards and scantlings bound for London," George replied. Henry was just about to say something when George stopped him, "I know! I know! You don't want to go to London. You want to go up north." Henry laughed and said, "You've got it skipper." Henry and George began to re-arrange the deal boards on Unity and slowly she stopped listing. Meanwhile, Jesse tied the horse up to a spike on the canal bank where there was plenty of fresh grass for it to eat. Dusk began to fall and the canal took on a different appearance as George jumped off Unity onto the towpath, "Right lads! We can't do much more today so I'm off to the Lamb Inn for a pint of ale. You lads can bed down in the hutch for the night. It has a couple of candles in there but don't leave them burning. I haven't got money to burn!" George then began to walk back along the towpath but after a few steps he suddenly stopped, thought for a moment and then shouted back, "Oh… and if you're really lucky you might find a couple of bottles of stout and some bread in the cupboard. The wife usually puts them in there for me, so help yourselves." And with that, George disappeared down the towpath into the darkness.

The following morning the hutches wooden bed boards had both Henry and Jesse up early. Jesse stuck out his stomach and pushed his fist into the base of his back before saying, "I don't know which is worse, being woken up by that bloody cockerel or these bloody bed boards." Henry laughed and said, "I know just what you mean." He then struggled out of his bed groaning with every movement. They slid back the hatch to reveal the morning drizzle which covered and wet everything in sight, "Ah, there you are. I was just about to knock," said George, who was wearing a scarf over his cap and the biggest overcoat Jesse had ever seen. Henry grabbed the little green bundle and took out the last of the bread and meat, he tore it in half and handed Jesse half. Jesse instantly took a large bite and said, "God that's tough!" "What did you expect its two days old!" Henry replied, as he bit into his bread and meat.

They both then stood at the back of Unity trying to chew the tough bread and meat. Their faces were in agony as their jaws began to ache from the activity. George laughed as he plonked down a brown paper parcel on the roof of Unity. It took a few seconds to open but once open the smell of bacon began to drift across the cold morning air. The smell instantly filled Henry and Jesse's nostrils. "Oh... I see you lads have already got breakfast," said George as he bit into a fresh hot bacon sandwich. The reply from Jesse and Henry was a faint grumble. George couldn't resist, he began to tease the lads. "How are the sandwiches lads?" He asked, whilst grinning all over his face. It took another couple of bites before George decided he'd better not tease the lads any longer so he looked across at them and said calmly, "I don't think I can manage three of these." He then wiped away the grease as it ran down his chin. It took a couple of seconds for Henry and Jesse to realize that George had brought sandwiches for all of them and a further couple of seconds before suddenly, there was a mad dash, as both grabbed their bacon sandwiches and divulged them almost instantly.

The old bread and meat was tossed overboard where even the ducks refused to eat it until it had been soaked and soften thoroughly by the canal. George hastily pulled a small flask of milk from his pocket. "Here, get that down ya, whilst I cast off. Henry you take the tiller, since you can't walk for long." Jesse took a long swig from the flask and jumped out onto the towpath. He quickly harnessed the horse and began leading it along the towpath. As they past the wharf at Hungerford, they could see Bill, who was using a crane to load up yet another barge with large crates. Bill looked up for a moment and waved. Jesse returned the wave as Unity slowly drifted by and passed gently under a red brick bridge.

It wasn't long before the horse began to slow down and Jesse shouted towards the barge, "George!" George instantly looked up at Jesse from the back of Unity and said, "What's the matter lad?" This infuriated Jesse because he'd asked George not to call him "lad." "Don't call me lad, my names Jesse, how many more times?" George smiled and then turned to Henry, "Touchy isn't he?" He said. Henry nodded his head in agreement and then George tried to appease Jesse by saying, "Alright Jesse, alright! What's the matter Jesse?" George emphasizing, 'Jesse' as he spoke. "The horse is slowing down for some reason," replied Jesse, who had by now stopped sulking and was feeling quite pleased that George had called him by his name. "Yes, he's seen the lock up front. He knows he has to slow down," replied George. Henry then butted in and said, "Oh, that's so we don't crash into anything little brother!" Jesse turned quickly to see Henry and George both grinning all over their faces. Jesse, trying not to let them see that he was bothered, said, "Oh... so you told him then." "Told me what little brother?" Asked Henry, who was still grinning and hoping that Jesse would admit to crashing the barge the day before. "Oh nothing," Jesse said sheepishly, as he jumped aboard Unity. He then quickly grabbed Henry and put him into a headlock, this caused Henry's cap to fall onto Unity's wet and slightly muddy deck. Jesse started to rub Henry's hair violently with the palm of his hand. "Make fun of me would ya! Laugh at my little incident yesterday, would ya?" Jesse cried as he continued rubbing Henry's hair. "And less of the little brother, I'm nearly twenty." Jesse emphasized every word by rubbing Henry's hair even harder. Just then George shouted from the front of Unity, "Come on you two, stop messing about. We've got work to do!" Jesse released Henry from the headlock and they both stood up straight. Both were grinning and

both had red faces. Jesse straightened his clothes and Henry picked up his cap. Jesse then playfully whacked Henry in the chest with the back of his hand before jumping out onto the towpath.

George shortened the towrope and then joined Jesse on the towpath. "Come on I'll show you how to operate the lock gates," he said to Jesse, who instantly became very excited at the prospect of learning how to operate the lock gates. As Jesse and George approached the lock, Jesse noticed a small house. The house lingered at the side of the towpath next to the lock and its garden could be seen and smelt for hundreds of yards along the towpath. There were baskets of flowers hung all over the house and at the front of the house, which faced the canal, there was a sign. It read… Dunmill Lock, Number 75. Please knock. This was followed by an arrow pointing to a small black wooden door. George knocked on the door and an old man appeared, "Usual George!" The man said grabbing a brown paper bag from a chair, which was just inside the door. George nodded and said, "Aye… the usual please." George sighed and took the paper bag from the man. He then, using just his thumb and index finger, gave the man some coins which he pulled from a small pocket in his waistcoat.

George began asking the old man how things were. The old man thought about the question for a moment before replying. He then turned and said, "Not so good I'm afraid. It's the new owners, Great Western Railways. They're not interested in the canal. They want me to retire because I'm too old." George turned to the man and said, "Well, if it makes you feel any better their cutting back all along the canal. They won't spend any money on anything. The mills, the locks, toll houses, and as for the maintenance, well, it's nonexistent in places. I'm only glad I work for Robins, Lane and Pinniger and not the new owners." George quickly turned to Jesse and said, "Come on Jesse get your back against this beam." George pointed to a large balancing beam which was attached to the lock gate. Jesse quickly lined up alongside George and was just about to start pushing when George stopped him and said, "On second thoughts, you'd better go and help the old lad on the otherside." George began to push the beam, "Go on then! He'll show you what to do."

Jesse followed the old man over the lock gates and stood at the side of him with his back against the balancing beam, "Right lad, start pushing with your legs not your back, got it!" Said the old man, who began pushing slowly, Jesse nodded his head and began pushing with all his might. "No lad, no, gentle pushing, don't rush, nice and steady, that's all that's needed." Jesse eased off and began pushing slowly, but constantly. "That's the idea lad," the old man said. Once the lock was open George shouted to the horse, "Come on boy!" The horse slowly pulled Unity into the lock stopping at just the right time and place so the barge didn't hit the second pair of gates. This amazed Jesse and made him smile, how clever of the horse to stop just in the right place and without being told, he thought.

The old man then gave Jesse a nudge and said, "Round here lad." Jesse walked around the beam and said, "I know, nice and slow." The old man nodded his head and both began to push the beam which closed the gate. Henry who was sat at the back of Unity looking very nervous about being locked between two pairs of large lock gates said, "What happens now?" Jesse shrugged his shoulders and said. "Search me!" "Over here lad," shouted the old man, who was waving a bent stick in the air. Jesse approached the old man cautiously, "Right lad, this is the Windlass." The old man handed Jesse the bent stick, which turned out to be made of metal. It had a square hole at one end and was very smooth at the other. Jesse looked at it puzzled and said, "What am I supposed to do with this?" He then began to laugh and lifted the Windlass into the air to show Henry what it looked like. Henry grinned at Jesse and said, "No good asking me. I've never seen anything like that before in my life." Henry shrugged his shoulders and Jesse turned to the old man, who said, "Go on then lad, open the sluice gates!" Jesse began to look around for a gate to open, "What are you looking for lad?" The old man asked Jesse, who was still looking puzzled, "The... what ya ma call it, gate," Jesse replied. The old man began to laugh and said, "Ya can tell you've not worked on the canals before. Come here," he put his arm around Jesse's shoulder and gently led him to the edge of the lock platform. He then pointed down to the bottom of the lock gate and said. "There's the sluice gate lad. Sometimes mistaken for the paddles, down there lad!" Jesse looked down at the gate and then looked back at the old man and asked, "And how am I supposed to get down there?" The old man then pointed across the lock at George who was already winding open the sluice gate on his side of the lock. Jesse copied George by inserting the Windlass onto a square ended shaft which ran to a mechanism on top of the gate. He then started to wind furiously and the sluice gate began to open allowing the water to pour out from the lock.

Just then there was a loud scream, "Jesse, we're sinking!" Jesse looked around to see Henry screaming and hanging onto the teller arm of Unity for dear life. He had the look of shear panic on his face as Unity started to sink into the belly of the lock. Jesse began laughing as Henry disappeared. He quickly ran to the edge of the lock and watched in amazement as the water disappeared as if by magic. Suddenly, Unity stopped and Henry looked up at Jesse and said angrily, "Get me out of here, quickly!" George, who was watching from the otherside of the lock, spoke before Jesse had the chance. "Won't be long Henry, we've just to close the sluice gates. Then we can let you out." George threw down a rope that he'd been using to steady Unity whilst she was in the lock. He then joined Jesse and quickly lowered the sluice gates before opening the lock gates by pushing once more on the balancing beams. Once open George shouted, "Walk on," to the horse and once more Henry and Unity were pulled from the darkness of the lock out into the morning sunlight.

After closing the lock gates and saying goodbye to the old man Jesse was keen to get to the next lock to practice what he had been taught. He quickly ran and caught up with the horse as George jumped aboard Unity and waved back to the old man who disappeared into the house. It wasn't long before Henry noticed that the barge seemed to be travelling at quite a speed. He was just about to say something to Jesse when George shouted, "Slow down Jesse, you're causing too much wash. I'll get a fine if we're caught!" Jesse began to slow the horse down and the speed of Unity returned once more to a more tranquil pace as she travelled along the canal. Jesse's keenness for operating the locks lasted for the next three locks, but then a sudden realization overcame Jesse, or was it tiredness from pushing the balancing beams? Either way at the ninth lock Jesse was definitely feeling the tiredness

from the opening and closing of the lock gates. Henry could tell this by looking at Jesse's face. The expression said it all, 'he'd had enough'. George too was beginning to slow down and when he shouted to Jesse that the next lock was to be the last of the day, Jesse seemed to get a second breath.

They came around a right-hand bend in the canal and there in front of them was the small town of Newbury, "The lock is just beyond that bridge up in front!" George shouted to Jesse. Jesse's head lifted and he put his hand over his eye brows to look off into the distance, sure enough there was a small bridge, it had people on it. Some were stood looking down at the canal and some were just crossing from one side to the other, "Seems like a busy place." Jesse said to George, "Aye lad, Newbury's a busy market town and that bridge is right in the middle of the town." George then nudged the teller arm and said to Henry, "Keep her steady Henry." As the bridge got nearer Jesse began to count how many people were using the bridge to cross from one side to the other, it passed the time. Then suddenly when they were nearly on top of the bridge Jesse noticed two people looking down at the canal from the middle of the bridge, they were wearing black! Jesse froze as he realized it was Earle and his sergeant. He quickly left the horse and jumped aboard Unity. "It's Earle," he whispered to Henry whilst pointing at the bridge with his head. Henry looked up onto the bridge and told Jesse to get inside the hutch quickly. Henry raised his jacket collar and pulled down his cap as Unity glided slowly under the bridge and the gaze of Earle's eyes.

160

Unity had cleared the bridge and as usual the horse stopped just in front of the locks, allowing Unity to glide gently to a stop, "Where's he gone now?" George asked, clambering down the side of Unity from the front. "He's not feeling well he's just taking five," Henry said as he began to hobble off Unity and out onto the towpath. "Come on, I'll give you a hand. I've seen how the locks work, it looks easy enough," said Henry. George hesitated and thought for a moment before saying, "Ok, if you're sure you can manage it." He then jumped onto the towpath at the otherside of the barge and began opening the lock gates. It took Henry a little longer to open his gate, partly because he could see Earle who had come to the edge of the bridge to watch the lock being operated. The last thing Henry wanted was to show Earle that he had a bad leg or was incapable of carrying out the work. This might have aroused Earle's suspicions and brought a closer examination.

All went well and Unity cleared the lock without much trouble. Henry had shut the last lock gate and was taking five minute's breather by sitting on the balancing beam before returning to Unity, who had just been tied up for the night by George. "That was easy enough," a voice said from behind Henry. Henry was startled and quickly spun around on the balancing beam to see Earle, who was stood looking down into the bottom of the lock. Henry didn't say anything at first. He just stood there dumb struck by the appearance of Earle. Earle spoke up again, "I said...," he looked at Henry. "That was easy enough." Henry knew he had to reply, so he spoke up using what he thought was a West Country accent. "Aye gov, the first two hundred lock gates are the worse gov, after that it gets easier." He then climbed down off the beam and began to head towards the safety of Unity's hutch. He tried desperately not to limp but before he'd gone five paces Earle suddenly shouted, "Stop!" There was a deafening moments silence and then Earle asked suspiciously, "Don't I know you?" Henry froze and without turning around he slowly said, again using the West Country accent, "No gov! I don't think so!" Earle removed his truncheon and slowly walked around Henry. He touched Henry on the shoulder with the truncheon and then looked deep into Henry's face before asking, "Are you sure?" Earle then took another good look at Henry, "You remind me of someone I went to school with." Henry then began to try and throw Earle off the scent by acting a little gormless, "Not I gov, never went to schools gov, spent all my life on the barges gov." Henry fingered his cap and quickly stepped aboard Unity. Earle watched as Henry slipped inside the hutch's two doors, Henry then quickly pulled the hatch back across the top of the doors to seal the hutch completely.

As soon as he was inside Henry quickly turned around and began watching Earle through a small gap between the doors. Earle was stood about twenty yards away talking to his sergeant. He pointed towards the barge a couple of times but didn't come any nearer. "Has he gone?" Jesse asked. He quickly joined Henry at the gap and put his own eyes lower down the gap. Jesse began peering out through the gap in the direction of Earle. "No not yet! I think he recognized me, but I'm not sure!" Both continued peering through the gap watching for any sign of movement towards them by Earle, when suddenly, George burst in and the hatch doors hit Henry full in the face. "What the bloody hell?" George said, tripping up over Henry and ended up flat on his face at the otherside of the hutch.

Jesse had begun to move away from the door and had been lucky not to have been hit in the face by the doors himself, "What's going on?" George asked as he picked himself up from the floor. There was a moments silence and then Henry replied, "Nothing, I just came down to see if our Jesse was feeling any better, that's all, why?" George picked up his cap and re-positioned it on his head before saying, "Hmmm... I suppose those two out there have got nothing to do with you two skulking around in here." He then pointed in the direction of Earle and his sergeant. Jesse answered quickly in an innocent voice, "Which two? Out where?" He leant forward and pretended to look out between the hutches double doors, "I can't see anybody, who do you mean?" George turned and looked to where Earle and the sergeant had been stood but they'd gone. It was late and George was tired, he couldn't be bothered to argue so he just said, "Ok, I'm stopping in the company hostelry tonight. My bones won't take those wooden beds anymore. You two are welcome to them. You can light the stove if you get some wood for it. There's plenty on the towpath," and with that George left saying, "See you in the morning."

Darkness fell and the canal moorings became very cold, Jesse had managed to gather some bits of wood from the towpath and had lit the stove, it gave off a reddish glow which lit up the whole hutch. After sitting there in silence for a few minutes staring endlessly into the red embers of the stove, Jesse looked across at Henry, who looked flushed in the red light, "What now?" Jesse asked. Henry groaned and fell back onto his bed before saying, "I don't know about you but I'm starving!" Jesse smiled at Henry and said, "We've had our hot meal today, remember the bacon sandwiches." The hutch fell silent again and Jesse started to prod the stove with an old twig. After a few minutes of prodding Jesse started to rummage around in his inside jacket pocket. Eventually, he pulled out the scam cards, "Bloody things," he said. He was just about to toss them into the fire when Henry said, "Wait! Don't throw them away, give em here!" Henry grabbed the cards from Jesse and said, "They might still be worth something, after all they promise you a job!" Jesse laughed and said, "I doubt it!" He continued to prod the stove. Henry started to read the cards. He leant towards the red light of the stove and started to sound out the letters of the words, he couldn't read. "Give em here," Jesse said, snatching the scam cards back. "Well I suppose we could still go to this mill in... err...." Jesse glanced down at the card and said, "Mirfield! It's as good a place as any, I suppose." Jesse returned the cards to his inside pocket and then Henry said, "Come on, it's time we got some food for ourselves."

Jesse followed Henry out onto the towpath it was dark, so dark, in fact, that Jesse could only just make out Henry's silhouette as he past in front of the only available light which was coming from the lamps above the bridge, "Where are we going?" Jesse asked Henry, who replied instantly, "To rob the poacher! Follow me!" Henry set off back down the towpath, after walking for about ten minutes they passed the Newbury boarder and headed out into the Berkshire countryside, "How much further?" Jesse asked, "Not much further our Jesse," Henry replied as he started to lean on his stick. They hadn't gone

162

much further when Henry's leg began to ache and eventually he had to stop. "Hold on for a moment our Jesse," Henry said as he leant up against an old mill wall. He took a couple of deep breaths and then gave his bad leg a good long rub. At the side of the old mill there was a small track, "Down here Jesse," Henry said pointing down the track. Jesse stared down the track and said, "It's awfully dark down there." "Stop being soft," said Henry leading the way down the track, Jesse reluctantly followed.

It wasn't long before Henry stopped and quietly said, "Listen!" Jesse froze instantly and began to listen, "What! I can't hear anything," he said as Henry tapped his nose with his index finger. Henry pressed the same finger onto his lips to indicate to Jesse to be silent, "Exactly!" Henry said. He then beckoned Jesse to sit down which he did. Both lads sat there in the darkness for over an hour not speaking or moving. The silence was deafening and Jesse was beginning to lose the feeling in his feet as the cold night air did its work. Just as Jesse was about to ask Henry what it was that they were actually supposed to be doing there, a loud squealing noise started about twenty feet further down the track. As soon as the noise started Henry was up off the cold floor and running towards the squealing noise. Jesse followed and nearly fell head long over Henry as he stopped suddenly to pick up a wriggling rabbit. Henry quickly gave the rabbit a chop at the back of the head which dispatched the creature immediately. The whole event was over and done within seconds and the deafening silence returned.

Jesse was puzzled as they returned to the towpath, "How did you know that trap was there?" He asked Henry, who had tied the rabbit onto his belt. "Living off the land for a couple of years you learn to recognize poachers. I saw one today from the back of Unity, he disappeared down this track. I didn't know where he'd laid his traps, so we had to wait until something got caught. However, what I did know is that the traps wouldn't be too far away from the track." The lads hasten towards Unity thinking all the time about one thing and one thing only, "Roast rabbit."

Henry's leg was in real pain by the time the lads reached Unity. Jesse could see the bridge lamps further down the towpath. However, he could also see some lights moving about on the towpath. Strange thought Jesse, he began to slow down, he grabbed Henry by the elbow and said, "Look! Can you see those lights near Unity?" Henry stopped and said, "Its Earle and that nosey sergeant of his, they've come back to search for us." Both lads stepped back into the shadows quickly and waited. It seemed like an eternity, but eventually, Earle and his sergeant were both satisfied that there was no-one aboard Unity and both turned and slowly began to leave, checking every nook and cranny as they went back towards the bridge. Finally, they disappeared under the bridge. Jesse was quick to come out of the shadows, but Henry quickly pulled him back saying. "Wait! Give em a couple of minutes, just to be sure." Jesse nodded his head and returned to the shadows.

Jesse puts some more wood on the stove and Henry handed him some rabbit meat which Jesse shoved onto twigs ready for roasting. It wasn't long before both lads had eaten their fill of roasted rabbit and were fast asleep. They didn't seem to be asleep for long when Jesse was awoken by the feeling of movement. "Henry, Henry! Are you a wake?" "Yes, I can feel it as well," Henry replied. Jesse quietly got up and leered through the gap in the double doors. To his surprise, he could see George operating the tiller. Jesse pushed open the doors and said, "You're keen aren't you?" George laughed and said, "Yes and so were those policemen, but just like you two, I don't need the police snooping around, especially around the tollstaff, so I set off a little earlier this morning just in case they came back, so get yourselves up and out here."

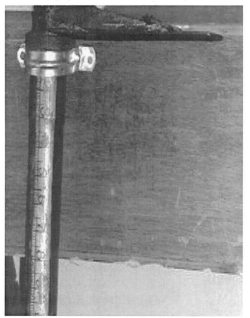

Jesse fingered his eyebrow and went back inside to put his jacket on, "Come on, it's only George." He told Henry, tapping him with the back of his hand on his foot. Henry stretched and climbed out onto Unity's deck, the sunlight made him squint as he took over the tiller from George. "Morning George," he said as George jumped out onto the towpath and started leading the horse. It wasn't long before Jesse was up and about. He joined George on the towpath as Unity approached the first lock of the day, "Not another one!" Jesse said exasperated. George laughed before saying, "Aye lad... there's only twenty one more before we reach Reading, you'll be leaving me then."

Jesse walked across the top of the lock gates and watched as the water began flooding out through the sluice gates. Unity slowly began to lower into the lock. George then threw a rope across at Jesse saying, "Here lad, wrap that around that bollard and steady her as she lowers," George pointed to a cast iron bollard at the side of Jesse. Jesse quickly looped the rope around the bollard and then allowed the rope to slide through his fingers as Unity lowered into the lock. When she reached the bottom Jesse un-looped the rope from around the bollard and threw the end of it down to Henry, who caught the rope and began coiling it up.

After two days of travel, Reading came into view and Jesse was getting sick of opening and shutting lock gates, his arms and legs ached from pushing the balancing beams. George looked into Jesse's tired face and said, "Right Jesse! I've got to trust you and Henry," there was a pause and Jesse looked back at George. "There's only one more lock before you reach Reading Wharf. I'm going to trust you both and allow you to take Unity through it, you should be alright. I've taught you both well enough." "Why where are you going?" asked Henry who had been listening in the background. George turned to look at Henry and said, "To get my nephew James. He's going to replace you and Jesse when you leave me at the Thames," and with that, George jumped clear of Unity and said. "I'll catch up with you at Reading Wharf, ok!" Jesse nodded his head and carried on walking at the side of the horse. George then disappeared down a small alley between two factories, turning to see Henry, who waved, as Unity floated past the alley.

They arrived at the last lock and Jesse opened the gates allowing Unity to glide in and gently come to a stop. Henry threw Jesse the rope to steady Unity, and he began to wind open the sluice gates. However, the sluice gates were exceptionally stiff and difficult to open. Jesse realized that he was going to need both hands on the windlass to wind open the gates, so he tied the steadying rope that Henry had given him to an old wooden bollard on the lock side. The bollard was old and well worn with the rope grooves of time. This freed Jesse's hands to do the winding, he began to wind open the sluice gates and the water began to lower, all seemed well and Unity started her descent. Henry was at the back of Unity leaning on the tiller arm, he grinned at Jesse as he disappeared beneath the lock edge. Henry had only just disappeared from Jesse's sight when there was a creak and the rope 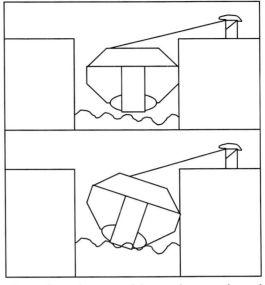 suddenly tensioned. Henry began shouting for Jesse, his voice echoed around the lock, "Jesse! Jesse! There's something wrong." Henry looked over the back of Unity and down at the black water. Jesse came rushing to the edge of the lock. He looked down at Henry, who had a very worried look on his face, "The water has gone down our Jesse but Unity hasn't!" Henry said as he began to panic.

The rope creaked again and then Jesse realized that the barge was being held by the steadying rope. The rope had stopped Unity from descending, and she was precariously hung in mid air about half way down the lock side, "Stop panicking our Henry," Jesse said sternly. "I'll close the sluice gates and refill the lock. It's not a problem!" Jesse disappeared from Henry's view and the sound of the water rushing out through the sluice gates stopped. Jesse re-appeared and began to reassure Henry by saying, "Don't worry our Henry all I have to do now is to refill the lock and you'll float back to the top, simple!" Jesse disappeared again and the sound of rushing water began to fill the lock again. Henry watched as the water began to rise, but then he noticed that Unity was beginning to lean, he began to lose his footing. He started to slide towards the lock wall. Henry realized that something was seriously wrong again, so he let out an almighty scream, "Jesse!" Jesse came to the edge of the lock just in time to hear a loud bang as Unity's load shifted, which tipped her even further. The water began to flow over the lower edge of Unity and Henry found himself trying to clamber up a by now wet and slippery deck.

Jesse quickly ran back to the lock gate and closed the sluice gates, the lock fell silent. After walking slowly back to the edge of the lock Jesse slowly looked down into the lock, hoping to find Henry and Unity still in one piece. Henry, who was by now sat on the top edge of Unity and clear of the water with his knees around his chin, was not amused, "What the hell happened?"

He asked. "You've tied the steadying rope to the bollard," a deep voice said from the otherside of the lock. Jesse glared across at an unshaven man who was stood looking down at Henry. The man had his hands in his pockets and a large grin on his face, "You're not the first to do it," he said lifting his cap to scratch his head, "and you probably won't be the last," the man said sarcastically. He then looked at the front of the barge and realizing he knew the barge, he asked, "Oh, its Unity, where's George?" "Why, who are you?" Jesse asked wondering what to do next. "I'm Arthur the lock keeper and by the looks of things the man who's going to get you out of trouble!" Arthur looked directly at Jesse who nodded in agreement. He then pushed Jesse by the shoulder towards the balancing beam and said, "Right lad go and open the sluice gates slowly, don't open them fully. Keep your eye on me and I'll tell you when to close them." Arthur then threw a rope down to Henry and said, "Tie that to the lowest edge of Unity, quickly!" Arthur then tied the other end of the rope to the horse and put tension on it. He signalled to Jesse by lifting his hand and Jesse slowly began to open the gates using the windlass. Slowly, the water entered the lock and Unity began to move slowly. Arthur watched as Unity began to rise slowly at the same time Arthur led the horse away pulling up the lower end of Unity, not allowing the water to flow over the lower edge. Eventually, Unity was level again and stood up right in the lock. Jesse closed the sluice gate and undid the steadying rope from the bollard.

Arthur helped the lads correct the shifted load and then said, "Right lads! Carefully does it the next time and don't tie up the steadying rope, eh!" Jesse grinned and nodded his head. Henry thanked Arthur from the back of Unity. Arthur then stood back and watched Jesse and Henry execute a near perfect lock descent. Unity was pulled gently from the lock as Jesse began leading the horse down the towpath. Henry steered Unity to the middle of the canal. Arthur stood and watched from the top of the lock as Unity gently glided out of sight towards Reading Wharf where Jesse tied her up and waited for George and his nephew to arrive.

They hadn't waited long when George arrived with his nephew James. James was a funny looking lad with a squint; he wore a new trendy bowler hat which he said sheltered his rather large nose from the rain and sun. "Come on then, let's get moving!" George shouted to the three of them as he clasped his hands together and jumped aboard Unity. Jesse walked at the side of the horse, but he allowed James to lead the animal. It wasn't long before they arrived at the Thames and George steered Unity to the bank. He then said, "Well, here ya go Henry; this is where we part company." George stretched out his hand to Henry, who shook it and said, "Thanks for putting up with us." George then helped Henry up onto the towpath as Jesse jumped down onto Unity and disappeared into the hutch, he re-appeared with the little green bundle. After throwing the bundle over his shoulder he jumped out onto the towpath and said, "Which way then?" George laughed and pointed up the river, "That's north to Oxford, up there! You might be able to cadge a lift if you're lucky."

Jesse held out his hand to shake George's hand and was shocked to feel a coin placed firmly in his hand by George. Jesse quickly looked at George, who said, "Its only half a crown. You'll need it and you've earned it." Jesse clasped the coin and smiled. George then handed half a crown to Henry and everyone began wishing each other good luck and after saying goodbye to one another Jesse and Henry began to walk away. They hadn't walked far when George shouted after them, "Oh and by the way Jesse!" Jesse stopped and turned around to look back at George, who then said, with a wide grin on his face, "Don't ever tie up the steadying rope, it can be very, very dangerous!" Jesse paused for a moment and thought about what George had said. He then realized that George knew about the incident in the lock. Jesse began to smile, the smile turned to laughter. He then fingered his eyebrow at George and turned to join Henry on the towpath. They both walked away and Henry began to laugh as Jesse told him what George had said. George watched as the laughing lads disappeared into the distance, he then set about casting off.

Chapter 8: Legging it Northward… at Last.

George and his nephew had delivered the deal boards and scantlings to London and were returning with a load of tin plated boxes through Newbury when they were stopped by the police. George pulled Unity over to the bank and jumped out onto the towpath. He quickly tied Unity to the nearest mooring ring, pulled out his handkerchief from his trouser pocket, and began wiping his brow free from sweat. The sergeant slowly approached George and said, "We understand that you have two young lads working for you on this barge just now." George thought about it and then said, "Only my nephew James," he pointed down the towpath towards James. Who waved from where he was un-harnessing the horse, "No, not him!" Earle bleated out. "Those other two little sods, where are they?"

Frantically Earle jumped aboard Unity and opened the doubled doors of the hutch. He stared into the darkness of the hutch, feeling sure that Jesse and Henry were inside. Earle waited for a moment for his eyes to adjust to the darkness and then shouted, "Come on out! I know you're in there!" But his shouts received an instant silence. "There's no-one in there sir," George said shrugging his shoulders. Earle, angry, quickly jumped back onto the towpath and pushed his way past his sergeant to approached George who was still removing the sweat from his face and neck with the handkerchief. "So where are they then?" Earle screamed in George's face. Just then the sergeant realized that Earle was becoming enraged by the situation and began to pull him back by the elbow in a bid to try and ease the situation. Earle quickly pulled his arm out of the sergeant's grip and stepped back away from George who calmly said, "I don't know who you're talking about. There's only the lad and myself working on this barge."

The sergeant stepped a little nearer George and began explaining that they were looking for two young lads. "One as run off without his release papers from the Chief Constable and the other.... Well, we think he's an escaped convict, if my partner in crime is correct," said the sergeant looking seriously at Earle who quickly reacted to the sergeant's doubtfulness by saying. "Of course it's him! It can't be anybody else! I didn't recognize him straight away but I never forget a face. I'm now bloody sure it was him!" The sergeant turned back to look at George and said, "We know you had two lads working for you because we watched them come down the canal towards the lock with you." George scratched his chin and thought for a moment but still said nothing. The sergeant, seeing George's reluctance to answer, took hold of him by the elbow and led him a little further down the towpath out of earshot. He then slowly whispered in George's ear, "Now listen, you don't want any trouble, do you?" George shook his head, "Well then, tell us who they were and where they were going and we'll say no more about the position." George looked puzzled at the sergeant and asked, "What position?" The sergeant grinned and nudged George before saying, "The position of that tollstaff on your barge." At the mere mention of the tollstaff George realized that he had no option but to tell the sergeant, "Their names were Henry and Jesse. They were going up north, or so they said. We left them at the Thames two days ago. We last saw them heading north towards Oxford. That's right isn't it James?" James nodded his head and Earle screamed, "I knew it! I was right! I never forget a face!" The sergeant had by now become very annoyed by an over excited Earle and said angrily, "Will you calm down." He then began to walk away from George and James thanking them for their information. "Come on you," he said to Earle who was still swooning over being proven right about Henry.

They hadn't gone far down the towpath when the sergeant put on a father like voice. "Now then Earle," he said, taking a deep breath and turning towards Earle. "It's all well and good knowing it was Henry but you can't go off chasing him all over the country, the chief wouldn't like that!" Their conversation eventually brought both of them to a stop and Earle said, "But we know its Henry, he's an escaped convict. Surely the chief will want him recaptured." The sergeant shook his head and said, "It's not that easy, you'll have to put in a request if you want to go after him." They then disappeared down a small street which led to the police station on Newbury High Street.

Meanwhile, Jesse and Henry had walked all day and most of the night when Henry had to force Jesse to stop. "I'm in agony our Jesse, we'll have to stop and rest," said Henry pulling back Jesse by his elbow. Jesse began to look around for somewhere to rest, "Over here our Henry." Jesse said, helping Henry onto a stone bench which was built into the wall. They'd sat there for sometime and Henry was beginning to nod when Jesse, whose bum was just beginning to feel the coldness of the stone, noticed a distant light. "Look over there Henry, Henry!" Jesse looked around to see Henry hard asleep with his head back against the wall. Jesse stood up and instantly made one of his

decisions. He set off towards the light leaving Henry asleep on the stone bench. He'd walked for about half a mile across open fields when he came across a small farmhouse with a candle burning in a small upstairs window. Jesse entered the farmyard and walked un-notice into the barn.

The barn was warm and full of dry straw, just the job, Jesse thought. Just then the sound of a large horse in the corner of the barn reached Jesse's ears. It reminded Jesse of his den back home in the barn and the sound's Titan use to make during the night.

Jesse waited for a moment, just to savour the memories. He then left the barn and headed back across the open fields to where Henry was still asleep. Jesse shook Henry hard to wake him, but Henry was so tired that Jesse had to slap him hard across the face to wake him up. Henry did eventually wake up but wasn't pleased by the way Jesse had done it, "I thought we were having a rest." Henry angrily moaned whilst rubbing his face where Jesse had landed the last slap. "We can't sleep here. Someone might see us. Anyway, I've found us a place just over there by that light." Henry looked across the fields at the distant light and said, "Do we have to?" Jesse snapped, "You ungrateful sod! Yes we have to, so come on. You can sleep when we get there." Jesse started off across the field and Henry gradually lifted his weary bones up off the stone bench saying, "You're a slave driver our Jesse." He then limped after Jesse, who was by now half way across the field.

Both lads covered themselves with straw and slept soundly until they were disturbed by the farmer opening the barn doors and saying good morning to his horse. Jesse quickly covered himself with more straw, so he couldn't be seen by the farmer who was beginning to harness the horse. Jesse watched the farmer through the gaps in the straw. Just then, from behind Jesse came an enormous snoring sound, it caught the farmer's attention immediately. He instantly turned and looked to where Jesse and Henry were laid. Slowly, the farmer walked across towards their position and shouted apprehensively, "Who's there? I know you're there. I've heard you." Jesse didn't answer at first, he just watched as the farmer picked up a pitchfork, which was resting against the barn wall. Grasping the pitchfork in both hands and looking very determined the farmer began shouting. "Come on then, let's have you!" The farmer began prodding the straw violently with the pitchfork.

Eventually, the prodding got too close for comfort and Jesse, not wishing to be stabbed with the pitchfork, jumped up out of the straw and shouted, "Don't stab me mister!" The farmer walked towards Jesse and pointing the pitchfork directly at him, shouted, "Outside!" Jesse slowly walked sideways in an anti-clockwise direction towards the door whilst keeping an eye on the points of the pitchfork as they followed him out through the door and into the farmyard.

Outside the barn the farmer began asking Jesse questions, "What's your name? Where are you from? Are you...?" But just before he'd finished asking the final question there was a sudden thud and the farmer fell to the ground groaning. As he fell Henry appeared in his place holding his walking stick by the thin end. "There! That'll teach him," Henry said tapping the handle end of the stick on the palm of his hand. Jesse was stunned at Henry's actions and couldn't quite believe what he'd just seen, "Have you killed him?" Jesse asked, still glued to the spot and looking down on a by now very still farmer. "No, he'll be alright." Henry replied as he frisked through the farmer's pockets for any coins he might have. "Come on, let's go," Henry said as he stood up. He then placed some coins in his pocket, "Waste not. Want not, eh!" He slapped Jesse's face gently and gave him a false smile as he set off back across the field towards the river. Jesse continued looking at the farmer for a couple of seconds more but a sudden movement convinced Jesse that he wasn't dead and that he'd better make tracks before the farmer came around from his ordeal.

It wasn't long before the pair had entered Oxford and both were ready for breakfast. Jesse suggested that they left the river and went into Oxford town centre to buy some food. "There's got to be some shops there where we can buy some pies or something worth eating." Henry agreed and they both jumped a small wall which led them to a street. The street was lined with terrace houses, all black and grimy from the mill chimneys which were nearby. After walking the length of the street and getting some funny looks from the locals, they came across a small butches shop on the corner of the street. Jesse and Henry approached the window of the shop, they gazed in. There, hung in the window were two chickens, a couple of rabbits and a hare. Underneath these unprepared creatures where pasties, pies and three types of sausages with an unprepared duck lying lifeless at the side of them. After a few moments of contemplation, Henry said, "Looks like the poachers have been busy." Jesse grinned and said, "I'm not bothered, this place will save us a walk. We can buy the pies from here instead of walking to the town centre." Henry hurriedly entered the shop and bought four pies. The shopkeeper double wrapped them in brown paper bags as Henry had requested. He returned and handed Jesse his pies saying, "One meat and kidney and one rabbit." Both lads walked back up the street with cheeks full of pie. They were just about to climb back over the wall when a small voice said, "Give us a bite of your pie mister, go on mister, please mister give us a bite!" Jesse looked back over his shoulder to see two shabbily dressed boys, neither had shoes on. The tallest of the boys repeated the request and then held out his hand. Jesse could tell instantly that the boys were starving; they reminded him of his own sometimes foodless childhood. Jesse stopped climbing the wall and walked towards the boys. "Ya poor little buggers," he said out loud. "Come on our Jesse, leave them. We haven't enough food for ourselves never mind feeding other folk!" Henry shouted from the otherside of the wall. Jesse

ignored Henry's advice and gave the boys half his pie. They instantly ran off back down the street clutching the pie. They disappeared into one of the terrace houses and Jesse returned to climbing back over the wall. It took a moment but eventually Jesse caught up with Henry, who was by now well into his pace along the path. "You're incorrigible!" Henry said spitting out a piece of grizzle from his pie.

It wasn't long before Oxford had come and gone and the lads had managed to hitch a ride on an empty coal barge heading back to Coventry along the Oxford Canal. It was very dirty but as Jesse had said at the time, "It was free and beggars can't be choosers," he'd also told Henry quite adamantly to, "Stop moaning about it. Otherwise the owner might decide to throw us off." Actually, Jesse too had thought that the coal dust very difficult to deal with, especially if you disturbed it and then breathed it in, it would make you cough. But if you were careful and kept still and didn't disturb the dust by touching anything, then it was quite tolerable. Anyway Jesse had decided to spend most of his time earning his keep by guiding the horse along the towpath and opening and closing locks for the barge owner, it seemed a lot better than sitting among the coal dust and coughing for most of the day.

The lads and the barge owner, whose name was Bill, had spent three long days travelling the canal before reaching, what Bill described as the black hole from hell! They came around a long left handed bend in the canal and Bill shouted from the back of the coal barge, "There it is, the black hole from hell!"

Jesse glanced around the horse and look to his front. Henry who had been resting his leg on a small three legged stool that Bill used to paint ornamental buckets on, also stood up and looked to the front. "What the hell's that Bill?" Henry asked looking a little afraid. "Don't worry it won't hurt you, it's only the Newbold Tunnel. It goes straight through yon mountain. It saves us going around. It shortens the trip by a good few hours as well," Bill replied as he lined up the barge with the middle of the tunnel.

Jesse reluctantly led the horse into the tunnel then Henry let out a shout, "Jesse! Are you alright up there?" The shout echoed the length of the tunnel. This made Jesse shudder with fright, having never heard such a thing before. Jesse quickly let go of the horse and returned to the barge, "What on earth was that?" Jesse asked as he stepped aboard the barge. Bill, who had lit an oil lamp and had hung it up on a long pole at the back of the barge, replied, "Oh…. It's only the devil shouting back." Bill tried very hard to keep his face straight and move back to allow Jesse to pass him. "That's enough for me. I'm stopping here!" Jesse said sitting down at the side of Henry who let out a loud laugh and said, "What's the matter our Jesse, scared of the dark?" Jesse quickly snapped, "No! But I don't fancy meeting the devil at the end of this tunnel!" Bill and Henry broke out into fits of laughter just as the barge burst out through the northern end of the tunnel into a sun drench forest of greenery. Which was just as well because the laughter echoes would have been tremendous and would have probably put Jesse off going through any more tunnels.

Jesse stood up and looked around for the devil, "It's only an echo Jesse, there's no devil! Bill was having you on," Henry said still trying not to laugh. Jesse pretended that he had known that all along and jumped off the barge as Bill steered the barge nearer the bank. "This'll do us for the night," said Bill. "Here tie her up Jesse." Bill threw Jesse a mooring rope which he used to tie the barge to a nearby mooring ring. Just then a young girl said, "Hello," she

 then pushed her way past Jesse and jumped aboard the barge, "Hello papa!" The girl said to Bill as she kissed him on the cheek. "Where's ya mother? I'm starving," Bill asked the girl. Just then from behind Jesse a woman appeared with a small child in her arms. "I'm here Bill Turner, don't you be worrying and yes I've brought your tea."

The woman looked Jesse up and down and then walked past him saying, "Aye and there's only enough for thine and mine!" She handed Bill a basket and they all disappeared inside the hutch. Henry and Jesse sat on the rim of the barge listening as the sounds of cutlery rattling and the tapping of forks on plates filled the air. "I'm off for a walk," said Jesse with annoyance in his voice. He grabbed his jacket and walked back towards the tunnel. As darkness began to fall Jesse stood for a moment at the entrance to the tunnel, he looked back down the tunnel. It sure is black, he thought as he cautiously began to look around. Because there was no-one about he let out an almighty shout, "hellooo, hellooo! Is there anybody there?" Jesse smiled as his voice came rebounding back at him. But then suddenly, a voice replied, "Yes there is, Hellooo, hellooo!" Jesse was so startled that he skedaddled quickly back to the barge where he found Henry preparing to bed down for the night in a small stopover shed used by crews and horses that worked on the canals. "What's the matter with you? You look as though you've seen a ghost or something," said Henry as Jesse joined him and the horse inside the small shed.

Henry was just about to close the door to the shed when Jesse said, "Leave it open a bit, if it gets cold, then I'll get up and close it." Henry paused for a moment and then realizing that Jesse was nearer the door than him, agreed by nodding his head and said, "Suit yourself." He then layed down on a pile of straw; shuffled for a moment, and then fell into a deep sleep. Jesse, on the other hand laid there looking out through the gap in the door as another long barge went cruising by in the darkness. The barge was lit by oil lamps on both sides. The horse also wore a lamp about its neck. Jesse then realized that it must have been the people aboard the passing barge that had replied to his shouts down the tunnel and not the devil as he'd first thought. Jesse fell asleep feeling comfortable that the devil wasn't close by and that it was just Bill's wild imagination that had him going.

The next morning Bill said goodbye to his family and the barge slowly headed north. They'd only been sailing for about two hours when they came to a junction in the canal. Bill on seeing the junction cried out, "Hawkesbury Junction!" Bill's voice deepened, and then he continued to say, "Or Sutton Stop Lock as it is sometimes known as." Jesse smiled at Bill and let go of the horse, he noticed that the lock had a small waterfall on one side, "Why the waterfall?" He asked Bill as the barge slowly pulled to a stop in front of the lock gates. "Oh that! It's to keep the waters of the Oxford Canal over there." Bill pointed to the direction they had just come from, "Separate from the Coventry Canal which is over there." He then pointed to the canal in front of

the barge. Jesse began opening the lock gates and Henry steered the barge into the lock whilst Bill chatted with the lockkeeper and paid the toll.

It wasn't long before Bill and Henry were sat in their usual places at the back of the barge steering it northwards. Jesse was quite content to guide the horse and watch the pleasant countryside pass them by, when they arrived at yet another canal junction, "Which way now?" Jesse shouted back to Bill, "Well... I'm heading up the right hand canal towards Ashby De La Zouch." Bill replied, and then, with his hand over his mouth, he turned to Henry and said, with a grin on his face, "That's French, don't you know." Henry laughed and said, "Never heard of the place." He then picked up the little green bundle which was lying on top of the barge roof and jumped out onto the towpath. "Suppose this is where we get off?" Henry said to Bill, "Afraid so, you need to follow the Coventry Canal as far as you can. Then take a right turn at a little place called Fradley Junction. The Coventry joins the Trent and Mersey there. Then head for the Macclesfield Canal it about half way up T and M, just past Harecastle Tunnel. That's a spooky wet place. Then, when you get...," Bill suddenly stopped talking and looked up at Henry and Jesse. They were both marching up and down the towpath doing chicken impersonations. Suddenly, Jesse stopped and said, "You lost us Bill at the first turn." Bill laughed, waved his hand at the lads and said, "I don't know why I bother, you two will need no help to get where you're going."

Before leaving Henry and Jesse both thanked Bill, "Remember to keep the sun on your right in the mornings and on your left in the afternoons and you won't go much wrong." Bill told them both in a caring voice. Jesse nodded and then Bill wished the lads the best of luck before pointing towards the left canal. "That's northwards lads, that's north!" Bill said adamantly. He then told the horse to move and jumped aboard the barge as it moved slowly up the right hand canal, "All the best then, all the best lads!" Bill shouted as the barge began to disappear down the right hand canal. Eventually, Bill gave a final wave, turned his back and was gone from view as the barge negotiated a bend.

The lads didn't have much luck hitching a ride along the Coventry Canal and ended up walking most of the thirty eight miles to the Trent and Mersey. Bill's tip about keeping the sun on the right in the mornings had paid off. Jesse had noticed that the sun was on the left after they'd passed a place called Fazeley Junction. And after nagging Henry for nearly five miles, he agreed to stop and ask someone where they were. It turned out that they'd gone down the Birmingham Canal by mistake and were heading in the completely wrong direction. They turned and walked back to Fazeley Junction and this time walked north to Fradley Junction. It had been an extra ten miles more than it should have been, but eventually; tired and weary they arrived at Fradley Junction where the Coventry Canal met the Trent and Mersey canal.

At the Junction, there was a pub called the Swan Inn, Henry suggested they lodge there for the night, get some decent food and take the chance to take a bath and get cleaned up. Tired and weary Jesse didn't argue he just followed Henry into the pub. The pub wasn't that clean inside, there was an old wooden table at the bottom of some steep stairs, which seemed to lead up to the roof space. At the table were sat four men, one of which had drunk his fill of ale and had fallen forward onto his arms to sleep. The landlord approached and asked, "What would sirs like?" He then wiped his greasy hands on a dirty apron and Henry answered, "A room and a bath with some food if you have some?" The landlord laughed and said, "As you can see we're full up," he pointed to other people who were in the room, some of whom were asleep sat on the floor.

Henry and Jesse paused for a moment, looked around the room and then asked the landlord if there were any out buildings where they could spend the night. The landlord looked sympathetically at the lads and said, "Tell you what I'll do, for a shilling you can spend the night in the barn. It's warm and dry in there and for good measure, I'll throw in a leg of lamb and a flagon of ale, how's that sound." Henry nodded his head eagerly at the mere mention of food. The landlord then rubbed his finger and thumb together saying, "I trust sirs can pay." Henry quickly gave the landlord his shilling. They were then shown through the crowded pub to a small passageway at the back which led to the backdoor of the pub.

The landlord opened the backdoor using a large key which he took out from under his apron. The backdoor led to a yard. "Across there," the landlord said pointing across the yard to the stables. Jesse and Henry walked out into the yard and the landlord began to shut the door. Henry quickly stuck his foot in the door and said, "Food landlord!" The landlord grinned and said, "Oh... yes sir." He went back into the pub and appeared a couple of minutes later with a tray and sure enough there, on the tray, was a large leg of lamb and a flagon of ale. Henry snatched the tray from the landlord and removed his foot from the door which was quickly slammed closed as soon as the foot was clear of the door. The sound of the locks and bolts being thrown echoed across the yard as Henry handed the tray to Jesse. He then took a long drink from the flagon. Jesse screamed at Henry, "Don't drink the lot!" Eventually, Henry replaced the flagon onto the tray and Jesse handed the tray back to Henry, whilst he took a drink. After drinking, they made their way across the yard to the stables where they could see a line of light around the stable door. Henry slowly pushed open the door to reveal a stable full of traveller's all with trays of lamb and ale, "Looks like we are going to have to share the accommodation our Jesse," Henry said with a smile on his face. Just then a shout came from inside the stable, "Shut that bloody door!" Henry and Jesse quickly shuffled inside the stable door and pulled it closed behind them blocking out the cold night air.

After cutting and sharing the lamb's leg, both lads took it in turns to swig off the last of the ale from the flagon. It was Jesse's turn to drink, but as he lifted the flagon to his lips, he noticed a chap watching him from the otherside of the stable. The man came closer and Jesse had no choice but to offer him a drink, which the man eagerly took. After wiping his lips the man asked, "Where are you from lads?" Henry quickly replied before Jesse had the chance to, "Wiltshire, as if it's got anything to do with you!" The man gave Henry a stare and then said, "I didn't mean to be nosey. I was just trying to be neighbourly sir." Henry apologized and said, "He was tired after a long journey." The man nodded as he accepted Henry's apology. Henry then layed down and pulled some loose straw over him. Jesse began talking to the man and discovered that he too was from Berkshire, but Jesse continued pretending he came from Wilshire, just in case Henry was listening. As they talked, they got around to the reason why they were there and what a surprise, when the man pulled from his inside pocket two tickets promising him free passage on the canal and a job up north. The tickets were nearly the same as Jesse's, the only difference being, these tickets had a different mill address on them. The man laughed and said, "All these people have tickets and are all travelling up north to find jobs. Some are heading for Huddersfield, some for Bradford and some for Leeds. There from all over the midlands and the south of England. Some are even running from the law!" Jesse began to feel uncomfortable but fortunately is feelings were short lived when a voice from the back of the stables shouted, "Give it a rest won't you, some of us want to sleep." The man crept back to his side of the stable whispering good night as he went. Jesse joined Henry, who was now fast asleep in among the warm straw.

The next morning the stable air was to say the least a little stale, Henry put it down to the poor watered down ale everybody had been drinking the night before. The landlord was up early trying to flog people sandwiches before they left, but after tasting the lamb and ale the night before Jesse and Henry had decided to decline his offer. The lads left the stable and walked out through the yard gate onto the canal towpath. Jesse stretched and then looked up the canal towpath; he nudged Henry and pointed with his head up the towpath. There in front of them was a long line of people carrying their worldly possessions. All were heading northwards along the towpath. Jesse looked at Henry and said, "We'll never get a lift from a barge with all this lot. We've got to get in front of them somehow." Henry agreed and said, "But how?" Jesse thought for a moment and then said, "Hang on here." He disappeared behind the pub and reappeared moments later riding a large shire. "Come on our Henry," he said holding out his hand. Henry grabbed Jesse's hand and was pulled up onto the back of the horse. Jesse kicked the horse with his heels and started screaming, "Coming through, coming through! Mind your backs!" As they made their way through the crowded towpath, Henry looked back to see the landlord of the pub waving his fist at them. Henry happily returned a signal of his own. Jesse didn't care he just kept kicking the horse forwards as he made his way through the scattering crowd.

After an hour, the crowd on the towpath began to dissipate and Jesse began to slow down to a slow trot. Henry tapped Jesse on the shoulder and slid down the side of the horse onto the towpath, "What are you getting off for?" Jesse asked, looking puzzled. Henry walked to the front of the horse and began to lead it at a nice steady walking pace, "I just fancied a stroll. Anyway, my bum was starting to hurt with all that bouncing up and down," Henry replied rubbing his bum. Just then Jesse's stomach began to rumble and Henry asked, "Are you hungry our Jesse?" Jesse turned and looked down at Henry and said angrily, "What do you think? I'm always hungry these days and the sooner we get to Mirfield and start earning some money the better as far as I'm concerned." Henry sensing Jesse's tone didn't answer him. He just carried on walking and guiding the horse. They'd gone about fifteen miles and the sun was high in the sky when Henry decided to break the silence by saying, "We're approaching another town. I can see it in the distance." Jesse looked towards the town and quickly snapped, "What's the good of that! We don't have any money left to buy anything." Jesse climbed down from the back of the horse and began walking in front of Henry with his head down, "What's the matter our Jesse?" Henry could see tears slowly crawling down Jesse's face, "I'm tired, hungry, and look!" Jesse pointed to the surrounding area, "We're in the middle of nowhere and with no money, no food and where the hell are we going to sleep tonight? I think we should go back." Henry lifted Jesse's head using his index finger and said, "How can I go back Jesse? The bastards will send me to the otherside of the world. You'll never see me again, is that what you want?" Jesse shook his head scattering his tears, "Well then, come on. Where's the Jesse I know? The lad who always manages to pull through," Jesse smiled and wiped away his tears with his jacket sleeve. Henry pulled out a florin and teased Jesse with it by holding it in front of his eyes. Jesse broke out into a grin and grabbed at the coin, but he wasn't quick enough, Henry quickly put it back into his pocket, "Where did you get that from you sod?" Asked Jesse amazed that Henry had any money at all. "Remember the farmer?" Henry said. Jesse nodded and Henry winked as he mounted the horse, saying, "I'm in front, come on let's get on." Jesse mounted the horse and put his arms around Henry as they sped off towards the town which happened to be Stoke on Trent.

The lads didn't spend much time in Stoke because they had to leave the horse in a field and were worried that the farmer might discover it before they

got back. They arrived back at the field with potatoes, carrots and some snowball turnips all tied up in Henry's jacket. Jesse gave the horse a carrot and was glad it was still in the field where they'd left it. They had also bought four bottles of stout which Jesse had tied up in his little green bundle. After a little feast, both lads set off along the towpath astride the horse.

They hadn't gone far when they came across two tunnels, one thin one and one slightly wider with a towpath. It seemed logical to the lads to use the tunnel with the towpath, so they both dismounted and Henry began to lead the horse towards the tunnel when a voice shouted, "Eh you! Where are you going with that horse?" Henry looked around to see a man on the otherside of the canal looking out through a stable door. The man came to the edge of the canal, put his hands on his hips and said, "That's a company horse. What are you doing with it?" Henry froze. He didn't know what to say. Luckily, Jesse came to his rescue and said, "We found it wandering on the towpath about five miles back. Why, what's it to you?" "I'm the stable master around here," said the man. Jesse smiled and said, "Oh you're just the man we've been looking for then." The man scratched his head and said, "What do you mean?" Jesse was quick to reply, "Well, the horse must be worth a bob or two. There must be a reward for finding it?" The man grinned and said, "Nice try lad, now just tie the horse to that ring on the wall and we'll say no more about this, eh!" Jesse thought for a moment and then Henry signalled, come on, with his head. So slowly, both lads started to walk through the tunnel leaving the horse tied to the ring as requested.

It wasn't long before the lads re-appeared at the otherside of the tunnel. Both were still laughing and joking with one another about Jesse's attempt to con a reward out of the stable master. They were both wet from the dripping ceiling of the tunnel and decided to lie on the dry stone wall and dry off for an hour. Jesse's eyes had only just closed when he heard voices and the sound of a horse trotting by on the muddy towpath. Quickly, he jumped up and shouted, "Any chance of a lift mate!" But then, as he focused his eyes on the back of the barge he realized it was a woman operating the tiller. Jesse blushed and quickly apologized, he then doffed his hat to the woman, who shouted, "You can ride on the front if you want!" Jesse quickly slapped Henry with his cap and began running along the towpath until he was in line with the front of the barge. He then jumped cleanly onto the front of the barge. Henry followed grabbing hold of Jesse so he didn't go completely across the barge and end up in the canal.

Henry settled on the roof of the barge and shouted back to the woman, "Where you bound for ma'am?" The lady flicked back the brow of her hat which was held in place with a large red ribbon and said, "Macclesfield, and call me Sarah." She then pulled her shawl up around her shoulders. Henry turned to Jesse and whispered, "A bit of a looker." He then made a kissing sound with his lips. Jesse quickly nudged Henry and said, "Shut up ya fool." He then turned his back on Henry and looked towards the horse, "Who's guiding the horse?" Jesse asked. Henry sat up and looked towards the horse, "Well someone is. I can see the little legs under the horse." Jesse quickly jumped onto the towpath and ran towards the horse. He stared around the front of the horse to find a small scruffy looking kid hanging onto the harness of the horse, "That's Samuel, he's my son!" Sarah shouted as she began to pull on the tiller. "Hi ya Sam," Jesse said, holding out his hand for it to be shaken. "My name's Samuel, not Sam!" Samuel growled. He then, with one clean swipe, wiped his snotty nose on an already snot covered sleeve.

Sarah began steering the barge around a left hand corner which led to two small locks. Samuel led the horse towards the locks whilst saying to Jesse, "Come on then, make yourself useful and get the lock gates open." Jesse looked at Samuel and said to Henry, "He's a cheeky little bugger, isn't he?" Henry just laughed and said, "You'd better do as you are told, otherwise the little boss will give you a thrashing with the frail." Jesse laughed and opened the lock. He watched as the barge slowly entered. As the barge passed him, he noticed that Henry wasn't laid on the barge roof at the front any longer but was now laughing and joking with Sarah at the back of the barge. "Keep ya mind on the job!" Jesse told Henry sternly. Sarah handed Jesse the windless and Henry began bending and acting like an old barge hand, "Aye boss aye… right you are boss." Henry began fingering his cap rim with a juddering finger whilst grinning at Jesse. Eventually, he burst into laughter with Sarah joining in. Jesse didn't say anything he just stomped off, "What's the matter with them two?" Samuel asked Jesse who was by now becoming very angry at Henry's behaviour, "Don't ask me! I'm no expert in the ways of love!" Jesse snapped. Amongst a lot of laughing and giggling, they eventually passed through the lock. Jesse jumped back aboard the front of the barge and threw the windless down onto the wooden decking. It clattered its way to a corner where it stayed stuck. Jesse could still hear the annoying giggles coming from the back of the barge and tried to block it out by whistling. He then began to act as if he wasn't bothered by the giggling and started to look around from his position at the front of the barge, what beautiful countryside, he thought. Just then he realized something was wrong, again the sun was on the wrong side. Immediately, he started to call Henry, but there was no answer, just more giggling. Jesse tried again to call Henry but this time he called as loud as he could, "Henry!" He screamed. Henry was annoyed by Jesse's interruption and screamed back, "What is it Jesse? What's up with you now?" "Were going the wrong way again, the suns on the wrong side again." Henry shook his head and said, "Oh, you're back on that one, are you?" Henry looked at Sarah and asked her quietly, "Are we on the Macclesfield Canal?" Sarah nodded her head and asked, "Why?" Henry replied quietly, "Oh... nothing, it's just him up

front, he's got some funny ways. He keeps imagining things." He then shouted back to Jesse, "Don't worry our Jesse. We're on the right canal heading north." "Jesse thought for a moment, looked up at the sun and then shouted back, "No, we're not, we're heading south." Henry again looked at Sarah who politely said, "North, south, who knows? All I know is that we're on the Macclesfield Canal heading for Macclesfield."

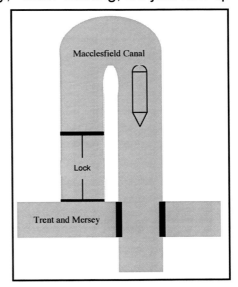

Furiously, Henry made his way hand over hand down the side of the barge to the front where he began snarling and screaming at Jesse. He was just about to give Jesse a real piece of his mind when the barge began to turn. The sun started to quickly move around from one side to the other. With head raised to the skies both lads watched in amazement and then Henry said, "Satisfied?" Jesse nodded and sat down next to the windless without saying another word. Henry returned to the back of the barge and said in amazement, "What happened?" Sarah laughed and explained, "The canal is like a u-nail here, it bends round just like a u-nail, first one direction then the other. Are we heading in the right direction for your friend now?" Henry hesitated and then answered, "I think so and he's not my friend, he's my brother."

By the end of the day Samuel began to tire of walking the horse along the towpath. He started moaning so Jesse took over for the last hour before darkness fell. The hour past quickly and Jesse pulled the horse to a halt. "That'll do us for today," Jesse said to himself as they arrived at a horse changing station just outside Macclesfield. Jesse led the horse to the stable and when he returned there was no sign of Henry or Sarah. He noticed light coming from the barge hutch and the thought of warmth and food came to Jesse's mind. He started to head towards the hutch when a small voice said, "They don't want disturbing. We've to sleep in the stables." Jesse turned around to see Samuel stood there holding a round loaf and a chunk of cheese, "Mum's said we've to get a bottle of ale from the pub and spend the night in the stables, come on, she's given me a tanner." Jesse looked back towards the barge and could see shadows moving through the crack of light that bordered the small hutch door. He tutted and then followed Samuel to the pub.

The next morning it was cold and a frost had penetrated the small hutch where the stove had gone out. Henry was the first to materialize from the hutch saying, "What's for breakfast my sweet love?" Sarah replied from still inside the hutch, "We need to light this stove first. Then I'll cook some bacon for breakfast." Henry, delighted by this said, "No problem my love, I'll fetch some wood." And with that, he tripped off down the towpath picking up wood as he went. Loaded up with arms full of wood Henry arrived back at the barge just as Jesse and Samuel appeared from the direction of the stable. Jesse rubbed his back and neck before saying, "I'm getting too old for lying on stable floors." "Never mind our Jesse, come and get some bacon down ya," said Henry as the wood wobbled in his arms. He clutched it tighter to stop it from crashing to the floor.

Samuel had already disappeared inside the hutch and harsh words could be heard coming from the hutch. When Henry and Jesse entered the hutch an awkward silence descended. Henry smiled at Samuel, who pushed past him saying, "What are you smiling at? Do you think you're the first?" He then stomped out through the hutch door and plonked himself down on the bench at the side of the tiller; his face was as long as a fiddle. Henry fed the wood into a small hole at the top of the stove, he then lit it. Sarah instantly covered the hole with a small black lid that clattered as it slotted into place. She then opened a small vent at the chimney and waited for the stove to draw; when it became hot enough Sarah covered the top of the stove with a large frying pan, which had been hung up on the wall of the hutch. She then opened a brown paper bag and took out a large piece of bacon; it went straight into the pan where it gave out a large crackle. Sarah turned and opened a cupboard. She took out a round loaf and began cutting it into slices using a knife which she took from the bottom of the same cupboard. Henry grabbed two slices of bread and shouted, "Come on then love, I'm ready for it!" He was expecting to receive the whole piece of bacon. However, his face changed when Sarah began cutting up the piece into four. "Do you think I'm made of money?" She said handing Henry his share of the bacon.

After breakfast, Sarah said, "Right! Got to go and collect my wages from the boss. Come on Samuel, you can come with me, instead of moping around here." She then turned to Henry and said lovingly, "See you when I get back. Ok!" Henry nodded his head and said, "Yes love. Jesse and I will clean up the barge and get it ready for loading." Jesse's head spun quickly but Henry calmed him before he had time to say anything by waving him off and puckering up his lips. Sarah and Samuel walked away from the barge along the towpath watched by Henry and Jesse. Just before they disappeared altogether Henry gave them a last wave and then quickly he turned to Jesse and said, "Come on brother, let's get going before they get back." Jesse was startled and said, "What! I thought you were all Lovie-Dovie with her." Henry laughed and said, "Don't be silly, it was lust, not love!" He tapped Jesse in the middle of his chest with the back of his hand, whilst grinning. Henry then descended into the hutch. He began looking around and grabbed the little green bundle from the corner of the hutch. Henry opened the bundle and laid it on the deck of the hutch saying, "We'll need this, and this, and that'll come in." After filling the bundle with all the items that Henry thought they might need, he finally grabbed the brown paper bag which contained the last of the un-cooked bacon and walked back up onto the tiller deck. Jesse seeing the brown paper bag said, "Henry you can't take that. It's all they've got." "No it isn't!" Henry snapped. "She's gone to get wages, hasn't she? She'll be able to buy some more, we can't, unless you've got some money!" Jesse fell silent and shook his head in disapproval as he stepped down onto the towpath. Henry threw the bundle over his shoulder and put his arm around Jesse saying, "Don't worry, they'll survive."

The lads left the boarders of Macclesfield glancing over their shoulders. However, they were still heading north and that was the important thing. They'd managed to cadge a few lifts here and there and all went well until they arrived at the junction between the Ashton Canal and the Peak Forest Canal. At the junction Jesse sat down on a black dry stone wall and began eating the last of the bread from the little green bundle, "There's not much left to eat," he said looking across at Henry, who was stretching and bending on the towpath. "I wonder where we are," said Henry, showing no concern for the food situation. "Don't know but there are two kids coming up the towpath, ask them where we are and which way we should go now." Henry looked down the towpath and laughed, "There only kids they won't know anything." Henry leant back against the wall and waited for the children to get close enough to ask them.

As they approached Henry noticed the tallest of the children had an umbrella with him so jokingly Henry asked, "Are you expecting rain lad?" The child stopped and said, "What's it to you mister?" Henry grinned and looked at Jesse. "We've got a right cheeky little bugger here our Jesse." Jesse nodded his head and said, "They remind me of when we were kids." Jesse jumped down off the wall, dusted his pant seat and walked towards the lads, "What's your name lad?" The lad thought for a moment and then replied, "James Higgins and that's my little brother John, he's four." Jesse knelt down so that his eyes were level with the lad's eyes and asked, "Do you know where we are lad?" Again James thought for a moment and then replied quickly, "Are you daft mister, were on the canal bank, look! Can't you see it mister?" The lad pointed to the canal and Henry laughed, "Told you they wouldn't know anything." Jesse thanked James and returned to the wall. After watching the children disappear down the towpath, Henry joined him, "What are we going to do now?" Henry asked.

Just then there was a loud wailing sound. It was coming from a warehouse on the otherside of the canal. "Must be dinner time," Henry said. The warehouse began to empty. Men and women came scurrying out from its doors as they made their way home for dinner. After a couple of minutes, the canal fell silent again. The silence was interrupted by a dishevelled looking man wearing a red and black spotted neckerchief. "Have ya seen two young lads here a bout's?" The man asked Henry who instantly recognized the man and didn't answer.

The man approached slowly, he suddenly became nervous for some reason. Henry, who was by now leaning on the wall at the side of Jesse, tried to make eye contact with the man, but the man quickly dropped his head and suddenly put his hands in his pocket as he hastily tried to pass them by. It was obvious that the man had recognized Henry. As the man drew level, Henry said, "Excuse me mate," the man didn't answer, he just continued past, but Henry was having none of it, he grabbed the man by the elbow and said, "I'm talking to you mate." The man looked up and instantly Henry was convinced it was who he thought it was, "Don't I know you?" Henry asked. The man was quick to reply and said, "No mate. I don't think so, you're mistaken." Henry stepped closer to the man and stared at him right in the face before slowly saying, "Yes I do, you were on the warrior with me. You're Tom Moore! I'd recognize that mucky neckerchief anywhere." Quickly, Henry grabbed the neckerchief and pulled it from around Tom's neck to reveal the hangman's mark. "There! That's the mark where the lads nearly hung you for thieving grub." The man quickly pulled his elbow out of Henry's grip and then looked closely at Henry. Acting surprised the man said, "Oh… it's you Henry. I thought you'd bought it in the fire." He pulled the neckerchief free from Henry's hand and began tying it back around his neck.

Henry grinned and said, "I thought those marines had done for you." Tom looked towards Jesse and grinning said, "They nearly did! I got a bayonet in the side and fell overboard." Tom lifted his shirt to reveal a large puncher hole where the bayonet had wounded him. Jesse jumped down off the wall and walked towards Tom to take a closer look, "This is my kid brother, Jesse." Jesse nodded his head and shook Tom's hand, "What are you doing up this way?" Tom asked tucking his shirt back into his trousers. "Were on our way up north to seek work, it's said there's plenty of work up north," Henry replied. At this point Jesse remembered what Henry had said about Tom Moore and what a nasty piece of work he was, so reluctantly Jesse decided to ask, "Can you tell us where we are? And which way is north?" Tom laughed and said, "You don't even know where you are!" He broke out into a full blown laughter fit. "It's not that funny," Henry said feeling a little uncomfortable.

After Tom had stopped laughing, he said, "Well. This place is called the Portland Basin and that way is Manchester along the Ashton Canal." Tom pointed up the canal towards a pub. "And that over there is The Ash Inn where you can buy me the best pint in Ashton whilst I think about which way you should be going to get up north." He chuckled and set off towards the pub, on the way towards the pub Henry, having no money, started to make up excuses to leave. Tom realized immediately Henry's predicament and set him at ease by saying, "Don't worry about the money, the innkeepers an old warrior resident." He winked his right eye and said, "If you know what I mean." Henry fell silent as they entered the inn but Jesse was still a little uneasy about Tom. Furthermore, he couldn't believe he was going to meet another escaped prisoner from the warrior. They sat down at a small table in the corner of the inn which was just out of sight of the doorway and waited.

However, it turned out that the innkeeper was quite a nice chap and was only too willing to feed them and allow them to stay in the stables overnight. But, he did insist that they be gone before dawn the next morning. "After all," he said. "I don't want to attract any unwelcome attention, now do I?" Henry

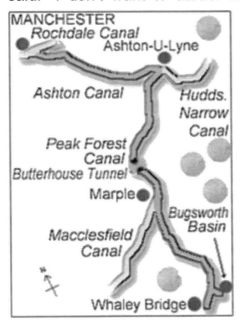

nodded and said, "Cheers," as he began supping the head off the first of three pints of stout which the innkeeper had laid on the table on a round tray. A couple of minutes later the landlord returned with bread and two types of cheese saying, "It's not much but since it's for nothing I suppose it'll do." Henry and Jesse were very grateful to the innkeeper and thanked him. They also reassured him that they would definitely be gone before dawn.

After spending an hour talking and drinking the pints of stout they quickly scoffed the bread and cheese. Henry burped loudly and said, "I needed that." Tom stood up and said, "Come on and I'll show you which way to go." They all stood up and began to walk back outside. They nodded to the innkeeper

who was busily wiping a glass at the back of a small bar as they left. Outside, they stood for a couple of minutes looking down the canal. Tom pointed out which way to go, "That's the Huddersfield Narrow Canal over there, it leads to Huddersfield and Yorkshire, it isn't far from Huddersfield to Mirfield so you'll soon be there," he said. Just then James and his little brother John appeared from under a bridge. James was twirling the umbrella above his head, "Arr! There are the little buggers I'm looking for!" Tom said angrily. He set off running after the lads shouting back from the top of a bridge, "See ya lads, hope you find what you're looking for up north, but remember hard work kills horses!" And with that, he waved and began chasing the lads up the towpath at the otherside of the canal.

Jesse and Henry decided to relax for a couple of hours by just sitting on the canal towpath. They just sat there among the long grass watching the barges sail by, "There are plenty of barges on this canal. We should be able to get a lift from here without much trouble," Jesse said whilst stretching. Henry stood up and said, "Come on our kid, let's get some sleep, it's getting late." Jesse stood up and both walked back to the inn.

The stables were at the back of the inn and were a little lacking in straw. On entering the stable they met a young barge hand changing his horse. "Not a lot of straw in here mate," Jesse said to the barge hand. Who turned and asked, "Why? Are you spending the night in here?" Henry spoke up and said, "Well we were hoping to." Leading the horse out of the barn the barge hand said, "There's more straw in the loft, that's where I usually sleep when I have to stop here, but the boss won't stop whilst there's daylight, so we'll be going onto the narrow canal." Jesse began to look around and saw a rickety old ladder leading up to a small straw filled loft.

Henry started to climb the ladder, "Close the doors our Jesse before you come up." Jesse ran towards the bottom of the ladder and said, "Cheeky sod! You close the doors!" He pulled Henry down by his leg and quickly sprinted to the top of the ladder before Henry had managed to get himself up off the floor. He then covered himself with straw so Henry couldn't find him. Eventually, Henry came to the top of the ladder and said, "Where are you? Ya bugger!" Jesse didn't answer. He just covered his mouth with his hands to prevent Henry from hearing his giggles. It was dark in the loft and the only light was a crack around a small door in the apex of the loft. Henry pushed open the door which allowed the last light of dusk to enter the loft. Henry stood for a moment looking out through the door at the exceptional views over the three canals that met at the basin. The canals seem to flicker as the last of the sun reflected purple on the surface of the water. Just then Jesse appeared from under the straw and said, "What ya doing?" Henry turned and said, "Oh nothing, just looking at the views, you can even see the front door of the inn from here. Look!" Henry pointed out through the door. Jesse came closer to have a look but before he reached the door Henry had grabbed him around the waist and was wrestling him to the loft floor saying, "Pull me off the ladder would you, think your tuff do you?" Both lads rolled around in the straw giggling and laughing until both tired of it. Eventually, Henry stood up and pulled out some straw from his hair, he closed the door carefully and the loft fell into darkness once more.

Next morning the lads were awoken by the innkeeper who was stood at the top of the ladder, "Lads, lads are you awake?" Henry sat up, rubbed his eyes and said, "Yes, we're ready for off as we promised." "You can't go just yet. There's something going on outside. There's a lot of police about." Henry stood up and walked to the ladder, "Ok, we'll sit tight until the coast is clear." The innkeeper put up a thumb and descended the ladder. Jesse stirred and asked, "What's going on our Henry?" Henry pushed open the small door and said, "I don't know, but there's a lot of police wondering about outside. Look!" He pointed towards the canal bank. Jesse eagerly joined Henry at the small door and began watching as two strapping police officers began dipping long poles into the canal, "What are they doing?" Jesse asked. "Looks like their fishing something or someone out of the canal," Henry replied.

After about ten minutes one officer shouted, "I've hooked one," other officers quickly rushed to his aid. Jesse began standing on his tiptoes to see what it was that the officer was pulling out of the canal. It appeared to be a small bundle of rags, which was pulled roughly onto the wharf and left there. Another, more senior officer, then arrived, he began examining the rags. Eventually, he began straightening the bundle of rags into a recognisable object. At that moment, reality struck home and to Jesse's horror, he began recognizing what it was the officer had pulled out of the canal. It was the small limp lifeless body of James, one of the lads he'd spoken to the day before. He knew it was him because he was still gripping the umbrella. "Poor little buggers, it's those lads we saw yesterday," Jesse said sadly to Henry, who drew back from the door and said. "That bastard has killed them. It must have been him. Why else would he have been chasing them like that?" Jesse thought for a moment and said, "What are we going to do?" Henry shook his head and banged his fist hard on the wall before saying, "What can we do? We can't do anything, we can't go to the police, now can we?" Jesse slowly had to agree and shrugged his shoulders.

But then suddenly, Jesse moved back from the small door and said, "God! It's Earle." Henry quickly rushed back to the door and peeped over the edge saying, "It can't be him we're too far north for him. How would he know we were here?" Henry spent a couple of minutes looking down onto the canal. By now he could see a couple of small black cloths covering the bodies of the two lads laid on the wharf. And there, stood with the senior officer, in deep conversation was Earle. "You're right our Jesse, its Earle!" Henry said to Jesse, who began to panic. "Calm down Jesse, it must be luck. He doesn't really know we're here. All we have to do is to wait!" Henry slowly closed the door, but left a small gap through which he could see what was going on.

It was a couple of hours later when a small black box coach arrived being pulled by a single black horse. The officer jumped down and saluted the senior officer. He then walked around to the back of the coach and opened the door which revealed layers of stretches. The officer pulled out the bottom stretcher and placed it at the side of the first bundle. There was then a short pause as the senior office went to the feet end of the bundle, gently and in one movement, they placed the body onto the stretcher. Again there was a short pause and then the body was carried back to the coach. It was slid into the coach and not a word was said, the process was repeated for the second bundle, again in silence. The only things to be heard was the coach door as the officer slammed it shut and the twisting of a squeaky handle as the door was locked.

Eventually, the wharf began to clear and the only person left standing on the wharf was Earle. He walked up and down the wharf for about ten minutes. You could see he was deep in thought by the expression on his face. Suddenly, and without warning a gust of wind caught the small door, and it swung open slamming against the wall. Henry quickly grabbed the door and closed it but the sudden movement had attracted Earle's attention, He stopped walking and looked straight up at the door. Henry quickly put his eye against the crack around the door to see what Earle was going to do. There was a long pause, Henry and Jesse held their breaths, Earle just stood there glaring up at the door. He started to walk towards the stables. He withdrew his truncheon and was just about to enter the stable when the innkeeper said, "Would sir like a breakfast? It's free to the boys of the constabulary this morning." Earle hesitated but then replaced his truncheon and said, "Why not."

Whilst Earle was inside the inn Jesse and Henry didn't hesitate, they slid down the ladder and out past the inn towards the Huddersfield Canal. They had to creep under the windows of the inn but once clear of the windows both made a run for it and they didn't stop running until the inn was out of sight.

Gasping for breath both lads slowed down and sat on a dry stone wall which lined the first part of the Huddersfield Canal, whilst sitting there Jesse began looking around, he spent a minute reading the sign, which read Whitelands Basin. Beyond the sign, there was a string of mill workers old dismal cottages. They were black and dirty curtains hung in the small windows which overlooked the canal, "Tell ya what." Jesse said attracting Henry's attention, "What?" Henry replied. "There are an awful lot of wool mills around here and if you ask me the workers don't seem much better off than we were back at home." "You're right there our Jesse. Look at the state of those cottages over there." Henry pointed towards the black cottages. Just as he did two burly police officers appeared from around the side of the cottages. Henry panicked and said, "Quick! It's the police!" He then quickly grabbed hold of Jesse and fell backwards over the wall pulling Jesse with him.

On the otherside of the wall, both lads' landed in nettles, at first they didn't feel anything, but as they spun around and quickly scurried back towards the wall to see what was happening. Their stings began to penetrate, "Did you have to pull me into the nettles with you?" Jesse screamed angrily. "Sssshh.... Or they'll hear you," Henry replied as he began staring through the gaps in the dry stone wall. Intensively both lads watched the cottages as more police arrived, "There's Earle!" Jesse said. He'd no sooner said the words when Tom Moore appeared in the cottage doorway. He was being wrestled through the doorway by the two burly officers, who eventually grounded Tom outside the cottage. With his knee firmly embedded in Tom's back the first officer cuffed Tom's hands behind his back. The second officer put some leg irons around Tom's ankles. Eventually, after much struggling, Tom was stood up and led away by the officers with Earle walking about two yards behind him.

Jesse stood up and brushed some of the nettles off his jacket. He then began looking around for some dock leaves to rub on his nettle stings. Meanwhile Henry had leaped back over the wall and with his hand over his eye brows he quickly scanned all around. Satisfied that there was no-one around, Henry quietly said, "It's all clear now our Jesse, you can come back over." Jesse held out his hand and Henry pulled him clear of the nettles. "Give us a bit of your dock leaf," asked Henry as he sat back down on the wall. Jesse tore a rather large dock leaf in half and handed half to Henry who began rubbing his nettle stings with it. They spent a few minutes in silence whilst they eased their stings with the dock leaves. Then Jesse said, "Do you think he'll tell Earle about us?" Henry paused for a moment before answering, and then said, "What! Tom Moore." Jesse nodded his head and Henry exclaimed, "He might be a murderer, thief and all round scoundrel but one thing he isn't and that's a

186

snitch, he won't say a word, honour among thieves and all that. Come on let's get moving before anything else happens around here." Jesse threw down his half of the dock leaf and began walking but then there was an almighty scream. It came from the same small cottage Tom Moore had just been wrestled out off earlier. The lads were stopped in their tracks by the scream. They both looked across towards the cottage and there in the doorway stood an old man. He had tears in his eyes. In his arms there was a small woman wearing a mill apron and shawl. The woman was distraught. She screamed, "My beautiful sons, my little sons!" Henry looked at Jesse and said calmly, "That must be the mother." Jesse, with a lump in his throat replied, "Aye... the poor woman. I hope they hang that bastard!"

They walked along the canal for quite some distance, neither felt like talking. They hadn't been able to hitch a ride but all that changed when they walked through a short tunnel. At the otherside, there was a short old chap sat at the back of his barge smoking a pipe and enjoying the morning sun. "Morning," Henry said politely. The old man removed his pipe, slavered a little and then lifted the pipe up to make a greeting gesture with it. He then replied, "Morning," in a very strong Scottish accent, "Any chance of a lift?" Jesse enquired. The old man returned his pipe to his mouth and through gritted teeth asked, "Why, where ya going?" Henry butted in and said, "Up north!" The man grinned and removed his pipe, "The north! I'm from the north and it's a mighty big place you're talking about, can you be a little more specific." Before Henry had time to answer Jesse quickly butted in and said, "Mirfield! Is it far?" The old man puffed on his pipe for a few moments more and then said, "Well as it happens, we're bound for Mirfield, the wife and I." Jesse couldn't believe their luck and quickly asked, "Any chance, we might cadge a lift? We can't pay ya but were both hard workers and we're quite prepared to work our passage."

The old man again resumed his pipe smoking and then after a few moments he stood up and said. "I'll tell ya what I'll do," he pointed his pipe at Jesse. "If you help me get through the locks and then help me walk her through at Standedge. I'll pay ya a bob each and that includes unloading when we get to Mirfield." There was a long pause and then the old man said, "Well, what about it?" Jesse looked at Henry, who gave a single nod of his head and shrugged his shoulders. Instantly, Jesse spat on his hand and shouted, "What have we got to lose?" He then jumped down onto the back of the barge and shook the old man's hand saying, "I'm Jesse, and he's Henry." The old man touched the rim of his cap with his pipe and then popped it back into his mouth saying, "McCullum," as he did so.

McCullum sat down on the hatchway edge and began calmly sucking on his pipe. Henry threw the small green bundle on to the roof of the barge and then sat down on a nearby wall to rub his bad leg, "What are we waiting for?" Jesse asked, looking around for a reason to stay. Calmly McCullum replied, "All in good time Jesse, all in good time." Just then the hatch door was slid all the way back by some old rheumatic fingers and the smell, it nearly knocked Jesse clean off his feet. "Arr.... Dinner is served," said McCullum as he knocked out his pipe into the canal. An old hunchbacked lady hobbled out of the hutch with a large spoon and a bowl. Jesse sat down at the otherside of the tiller and began savouring the smells. He watched intensively as the old man spooned up what looked like stew.

After a couple of spoonfuls McCullum turned to Jesse and said with a glint in his eye, "Aye… the old lass make's the best stew this side of Manchester." He then slurped another large spoonful into his mouth. It wasn't long before McCullum began to feel guilty and every spoonful became harder to swallow, "Oh for Pete's sake!" He said frustratingly. He stood up and shouted, "Agnes, you'd better bring these lads something to eat before they eat me." Instantly Agnes appeared at the hatch with two bowls in her hands saying in anticipation, "I thought as much. They both looked so hungry so I've already prepared two more bowls." Agnes bent down and placed the bowls on the deck of the barge. She placed a large spoon at the side of each bowl and returned to the hutch. Jesse and Henry didn't wait to be invited to eat. Rudely, they both eagerly slurped away all the stew until the last drop had disappeared from the bottom of the bowl. After finishing, Henry exclaimed, "That was the best stew I've ever tasted." Jesse nodded his head in agreement and then continued to lick the bowl clean, "Put your bowls down there lads and let's get started," the old man said pointing to a space just in front of the hatch. Henry grabbed a long pole which ran down the side of the barge and began pushing the barge away from the wharf, "Right Jesse, pull her on." Henry shouted as the barge floated into the middle of the canal. Jesse quickly removed the horse's nosebag and began leading it down the towpath towards the first lock.

It wasn't long before they came across the first of the locks, then another, then another. Jesse began to get fed up with the locks and as he approached another lock he turned and said to McCullum, "This lock is numbered 32W, how many more of these bloody locks are there before we reach Mirfield?" The old man's face lit up and a broad grin began to establish itself across his face, he hesitated for a moment and then replied, "Oh, there are seventy four locks altogether." Jesse's face sank at the prospect of seventy four locks having to be opened and closed before reaching Mirfield. McCullum, trying not to laugh, could see that Jesse wasn't happy so to relieve his anxiety, he said, "Don't worry Jesse you've already done thirty two of them on this side, you've only got forty two left on the otherside to do." McCullum couldn't help himself but the expression on Jesse's faced began to make him laugh. He quickly took a swig of his tea from a dirty cracked mug which was sat on the roof of the barge to try and hide his laughter. By this time Jesse was beginning to realize what McCullum had said, suddenly he stopped what he was doing and said, "Hang on a minute. What do you mean, thirty two on this side and forty two on the otherside, the otherside of what?" McCullum lifted his head, looked down the canal towards the hills and pointed, "Of that!" He said. Jesse and Henry both looked off into the distance at what McCullum was pointing at and there, in the distance, was a black hole, it stood out against the lush green backdrop of the hillside grass. Jesse and Henry both said surprisingly, "It's a tunnel!" McCullum wiped a run of tea from off his chin using the back of his hand, "Aye, but this is not just any old tunnel! This is the Standedge Tunnel! It's the highest, the longest and the deepest tunnel in the world. And if we don't hurry up we'll lose the light and won't get there tonight." Jesse began to rush back to the horse when McCullum shouted after him, "Nice and steady Jesse. We won't get through the tunnel tonight anyway. There's usually a queue so don't rush, nice and steady, and we'll get there before dark. Then you and Henry can spend the night in the Transhipment Shed." Sure enough as darkness appeared the barge arrived at the wharf in front of the tunnel and just as the old man had predicted there was a queue of three barges waiting patiently to go through the tunnel.

Jesse put the horse into the stable for the night and then joined Henry and the other men who were inside the Transhipment Shed. The shed was lined with straw and had blankets running down both sides. Jesse picked the first blanket he came to that was empty and laid flat out on it. Henry took the next blanket and then asked out loud, "I wonder why this is called a Transhipment Shed?" He then tucked the little green bundle under his head for a pillow. Just then a voice from the next blanket said, "It's the shed where the goods were kept and transferred from the barges to pack horses for the trek over the mountain back when there was no tunnel. Now that there is a tunnel and there's no need for goods to be transferred, the shed is used as a sleep over for bargemen and their crews whilst waiting to get through the tunnel. "Are you a bargeman?" Henry asked the stranger, who replied, "No, I'm a legger. I work in the tunnel." Henry shrugged his shoulders and looked at Jesse. Who also seemed mystified by the man's occupation and just shrugged his shoulders back at Henry. Henry was by now pretending he knew what the man's occupation was. "Oh right, I see," Henry said as he turned over and closed his eyes.

The next morning Jesse and Henry were up early, they decided to get a closer look at the tunnel. They lazily walked towards the stone entrance of the tunnel. As they approached, to the right of the entrance, they noticed a group of hard weather worn men stood talking below a sign. The sign read, 'leggers 1s 6d each.' The men were wearing clogs or boots with steel segs on the soles. Some of them had chopped off the lower legs off their trousers and were showing long bright red socks. At the side of the men were planks of wood stacked up against the wall. On the floor in front of the planks were long scruffy red leather cushions, which were well worn. Jesse and Henry sheepishly ignored the men and began to look down the tunnel, "Henry can you see the other end of the tunnel?" Jesse asked Henry who was staring down the tunnel and rubbing his eyes. Henry had another good look and then replied bluntly, "No, afraid not!"

Just then out of the black darkness of the tunnel came a light, faint at first, but as it got nearer it began to flicker in the wind of the tunnel. It was a barge with a candle on the front of it. As the barge approached, two men became visible, they were laid on their backs, their legs were out stretched, and they appeared to be walking along the ceiling of the tunnel, "What the hell are they doing?" asked Henry. Jesse looked into the tunnel and replied, "I don't know but it looks very iffy. What if they fall in? The barge would run straight over them!" Both lads stood there watching as the men legged closer and closer to the end of the tunnel. "Mind your back!" The men shouted as they gave a final push on the ceiling of the tunnel. The barge slowly floated out of the tunnel and the men rolled backwards off the plank and stood up. The first man then threw a rope to the men stood waiting. One of them caught it and pulled the

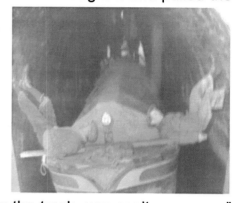

barge towards the wharf where he tied it up as it bumped its way along the water's edge of the wharf. The men on the barge then stretched and jumped down onto the towpath.

Suddenly, McCullum appeared from the barge hutch and shouted, "Come on then lads. It's our turn to go through. Henry, since you've got a bad leg you'll have to take the horse over the hill." Henry stood there with a gaping mouth, stunned by McCullum's words. "Go on then. Get on with it. Just follow the track, you can't go wrong," said McCullum as he untied the barge. Henry shut his mouth and disappeared in the direction of the stables. McCullum then turned to Jesse and said, "Right Jesse! Grab that plank and put it along the front of the barge." Jesse reluctantly took the plank and laid it across the front of the barge. McCullum then threw down a red leather cushion which landed on top of the plank with a dull thud, "Right! Get your back against that cushion," McCullum said as he lay down on the otherside of the cushion. Jesse looked at McCullum and then said, "You're kidding me, right!" "Oh you're not going to welch on our agreement, are you?" McCullum blurted this out so everyone could hear. Jesse hesitated and didn't say anything he just looked down at the place where he was supposed to lay and shook his head. McCullum chirped up again and said, "A deal's a deal. You said you would help me walk her through the tunnel and unload for a shilling. That's the deal!" Jesse, who had never gone back on a shaken agreement in his life, said, "You conned me old man, you conned me," and with that Jesse layed down on the plank opposite McCullum.

McCullum was careful not to let Jesse hear him grinning as he told him how easy legging was, "Right Jesse, legging is easy," he said. "All you have to do is walk slowly along the ceiling of the tunnel as if you were walking up a hill." The barge entered the tunnel and Jesse began walking along the ceiling, "Nice and steady put one leg over the other and grab the plank behind you with both hands." McCullum told Jesse, who was still feeling nervous and as he looked down into the murky waters of the canal, he thought to himself. I'd better not end up in there. Otherwise there'll be trouble. The barge slowly began to make its way along the tunnel. Jesse occasionally looked back to see the light at the start of the tunnel beginning to disappear as the tunnel began to bend. Jesse started to pass the time by watching the bricks in the ceiling pass him by. Well, it was the only thing he could see in the candle lit tunnel. Occasionally, the bricks would change slightly in colour, sometimes there be no bricks at all, just solid rock.

Three hours later the sweat was pouring out of Jesse and his legs felt like they were about to fall off, not to mention his back that was being rubbed clean of skin. In agony Jesse screamed, "How much further old man?" The old man took a long puff on his pipe which for a moment added a red glow to the ceiling. "Oh about another hour," the old man replied, trying not to laugh. Jesse couldn't believe that the tunnel was so long, he kept looking forward down the tunnel into the abyss in the hope of seeing the light, but there was no sign. Then just as he was about to give up hope, he saw a light, it was an unusual light, it certainly wasn't the sort of light that you would associate with daylight. Jesse kept watching the light, and then he suddenly realized it was getting closer. The light was nearly upon them when Jesse realized it was another barge coming the other way. Quickly, Jesse began to panic, "McCullum! Old man! There's another barge coming towards us, we're going to crash!" he screamed. McCullum replied calmly, "Don't worry Jesse. You can stop legging for a moment now." McCullum got up and walked to the back of the barge. He mumbled something in his Scottish accent as he went but Jesse didn't quite catch what he'd said. McCullum gently grabbed the tiller and pushed it hard over. Slowly the barge drifted off to one side allowing the other barge to pass by slowly. It was a close run thing, so close in fact, that Jesse thought the barges were going to become wedged between the walls of the tunnel. Jesse stood in the candlelight watching as the other barge past by. But then suddenly there was a loud crack, a splash, followed by loud laughter coming from the other barge. Jesse spun around to see that the plank of wood had gone along with the red leather cushion. McCullum quickly came back to the front of the barge and said furiously, "Didn't you lift the plank like I told you to?" Jesse just stood there shaking his head. McCullum peered over the front of the barge and there about six feet away was the plank drifting away from the barge, "Quick!" McCullum said to Jesse. "Get in and get it out before it disappears altogether." Jesse without thinking jumped over the front of the barge and retrieved the plank of wood. There was no sign of the leather cushion.

It took another hour to leg their way to the end of the tunnel where they found Henry waiting for them with the horse. "You took your time," Henry said grinning all over his face. Jesse threw him the rope and said, "Very funny." Henry began pulling the barge towards the wharf when he noticed that Jesse was dripping, "What happen to you? You look wet!" He said as he tied up the barge to the first mooring ring. Just then McCullum butted in and said, "Oh, he went for a swim in the tunnel." Henry started to laugh, he laughed even louder when Jesse began wringing out his jacket and cap. Just then Agnes appeared with tea and biscuits. "Here get this down ya," she said placing the tray on top of the barge roof. She then grabbed Jesse's jacket and cap and took them into the hutch to dry them on the small stove. The three men sat on deck supping tea and crunching on the biscuits whilst talking about the day's events. After a while, even Jesse began to laugh as he saw the funny side of getting wet whilst retrieving the plank.

After tea Jesse resumed his duties and began leading the horse along the towpath to the first lock. The lock sign read in big black letters on a white oval plaque "42E." Henry shouted from the tiller, "Hey Jesse, look! Lock forty two!" Jesse walked back to the barge and said to Henry, "Aye and you're going to do the first ten whilst I sit at the back of the barge shouting orders out like you do!" Henry, realizing Jesse was exhausted from his legging, didn't argue, he just got up and began opening the lock gates whilst Jesse took a well deserved rest hanging onto the tiller. As they sailed into lock 42E Jesse just sat there feeling fed up and wondering how long it would be before they reached Mirfield. His mind was soon put at rest when the old man tried to cheer him up by saying, "Never mind lad. You'll soon be there. Only 42 more locks to go." Jesse nodded his head as the barge sank into the belly of the lock.

Chapter 9: Mirfield, Procession and Hard Graft.

It was early afternoon before the lads had finished unloading McCullum's barge. The thrifty McCullum paid the lads the shilling he'd promised them, it was all in pennies and ha'pennies, which he had taken from an old tin box that he kept somewhere in the hutch. Henry moaned about the weight of the coins and said, "All this lot will put holes in my pockets." But Jesse, who didn't mind the coins, told Henry to, "Stop moaning, it all spends doesn't it?" Henry sighed and lifted the small green bundle off the top of the barge where he'd left it and threw it over his left shoulder. Whilst doing this McCullum chirped up from the back of the barge and said, "The wife's put you some bread and cheese in your bundle for later, don't thank us for it. It's a bit stale and has been sat on the table for over a week so get it eaten as soon as possible." McCullum then stretched out his hand towards Henry, who shook it vigorously before shouting down into the hutch, "Thanks Agnes, you're a gooden!" Henry turned to Jesse and said, "Come on then, let's get moving." Jesse took a folded cap from his pocket and plonked it on his head. He shook McCullum's hand and touched the rim of the cap with his finger as Agnes appeared at the hutch door. She nodded in acknowledgement and smiled gently. The lads began to walk away from the barge along the towpath. They'd only gone a couple of paces when McCullum shouted after them, "Oh and before I forget, there's an inn just over there by that bridge, it has decent clean lodging and food for those that can afford it."

Jesse and Henry nodded and set off again. When they'd reached the bridge, they climbed the towpath up onto it, where they stood for a moment to admire the view. In the distance, they could see the mills and houses of Mirfield, "Wonder if that's Butt End Mills over there?" Jesse asked. "Probably, it's certainly big enough." Replied Henry as he began waving at the McCullum's barge as it bobbed up and down on the windy waters of the canal. McCullum and Agnes were sat at the rear of the barge on either side of the hutch enjoying some tea. They both waved back and gave big smiles, which Jesse and Henry returned before descending down the otherside of the bridge towards the inn.

As they approached the inn, Jesse said, "The Ship Inn. Well it certainly looks alright. Shall we dump the bundle and get a room before we go and see if these cards are genuine or not." "Aye, we might as well but leave the negotiations to me," Henry replied. The lads entered the inn and were greeted by a hobbling woman with a very bad stoop and a stick. She politely asked, "What can I do for you two then?" She made her way towards a small bar in the corner of the lounge. Henry stepped forwards and said very politely, "We'd like a room please." The woman sat down on a long three legged stool at the otherside of the bar and waited for a while until she caught her breath. She then quickly fingered through a grubby looking book, she hummed and ahhed for a while and then said, "You're in luck. We've got just the one room left and that's two shillings a week with food. In advance please," she quickly held out her fingerless glove covered hand to receive the money. Henry looked across at Jesse, who was shaking his head furiously but Henry continued to negotiate with the woman. "Tell you what I'll do," he said. The woman stopped Henry quickly by saying, "That's the price, take it or leave it!" There was a moments silence and then Henry quickly said, "Ok! We'll take it." Jesse looked to the ceiling in disgust and sighed. He then pulled out the pennies and ha'pennies from his pocket and slapped them down on the bar. "Some negotiator you are," he said removing the bundle from Henry's grasp. "What choice do we have our Jesse?" Henry murmured as they began to follow the old woman upstairs to the room.

At the top of the stairs, they walked down a short dark dismal passageway and at the end the old woman opened a latched locked door which led into the room, the door creaked as she opened it, "There you go. You'll have to share the bed but it's a nice room with a good view of the canal bridge," she said with a grin. Henry and Jesse nervously squeezed past the old woman to enter the room and tested the bed by sitting on it. The old women stood by the door pointing out the good features of the room, which didn't take long. She finally finished by saying, "Tea is served at six sharp in the front lounge. Those that come late don't get any, so don't be late!" And with that, she shut the door and left the lads to look over the room.

It wasn't long before the lads had settled into the room and decided to go and look for some work in the mills they had seen from the bridge, so they walked back along the passageway to the top of the stairs. As they descended the stairs, they could hear voices. About halfway down Henry stopped and put his index finger over his lips. They listened for a moment and then Jesse said in a whisper, "I know that voice." Henry looked back at Jesse and replied, "Yes me too." They slowly descended the rest of the stairs and began to peer around the corner into the lounge.

To their astonishment, there sat at the bar was McCullum, who turned and with a large grin on his face, said, "Ok lads, settled in alright." Just then the old woman appeared and gave McCullum a tankard of ale and some money. Jesse could tell by the sound of the money clanking into McCullum's grubby little hands that it was the pennies and ha'pennies that they had been paid by him, "Have you met my sister?" McCullum said to Henry and Jesse with a smug look on his face. Jesse looked straight at Henry and said in a squeaky voice, "but leave the negotiations to me," Jesse's voice then returned to normal before he continued to say, "Some negotiator you are!" Henry pushed Jesse out through the front door by his left shoulder blade and said, "How was I supposed to know that she was a relative of his?"

Outside the pub Jesse pulled out the scam cards from his jacket pocket. They were a little faded and the black ink had run slightly, but they were still legible. He lifted

Henry Wheatley's and Sons Ltd.
Butt End Mills,
Chadwick Folds Lane,
❧ Mirfield, Yorkshire. ❧

Promises to give the bearer of this card a position in the above mill at a weekly income of 5/- and a place to stay.

them aloft and shouted out loudly, "Now to see if these bloody cards are a scam or not. Let's find Butt End Mill!" They set off back over the bridge onto the main road. At the first tee junction, there was a directional sign with two arrows pointing in opposite directions. The arrow pointing left said in large capital letters 'HUDDERSFIELD' the other arrow read 'DEWSBURY' and pointed to the right. Just below the Huddersfield arrow there was a smaller arrow which read, 'Mirfield' in smaller letters. Both lads turned left and walked towards Mirfield.

They hadn't been walking long when Henry asked, "Are you sure we are going the right way our Jesse?" He began to limp on his bad leg and started to reckon on that it was beginning to ache, "Yes, I'm sure this is the right way. There's only two ways to choose from and the other way leads to Dewsbury." Henry reluctantly continued to walk through Mirfield. They passed a small butcher's then a large hotel called The Black Bull Hotel. After that, at the cross roads, they passed a small bank and some small shops which lined the road. Onwards they travelled along the road, the small shops turned into small houses, little black houses, which again lined the road. Eventually, the houses began to dissipate and the road began to bend as it left Mirfield and headed

out into the open countryside. Eventually, all that could be seen was the river, "Well there's no sign of a mill out here our Jesse," Henry said hoping that Jesse would turn back. "Oh no, then what's that over there?" Jesse said pointing down a steep hill towards a massive mill complex.

They started to descend the hill, stopping occasionally to stand on their tip toes. This enabled them to look over the wall at the mill, which seemed to get larger and larger everytime they stopped to look. Eventually, they arrived at the main gates. The gates were enormous and were painted in a shiny bottle green colour. Jesse tried to open one of the gates, but it was locked. Just then, from a small office just inside the gate, a man appeared dressed in a very smart black and gold uniform. "Come on lad! You'll have to move from there," he said inserting a large brass key into the lock of the first gate. As the man started to open the gates Jesse began explaining to him why they were there, but the man didn't seem interested and began to push Jesse back using his fist, which had a bunch of keys clinched tightly in it. After two or three steps backward Jesse started to push back whilst still trying to explain things. The man didn't listen he just continued to open the gates whilst Jesse followed him around pointing at the cards. Eventually, the man became annoyed and after some effort. He managed to push Jesse back onto the footpath, still annoyed the man said, "Look, just stay there and I'll come and see you in a minute." The man then quickly returned to the small office and pressed a large red dome shaped button at the side of the door which set off a very loud clackson. It was so loud that Jesse had to cover his ears with his hands.

Immediately there was a low rumbling sound which started to get louder and louder until eventually, from every corner of the mill came workers, workers all eager to get home. Jesse now understood why the man had been so keen on moving him back away from the gates. He'd have been crushed in the rush. Jesse and Henry stood well back against the wall, but still they were getting dragged along by the sheer volume of workers. Eventually, Jesse managed to pull himself up onto the wall. "Up here our Henry," Jesse shouted, holding out a hand by which he pulled Henry up onto the wall. It must have been about fifteen minutes before the stream of workers began to ease up enough for Henry and Jesse to jump back down off the wall, "By, that was a near thing our Jesse," Henry said, dusting the back of his trousers with the palms of his hands. Just then the man re-appeared still holding the bunch of keys, "Aye, you can get hurt right easy at home time around these gates, you've got to be very careful! They'll run you down, they don't care!" Jesse quickly held up the scam cards and said, "We've come about." The man stopped Jesse quickly by saying, "I know why you're here lad. Do you think you're the only one?" Jesse instantly dropped the cards and the man continued, "There no good today lad!" "I knew it, there a bloody scam!" Jesse screamed with disappointment. Instantly, Jesse lifted the cards up to chest height and was just about to tear them in half when the man stopped him, "Stop! What are you doing?" he shouted. Jesse hesitated and the man said, "There no good today but they'll be alright tomorrow when the foreman comes back, he's gone home for the day, today." Henry, who was surprised, then asked, "So their real then." "Oh yes, you can get a job here with those cards." Jesse shouted a victorious, "Yes!" And then he punched the air with his fist. The man started to shut the gate and said, "Come back in the morning at six sharp!"

The next morning it was cold and very dark when Jesse and Henry had to drag themselves from their flea ridden bed at the Ship Inn. The darkness seemed to get darker as they staggered their way along the passageway and down the stairs to the front door. Once outside they set off towards the mill along a frost covered road, the only light to show them the way was that of moonlight, which kept disappearing behind low clouds. As they passed The Black Bull Hotel, Henry began to feel that there was something not quite right, his pace began to slow, "What's the matter with you?" Jesse asked, thinking that Henry's leg was playing him up again. "There's something wrong here our Jesse." "What do you mean?" Henry stopped suddenly and said, "Haven't you noticed anything?" There was a pause and then Jesse snapped, "What?" "Where are all the workers?" asked Henry as he looked around. Jesse began to do the same and then quickly replied, "Their probably already hard at work in the mill. Come on, let's get on." Jesse turned and set off towards the mill at a much quicker pace.

It wasn't long before the lads arrived at the mill gates, again they were locked and the whole place was in darkness. Jesse placed his head between the metal bars of the gate and shouted, "Hello! Is there anybody there?" He waited for a moment only to receive a silent reply. He tried this several times and each time he received the same silent reply. On the last occasion the silence was broken by Henry, who began to laugh, this annoyed Jesse, who quickly snapped. "What are you laughing at?" Henry stepped forward and put his hand on Jesse's shoulder, "What have we come to," he said, shaking his head. "Here we are on a cold frosty morning, miles from home, begging for hard work. We must be mad!" Reality struck home for a moment and Jesse began to see the funny side of the situation, he sat down on the kerb edge to think. He slowly said out loud in desperation, "Where is everybody?" There was a moment of deadly silence then Jesse turned to Henry and said quietly, "What do you think is going on our Henry? Where is everybody?" Henry sat down at the side of Jesse, took off his cap and put his arm around Jesse's shoulders before saying, "There's got to be a perfectly reasonable explanation our Jesse, people don't just disappear." Jesse nodded his head in agreement and then made one of his decisions. "Alright then," he said. "We'll wait for a while and if no-one comes; we'll go back to the inn and try to scrounge up something for breakfast, deal!" Henry nodded and both lads sat there waiting for something to happen.

After an hour and a half bums were beginning to turn numb by the cold pavement and nothing had happened, no-one had come. Jesse stood up and said angrily, "That's it, come on, let's go and get some breakfast." He then stomped off up the hill followed by Henry, who had to stand up and start running straight away in order to catch up with Jesse. Out of breath and still

panting both arrived at the top of the hill and came to a halt further along the road outside The Black Bull Hotel. By this time dawn had broken and the sun was laid low in the morning sky causing long shadows across the face of the hotel. Jesse sat down on the top step of the entrance to the hotel. He rested his forearms on his thighs and interlocked his fingers, "Well! What are we going to do now?" He bellowed at Henry, who was by now becoming fed up with Jesse always snarling at him, and said, "I don't know but don't take it out on me. I thought we were going back to the Ship Inn for some breakfast?" Henry sat down on the steps facing the other way and a silence descended over the pair.

All of a sudden, there was a scraping noise followed by a couple of large clunks and then a bang as the bolts of the hotel door were drawn back. The door eventually opened and there stood at the door entrance was a portly man with a black and white striped apron on and a Straw Boater, tilted to one side. "We're not open yet," he said in a very posh voice, so posh in fact that Jesse and Henry stood up quickly thinking they were talking to gentry. Henry removed his cap and asked politely, "Excuse me sir." The landlord stopped what he was doing and looked up. "Can you tell us where everybody is?" Henry asked. The landlord instantly replied, "At the church, at the church young man," and with that he sped off back into the hotel.

The lads stood and watched him disappear from sight down a long dark passageway. However, just as Jesse was going to suggest that they return to the Ship Inn, the butcher, whose shop was just across the yard from The Black Bull, came to the door of his shop. "Aren't you lads going to, 'the do' then?" He asked, wiping the blood from his hands on the already blood stained apron. "What 'do' is this then?" Jesse asked. The butcher let go of his apron and it returned to its normal position, loosely hanging down in front. "It's 'the do' of the year. There's going to be a procession, a party and there's plenty of buckshee food going." The butcher said placing a small sign in front of his shop. At the mention of food Jesse and Henry's ears began to wag. Jesse quickly stepped forward and said, "Well, point us in the right direction then. We'll eat a buckshee anytime of the day, won't we our Henry?" Henry nodded his head and the butcher began to laugh. "You're not from around here, are you lads?" The butcher said trying not to laugh. He then said pointing down the road, "Go down there until you come across a lane on your left. It's called Church Lane, go up Church Lane, you can't miss the church. It's on your right about half a mile up."

Jesse and Henry set off towards Church Lane. They hadn't gone far when they were suddenly stopped in their tracks. In the distance, they could hear music, "What's that?" Henry asked. Jesse pointed down the road towards a crowd of people who were fast approaching them, "Looks like the processions on its way," he said. Both lads stood there waiting for the procession to approach. The nearer it got the bigger and louder it got as people began to come out of their houses to join the procession. Everybody was throwing flowers and strips of paper made from old newspaper and brown paper bags. At the front of the procession was a brass band followed by a tall skinny chap carrying a large flag, it had some writing on it but Jesse couldn't read it as it wagged about in the morning wind.

By the time the procession arrived at where Henry and Jesse were stood the crowd was so large that both of them had to move back. Henry climbed up an old stone mounting block to gain a better view. He was soon joined by Jesse and two other chaps who were also getting crushed by the crowd. The crowd then stood and began to wait. After standing there for a couple of minutes, Jesse as usual became his self and after ten minutes, he was really feeling the pain of intolerance, so he quickly turned to the bloke who was stood next to him and asked, "What are we all waiting for?" "For our Billy and Sally, their getting married at the church today," the bloke then fell silent and Jesse continued to wait.

It wasn't long before another type of music could be heard in the distance, and Henry turned to Jesse, who was by now ready to leave, and said, "Looks like the main events about to start our Jesse." Henry turned his head back to the front just in time to see in the distance another marching band approaching, this time they were playing drums and what look like penny whistles. They looked very smart in their bright green uniforms, especially when the gold trim caught the sunlight. They were being led by a fat man who was twirling a baton, when the band reached where Jesse and Henry were stood watching the fat band leader stopped twirling his baton and threw it high into the air whilst doing a spin, he then caught it again before moving off very smartly, the crowd applauded and gave a little cheer.

Behind the band came a small open top coach being drawn by two beautiful black shires. In the coach were the bride and groom who were sat looking forward and waving to the crowd. Facing them in the coach was a group of children, all of different ages, sizes and colourings, Jesse counted two girls and four boys, two of which were knelt up facing forwards, "Whose children are those?" Jesse asked the bloke stood next to him. "Their Sally's children," the bloke replied before falling silent again. Jesse waited for a moment and watched as the coach carrying the children past by. Then a thought occurred in Jesse's head, he slowly turned to the bloke and said, "I thought you said she was just getting married today." The bloke grinned and said, "Aye, she's quite a character our Sally is, you might say she put the cart before the horse." Jesse turned red and was startled by what the bloke had said. Embarrassed, Jesse managed to reply, "Oh I see." The bloke laughed, jumped down off the mounting block and said, "I doubt if you do." He then disappeared into the crowd.

Jesse continued to watch the procession as floats of all shapes and sizes passed him by. The floats were suddenly interrupted by ten horses ridden by both female and male riders. The riders were dressed in costumes, which looked like flags. Henry looked at Jesse and shouting above the noise of the crowd said, "Look our Jesse." He pointed to some small ponies which were following the ten horses. Jesse scanned the ponies and then replied, "Aye... they look like Jerusalem ponies to me." Henry agreed and began laughing at some of the riders whose legs were too long to ride the ponies. Their legs could be seen dragging on the ground. Henry laughed even louder when he saw a pony escape from beneath a tall chap's legs as he stood up for a moment to light his pipe. It didn't take long for the chap to pull the pony back beneath his legs, about four strides.

At the back of the ponies came an old gent dressed in a very ceremonial gown carrying a long staff with a bauble on it, "Whose he?" Jesse asked out loud. "That's old Jim Haley," a giggling voice said from the front of the crowd. Jesse quickly searched the heads to see who it was that had spoken. At first he couldn't see who had replied to his question, but then a woman with hair as black as a raven turned and smiled at him with the most beautiful lips Jesse had ever seen. The smile eventually disappeared and was replaced with girlish giggles. Jesse tugged up his belt, grinned to himself and then acknowledged the woman by tapping his cap with his finger. The giggles got louder as another girl joined in. Jesse nudged Henry, who was too busy watching the procession to notice the girls, but after a second nudge. He stepped down onto the same step as Jesse to get a better look at the girls. "A nice pair of fillies," Henry said whilst grinning at Jesse. This made the two girls giggle even more, but then, still giggling, they disappeared into the crowd. "Awe, you frightened them off now, with your ugly mug," Jesse said feeling a little disappointed that he hadn't had time to introduce himself. Henry just laughed and continued watching the end of the procession.

Just then someone from the crowd shouted, "Buckshee hot ale and rum at The Bull!" The crowd frantically surged to the right pulling both Henry and Jesse clean off the mounting block. They were dragged back along the road towards The Black Bull Hotel where the crowd dissipated into the square at the front of the hotel. By this time, the landlord was busily serving out the ale from a large pot which was being heated over an open fire. At the side of the pot a queue had begun to form. "Over here our Henry," Jesse said joining the queue which was moving quickly, so quickly, that Jesse was forced to grab a tankard off of a table on his way to the hot ale.

Arriving at the hot ale Jesse held up the tankard and the landlord slopped hot ale into it, "Move on, move on!" The landlord shouted everytime he filled a tankard. The queue continued past a second table where women were giving out tots of rum in small crystal glasses. "Hurry up and you can have another one," a voice said. Jesse looked up to see the raven haired girl. "Thanks!" Jesse said quickly swigging back the first glass of rum. The girl had just enough time to fill the glass a second time before Jesse was pushed on by the force of the queue. However, Jesse did manage to blurt out one question at the girl, "What's your name? To which the girl replied, "Eunice, Eunice Schorah!" She then disappeared from sight as Jesse was pushed on further by the queue.

The hot ale and rum were slowly coming to an end, some drank more than they should have, when the brass band struck up and began marching off with everybody following, by this time the housetops were full of people waving and cheering. Henry and Jesse tagged along looking for more freebies. The procession walked back along the road and turned left up Church Lane towards the parish church where it arrived at ten o'clock precisely. The bride

and groom stepped down from the open top coach and walked slowly up the path towards the church door, waving to the crowd as they went.

Arriving at the door, the vicar received them and the church clock began to strike ten. There was a mad rush and the church pews downstairs quickly became full. No-one was allowed upstairs because the rector said, "The weight of so many people would cause the floor to give way," so many of the crowd instead sat silently outside among the gravestones, trying to hear the service through the open doors and windows of the church.

The service had gone on for about an hour and Jesse had become bored with standing around and doing nothing, so he began to look around for somewhere to sit. Henry, whose leg was playing him up, had already found somewhere to sit. He was sat down on a nearby gravestone. However, Jesse refused to sit on a gravestone or walk on the graves as some had done, he found this very disrespectful, instead he walked back to the churchyard gate and sat on the wall. He'd been sat there for about ten minutes when he noticed Eunice approaching. "Hello again," she said. Jesse immediately jumped down off the wall and then Eunice politely asked, "Haven't they finished yet?" She looked towards the church. Jesse shook his head and then said, "Won't be long though." Just then the church bells began to ring and Eunice and Jesse laughed as they both said together, "There they are now." Eunice moved back from the gate and handed Jesse a handful of rice from a small brown paper bag she had pulled from her coat pocket. Both began to throw the rice over the bride and groom as they came down the churchyard path and clambered aboard the open top coach.

The band struck up again for the return journey and set off up a steep hill called Lee Green towards the King's Head, a long procession followed. At the King's Head Jesse and Eunice sat at a small table slightly away from the crowd and had refreshments, which consisted of a glass of best bitter and some small bread puddings. Eunice could see that Jesse was practically starving by the way he'd scoffed four puddings and swilled them down with two glasses of bitter before he lifted his head to talk, "When was the last time you ate?" Eunice asked trying to remain within the boundaries of politeness. Jesse was quick to reply, "Two days ago on an old barge," he said wiping a run of bitter from his chin. This led to Jesse explaining where he was from and how he'd gotten there. They'd sat there for over an hour when the crowd began to move again. Neither Jesse nor Eunice moved from the table and as the crowd began to disperse, Henry appeared. "Arr... there you are, thought I'd lost you forever." He said approaching the table whilst still eating a pudding.

Jesse stood up and introduced Henry to Eunice. Henry then said, "Come on our Jesse. I'm told there's more free grub at the Wilson Arms which is the next pub." Henry started off after the procession but stopped after about ten paces. He realized that Jesse had sat back down. Henry turned and repeated his request for Jesse to come. "You go on we'll catch you up in a moment, we're just talking," said Jesse. A worried expression came over Henry's face, "Don't worry," Jesse said. "We won't be long. You go on; you'll miss the free grub!" Henry shook his head and reluctantly ran after the procession. Jesse continued talking to Eunice and time just flew by un-noticed. Eventually, Jesse stood up and said, "Let's catch up with the procession and make a night of it." Slowly Eunice stood up and said, "I can't! I've got to get back." Jesse was surprised by this answer but not wanting to appear rude, he quietly said, "Are you sure?" Eunice nodded her head and slowly started to walk back down the road towards the church. She waved gently before she disappeared off the end of the road.

Jesse, still trying to understand Eunice's decision, began going over things in his mind to see if he had said or done anything to offend Eunice. However, by the time he'd caught up with the procession at the Wilson's Arms, he had decided that he hadn't and put it to the back of his mind as he began searching for Henry amongst the crowd. Who had by now been drinking for most of the day and were well on their way to becoming very inebriated. Even the groom had become drunk and was busily going around showing everybody a straw arm which had been made for him by the locals of the pub. They said it would help him in his sex life, since he'd lost his own arm in a quarry stone crushing machine a year before. Jesse couldn't help grinning when the arm kept falling off and the drunken groom kept trying to shove it back up his sleeve as though it would stay on, eventually, someone tied a piece of string around the groom's sleeve which held it in place.

After searching all areas outside the pub, Jesse ventured into the pub and eventually found Henry enjoying a large supper in the backroom. As soon as Jesse entered the room Henry's shouts could be heard. "Jesse! Jesse! Over here." Jesse, who was slightly embarrassed by Henry's shouts, slowly sauntered across the room to where Henry was stood. "Come on our Jesse get some of this grub down ya, its buckshee, free!" Henry said filling his cheeks with more ham from the plate. He then took a swig from a large tankard to wash it down before wrapping his arm around Jesse's neck. The ale coloured slaver ran down Henry's chin which he quickly wiped away with an already ale stained sleeve. Still chewing, Henry leant towards Jesse's ear and quietly whispered, "What have you done with that bit of skirt then?" Immediately Jesse shrugged off Henry's arm and angrily replied, "You've had enough bruv. Come on let's get back." Jesse loaded some items of food into his pockets, anything that was close at hand. He then pulled Henry by his sleeve out into the night air.

It took about an hour to walk back to the Ship Inn where they were received by the words, "You're too late for supper. It finished hours ago." Jesse and Henry ignored the old woman and ascended the stairs to the cold dismal room at the end of the corridor. There they had a small party with the food that Jesse had collected. They only had water to drink but as Jesse said at the time, "beggars can't be choosers," and with that, they got into bed fully dressed, pulled a holed filled blanket over them and went to sleep with full bellies.

The next morning the lads arrived at the mill and were taken down endless corridors, which were painted half bottle green and half cream, cream being the colour upper most of the two. Eventually, they were told to sit down in two very comfortable chairs, which were outside a frosted glass door marked Mill Manager. At the otherside of the door, the cream colour of the corridor was replaced by frosted glass. Jesse could see shadows of people moving around through the frosted glass as he sat down.

Ten minutes had past and Jesse had begun to twiddle his thumbs as he nervously waited to go into the office. After about another ten minutes the door suddenly opened and two shawl covered women and a well dressed man hastily left the office. The women ran back up the corridor, glancing back before disappearing around the corner at the top of the corridor. The man, without stopping or looking at either Henry or Jesse sharply said, "You can go in now." He then walked quickly across the corridor and entered another office, shutting the door behind him. Jesse and Henry stood up and slowly

202

walked into the office where they came face to face with the Mill Manager, who was sat behind a large desk. Jesse began scanning the top of the desk which was full of bits and pieces but his eyes suddenly stopped at a large green blotting pad, which was directly in front of the manager. On top of the pad was a pile of scam cards. "I see we're not the first then," Jesse said jokingly as he pointed at the cards.

The manager's eyes peered critically over the top of his half rimmed glasses and said sternly. "Remove your caps and stand up straight when you come into my office from now on." Henry quickly removed his cap and stood up straight. Jesse, however, was still scanning the desk and had not heard the manager's comments. Henry swiftly nudged Jesse, who speedily returned to reality by removing his cap and lining up with Henry. "Cards please," the manager said holding out his hand. Jesse produced his cards and then the manager stood up and snapped his fingers at Henry. Henry shrugged his shoulders and said, "Oh! I don't have any cards. I was hoping to get a job with my brother's cards." The manager tutted and said, "I see." He then sat back down, pushed his glasses up his nose and said, "Well, as it happens, we do need strong lads, so it shouldn't be a problem. I'll introduce you to our Overlooker." The manager pushed a button and a distant bell rang.

Suddenly, in walked a man dressed in a long green coat, "This is Benjamin. He's one of our Shed Overlookers. What he says goes, got it!" Henry and Jesse eagerly nodded their heads and the manager then turned to Benjamin and snapped, "All yours then." Benjamin turned and walked back out of the office half expecting Henry and Jesse to follow him, when they didn't, he shouted, "Come on then!" Jesse quickly pushed Henry forward towards the door and as both were bungling each other out the door and down the corridor towards Benjamin, a shout rang out. "Shut the bloody door!" It was the manager screaming from behind his desk. Jesse quickly ran back, fingered his cap at the manager and pulled the door too. The manager then leant forwards. Placed his head in his hands and began making a groaning noise whilst shaking his head.

Jesse and Henry were led across a cobbled yard to a large green door which Benjamin pulled opened sideways. The door, which was controlled by a weight at its side, allowed the noise from the looms to escape, it was absolutely deafening. However, before entering Jesse rubbed his hands together and said, with a large grin on his face, "Right Benjamin lad! What's the first Job?" Benjamin looked at Jesse and viciously growled, "First off!" But before finishing his sentence Benjamin suddenly grabbed Jesse and pinned him up against the wall, "You don't call me Benjamin. I only allow the Mill Manager to call me that. The likes of you can call me Mr. Schorah, got it!" He then threw Jesse into the shed. Jesse laughed and walked back towards Benjamin. He then pretended to be a hunchback and put on a sombre facial expression, doffed his cap and started to limp past Benjamin slowly. He then began grovelling, bowing and using his index finger over one eye, he said in a scrawny voice, "Right Sir Ben! Anything you say Sir Ben! Dob, dob, dob, Sir Ben!" Henry started to laugh but Benjamin didn't see the funny side of Jesse's gestures and quickly became angry, he began to glare at Jesse.

Instantly, Henry could see that Benjamin was going to say something Jesse might regret so he tried to relieve the situation by quickly saying, "He's only clowning Mr. Schorah. He doesn't mean anything by it, honestly he doesn't." Benjamin's reply was swift and to the point, "I hope you two aren't going to be trouble, because if you are? I'll have you both out, right sharp!" Henry reluctantly smirked, pulled up his belt and then joined Jesse who was by now limping down the aisle between the looms. Henry called after Jesse, "Jesse! Jesse!" Jesse turned and Henry said firmly, "Stop winding Mr. Schorah up our Jesse. We can't afford to lose these jobs." Jesse, because of the noise, pretended he couldn't hear Henry and cupped his ear before saying, "What! Who, Mr. Who...?" Henry put his mouth right up to Jesse's ear and said loudly, "You know what I mean." Jesse nodded and replied, "Well, who does he think he is? Mr. Schorah indeed," Jesse was then suddenly stopped by a thought, "Schorah, Schorah, where have I heard that name before?" He thought for a moment longer and for the life of him, he couldn't think where he had heard the name before. After a while, Jesse dismissed the thought and started work. It was a long hard day and at the end of it Jesse and Henry were offered accommodation as the scam cards had promised. The offer had come from another Overlooker named Will Sykes who had a London accent and had befriended Jesse earlier in the shift. "Down here lads," he said leading Jesse and Henry down a stone stair well. "It's not much but we call it home," said Will pulling back a badly painted green door. As soon as the door was opened it released a rancid stench which instantly struck Henry and Jesse full on, it was so bad, it nearly knocked them clean off their feet. The stench was horrendous, it was a sort of mixture of urine and boiled cabbage, and it reminded Jesse of the Kaile broth back home. Instantly, Henry put his sleeve over his nose and mouth and said, "My God! What's that stench?" Will inhaled and took in the full aroma escaping from the cellar, "Oh, that's the tea, boiled cabbage by the smell of it, lovely!" He said smacking his lips. Henry, who was by now beginning to gip said, "That's not just boiled cabbage, it smell's more like piss to me." "Oh that! Don't worry about that! You'll soon get used to that! When you've been down here for a couple of days you won't even notice that particular smell." Jesse and Henry entered the cellar and began to focus their eyes in the dim light. The green door slammed behind them and Will, patting Jesse on the back, said eagerly, "Go on lad, choose a bed. There's plenty, especially at the bottom end." He then disappeared into a smaller room off to one side where a cloud of steam smelling of cabbage was emanating from a slightly open serving hatch.

Jesse and Henry slowly started to walk the length of the cellar, which was lined by rusty metal bed frames. Wooden benches and bare tables ran down the middle of the cellar. In the wall above the bed frames were half used candles perched in small blackened holes. At the foot of some of the bed frames were rolled up striped mattresses, some with holes in that were so big you could put your hand through them. As the lads reached the middle of the cellar some of the bed frames had the same striped mattresses stretched out flat on them. This was to allow the large stains in the middle of the mattresses to dry. Henry, holding his breath slightly, walked closer to inspect one of the mattresses, "Told you it smelt like piss, didn't I?" He said pointing to the stained mattresses. But by now, Jesse had become disinterested in what Henry had to say about the stench. He only knew one thing, and that was, he was beginning to feel distinctly unwell by the rancid stench.

Jesse walked backwards onto a bed frame and used the bottom of the bed frame to slowly lower himself down onto the corner of one of the mattresses. He'd only just sat down when Jesse felt his foot hit something under the bed. It was a metal bucket, over it went, the content spewing out over the floor and the smell from the spillage instantly made Jesse sick. Henry laughed and said, "Trust you to kick over the slop bucket!" That was enough for Jesse; he stood up, wiped his chin and said, "That's it! I'm off back to the Ship Inn." Briskly he walked back to the green door and began climbing the stairs. He hadn't gone far when he was stopped by a crowd of boys coming down the stair well. Jesse quickly stood back up against the wall and watched in disbelief as the unshod boys as young as seven, wearing very poor clothing, past him. They were followed by girls and old women who weren't much better dressed. They were wearing dirty long aprons and holed shawls, some, however, did have shoes. At the back of them came Benjamin who was carrying a thick black leather strap. He quickly tried to hide the strap when he noticed Jesse stood up against the wall. Knowing Jesse had seen the strap, Benjamin angrily said, "What are you looking at?" Jesse quickly stepped past Benjamin saying, "Nothing Benny, nothing at all pal." Jesse disappeared quickly up the stairs leaving Henry, who was following, to take the brunt of Benny's scorn, "I'll have him. I'll have him yet, you see if I don't!" Benny said angrily to Henry who didn't say anything. He just grinned and walked quickly past Benny saying, "Night Mr. Schorah!"

The next morning Jesse and Henry were quartered for being late. Both of them knew they were in for a rough telling no matter how hard they ran. Jesse suddenly stopped running and whilst still panting said, "What's the point of running, we're still going to get told off." Henry grabbed Jesse by the sleeve and pulled him on saying crossly, "The later we are the more money we lose, stupid, now get moving!" The pair arrived at the mill which was in full production. Jesse pulled back the door to find Benny stood there waiting for them. "You're lucky I'm in a good mood this morning," he said, whacking the leather strap across his hand. Jesse wondered at that moment if Benny had intentions of using the strap on him and Henry, but he didn't. Instead he just pointed the strap at Jesse and said, "Today you are going to learn how to scavenge." He then altered the direction of the strap towards Henry, "And you go and see Will, he's across the yard in the Fuller Shed." Henry turned and went back out into the yard whilst Jesse was led down the length of the weaving shed and out the back door to another long shed, "What's in here?" Jesse enquired as Benjamin opened the shed door, "Spinning!" Was the reply, it meant nothing to Jesse so he just followed in silence.

Half way down the shed Jesse was introduced to a small frail looking lad, he cowered as Benjamin approached. "This is Tom. He's going to show you how to scavenge." Tom nervously gave a small nod to Jesse who was stood there holding his hand out ready to shake Tom's hand. Benjamin growled and automatically gave Jesse's hand a whack with the strap, "Enough with the formalities, get on with the work!" Benjamin roared fiercely. Jesse's hand recoiled instantly and was shoved under his arm pit to try and take the sting out of it. Tom instantly scurried under a machine which seemed to have endless moving parts about it. Still grumbling Benjamin turned and walked back down the shed and out through the door leaving Jesse still nurturing his hand and looking around to see if there was anything that might soothe the pain. Just then Tom reappeared from under the machine. "Dip it in the cistern," he said pointing to the corner of the room where a large cast iron cistern full of cold water stood. That's handy thought Jesse as he dipped his hand in the cistern, "You've got to watch Benny the Bastard. He's a sod with that strap," said Tom as he approached Jesse, who was beginning to grin. "What did you call him?" Jesse asked. "You heard. Benny the Bastard! Because that's what he is," Tom replied as he sat down beside Jesse who waggled his hand in the cold water and then said, "He can't be all that bad." "Oh yes! And how would you know?" Tom asked. Jesse thought for a moment and then waggled his hand again in the cold water. "You see that cistern of water you've got your hand in." Jesse reluctantly replied, "Yes." "What do you think it's for?" Jesse shrugged his shoulders and said, "For us to take a drink from if we get thirsty." Tom screamed with laughter and then said, "The young

apprentice's call it Benny's Bath!" Jesse laughed and said, "Whatever for?" Tom gave his nose a wipe with his sleeve and replied, "Because if you nod off which sometimes the young ones do and Benny catches you. He'll pick you up by your ankles and dip your head in that cistern." Jesse laughed and said, "You're joking!" "You might think it's funny but the last time he did it, he nearly drowned the lad. It took ages to bring the lad round." Jesse, realizing that Tom was serious, immediately stopped laughing and said, "Well, I'm a bit too big for him to do that to me." "Yes, he'll just whack you with the strap," Tom replied.

They'd sat there for a couple of minutes watching the machines going backward and forward when Tom chirped up, "Come on then. I'll show you the first job." He then picked up a small hand brush and disappeared under a machine. Jesse watched as Tom brushed down the wheels which had pieces of cotton stuck to them. He then made his way to the back of the machine brushing the loose pieces of cotton as he went. Eventually, he reappeared and said, "Right, your turn!" He handed Jesse the brush, "I can't get under there! I'm too big," said Jesse. Just then a cold breeze hit Jesse's face, Tom's head quickly lifted and spun around to look at the shed door, "Benny, quick get working!" Instantly Tom disappeared under the machine and began to sweep vigorously. Jesse wasn't as fast and was caught by Benny, "Are you going to do some work?" Jesse quickly replied, "Yes! I was just going to," but before Jesse had finished talking Benny had started to lift the strap. Quickly,

Jesse ducked under the machine and began sweeping and the strap hit the post of the machine with a loud whack.

Benny walked past and left Jesse sweeping vigorously. As soon as Benny had gone, Tom quickly reappeared and ran towards Jesse, who was still innocently sweeping the cotton from under the machine. Trying to warn Jesse, Tom screamed as loud as he could, "Jesse! Watch the mule!" Jesse turned to see the mule coming straight at him. Tom slid at Jesse kicking his legs out from under him. "Lay flat quickly!" Tom screamed. Jesse quickly layed as flat as he could on the grease covered wooden floor and the mule went slowly hissing over his head. Jesse was about to move when Tom told him to, "Stay down!" The mule was returning to its original position at the front of the machine missing Jesse's head by inches.

Jesse crawled clear of the machine, stood up and dusted some pieces of cotton off his jacket and trousers. He then turned to Tom and thanked him for his help in escaping the machines clutches. Tom grinned and said, "You've got to be careful these machines don't mess about, they will kill you! We've had two deaths this year already. Who do you think you are replacing?" Just then Benny returned and saw the two of them talking. He wasn't amused and walked straight towards them saying, "What are you two doing? Get on with your work!" He lifted the strap, Tom disappeared instantly but Jesse pulled up his belt and stood firm. Benny didn't land the strap. Instead he hesitated and pointed it at the middle of Jesse's chest saying, "You're trouble lad but I'll soon lick you into shape." Jesse grinned, fingered his eyebrow and then returned to collecting the pieces of cotton from under the machine.

Daylight came and one of the girls whose job was that of a piecer, a pretty girl by the name of Sarah, went to get the breakfast. She returned moments later with half a dozen tin cans, three in each hand. She separated the strings and handed a can to Jesse who looked wondrously into it, "What's this?" Jesse asked. "You don't expect me to eat this, do you?" Tom, who was coming to get his breakfast, quickly said, "It's watered down porridge with oatmeal and onion and if you don't want it. I'll have it!" Sarah handed Jesse a chunk of bread saying, "That's for dunking." Tom sat beside the cold water cistern and began gobbling his breakfast only stopping on occasion to breathe and to remove the pieces of airborne cotton that had landed in the can. Sarah returned to the front of the mule and continued working whilst taking the occasional drink from her can. She stuck the bread into the front of her apron for later. Jesse was just about to sit down to eat his breakfast when Benny returned, "Ahhh breakfast!" He said. Jesse reluctantly nodded and smiled, but Benny, wanting revenge for Jesse's arrogance earlier, quickly whacked the can with his strap and sent it flying through the air, it smashed against the wall and rattled to the floor spilling all its contents. "You've not got time for that, oh and by the way, clean that mess up!" Benny said pointing at the wet wall and floor whilst laughing. Jesse was furious and was going to retaliate but he was quickly pulled back by Tom who shook his head and pointed to three other Overlookers who were watching the proceedings. "Those are his mates and they're waiting to have you, you'd better be careful." Jesse realized he was out numbered. He also remembered what Henry had said about keeping the jobs. So reluctantly, he calmed himself down and decided to try to behave himself for the rest of the day.

Darkness came and the mill lamps were lit. Jesse, tired, exhausted and craving for his tea asked Tom, "What time is it?" Tom laughed and said, "What's that! Who knows?" Jesse began looking around to see if he could find a clock, "Don't bother looking for a clock. The masters don't allow clocks in the mill or watches!" Jesse walked to the window and said, "I need to be back at the Ship Inn for tea at six o'clock otherwise I don't get any." Tom laughed and said, "You can't leave until the clackson sounds and Benny's the one who says when that happens." Jesse went back to work and it was another four hours before the clackson was sounded. He trudged wearily to the front gates hardly able to walk with pains in both his legs and back from bending all day. At the gates he met Henry who was too tired to even talk. Both walked back to the Ship Inn along the canal and not a word was said.

Arriving at the inn which was all in darkness, Jesse said, "I suppose we've missed tea again." Henry groaned and said, "It looks that way. I'm starving as well." They began to wearily climb the stairs when Jesse suddenly said, "Stop!" Both lads stopped and listened. Henry then said, "What?" Jesse sniffed up and said, "Can't you smell that? It smells like the pig sty on the farm back home." Henry giggled and then said, "Oh that's me! I've been walking in pig shit and urine all day, it's called fulling. It does something to the cloth but all it's done for me is turned my feet green and give me a bad smell." At the top of the stairs they walked down the passageway and open the latch door into the room. Jesse lit a small candle and rolled onto his bed, he then noticed a plate with two thick slices of bread on it at the side of his bed. There were also a couple of tankards of ale. "Good old Mrs. McCullum," Henry said grabbing a slice of the bread. The lads sat on their bed enjoying the ale and bread whilst describing their day to one another. Eventually, they fell fast asleep.

The days were long and tiring, the work was dangerous and made even worse by the frequent visit from the Overlookers, who thought nothing of giving you a whack with the strap. Eventually pay day came and Jesse queued at the little window at the bottom of the shed. The window was always half open on pay days. When Jesse arrived at the window, he said his name and waited. There was a rustling sound and then Jesse received a small brown packet shoved under the lower part of the window from Benny who was sat at the otherside of the window. The packet had figures on the front of it. Eagerly, Jesse opened the packet and tipped out three shillings, "What's this?" Jesse screamed angrily. The queue fell silent and all heads turned towards Jesse. This was followed by Benny snatching back the packet and saying, "What!" "I

208

was promised five shillings a week," Jesse raged. Benny shut the window and started to study the front of the packet; eventually he reopened the window and said, "That's right! Five shillings a week, less two shillings for board and lodgings, equals three shillings." He then promptly shoved the packet back towards Jesse and said, "Perfectly correct!" Jesse, who was trying to remain calm, said, "But I don't lodge here. I lodge at the Ship Inn." Benny put his face nearer the window and said angrily, "You were offered board and lodgings, weren't you?" Jesse nodded slowly, "Well then, it's not the companies fault if you don't use them. It's there for you to use." Benny then shut the window and turned to look at another Overlooker who together with Benny began to howl with laughter. Jesse put the money in his pocket, turned and slowly went back to work.

When he got back to the machines Sarah was waiting, "You don't look happy," she said. Jesse sat down on a small stool which was kept out of sight of the Overlookers and said, "They've robbed me." Sarah came closer and said, "The old board and lodgings routine." Jesse could only nod in reply, "If it makes you feel any better it's the same for everybody," Sarah said sympathetically, trying to cheer Jesse up. Jesse didn't disbelieve Sarah but all the same he wanted verification. "Let me see your packet then," he said standing up. There was then an uncomfortable silence and Sarah began to blush. Jesse thinking he'd cause Sarah some embarrassment began to apologise. "Oh it's not you Jesse but I don't get my wage packet at the same time as you," Sarah explained. "I'll show it you later though," and with that, Sarah walked away. Jesse stood there for a few moments feeling that something wasn't quite right and when Tom arrived, he asked, "What was all that about?" Nudging Jesse from his trance like state, "I'm buggered if I know!" Jesse replied.

He then took a drink of the watered down porridge that was costing him two shillings a week. Just then Benny appeared at the bottom of the shed. Tom did his usual disappearing act under the machine and Jesse disappeared quickly behind the back of one. He watched through a gap in the machine as Benny approached. However, about halfway up the isle Benny stopped, he was approached by Sarah, who walked straight towards him. Both disappeared into a small side room. About twenty minutes later they both reappeared and separated at exactly the same place they had met. Sarah walked back up the isle towards the machine and Benny went in the opposite direction, eventually disappearing out of the door at the bottom of the shed. Jesse came from behind the machine and walked towards Sarah. As soon as he reached her she pulled from her apron pocket an unsealed brown packet. "Here's my packet!" She said, showing Jesse her deduction. Jesse still not realizing what was happening said arrogantly, "And when did you get that?" Again Sarah blushed but this time it came with anger, "Mind your own bloody business!" She said before furiously stormed off. It wasn't until later, when he was talking to Tom that Jesse began to understand the situation. He was told that all the young girls in the mill get their packets that way, and it was nothing to be ashamed of. Jesse realizing he'd upset Sarah decided he would apologise, which she accepted with a nod.

That night Jesse met Henry, who had also suffered the same robbery, in the mill yard. They both decided a good pint and a pie was in order after a gruelling week of work in the mill. They both set of towards the Ship Inn but on their way they came to The Black Bull Hotel. The smells were too much for the lads. "Smell that our Jesse," Henry said inhaling a large portion of the smell. Jesse didn't hesitate and was already making his way through the door before Henry had even finished talking. Inside the hotel, the sound of cutlery rattling on plates could be heard as customers scraped their plates clean of meat and potato pie. Jesse knocked on the bar and shouted, "Two portions of pie and two pints of ya best landlord." But no-one appeared so Jesse started to knock again. He was just about to repeat his order when a woman's voice screamed from the back kitchen, "I've heard ya! I'm not deaf you know!" Jesse stopped knocking instantly and the woman appeared. She wiped her hands with a cloth. "Oh it's you," she said putting the cloth on the bar. Jesse started to blush as he realized it was Eunice, the girl from the procession. "I didn't realize you worked here," he stammered. "Well I do! So what can I get you?" she asked. Jesse, whose tone had changed, politely repeated his order. He finished speaking with a sort of pathetic smile which always made Henry laugh. Eunice poured two pints of ale and told the lads to sit in a corner, while she prepared the food. Both lads took a swallow of the ale and went to sit down. Ten minutes later Eunice arrived with two bowls piled high with pie. Henry realizing it was an extra large portion said, "I'll come here again." Eunice replied by saying, "Don't expect it all the time. The landlords out today," she winked at Jesse, threw two large bent spoons onto the table and walked back to the bar where other customers were waiting. Henry nudged Jesse and said, "You're in their lad." Jesse began to blush and replied, "Eat ya pie our Henry."

They'd eaten the pie and had happily consumed two pints of ale when Henry began to feel tired, "Come on our Jesse let's get back." Jesse hesitated and replied, "You go on. I'm going to have another pint." Henry grinned, stood up and before leaving told Jesse not to be late. Jesse nodded and walked to the bar where he propped it up for another hour. Eventually, Eunice threw her shawl over her head and said, "Come on then if you're going to walk me home." Jesse swigged off the last of his ale and followed Eunice out of the hotel, "You can only walk me as far as the street corner, after that I have to walk alone to the house." Jesse nodded and Eunice linked his arm. As they walked Jesse began to wonder why Eunice wouldn't allow him to walk her to the house. Eventually, he couldn't stand it any longer; he just had to ask, "Why won't you let me take you all the way home, is it your father?" Eunice laughed and said, "My father's dead. It's not him you've to worry about. It's my bastard of a husband." Jesse quickly dropped Eunice's arm, stunned, he said, "You're married!" "Yes, if you want to call it that." Eunice began explaining her predicament and how bad her husband was to her as they walked the rest of the way.

Eventually, Eunice pulled Jesse to a stop by his elbow and declared, "Here we are then, Stevenson's Row." She then looked closely at Jesse and said, "Don't be mad at me," she came closer and got hold of Jesse's lapels, her body touched his and she nibbled at Jesse reluctant lips. After a moment Jesse began to respond, they cuddled and canoodled for about ten minutes. "It's getting late and I've to be up early in the morning," Jesse said as he broke the tender clinch between them. Eunice nodded and started off down the street, Jesse shouted after her, "When will I see you again?" Eunice turned and replied, "You know where I work, don't you?" Jesse shrugged his shoulders and quickly replied, "Suppose!" He then watched Eunice walk the rest of the way down the street, Jesse estimated that the house was about halfway down the street. But Eunice wasn't stupid and when Jesse had gone she came back up the street to her real house.

Jesse's way home was lit by a crescent moon and as he blew on his cold hands, he approached the Ship Inn feeling on top of the world. That evening's events had brought back memories of a young Irish girl named Megan and the warm summer's evening he'd spent with her back home on the farm in his youth. Jesse pushed opened the inn door and entered. As he stepped across the threshold he got the feeling that something wasn't quite right. "Is that you Jesse?" A voice called out from the lounge. Jesse peered into the lounge to find Mrs. McCullum sat at the bar with a small candle burning. In front of her was a small tankard which she kept taking a sip from as Jesse approached her. "You still up Mrs. McCullum?" Jesse asked beginning to feel a little easier. "Can I have your shilling? Henry's already paid me his earlier."

Jesse entered the candle light and dug deep into his trouser pocket. He rummaged about for a moment and then produced a shilling which he was just about to hand to Mrs. McCullum when she quickly snatched it from his grasp. This startled Jesse for a moment, "You're a bit keen aren't you!" He said pulling his hand back quickly. "Aye lad, you've got to get it when it's there, that's my motto." Mrs. McCullum replied. She then stood up and pushed the small stool she was sat on under the bar before saying, "Oh, and by the way, there someone here to see you." She gestured with a scrawny finger to a darkened corner of the room behind Jesse. Jesse quickly spun around to find Earle stood there grinning and Henry, who was sat on a stool and handcuffed with two officers flanking him. "Hello Jesse," Earle said in a subtle tone.

Chapter 10: Mirfield, the Mill and Running Away.

Jesse was stunned for a moment, but it was only for a moment. Mrs. McCullum saw to that as she shoved past him still clinching his shilling. "Close the door behind you when you leave," she screeched. "I'm off to my bed!" She then cackled, stretched and began to climb the stairs. Everyone in the room waited for the sound of her footsteps to stop echoing around the inn before Earle said, "You'd better come and sit down." Jesse walked calmly towards a chair which loitered at the otherside of the table from Henry. He sat down with only one thing on his mind and that was going back home, the farm and being ridiculed by Amos. He was determined that that wasn't going to happen.
Earle grabbed a chair from another table and placed it at the side of Jesse. He sat down and placed a small black leather notebook neatly on the table which he'd taken from his breast pocket, "Now then!" He said looking at Jesse who immediately started to babble. "I'm not going back. I've got a job, it pays good money. I've got plans!" Henry laughed and said, "Oh Aye! And how was the lovely lady?" Jesse's face changed and he struck out at Henry's ankle under the table with his boot. "Shut ya face!" He said angrily. Earle coughed and said firmly, "Now lads, settle down." Henry still flinching from the kick leant forward towards Jesse and whispered, "You're going back to that bastard Amos," he then broke out into laughter. Earle quickly pushed Henry back to his original position and said, "Actually, it's not Jesse I've come for, it's you!" Henry instantly fell silent and looked at Jesse, who said, "What do you mean?" "Well, the laws regarding farm workers have changed," Earle said. He opened his notebook and then continued to say, "You no longer have to be released by the chief constable." Jesse was pleased by this news and punched the air. "Does that mean I can stay?" He asked. Earle nodded his head and then turned to Henry, "The real reason why I followed you this far was you Henry! I was the only one at our station who could recognize you and you're still a fugitive." Henry glared at Earle and said with a bitter tone in his voice, "I don't suppose there are any changes in the law for me then?" Earle lifted the notebook from the table and said, "Well, it's not as bad as you might think, yes we have to arrest you and take you in...." He then stopped speaking for a moment, thought for a second and then began scanning his notebook. Henry sat there impatiently watching Earle's eyes move left to right across the pages of his notebook. "Ah, here it is," he said, holding up the notebook at an angle so as to catch the candle light. "Did you know a Tom Moore?" Earle asked. To which no-one answered, the silence was deafening. Henry looked at Jesse and slyly, with his eyes, tried to indicate to Jesse to keep quiet but Jesse misunderstood and began to open his mouth. However, before Jesse could utter a word Henry spoke up, "Yes I knew Tom!" He stammered, "So what? He's dead!" Henry sat back in the chair thinking that that was the end of that but Earle shook his head and said, "You know full well he's not, he's on trial in Liverpool for murder." Henry angrily banged the table with cuffed fists and replied, "Look, as far as I know Tom was killed aboard the Warrior. I saw him run through by a marine's bayonet just before I jumped overboard." "Is that the

last time you saw him?" Henry nodded and Earle asked, "Are you sure?" At this point Henry angrily jumped up and said furiously. "Of course I'm sure! Now come on let's get on with it." One of the other officers stepped nearer Henry and shouted, "Sit down!" He quickly pushed Henry back down into his chair by the shoulder. Earle turned his attentions away from Henry and began to focus on Jesse who just shrugged his shoulders and remained silent.

Earle blasted out a couple more unanswered questions about Tom Moore and the murders on the canal. He then sighed and to show his disgust at Henry and Jesse, he angrily slapped his notebook shut and returned it to his breast pocket. Again, Earle sighed, but this time he stood up whilst doing it. "Come on then," he said. "We're wasting our time here and we've to get back." Henry stood up and started off towards the door with the officers in close pursuit. About half way across the lounge Henry turned suddenly, stuck his cuffed hands into the air and said, "Quickly Jesse, take the rest of my money from my trouser pocket! I won't need it where I'm going." Jesse literally dived towards Henry's trouser pocket and stuck in his hand. After rummaging, Jesse pulled out a mix of old bronze coin and a couple of silver ones leaving the pocket quite empty. Henry then disappeared out through the front door of the inn still being escorted by the two officers. Jesse now found himself alone with Earle. "Where are you going to take him?" Jesse asked quietly. As soon as the question was asked the mood of the room turned quite sombre and Earle quietly returned to his seat. "You've both led me a merry dance," he said shaking his head. "And I still think you met Tom Moore but I can't prove that you did." Jesse smiled reluctantly and Earle took a deep breath, he then said, "Henry won't be transported to Australia because the law doesn't do that

anymore. They stopped doing that about six months ago." Jesse lifted his head slightly and managed another reluctant smile. He then asked, "So where's our Henry going to end up?" Earle rubbed his chin, stretched and said, "Probably the local prison in Wakefield. There's no point in dragging him back to Newbury with me. Anyway, you'll be able to visit him if the prison is near enough. I think Wakefield  Prison is only about ten miles away." Jesse nodded his head thankfully and Earle got up to leave. He held out his hand, "I'll see ya then Jesse," he said quietly. Jesse shook hands and Earle made his way towards the door but just before he left, Jesse couldn't help himself, he just had to ask. "How's Aunt Em?" Earle turned his head slowly and said, "She's fine, she misses you." Jesse again lifted his head slightly and smiled, "Tell her I'm alright and doing well. Give her my love, won't you?" Earle nodded, put his helmet on and ducked to negotiate the door. Jesse then placed a curved hand around the back of the candle and blew it out before climbing the stairs to the bedroom. He watched from the bedroom window as Earle mounted the front of a small black police wagon containing Henry. The wagon drove off and as Jesse watched it disappear from sight, he promised himself one thing. He would visit

Henry as soon as he could afford to go to Wakefield or wherever it was they put Henry.

The following weeks were very lonely for Jesse, he'd seen Eunice a couple of times, which had helped, but when he got back to the lodgings, that's when he missed Henry the most. He missed the quiet conversations they used to have when they were laid in bed on a night before they fell asleep, he missed Henry's cold feet stuck on his back during the night, but most of all, he missed Henry when he woke up on cold dark mornings and there was nobody there to kick him out of bed, which made it hard for Jesse to get up.

It was on one of these cold dark mornings when Jesse had dragged himself out of a warm bed and was making his dreary way, still half asleep, to another agonizingly long day in the mill, when he was rudely and scarily fully awoken by Eunice who approached him from out of the morning darkness, "My God woman! You scared me half to death!" Jesse said holding his chest and stepping back for a moment. It took a moment but Jesse quickly realized that something was wrong. Eunice quickly turned away and stepped back out of the lamp light. Jesse took a deep breath and began to calm down, he then asked, "What on earth are you doing out here at this time of the morning?" Eunice didn't answer so Jesse grabbed her. Instantly, he could feel Eunice shivering. Although it was obvious that she'd been there most of the night, Jesse tried to show concern by asking, "How long have you been out here? You're freezing!" Again Eunice didn't answer so Jesse quickly pulled her towards him and threw his arms around her. He instantly began rubbing her back in a vain attempt to warm Eunice up. Eunice resisted at first but eventually by shear force Jesse managed to pull Eunice around into the lamp light, he then turned her head to face him and pulled back her shawl to expose a battered face.

Jesse gasped and could feel the rage instantly beginning to build up inside him. He slowly moved Eunice's face from side to side examining every quarter for bruises and cuts. Although not calm inside, Jesse managed to ask Eunice calmly, "Who's done this or need I ask?" At that moment Eunice could no longer contain herself. She broke down into floods of tears and leant into Jesse's shoulder. This made Jesse quiver with anger. He pushed Eunice away and screamed, "I am going to sort that bastard out, once and for all!" He then began to walk quickly down the road towards Stevenson's Row leaving Eunice crying and screaming. "Jesse don't, come back! Please come back!" Realizing that Jesse wasn't going to come back Eunice started to chase after him. She struggled, but eventually, Eunice managed to grab Jesse's arm and pull him to a stop. Wiping the tears from her eyes she babbled, "You can't, Benny will kill you! He doesn't care who he hurts!" Jesse suddenly stopped resisting Eunice's hold and stopped pulling. The mere mention of the name Benny instantly made Jesse realize where he'd heard the name Schorah before, "Benny, Benny! You mean Benjamin Schorah?" Eunice nodded her head slowly and Jesse began to grin. Slowly, the grin got wider and wider; he turned to face Eunice and said, "You mean Benny the bastard is your husband!" Jesse began to laugh as Eunice stopped crying, "Yes," she said. Jesse laughed even louder which puzzled Eunice. The expression of puzzlement on Eunice's face made Jesse laugh even more. Eventually, Eunice became annoyed by Jesse's laughter and stamped her foot hard to show her annoyance, she then asked, "What's so funny?"

It took a few moments, but eventually Jesse stopped laughing and began to pull himself together. He sat down on a small wall and started to answer Eunice. "I was so worried about seeing you," he said, wiping some slaver from his chin, "You being married and all. I felt so guilty. But now I know who you're married to and I know the things he gets up to in the mill, I no longer feel guilty about seeing you! He's a right bastard!" Eunice, looking annoyed sat down on the small wall at the side of Jesse and said angrily, "Oh... I'm glad about that!" Jesse slid along the wall towards Eunice and said lovingly, "I didn't mean it like that," he gave her a small peck on the cheek and put his arm around her.

The pair sat on the wall for quite sometime, thinking, not saying anything to one another. However, as daylight broke over the tops of the small houses which lined the road, Jesse said, "I've got to get to work." Eunice nodded and stood up; she dragged Jesse up and linked his arm as they started to walk towards the mill. As they walked Jesse asked, "What are we going to do

now?" "I'll go back home," Eunice replied. "Benny will be at work by now." Jesse nodded his head and said, "Aye, he's probably waiting to quarter me." They arrived at Newgate, which was the road that led down to the mill and Eunice stopped.

A weary horse slowly trotted by pulling a fully loaded cart, a postman pushing his bicycle, said, "Morning!" Has he past both of them. Eunice

became scared for a moment but she shuddered herself free of it. "I'd best not go any further Jesse, someone might recognize me!" She said looking into Jesse's eyes. Jesse agreed and said, "Will you be alright?" Eunice nodded her head and unlinked Jesse's arm, "Yes. I'm safe, whilst he's at work. It's when he gets home, if I stay, I'll be in for another beating for staying out all night." Without hesitation Jesse jumped in and said, "Don't stay then! Come and stay with me at the Inn. Just get your things together today whilst he's at work and I'll meet you tonight, alright?" Eunice was relieved and smiled. She nodded her head eagerly and said, "Ok, I'll be at the top of Stevenson's Row at eight, alright?" Jesse leant forward and tenderly pecked Eunice on the lips, "Yes. Ok!" He said as Eunice started to walk away. Jesse stood there for a moment watching Eunice. She didn't look back, not even when she turned the corner and disappeared down Stevenson's Row.

When she'd gone Jesse quickly set off down Newgate towards the mill. It was funny, but as he walked, he realized that he wasn't bothered about being late anymore. He even started to slow down to a stroll. He put his head up high and decided that life was good. This pleasurable feeling was short lived as Jesse let the door slam behind him as he entered the spinning shed. A scream was bellowed the length of the shed as the sound it Benny's ears, "You! Ya little sod! What time do you call this then?" Jesse looked down the aisle to see Benny bearing down on him with a strap which landed squarely across Jesse's shoulders. Jesse's snarled and turned to face Benny who instantly grabbed Jesse by the throat. He then pinned him to the shed wall thumb and fingers pressing hard against his windpipe. Benny leant forward and with his face about an inch away from Jesse's, he screamed, "And where the hell have you been ya little bastard?" Jesse in his anger nearly said, "Having a continuing affair with your wife." But since the grip on his throat prevented this, Jesse decided to act like an imbecile and to squirm is way loose of the grip. Eventually, after some moments, Jesse managed to wriggle free of Benny's grip and whilst cowering and with his hand trying to reopen his throat, Jesse whimpered, "Slept in Mr. Schorah." He then coughed and spat to clear his throat. Benny growled with anger and screamed, "Being late is going to cost ya lad, now get on with your work!" Benny then cracked the strap once more across Jesse's back whilst throwing him up the isle towards the spinning machinery.

Waiting to meet Eunice made the day seemed longer than usual, it was certainly very tiring, and as usual it got dark and no-one moved towards the shed door, they just continued to work as usual. Occasionally, Benny would walk the length of the shed snarling here and there at frail timid workers who cowered if they thought Benny was snarling at them. Jesse bided his time and waited until he thought it was nearly a quarter to eight before deciding to leave. He watched Benny pass by whacking the strap across his hand as he walked, he then made his move, he quickly crept out of the shed taking care that the door didn't slam behind him. He quickly walked across the yard and out through the gates. It took about four or five minutes to reach Stevenson's Row and just as Jesse arrived, he could hear the sound of the mill claxon going off, in the distance, this meant that Benny wouldn't be long behind him. This made Jesse very nervous, and it was cold stood there in the street.

It wasn't long before Jesse began to feel the cold, so he tried stamping his feet and blowing into his hands as he waited. The longer he waited the colder it became and the more nervous he became. After all he thought, the last thing I need right now is Benny to catch me with Eunice. Just then a voice from behind Jesse said, "Hello Jesse." Jesse was startled and spun around quickly, thinking it was Benny. However, his heart stopped racing when he realized it was only Sarah that was stood behind him, "You were off a bit sharpish tonight weren't you?" Sarah asked. Jesse smile sheepishly and said, "Aye. I had some business to attend to." "What are you doing here then?" Sarah asked Jesse politely. Jesse thought for a moment before answering, "Err, Oh, I'm, err, I'm meeting someone here and then we're going on." he stammered. Sarah adjusted her shawl and said, "Well I wouldn't wait here for too long if I were you. Benny's coming and it's going to rain. Mind you, it's cold enough for snow!" She then walked briskly past Jesse and down Stevenson's Row.

Jesse was by now becoming extremely nervous and started to stare down the row of houses. There was still no sign of Eunice. "Where is she?" He murmured to himself. He blew into his hands once more and then began to say quietly to himself, through gritted teeth, "Come on! Come on, where are you?" He'd said it about eight times when Eunice appeared wearing a long blue coat and carrying a large grey bundle. She disappeared for a moment as Sarah eclipsed her on the footpath, but she reappeared again as Sarah past her and said, "Hello Mrs. Schorah." Eunice acknowledged Sarah with an apprehensive nod and Jesse began to walk quickly towards Eunice. He quickly removed the bundle from her hand and hastily pulled her down a small ginnel between the houses, "quiet!" Jesse whispered.

They waited for a moment. The only sound was their deep breathing and thumping hearts. From the darkness of the ginnel, they watched as Benny passed beneath the lamp light at the front of the ginnel. Just then there was a baby's cry from beneath Eunice's coat. Jesse turned and whispered angrily to Eunice, "What the hell is that?" He then looked back to the front of the ginnel where Benny had reappeared under the lamp light. Both of them held their breaths as Benny glared longingly down the ginnel. Jesse and Eunice slowly moved further back down the ginnel when they thought Benny was going to enter the ginnel but a voice from further up the row stopped him by saying something to Benny. Jesse couldn't make out what was being said but he recognized the voice as Sarah's. Benny walked towards Sarah, put his arm around her and entered her house, leaving it clear for Eunice and Jesse to make their escape.

They ran from Stevenson's Row like the wind but eventually Eunice had to stop and sort out the baby, which was beginning to slip from under her coat. Jesse then drew breath and leant against a lamp post, he put down the grey bundle to rest his arm, "I know it's a stupid question, but whose baby is it?" Eunice began to cry and she blubbered, "It's mine, she's my daughter. I was going to tell you, honest I was. But the moment never seemed right to tell you." Jesse shook his head and said, "I wished you'd told me." Eunice approached Jesse and opened her coat. By the light of the lamp she revealed the baby. Jesse looked into the coat and saw a small face smiling back at him. Jesse could only grin and look away, thinking he must be mad. "This is Emily Louise, isn't she beautiful?" Eunice said in a proud voice. She then smiled at Jesse and beckoned him to look again. Jesse peered once more into Eunice's opened top coat and his heart melted. He had to admit that the child was indeed beautiful but then he said, "I don't know what we're going to do now? A baby, it's just added to our problems!" Jesse rubbed his chin and thought. He then said, "My plan was to sneak you into my lodgings after Mrs. McCullum had gone to bed, but now, with the baby, she's sure to catch us." Eunice fastened up her coat and grabbed Jesse by the arm, "This baby is no trouble!" she said adamantly. "She only cries if you let her get hungry. Keep her fed and you keep her quiet, so come on and show me these lodgings." Eunice began pulling Jesse by his arm. He was still unsure but decided whilst walking at the side of Eunice that he had no alternatives. So he grabbed Eunice's wrist, wrapped it around his arm and said, "Come on then, let's go home."

They arrived at the inn, and as usual it was all in darkness. Jesse opened the front door quietly and led the way up the stairs feeling his way towards the room. Arriving at the room door Jesse quietly opened the latched door and allowed Eunice and the baby to enter before he followed. Quickly he shut the door behind him. Relieved that they'd gotten to the room without being discovered, Jesse quietly walked across the room to the table and lit the small candle which was in the middle of the table. The room lit up to reveal Eunice breast feeding the baby. Jesse became slightly embarrassed by this and sat on the bed facing away from Eunice. The sound of the child sucking echoed around the small room, "Can't she do that any quieter?" Jesse asked, thinking Mrs. McCullum would hear it. Suddenly, the sound stopped and Eunice got up. Then, as all women would do, she examined the bed. "This bed is disgusting!" She said pulling back the sheets. "How much do you pay for this room?" Jesse reluctantly replied, "Two shillings a week with food mind," "Huh what food, this food?" Eunice said pointing at some ham and bread on the table. Jesse altered his position on the bed and said nothing. He broke off a piece of bread and shoved some ham into his mouth followed by a bite of the bread. Eunice knelt down and began opening the grey bundle. She pulled out two immaculate white starched sheets that had been ironed flat. Then from her skirt pocket she pulled two safety pins and began making a bag with one of the sheets, she then placed Emily into the bag and delicately laid her down on the bed. She laid the second sheet over the top of her to keep her warm in

the cold bedroom that Jesse called his lodgings.

Jesse had sat on the edge of the bed for sometime and had said nothing. Eunice looked across at him and said, "Penny for them." She pushed Jesse along the bed so she could sit up beside him. She grabbed his hand and held it tightly, the candle light flickered and their eyes met. Jesse leant towards Eunice in an attempt to plant a luscious kiss but she held him off and said, "You seem distant, are you annoyed at me?" Jesse shook his head and said, "No. I was just thinking about what we were going to do next. I don't have any family up here to help us." Eunice placed her index finger across Jesse's lips and said calmly, "No, but I do, so come on let's go to bed and we'll talk about it in the morning."

The following day Jesse and Eunice got up early to avoid confrontation with Mrs. McCullum and set off towards Cleckheaton where Eunice had a sister. Eunice explained that her sister, Emily, lived with her daughter Florence in a small back to back house at a place called Quarry Terrace in Cleckheaton, which was about ten miles away, and that they would be able to stay there whilst they got on their feet. Eunice continued to say that Emily had lost her husband two years earlier in an accident at the wire mill in Cleckheaton and would be only too pleased to have paying lodges. Jesse laughed and said, "Paying lodges! I can't even get my wages from the mill!" Eunice dug deep into her skirt pocket and pulled out a sow's purse. "Here, that should keep us going for a while." She threw the purse across at Jesse who quickly undid the strings and squinted in through the top of the purse. Surprised, he said, "Well who's a clever girl then." Jesse began shaking the purse which caused the coins to toss and turn over in the bottom. "There must be at least, oh... three pounds or more in here. Where did you get all this from?" Jesse asked. Eunice looked hard at Jesse and snapped, "Hard graft and crafty saving." She then flicked her hair back with her hand and continued to walk towards Cleckheaton with Jesse, still counting the money, following closely behind.

After a three hour trudge along lane and over dale. Jesse, Eunice and baby Emily arrived at Quarry Terrace and a bleaker place Jesse had never seen. Quarry Terrace consisted of a row of twelve black terrace houses divided by fall pipes. Each house had a small set of steps, which descended steeply from the front door down to the grey stone slabs of the pavement. Some of the houses were back to back and some were through houses, which meant that the through houses had the luxury of using a backyard for things like drying and washing clothing. This bleak terrace was isolated from surrounding houses on all four sides by heavy industry. At the back of the terrace, there was a horrible smelling foundry, which bellowed black smoke all day, everyday. At the front of the terrace was, as the name suggests, a quarry with kilns, which also bellowed out acrid smoke most of the day. The quarry, whose owners owned the land, piled slack at the end of the terrace which blocked out the light from the last two end houses. On both sides of the 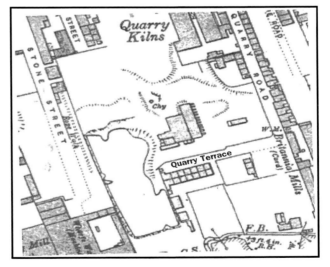 terrace were two large wool mills, which operated twenty four hours a day. Both had their own sounds and stenches, which spewed out relentlessly come rain or shine. However, as Jesse was to find out, what the terrace lacked in beauty and scent, it made up for in camaraderie and neighbourly help.

About halfway down the terrace Eunice stopped, she looked up at a house and then approached it slowly. She climbed the steep steps to the front door and then knocked, but there was no answer, so she knocked again, only this time a little harder. After a moment of silence Jesse stepped up and said, "Here, let me try!" But just as he was about to knock a voice from the otherside of the door echoed around the small front room which the door led to, "Who is it?" Eunice called back, "It's me Emily, come on, let us in, it's bloody freezing out here!" There was then the sound of scraping bolts and eventually the door began to open slowly. A small drawn face of a woman appeared around the edge of the door. She coughed and then said in a hoarse voice, "Oh it's you Eunice. I thought you were the landlord." Eunice kissed Emily on the cheek and then asked, "Are you well sister?" Emily didn't answer. Instead she started to walk back to her chair. Eunice looked seriously at Emily across the room. Then showing concern for her sister Eunice quickly followed Emily towards the chair which was positioned in front of a smouldering fire at the front of the room. "You need some more wood on that fire," Eunice said poking at the grate. Emily sat down and began to cough

again. Eunice placed her hand on Emily's shoulder and said, "You're not alright, are you?" Emily shook her head and began to cough even harder. She began spitting blood which she caught by placing an old piece of cloth over her mouth. Eunice paused for a moment and began to look around her. She suddenly noticed the condition of the room, it was absolutely filthy and she could see that no cleaning had taken place for sometime. Eunice undid her coat and took out the baby; she gently laid the baby down on an old rickety bed which lingered in the corner of the room. After ensuring that the baby was safe from rolling off the bed by positioning a pillow at the outside, Eunice rolled up her sleeves and turned to face Emily and said, "Come on girl, we'll soon get this place ship shape and Bristol fashion."

Eunice began gathering up dirty washing from around the room and started to chat. The chat was filled with queries and questions which Emily simply couldn't answer. All she could do was to cough. Eunice's talking was endless. It wasn't long before Emily had become annoyed at Eunice, she tried in vain to wave the old piece of cloth she was using as a handkerchief at Eunice to try and stop her from talking so much. But eventually, it took the intervention of Jesse who had a reluctance to enter the room to stop Eunice from talking. "She's got the consumption, can't you see?" Jesse said from the doorway. Eunice became quiet and looked towards Jesse who pointed at Emily with the flat of his hand.

Instantly, Eunice gave Jesse a glare, and he immediately shut up. The room became silent and Emily started to control the coughing, it slowed as she replaced the cloth over her nose and mouth. She then said, "I've not been well and haven't been working for a while, but I'm on the mend now and hopefully I will get back to work tomorrow." Eunice's nodded and then began to search around the room, "Where's Florence?" she asked. "In the drawers over there," Emily said pointing towards a set of tatty drawers under the room window.

Eunice slowly walked across to the drawers and knelt down in front of them. There in the bottom draw was a scruffily dressed little girl of about two years old. Her feet and hands were as black as coal and her arms were folded in a vain effort to keep warm, she was hard and fast asleep. Jesse peered into the draw over Eunice's shoulder and said, "Poor little mite." Eunice pulled up an old blanket and laid it gently over Florence's body, "She'll be alright." Eunice said tucking in the corners.

Just then there was a knock on the door, instantly Emily began to panic, "Quiet! Quickly, get down!" Jesse and Eunice quickly ducked and sat under the window next to the drawers, one on each side of them. The knocking continued and this time it was accompanied by a voice screaming, "Come on! I know you're in there, open up!" Jesse looked across at Emily and mouthed, "Who is it?" Emily, who was by now hiding under the bed and trying her best not to cough, replied, "The landlord, he's after his rent." She then gestured by rubbing her first two fingers and thumb together. Jesse stood up, coughed and then straightened his jacket. "Leave this to me," he said strutting towards the front door. "I'll sort this out!" Jesse pulled opened the door and was met by an irate landlord dressed in very smart clothing and wearing a top hat. As soon as the door was open wide enough the landlord stepped forward and began trying to push his way past Jesse using his walking stick. However, Jesse was having none of it. He hooked the landlord's arm in his and pulled him back down the steps onto the pavement. Taking a small cigar from his mouth the landlord snarled, "Who are you sir?" Jesse remained calm and replied, "The man of the house sir and who might you be?" "The name's Bartholomew Smith, the owner of this property sir." The landlord instantly drew his card from his pocket as if he was drawing a sword from its sheath and handed it to Jesse. Then once again the landlord tried to push his way past Jesse but Jesse raised his right hand and firmly placed it on the landlord's chest whilst he read the card, "Easy, easy sir. What is it that you want here?" Jesse asked, knowing it was the rent.

The landlord was by now becoming very frustrated and said, "As if it's any of your business, sir. Its eight weeks rent I'm after." He then began to push against Jesse's right hand, trying once more to gain access to the house. Jesse quickly with his left hand reached into his jacket pocket and pulled out the sow's purse that Eunice had given him. He quickly made the coins rattle by throwing the purse slightly into the air and catching it again. Instantly, the landlord stopped pushing against Jesse's hand and looked towards the purse. "Now then sir, can we sort this out like gentleman?" Jesse asked giving the landlord a little push with his hand and a wink with his eye. The landlord took the hint and stepped back. He removed his tall top hat and smiled excitedly at Jesse. "We certainly can sir!" He said wiping slaver from his chin whilst pulling the rim of his hat through trembling fingers. "How much is owed sir?" Jesse asked pushing out his chest and standing proud. The landlord took out a small black leather book from the inside pocket of his coat and mumbled for a moment. He did a small sum using a black pencil and then proudly said, "Eight weeks at half a crown a week. That's a pound to you sir." Jesse sat down on the door steps and counted out twenty shillings from the purse which the landlord eagerly collected. He then made adjustments in his book, doffed his hat and disappeared off the end of the terrace.

Jesse went back in doors slamming the front door behind him. He then said out loud, "Well that's blown a big hole in your money!" He looked at Eunice and said, "I suppose I'd better go and find some work before this money runs out altogether." Eunice nodded and replied, "Yes. But leave us half of what's left. I need to get milk and food for us, and Florence will need feeding when she wakes." Jesse took out the money and counted out ten shillings. He placed them in a pile on top of the drawers, kissed Eunice and said, "I'll see you later, ok?" Eunice nodded back and Jesse left the house. He hadn't gone far down the terrace when he noticed in front of him a large mill complex. It had a sign on it saying Britannia Mills. I'll try there, Jesse thought to himself. But as he approached the mill he could see a large brown sign on the gate, it said in golden letters. 'No Vacancies'.

Disappointed Jesse walked towards the top of the road and turned down Westgate Hill towards Cleckheaton. He was about halfway down the hill when he noticed a small sign in a grocer's window which read. 'Vacancy: man needed to assist with large deliveries of hay and straw'. Jesse looked at the notice and immediately thought, "That'll do me." He quickly entered the shop and where he found a bedraggled old woman sat in the corner of the shop behind a wooden counter. The shop had the unusual smell of hay and straw mixed with fruit and vegetables. There was also the aroma of fresh baked pies lingering in the background. Jesse inhaled the aroma and said, "By. That reminds me of home." The old woman stood up and said, "Can I help you sir?" Jesse removed his cap and said, "Yes. I've come in about the vacancy in the window." The old woman walked towards a door at the back of the shop, opened it and shouting in an upwards direction, shouted "Dad! There's another chap here about the vacancy." There was then the sound of footsteps, odd footsteps, from the upper floor. Jesse followed the footsteps, with his eyes across the ceiling and down the stairs. The odd footstep sounds suddenly stopped at the otherside of the door and an old man appeared in a brown coat. He wiped the sweat from his brow and hands using a gray handkerchief. He then shook Jesse's hand and said, "Hello! My name is Mr. Hillard. So you want the job, do ya?" Jesse nodded his head and replied, "Yes please."

Mr. Hillard limped towards the old woman and said, "Well, as you can see, I have only one good leg. I broke this one some years ago and it's never been the same since." Jesse looked down and said, "Oh, I see." Mr. Hillard leant against the wooden counter and said, "I need a good strong man to help me deliver the bales of hay and straw, we supply to the local area." Jesse thought for a moment and then asked, "How big is the local area?" Mr. Hillard scratched his balding head without removing his cap and said, "Well I suppose it's as far over as Mirfield and parts of Huddersfield and up to Gomersal and on towards Bradford." Jesse then curiously asked, "And how do we get bales of hay and straw to those places." Mr. Hillard beckoned Jesse towards the door. He walked him through a back room and out into a yard where there were two carts and a stable. The top half of the stable door had been left open. Jesse looked inside and saw a nice size shire horse, "Is he a gooden?" Jesse asked pointing at the horse. Mr. Hillard came and leant on the bottom half of the stable door at the side of Jesse and said, "Do you know

anything about horses then?" Jesse laughed and said, "Do I!" Jesse shook his head and said, "Listen. I've lived on farms all my life growing straw and hay and using horses to plough the fields to grow the stuff in, there's nothing I don't know about horses, straw or hay!" Mr. Hillard was pleased to hear this and said, "Oh you'll know the difference between good straw and bad then?" Jesse was quick to reply and said, "I can smell bad straw."

He then opened the door and entered the stable. "Not bad," he said as he began to slowly stroke the horse. Mr. Hillard could see straight away that Jesse had a way with horses, "He seems to like you." Mr. Hillard said smiling at Jesse, who turned and said, "You've got a good horse here, I can see that." Jesse patted the horse firmly on the neck and picked up its nose bag which was lying on the stable floor. He confidently hung it up on a nearby post and Mr. Hillard opened the door for Jesse as he came out of the stable. "Do you know you're the first person to get that close to that horse, he usually throws a fit if anyone goes near him." said Mr. Hillard, closing the bottom door. Jesse smiled and sat on a bale of straw. "Well! Have I got the job or not?" He asked. Mr. Hillard thought for a moment and then held out his hand before saying, "Anyone who can manage that horse has got to be the man for the job." He then shook Jesse's hand and said, "Welcome! Come on in doors and we'll celebrate with a tankard of ale." Jesse smiled at Mr. Hillard who led the way into the backroom where his wife had already laid out two tankards of ale.

Time past and the ale flowed, but eventually, Jesse had to leave. He said his goodbyes to the Hillard's and set off walking back to Quarry Terrace. Arriving on the terrace Jesse said, "Good evening," to the lamp lighter. Who had just lit the only lamp on the terrace and was on his way to light the next lamp on Quarry Road. Jesse had by now become a little wobbly from the mixture of air and ale, so he used the lamppost to hold himself up for a moment. He took a deep breath and tried to compose himself by straightening his jacket before entering the house. After a little shake and a wobbly step forward, Jesse smiled to himself, as he wobbled up the steps towards the front door. It was a rare moment of elation for Jesse, he felt on top of the world. It was the first time since leaving White's Farm that he felt a sense of belonging and felt he was going to enjoy life working for old Mr. Hillard delivering hay and straw.

The next day Jesse was up early and keen to get started on his new job, he kissed Eunice good-bye and gave her the last of the money from the purse. "Don't spend it all at once!" He said leaving the house by the front door. Eunice watched Jesse disappear off the end of the terrace through the grime stained window of the front room. He waved, just before he turned the corner at the end of the terrace.

Jesse arrived at the shop on time and eager to start. Mr. Hillard quickly gave Jesse his first orders, "The cart is out the back and you know where the horse is." Mr. Hillard said. He then handed Jesse some order sheets which he hurriedly explained to Jesse as they walked around to the back of the shop. Jesse quickly harnessed the horse to the flat cart and said, "Right! Where are the goods?" Mr. Hillard looked at Jesse a little puzzled and asked. "What do you mean? Where are the good?" "The straw and hay," Jesse exclaimed. Mr. Hillard laughed and said, "Forgive an old man, the minds not what it was. You have to pick up the goods from the farms. We don't keep it on the premises, we don't have the room. Come inside and I'll draw you a map." Jesse entered the backroom and instantly the smell of fried bacon hit his nostrils, "By... that smells good, is that your breakfast I can smell?" Jesse asked Mr. Hillard who was by now sitting down at a thick wooden table in the middle of the backroom. "No. It's not my breakfast." he said grinning. "It's our breakfast you can smell. Sit down lad and eat! You can't go out delivering on an empty stomach. Anyway, it's part of your wages, breakfast!" Jesse sat down and reluctantly said, "Aye, we didn't talk wages yesterday, did we?" Mr. Hillard shook his head and said. "No, we didn't and I'm afraid to say the job only pays ten bob a week, that's why we throw in a breakfast and two pints of ale on an evening." There was a silence and then Mr. Hillard looked hopefully at Jesse and said, "I hope that's alright Jesse." Jesse thought for a moment and then, not wishing to be seen to be too keen, said, "Aye. I suppose it'll have to do for now." Jesse smiled reluctantly knowing it was far more than he had been getting in the mill. Mr. Hillard smiled satisfyingly back at Jesse thinking he'd gotten Jesse reasonably cheap. He would have offered him twelve bob if he'd have complained.

Jesse enjoyed a hearty breakfast with Mr. Hillard. They chatted and nattered for sometime. Jesse told the story of his life on Whites Farm and how he'd journeyed along the canals to Yorkshire. Mr. Hillard then gave Jesse instructions on how to get to Woodside Farm where he was to pick up fifteen bales of hay and deliver them to the train station in Cleckheaton. Mr. Hillard got a pencil and a brown paper bag from behind the shop counter. He wetted the point of the pencil with an outstretched tongue and laid the bag flat on the table. He put on his glasses and started to draw Jesse a rough map of how to get from the shop to the farm and then the shortest route from the farm to the train station. He finished it off by saying, "There you go. You won't get lost with that." He underlined and circled the train station and handed the bag to Jesse. Jesse smiled and put the map in his pocket, "Better get started then." He said rising from the table. Mr. Hillard nodded and Jesse walked out into the yard. He mounted the waiting cart and slowly started off down the road towards his first pick up at the farm.

Things went well for Jesse over the next six months. Eunice had joined Emily in the mill and was at least earning some money. The children, Florence and baby Emily, were being looked after by a neighbour called Mary Taylor, who had children of the same age as Florence and therefore was quite happy to look after each child for a shilling a week and as she had said at the time, "I'm at home anyway so I might as well earn a little extra spending money."

Jesse's new job was also going well, he had quickly become familiar with the surrounding area and had built up quite a relationship with the farmers and customers where he delivered and collected straw and hay from. The Hillard's had also become good friends, treating Jesse, as if he was their own son. Jesse was even allowed to call Mr. Hillard, Wes, on account of his name being Wesley.

However, all this was to change, when one morning, Jesse had enjoyed his usual hearty breakfast and was busy harnessing the horse to the cart, when Mr. Hillard suddenly shouted Jesse into the backroom of the shop, "Right Jesse!" He said shuffling some papers around, "Pick up ten bales of hay and ten of straw from the farm and deliver it to." Mr. Hilliard began riffling through some more papers and then said, "Arr... here it is, The Black Bull Hotel in Mirfield." Jesse's face must have changed instantly at the mere mention of The Black Bull Hotel because Mr. Hillard, who was quick to notice, said, "Is everything alright Jesse, you look worried." Jesse smiled reluctantly and replied, "Yes. I'm alright." Jesse took a moment and composed himself before saying, "Come on then, give me the invoices. I've got to get on!" He snatched the invoices out of Mr. Hillard's hand and marched out into the yard. It wasn't long before Jesse was out on the open road heading towards the farm. He quickly picked up the straw and hay from the farm and hadn't said much to the farmer or his sons. Who usually helped him load the cart and by the time Jesse had reached the Mirfield's boarder his mind had gone into over drive, "What should I do if someone recognizes me? Or even worse, what if I bump into Benny?"

These thoughts kept going around and around in Jesse's head and had completely distracted him from his driving. When there was a loud scream from the front of the cart, "Hey, watch where you're going!" A voice said. Jesse quickly pulled on the rains and stood up to see whose voice it was. From in front of the horse appeared Sarah. "Hello Sarah," said Jesse. Sarah looked up and put her hand over her eyes to shield them from the strong morning sun light, so that she could see who it was that had nearly run her over. Jesse jumped down from the cart and said, "It's me, Jesse!" "Oh, you're a fine one, running off like that! Not saying goodbye or anything. I thought we were friends?" Sarah said looking annoyed at Jesse. "Oh don't be like that," Jesse replied. He then apologized and then, trying to change the subject, asked how things were. Sarah shrugged her shoulders and said, "As if you cared!" She had just started to walk away when Jesse asked out loud, "How's that bastard of an overlooker, Benny!" Sarah turned quickly, her face scowling, but then as she realized that Jesse didn't know about Benny, her tone altered. "Don't you know?" She asked politely. "Know what?" Jesse asked, showing a little concern. Sarah stepped nearer to Jesse and said, "He's taken to his bed these past weeks. It's said he might die." "Well, I can't say I'm sorry to hear that!" boasted Jesse. He then began to check that the load hadn't moved by the sudden halt of the cart. He slowly walked around the cart checking that all the fastening ropes were still tight. He twanged each one individually intern as he past them. Eventually, Jesse arrived back where Sarah was stood. He could see she was quite upset by what he'd said, so, quietly he leant over and whispered in her ear. "Is it bad lass?" Sarah wiped her nose and nodded, she then answered quietly, "As bad as it gets, and he's always asking for Eunice and Emily." Jesse stepped back and rubbed his unshaven chin. He thought for a moment and then said reluctantly, "I'll tell her. But I can't promise anything." Jesse jumped back up onto the cart, clicked the horse and shouted, "Get on!" The horse began pulling.

It took Jesse another hour to deliver the hay and straw to The Black Bull Hotel but as he turned and headed back towards Cleckheaton he wondered how he was going to tell Eunice the news about Benny, he knew it would upset her. The journey back seemed endless and it was getting dark by the time Jesse arrived back at the yard. He quickly put the horse and cart away and made sure everything was secure. Still thinking, he headed for the gate and the road home. Mr. Hillard had seen Jesse leaving and had shouted, "What about your ale?" But Jesse paid him no attention and just continued on his way. Mr. Hilliard just assumed Jesse hadn't heard him but the truth of the matter was Jesse was still trying to figure out a way of breaking the news gently to Eunice.

Fifteen minutes later Jesse entered the house on Quarry Terrace and the warm air from a raging coal fire, that Eunice had lit, hit him full on. He could smell food cooking. "Is that you Jesse?" Eunice shouted from the small kitchen at the back of the front room. Jesse dropped his cap onto a wall peg before taking off his jacket; he dropped the jacket over the top of the cap and walked towards Eunice. Eunice leant backwards so she could see Jesse through the kitchen door. "Tea won't be long," she said as Jesse approached. Instantly, with the expression on Jesse's face, Eunice knew something was wrong. "What's wrong with you?" she asked, wiping her hand on her apron. Jesse unwillingly replied, "I've got some news for you." Eunice became very excited and said, "Oh good, I've got some news for you too. We'll swap news after tea upstairs." She then turned and re-entered the kitchen saying, "I hope its good news!"

Eunice began serving tea which everybody ate quietly. The silence was so noticeable even Emily had mentioned how quiet everybody was. Jesse reluctantly smiled and said, "Aye, I think we're all just tired, aren't we?" Eunice nodded and then gave Jesse a quick smile. She waited for a moment and then gave Jesse the nod which usually meant she wanted Jesse to go upstairs to their bedroom. The bedroom wasn't much and it suffered badly from damp. Especially in one corner where there was a particularly large damp patch covered in black mould. The window, of which there was only one, leaked when it rained in a certain direction. However, despite all of this it was the only place in the house where Jesse and Eunice could relax and have time on their own. Jesse had entered the bedroom first and sat on the bed. Eunice was slightly out of breath as she entered the room carrying baby Emily. "By those stairs are steep," she said patting her chest whilst trying to regain her breath. She placed baby Emily down on the bed, wrapped her shawl around her and then sat beside Jesse.

They both turned to face each other and Eunice grabbed Jesse's hands. She rested them on gently on her lap. Still holding Jesse's hands tightly Eunice said excitedly, "Right then, come on, let's hear your news first." Jesse hesitated; he squirmed a little and then awkwardly said, "Well it's about Benny." Jesse then waited for a moment and tried to gauge Eunice's feeling from the expression on her face. Eunice pulled Jesse towards her and said, "What about Benny?" Jesse looked deep into Eunice's eyes and said, "He's poorly. I bumped into Sarah today. She said Benny had taken to his bed these past weeks." Eunice took a deep breath of relief and said, "Oh is that all. I thought it...," she stopped speaking and looked at Jesse, whose head had sunk deep into his chest. "It's worse than that isn't it?" She asked. Jesse nodded and said, "Yes, I'm afraid so. She said he might be dying."

Eunice immediately stood up and stormed across the room to the door where her best blue coat was hung up. "I must go and see him straight away!" She said buttoning up the coat. Jesse was shocked by this and said, "What now! It's late and it's a good two hours walk to Stevenson's Row." Eunice ignored Jesse's pleas and just pushed past him as he tried to talk sense to her. She refused point blank to wait until morning and began descending the stairs. Jesse followed Eunice out onto the terrace and began shouting after her. "What about baby Emily?" "Ask Emily to put her to bed for me," came the reply as Eunice disappeared quickly off the end of the terrace.

The night was very dark and Eunice arrived on a lamp lit Stevenson's Row. The whole row was quiet. A cat dashed across the front of Eunice which startled her for a moment. She arrived outside the house and looked up the path towards the front door, all seemed quiet. At the window there was a stream of light. It was coming from a slit in the curtains where both halves met in the middle. Eunice slowly approached the door and knock quietly. The door opened slowly and Sarah appeared, "Oh it's you." She said, opening the door wider to allowed Eunice to enter the house.

Meanwhile back at Quarry Terrace Jesse had gone to bed and was laid awake waiting for Eunice to return. He tried in vain to sleep, first he'd lay one way, then the other, he shuffled the pillows but still his eyes would not close. His mind was revolving, going over and over again about how Eunice had reacted to the news about Benny. Questions began to emerge in Jesse's mind, "Did this mean Eunice still loved Benny? Or, on the other hand, did she love him? Will she be coming back?" The hours past and the questions continue to haunt Jesse until the early hours. He couldn't find answers to the questions no matter how hard he tried but eventually, he fell asleep. Well, if sleep is wakening every hour to check the empty bed beside you.

Morning came and Eunice was still nowhere to be seen. Jesse looked across at the un-slept on pillow and realized that Eunice must still have some feelings for Benny. Why else would she have stopped out all night? Thought Jesse as he sat up in bed and scratched his head. He began to dress quickly, but all the time his heart was yearning for the company of Eunice.

By the time Jesse had arrived at work that morning, his mind was working overtime. Jesse just couldn't concentrate, his mind was elsewhere. Mr. Hillard had watched Jesse trying in vain to harness the horse and making a complete ash of it. Eventually, Jesse threw down the rains and walked into the backroom. "Morning Jesse," Mr. Hillard said as Jesse sat down for his breakfast. Jesse didn't answer and only picked at the breakfast. "What's the matter Jesse?" Mr. Hillard asked, seeing that things weren't right. "I need a favour Wes," replied Jesse. Mr. Hillard sat down opposite Jesse and said, "What's that then?" Jesse hesitated and then asked, "Can I borrow the horse and the small cart this morning? I need to go across to Mirfield on family business." Mr. Hillard grinned and said, "Phew! I thought you were going to ask me for some money then." Jesse tried to grin but was unable to. Mr. Hillard could see by Jesse's expression that there was something seriously wrong so he quickly replied, "Yes Jesse. No problem, take the horse and small cart. We don't have a lot on this morning anyway." Actually the shop was quite busy but Mr. Hillard was trying to make Jesse feel a little better by pretending it wasn't. He continued with the pretence until Jesse had left the room, which he did without saying anything. Mr. Hillard watched through an open backdoor as Jesse mounted the cart. He then shouted after him, "I'll keep this for you until you get back then, shall I?" Showing the plate of full breakfast to Jesse as he left the yard, Jesse looked and then nodded.

Jesse had gone about halfway to Mirfield when he noticed a bundle of rags at the side of a dry stone wall about a hundred yards in front of him. He slowed up as he approached the rags. He then identified the blue coat, it was Eunice. Jesse pulled the cart to a stop and waited. He didn't say anything, he just sat and waited. The bundle of rags began to move slowly and eventually Eunice's face appeared from beneath crossed arms. The tears were streaming down her face. "He's gone," she moaned. "He's gone!" Jesse jumped down off the cart and walked around to Eunice. Grabbing her by the elbows Jesse picked her up from the floor. "Come on lass," he said trying to comfort Eunice, who was still crying. Jesse gently pulled her into him and then Eunice let go the most agonizing scream that Jesse had ever heard. It sent shivers down Jesse's spine. He didn't know what to do. So he just clung onto her softly. After about ten minutes Jesse slowly began to release his grip. He turned Eunice and led her to the back of the cart. He helped her up into the back of the cart where she flopped down and laid lifeless on half a horse blanket which Jesse had spread across the bottom of the cart. He put the other half over Eunice to keep her warm and then returned to the front of the cart. After turning the cart around by leading the horse by hand, Jesse mounted the cart and headed back towards Cleckheaton. The road was quiet, so quiet, that Jesse could hear Eunice still whimpering in the bottom of the cart.

They'd travelled a good proportion of the way back before Eunice stopped whimpering. She sat up and wiped her nose on a folded back coat sleeve which was already wet from previous wipes. It took a moment but eventually she decided to join Jesse at the front of the cart. At first she didn't dare say anything, she just sat there. However, eventually, Eunice plucked up the courage to grab Jesse's hand. She placed it in her lap and asked, "Are you alright?" Jesse didn't answer and had to be encouraged with a nudge in the ribs from Eunice, "Course I'm alright. It was you I was worried about." Jesse replied. "I'm sorry but I couldn't leave him to die alone, could I?" Jesse thought for a moment and then said, "Suppose not."

They travelled on a bit further and both were trying to break the silence by thinking of something to say. It was broken by Jesse, who began to relent a bit and started to ask Eunice's things like, "Are you alright?" And, "Do you still love me?" To which Eunice nodded gently. Then from out of the blue Jesse remembered that the night before Eunice also had some news to tell him. He looked down at Eunice and said calmly, "Well, I gave you my news, now, what about yours?" Eunice cuddled closer to Jesse and said, "Oh yes, I almost forgot, we're going to have a baby!"

Chapter 11: Beneficial Deaths.

Jesse had decided it was time he visited Henry in prison. He'd asked Mr. Hillard if he could borrow the small cart on the following Sunday. Eunice had intended to travel to Wakefield Prison with Jesse but on the Sunday morning she was so tired after spending an un-settled night with the baby constantly kicking, she'd decided to stay at home and rest. Jesse was worried and said that he could put the trip off if Eunice had wanted him to. "No you go," she said pulling Jesse on towards the front door. "Henry will be pleased to see you." she said going back up the stairs to bed. Jesse, still looking worried, watched as Eunice ascended the stairs. She waved from the top and blew him a kiss. Jesse smiled and waved back before leaving by the front door which he slammed behind him to make sure it was closed properly.

Jesse arrived at the yard to the sound of church bells ringing across Cleckheaton. He quickly harnessed the horse to the cart and set off towards Wakefield Prison. The journey was uneventful and after two hours of boring bum aching travel Jesse arrived in Wakefield. The whole place was quiet and the only people who were about seemed to be all walking in the same direction carrying baskets or small bundles. Jesse asked an old lady who was selling pegs at the side of the road which way the prison was. She replied, "Follow the crowd sonny. Follow the crowd." She then lifted a bony finger and pointed in the same direction that the people were walking. Jesse thanked the old lady, doffed his cap and followed, what had by now, become a long procession of people and carts heading towards the prison. The procession led straight to the front gates of the prison which were black and absolutely enormous. The sheer size of both the gates and the surrounding walls had startled Jesse at first. He couldn't believe how high they were.

The long procession turned into an orderly queue in front of a smaller door which languished inside the left prison gate. People began sorting out baskets and bundles, people began laughing and chatting, it was the happiest queue Jesse had ever been in. He jumped down off the cart and put the nose bag on the horse, whilst he waited for something to happen. He began chatting to a very plump lady who wasn't averse to showing a very large cleavage. Jesse thought the woman had a peculiar way about her, she seemed to get rather close to Jesse, and in fact, Jesse could have sworn that she was rubbing against him at one stage of the conversation. Jesse quickly stepped back and was about to say something to the woman when the small door opened and out stepped three warders.

Everybody in the queue began to pick up rested baskets and bundles and began to shuffle forward to where the first warder began to check the baskets and bundles. The second began flipping people's arms up into the air, whilst he searched their person. The third warder approached Jesse and said, "Put your horse and cart over there sir." He pointed to a gate across the road where another warder was stood waiting. Jesse led the horse across the road and removed its nose bag. Approaching the gate the warder said, "In here sir. Un-harness the horse and let him run free in the field sir." Jesse nodded and then the warder gave Jesse a ticket. "Here you go sir. You'll need that to get them back." He then placed a ticket on the horse's yoke and the wheel of the cart. Jesse started to walk back across the road to join the queue or what was left of it, when a bell rang out from inside the prison. The warder from the field flew past Jesse at a great speed and entered the small door which was suddenly slammed shut in Jesse face. Jesse knocked on the door and shouted, "Hey, what about me?" But a voice from behind him said, "Don't bother lad, they won't let anybody in or out until the second bell."

Jesse turned to find a small man sat down on the pavement with his back against the prison wall looking up at him. "Take a seat lad," the man said handing Jesse an apple from his bundle. Jesse sat down at the side of the man and took a bite from the apple. The man began to explain that when the first bell rings, it means someone is trying to escape or someone is fighting inside and that means that the prison is closed until they have accounted for everybody or they've sorted out the fighting, "It'll open again when the second bell rings," the man said grinning. "How long will that be?" asked Jesse. There was a moment silence and then a second man further down the queue said, "How long's a piece of string?"

After an hour Jesse was becoming bored, so he began walking up and down. He began thinking about Eunice and the baby and whether or not it was still kicking her. I wish they'd hurry up he thought. Just then there was the sound of a bell and bolts being drawn back. The small door began to open, "Come on lad. We can go in now," the man said getting up from the pavement. The first warder approached Jesse and said firmly, "Basket or bundle please!" Jesse looked at the warder and replied, "I don't have a basket or a bundle." The warder then said, "First timer hey. It's always the same the first time. You'll bring one the next time no doubt." He then passed Jesse onto the second warder who patted him down and said, "Give that man over there the name of the person you've come to see." He pointed to a desk where a man wearing spectacles was sat. Jesse quickly gave the man Henry's name and after he'd wrote it down in a small note book, Jesse was told to go through another small door to the left of the man. However, his way was blocked quickly by warders, who were screaming, "stand back please, out of the way please." One warder put his arm across Jesse's chest holding him firmly in the corner of the room. There was then a huddle of warders struggling with a man who had a high forehead. The man was swearing and screaming abuse at the warders. Two of the warders kept hitting the man on the back of his legs with their truncheons. Jesse watched in amazement as the man was dragged past him spitting and screaming. The huddle hurriedly squashed through the small doorway and the man was dragged away out of sight. When the rumpus had passed and everybody, including Jesse, had calmed down, the warders began showing people through into a long room. The room had long high barred windows to one side which made the room feel bright and airy. Jesse looked down the room for Henry but the only thing he could see were rows of small square tables being patrolled by warders.

At some of the tables visitors and inmates were sat scoffing food from baskets and bundles. Jesse began slowly to make his way down the room, scanning each table as he went. Eventually, right at the back of the room, he noticed Henry sitting at a table waiting patiently for him. As soon as their eyes met Henry stood up. Jesse walked quickly towards him and they met over the table. Jesse stretched across the table and enjoyed a back patting hug with his brother, which was a little short lived as a warder pushed a truncheon between them and screamed, "No touching, sit down!" Jesse sat down facing Henry and said, "What a performance! I've waited over an hour and a half to get in here." Henry laughed and said, "Aye, a couple of the lads got a bit restless and decided to try and do a runner. They were in the next pad to me." Henry began to look under the table and then he looked to both sides of Jesse, who asked, "What are you looking for?" Henry expectantly looked at Jesse and asked, "Where's the grub then?" Jesse apologized and said, "I didn't realize that you could bring things into the prison." Henry wasn't happy about it but realized that Jesse wouldn't have known, so, trying to ease Jesse's guilt, he said. "Bring some the next time, won't you?" Jesse nodded his head and promised he would, he then began to tell Henry of the man with

the high forehead being dragged across the front of him whilst still being hit by the warders, "Aye, that'll be Charlie Peace; he's a nasty Peace of work."

Henry smirked to himself at his play on words. Jesse grinned and leant forwards on the table as Henry began to tell him how Charlie had tried to escape using a small ladder he'd smuggled into his cell, whilst he was doing some repair work for the head warder, "He was put up to it by his cell mate." Henry said, but then he suddenly stopped talking as a warder slowly passed the table. "Elbows off the table, please," the warders said to Jesse, who instantly sat back and removed his elbows from the table. Henry's eyes moved with the warder, watching every move he made as he past. When Henry thought the warder was far enough away from the table he began to talk again. "Like I was saying; he was put up to it by another chap named Jack Sheppard. I had a run in with him some weeks ago. We're alright now though, but I still give both Charlie and Jack a wide berth. Their trouble, I don't go near them, unless I have to!" Jesse nodded and said, "Aye that's the way, keep your nose clean, that's the best way." Just then a burly warder began ringing a large brass bell which had sat on a table at the end of the room. "Well that's it our Jesse," Henry said rising from the table. "Come again, won't you. And bring some grub next time." Jesse agreed and shook Henry's hand before turning to walk back up the room. Jesse looked back when he reached the top of the room but Henry had disappeared among a crowd of prisoners.

Jesse rifled through his pocket for the ticket, on finding it, he reclaimed the horse and cart. He'd just mounted the cart when he heard someone calling his name. Instantly, Jesse looked up above the prison walls at the prison buildings. He could see a dark green cloth being waved from a cell window, it was Henry. Jesse was so pleased that he stood up on the cart and began waving vigorously back at Henry, who he could just see peering at him through the bars of his cell window. This was an image of Henry that was to stay with Jesse for some weeks.

Jesse arrived back at the yard well after dark and was beginning to feel the tiredness of his journey. He locked the yard gates, yawned and then stretched as he began the walk back up Westgate Hill towards home. He arrived on the terrace and could see a small crowd of people hanging around the front door of the house. Instantly, Jesse thought of Eunice and began running along the terrace, he cleared the steps by the front door in one bounding leap, nearly knocking half the people off the steps. He quickly entered the house and hurled himself towards the stairs where he was stopped and pushed back by Emily, "What's the matter? Is it Eunice, is it?" Jesse was so flustered by this time that the words just blurted out spraying Emily with spit. "Calm down." Emily said wiping her face with her hand. "She's only in labour; Annie Naylor is with her, she knows what she's doing." Jesse put his hand over his forehead. His mind began flashing back to Percilla, "Only in labour! Only in labour." he ranted. "And who the hells Annie Naylor?" Emily smiled and touched Jesse on the nose with her index finger, "She's a very good neighbour and friend who's helping to deliver your baby." Jesse began striding up and down the front room. "Come on lad, this is no place for you," a voice said from the crowd at the front door. "Aye take him down the pub Arthur." Emily said carrying a large pan of water up the stairs. "Arthur Sugden is the name. I live just down the terrace. Come on lad let's go to the Punch Bowl for a pint."

Jesse didn't take much persuading. He pulled out his cap from his jacket pocket and plonked it on his head. He followed Arthur out through the front door and down onto the footpath where their way was blocked by a big chap who asked, "Any news yet Arthur?" "Not yet Daniel, but you know what these things are like." Daniel nodded his head and said, "Aye! Only one thing left to do then and that's to go down the pub." Arthur agreed and Jesse said nothing. That was until Arthur realized he hadn't introduced Jesse and Daniel. Daniel turned to Jesse and held out the largest hand Jesse had ever seen, it was like a shovel. "Daniel Naylor. It's my wife who's looking after your missus; she knows what she's doing, so don't worry." Jesse shook hands and found Daniel's grip tight, his hands were as hard as rock from, as Jesse was to find out later, digging holes for Cleckheaton Council.

Three hours later Jesse, Arthur and Daniel returned to the house a little worse for wear. The house was quiet, which worried Jesse at first. He slowly opened the front door to find Emily sat waiting in front of an orange glowing fire. The cold air from the opened door caused Emily to turn and look, "Arr... there you are, about time too." Jesse panicked for a moment and quickly asked, "Is everything alright?" There was then a heart rendering silent moment followed by Emily nodding. "She's waiting for you upstairs." Jesse headed straight for the stairs whilst Arthur and Daniel walked towards the fire and began warming themselves. Jesse stood at the top of the stairs for a moment. He began straightening his jacket and patted down his hair with a licked hand before slowly entering the bedroom.

The bedroom was bathed in yellow candle light and Eunice was sat up in bed holding a small bundle of cotton cloth to her breast, "What did we get?" Jesse asked quietly. Eunice looked up at Jesse and replied, "A girl. She's beautiful." She then peeled back the cloth to show Jesse his daughter. He leant forwards, kissed Eunice on the cheek and the baby on its forehead before saying, "What are we going to call her then?" Just then the front door slammed and Emily could be heard coming up the stairs. When she arrived at the top of the stairs Emily shouted, "Goodnight." Jesse and Eunice both replied together, "Goodnight." They heard Emily's bedroom door close and Jesse kicked off his boots which landed in the corner of the room. Jesse then sat on top of the bed and said, "I like Harriet. I have a sister named Harriet." Eunice thought for a moment and then replied enthusiastically, "Harriet it is then." Jesse smiled and lifted Harriet off of Eunice whilst looking around. Jesse smiled again as he saw a couple of drawers at the bottom of the bed. One contained baby Emily and the other was obviously for Harriet. Jesse quietly walked towards the drawers and laid Harriet down in the empty one. He then pulled up a cover and quietly whispered, "There you go my beauty. It isn't much but things will get better, I promise." He kissed his finger tips and touched Harriet's forehead with them.

Harriet wasn't a baby for long and before Jesse knew it she was toddling around the house shouting for daddy. Everyday the doting Jesse made sure he arrived home from work carrying two pieces of strawberry twist rock in his pocket. The girls would be sat on the front doorstep waiting patiently for Jesse to appear on the terrace. Immediately, he did, the girls would rush towards him screaming and jumping up at him. However, on one particular day the girls weren't sat waiting, which immediately had Jesse worried. He stepped up the pace as he walked towards the house. Jesse opened the front door to be greeted by silence. He quickly entered the front room thinking something was wrong and was just about to shout, "Eunice" when suddenly from the small kitchen and from behind the furniture came cries of, "Surprise!" Jesse looked startled as the girls and Eunice ran at him, "What, what?" Jesse asked looking around the room. Harriet quickly clambered up Jesse and planted a kiss on his cheek; she then threw her arms around his neck. The room went quiet and Emily appeared at the kitchen door, she gestured to someone who was just out of sight. "It's Uncle Henry," Harriet said pointing to the kitchen door. "Hello our Jesse." Henry said, walking out from the kitchen. Jesse quickly put Harriet down and hugged his brother with a tear in his eye. "They let you go then." Jesse said looking Henry in the eye. He then hugged Henry again before saying, "Come on. Sit down our Henry." Jesse led Henry towards the table and pulled out a chair, which Henry politely sat on. The rest of the family eagerly gathered around the table and waited for Henry to say something.

Henry spent the next hour explaining to everybody how he had become free and how he'd manage to find them. Jesse then asked, "Whatever happened to Charlie Peace that nasty Peace of work?" Henry grinned and said, "I'm surprised you remembered him." He paused for a moment and then said,

"Well, it's a bit of a sad story really." He paused again and took a deep breath, "He was transferred to another geol after trying to escape again, one in Leeds, I think. They call it Armley Geol, where rumour has it, he was hung!" on the word hung everybody became silent, which was only broken when Emily, bounding towards the kitchen, said, "come on let's have some tea." Jesse lit a candle and placed it in the middle of the table. He then told Henry, "you'll stop, won't you our Henry?" Henry nodded his head and said, "Aye I'll stop for tea, but then I'm off back to my lodgings in Dewsbury, it's a good hour's walk. I want to be back before it gets too late."

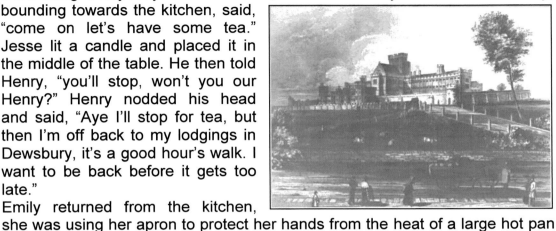

Emily returned from the kitchen, she was using her apron to protect her hands from the heat of a large hot pan she was carrying. "Here you go, get this down you and you'll want for nothing." she said placing the hot pan in the middle of the table. Eunice lifted the pan lid and smelt the steam, "hmmm stew, my favourite." she said picking up the ladle from the table. It wasn't long before the conversation stopped and all that could be heard was the slurping of the stew. "This is good." Henry said looking up for a second helping, which Emily gladly provided. As they were coming to the end of the meal Eunice stood up and banged the ladle on the side of the pan. This got the attention of everyone around the table, "since we've got family visiting, this seems the appropriate time for me to make an announcement." The room fell silent and all eyes were on Eunice. "Come on then." Jesse said impatiently. Eunice stepped back away from the table and rubbed her stomach a couple of times before holding down her skirts to reveal a little bump, "the baby will be here in five months." she announced proudly. Henry Jumped up and shouted, "congratulations our Jesse, you old scoundrel you." He grabbed Jesse's hand and began shaking it vigorously.

It took a moment before Jesse realized what Eunice had said, but when he did, he walked across to Eunice and said sternly, trying not to grin, "you know what this means, don't you?" Eunice looked puzzled at Jesse and said, "Yes, we're going to have a new baby." Jesse grabbed Eunice and lifted her off her feet; he pecked her on the tip of her nose with his lips and said, "No, it means we're going to have to get married now." Jesse slowly lowered Eunice back onto her feet and then said seriously, "you know that the Reverend Maude wasn't happy about you having Harriet out of wedlock. He'll hit the roof if we tell him that you're going to have another." Eunice nodded and deflated, she sat back down at the table, "you're right. He'll go mad." Henry and Emily joined Eunice at the table. The candle flickered as everybody thought about the situation. Henry then said, "Well, what's wrong with getting married?" Jesse walked back to the table, "it's the cost of it all, and the Right Reverend Maude is a right stickler for things to be done right." Eunice sighed and said, "There's only one thing for it. I'll have to go and see Reverend Maude first thing tomorrow morning and see what he has to say." Jesse grinned and said, "Rather you than me!" Eunice quickly turned and snapped, "Why, you're

coming as well." Henry broke into laughter and patting Jesse on the back, said, "I think that's my queue to leave our Jesse." Henry got up and left by slamming the front door whilst shouting back, "I'll see you all later." Jesse's reply was a short grunt.

Emily quickly gathered up Florence, "Time for bed young lady, goodnight everybody." she said, disappearing out of the candle light towards the stairs with Florence in her arms. Jesse again replied with a grunt and began piling up the used bowls from the table. Eunice, who was slightly annoyed at Jesse for not wanting to come and see the Reverend Maude with her said, "and you, stop right there, whilst I put these two to bed." She picked up the girls and like Emily disappeared towards the stairs with them. Jesse could hear Eunice talking to the girls in the bedroom above, but eventually, it when quiet and Eunice entered the room and sat back at the table opposite Jesse. "Now then." she said resting her arms on the table. "What's all this nonsense about the cost of us getting married?" "Well how can we afford to get married on my wages and that pittance you earn at the mill?" Eunice took hold of Jesse's hands across the table and quietly said, "I have a small confession to make." Their eyes met and Eunice said nothing for a moment, she gripped Jesse's hands slightly tighter and said, "You see, when Benny died, he left me a small legacy, enough to get married again and a fresh start." Jesse's eyes opened wide at this news, "why didn't you tell me

this before now?" Eunice was quick to reply and said calmly, "I was saving it for a rainy day. And it looks like that rainy day is here." Jesse nodded his head and apologized for not wanting to come with her to see the reverend. They kissed and then Eunice accepted Jesse's apology before blowing out the candle and leading him upstairs by the hand.

The following day both made the trek to the parish church at Mirfield to find the Reverend Maude performing a funeral. Jesse removed his cap as the entourage slowly passed them by, "looks like the reverends going to be busy." Jesse said to Eunice, thinking it was perhaps a good enough excuse not to see the reverend. But Eunice was determined; she smiled reluctantly and said quickly, "we'll wait. We can sit over there." Eunice pointed to a small bench in front of the church where both of them sat down. They watched as the funeral took place, which seemed to take forever. Eventually, the reverend bid the funeral goers a handshake farewell at the graveyard gate. After the last one had left the reverend headed back up the

236

path towards the church where Eunice and Jesse were sat patiently waiting on the bench.

"Ah, Mrs. Schorah, we haven't seen you in church for quite sometime." The reverend said as he approached Eunice and Jesse. Eunice apologised and told the reverend that after her husband had passed away, she'd been living in Cleckheaton. The reverend sat down between Jesse and Eunice, he placed his bible on his lap and said out loudly, "in sin, no doubt!" this made both Jesse and Eunice cringe slightly. "Well, we are hoping to put that right." Eunice told the reverend, thinking this would calm him down a little. But the reverend continued to bellow more obscenities, "marriage, marriage woman, that's the only thing that will relieve you of this sin. And is there a bastard child involved in this fornication?" Eunice nodded and looked at Jesse, who was beginning to turn red with anger. Eunice could see Jesse was about to explode at any minute. The reverend continued his ranting about the sins of the flesh and all manner of other things that Jesse had never even heard of, let alone tried. Eventually, to stop himself exploding Jesse managed to stop the reverend by quickly blurting out, "We want to get married!" The statement brought the reverend to a quick stop, and he paused for a breather before saying, "oh! I see. Well you can't get married here." This revelation seemed to shock Eunice more than it did Jesse, who looked at the reverend startled and asked, "Why not?" the reverend began to un-muddle himself by fingering his ear for a moment and then said. "Well not in this church at least! You see, you're in the wrong parish to be married in this church. You'll have to be married in Cleckheaton at their parish church." As the reverend turned to walk away he could see the disappointment on Eunice's face, so calmly, and trying to reassure Eunice, he said, "that's unless you move back into this parish, then you can get married here at Saint Mary's Church."

The reverend had given both Eunice and Jesse food for thought and their journey back to Cleckheaton was quiet and a reflective one. By the time they'd arrived back on the terrace both of them had ideas on what they should do next. They arrived in front of the house and Eunice spoke first. "I don't want Emily knowing our business, so don't say anything. If she asks, just say everything went fine and we are waiting for a date for the wedding." Jesse nodded his head and they both entered the house to find Emily laughing and joking at the table with Henry. Harriet and Baby Emily came running the moment they saw Eunice. She received them with open arms. Eunice gave them both a big hug and a kiss on the forehead whilst Jesse joined Henry at the table. There was a long sigh as Jesse sat down at the side of Henry, who instantly asked, "How did it go then our Jesse?" Jesse smiled and said, "Fine, we're just waiting for the date." Emily looked at Eunice and said, "Is that all? No telling off from the Reverend Maude. I don't believe that!" Eunice walked closer to the table and replied, "Oh we got our telling off alright. Didn't we Jesse?" Jesse nodded and said, "Oh yes love." Henry knew Jesse better than this, he knew something wasn't quite right in the way Jesse was behaving and talking. But decided not to push him on it, instead he blurted out, "Oh by the way, I need a favour." Jesse and Eunice both looked towards Henry. There was a pause and then Jesse said, "If its money you're after, forget it." Henry laughed and said, "No, I want you to watch Florence tonight." Eunice smiled at Emily knowing instantly why. But it took Jesse a little longer to twig what was happening. It wasn't until Eunice had said, "Jesse!" and used her head to point at Emily that Jesse realized that Henry wanted to take Emily out. "Oh... I... we'll look after Florence. No problem. You two go and enjoy yourselves." He then winked at Henry, who was grinning all over his face.

Over the next three weeks Henry and Emily's relationship flourished but the same could not be said of Jesse's and Eunice's. There's was in a state of limbo, not knowing what to do. However, life sometimes leads you to a solution and destiny was about to play a part. Jesse had had an early breakfast and before leaving the house he'd kissed Eunice goodbye at the front door. He'd arrived at work by eight and harnessed the horse to the flat cart before entering the back of the shop by the backdoor as usual, "morning, morning Mrs. Hillard." Jesse said looking around for Mr. Hillard, "what have you done with him then?" Jesse asked jokingly. Mrs. Hillard shuffled forward on her walking stick and replied, "Oh he's not well this morning, so he's having a lie in." Jesse paused for a moment and then said, "Hope it's nothing serious?" "No, he'll be up later. Your first orders are on the desk. It's The Black Bull Hotel in Mirfield, they want a dozen straw and a dozen hay." Jesse grabbed the invoice and shouted, "See you later then," as he stomped out through the backdoor and across the yard to where the cart was.

It wasn't long before Jesse arrived at The Black Bull. He tied the horse and cart to the ring at the side of the building and began unloading the hay and straw. It was hard work humping the large bales around to the back of the hotel where the landlord insisted they went in a neatly stacked pile. Jesse had continued unloading the bales for sometime when he noticed a small shack at the very back of the pub yard. At first he thought nothing about it, but then, after a few trips backwards and forwards to the cart, Jesse decided to take a closer look. He stepped up onto an old crate which could barely hold his weight, and peered in through a small window which was high in the back wall of the shack. The inside was old and dusty with spider webs hanging from the ceiling. Across the otherside of the shack Jesse could see two more windows with a small door in the middle of them. Eager to try the door Jesse stepped down off the crate and began making his way around to the front. At the front of the shack there was a row of roof tiles leaning against the wall. Jesse tried the door, but it refused to open, no matter how hard he pushed.

Eventually, frustrated, Jesse gave up. He turned and walked across a small front yard using a well worn grassy path. The path led from the front door of the shack to a gap in a low wall that surrounded the shack. Jesse sat down on the wall and watched as men with flat caps and rolled up sleeves, rolled bowls over a square of velvet green grass. But as usual, after a few minutes, Jesse began to get bored, partly because he didn't understand the game, and it seemed like an awful lot of effort for nothing. He was just about to leave when the smell of beer penetrated his nostrils. He instantly looked around to find that the draymen had arrived with a delivery of beer, best beer. Jesse quickly stood up and walked back to the front of the hotel, he nodded politely to one of the draymen who returned the compliment before quickly disappearing inside the hotel. It seemed to take an age to finish unloading the rest of the bales, but eventually Jesse entered the hotel. He walked straight towards the bar where he found the landlord in deep conversation with the drayman, "I suppose you want paying now." The landlord said to Jesse, who just nodded and then waited, whilst the landlord disappeared through a door at the back of the bar.

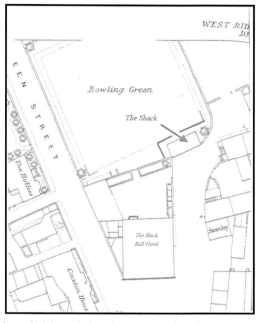

Jesse began to feel uncomfortable and for a moment a silence descended, "come on mate, get a pint whilst you're waiting." The drayman said breaking the atmospheric silence and pointing to a tankard on the bar. Jesse smiled, stepped forward and took a good long swig from the tankard. He then wiped away the froth from his mouth with the back of his hand and said, "By, I needed that!" Just then the landlord arrived back and placed six half crowns on the bar and said, "There you go, fifteen shillings." Jesse thanked the landlord and quickly picked up the half crowns before gently dropping them into his jacket pocket. There was a pause and Jesse got an uneasy feeling that he wasn't wanted. A few seconds past and the uneasiness became unbearable so Jesse quickly swigged off the last of the beer from the tankard and started towards the door saying, "must get back." However, just before he left, he turned to the landlord and asked, "What's that old shack out the back for?" The landlord thought for a moment and then said, "Oh the old bowls store. It's where the Masonic Lodge members used to keep their bowls, but they don't use it anymore. It's up for sale or you can rent it if you want to." Jesse didn't say anything he just fingered his eyebrow and said, "Thanks" before leaving.

Jesse arrived back at the shop. He put the horse to bed and made sure it had food and water for the night. The last job of the day was to drag the cart to the top of the yard so it couldn't be seen from outside the yard. Jesse thought it was a waste of time but Mr. Hillard always said, "It made it harder for thieves to steal it." Jesse grabbed the cart by the harnessing arms and like a horse he began to pull the flat cart across the yard. About halfway across the yard Jesse suddenly stopped, he looked up, it was very quiet, he thought. Jesse got an uneasy feeling that something wasn't quite right. He slowly put down the harnessing arms and walked towards the backdoor, cautiously he entered. There was no-one about. He walked through the backroom and into the shop, assuming that he would find Mr. and Mrs. Hillard there, but there was no sign of either. After standing still and listening intently for a moment the only thing to be heard was a deadly silence. Jesse decided to walk towards the front door, maybe their outside, he thought, but the front door was locked and the closed sign was facing outwards.

"Most unusual," Jesse said to himself. He walked back to the bottom of the stairs and shouted, "Anyone at home?" The reply wasn't instantaneous but eventually Jesse heard, "up here Jesse, come on up." Jesse climbed the stairs and entered the bedroom at the top. The bedroom was dark and there, sat at the side of the bed, was Mrs. Hillard. Jesse quickly scanned the darkened room for Mr. Hillard. His eyes stopped at the bed. Mr. Hillard was laid flat in the bed with only his face and shoulders showing. The sheets had been pulled tightly over him and tucked in hard under the mattress. "He just slipped away." Mrs. Hillard snivelled. Jesse hung his head and knelt down beside Mrs. Hillard. Gently, he put his arm around her and said, "I'm awfully sorry Mrs. Hillard. He was a good man." Mrs. Hillard nodded and wiped her nose. "How long has he been gone?" Jesse asked reluctantly. "Oh not long after you left, a friend and I washed him and laid him out. All we've got to do now is to wait for the vicar to come and tell us when he can be buried." Mrs. Hillard again wiped her nose.

A week later Mr. Hillard was laid to rest and Jesse was invited back to the wake at the shop, where family and friends met in the usual manor. There wasn't much family, an old aunt, a sister, who was knocking on a bit herself and of course Mrs. Hillard. The friends consisted of the butcher from across the street and two neighbours whose only interest seemed to be the little spread Mrs. Hillard had set out on the backroom table. Jesse sat at the table and began to wonder whether or not he still had a job. He didn't think Mrs. Hillard would run the shop on her own, her being old and not very good on her feet. Still wondering, Jesse grabbed a bottle of stout, which was sat on the table with some others at the back of the food. He took a good long swig from the bottle and then nibbled at a sandwich before munching on a rather large piece of pork pie. He took another swig and as he downed the bottle he found Mrs. Hillard had appeared in front of him, "now then Jesse." she said as she sat down at the otherside of the table. "We need to talk." she said politely. Jesse nodded his head and smiled but deep inside he feared the worst, "no job!" "Give it quarter of an hour." Mrs. Hillard said looking around the room, "by then these parasites will have left." Jesse agreed by grinning and again nodded his head.

It wasn't long before everyone began to leave. The last one being the butcher, who bowed, kissed Mrs. Hillard's hand and then expressed his sincere condolences before he finally left. Mrs. Hillard quickly pushed the door closed and slammed home a bolt before pulling down the blind, making sure the closed sign was outwards. "There, they've gone!" she said limping back to the table. She took a moment to catch her breath, coughed and then said, "now then Jesse. I bet you're wondering if you've still got a job or not." Jesse, still fearing the worse quietly replied, "Yes." He took another swig from the bottle and waited. "Well it's like this Jesse. I can't run the shop on my own. I'm too old for that and with my legs and all, I just can't do it." Jesse was so sorry to hear this news, although it's was only what he had expected.

There was a moment's silence and Jesse slowly took the last swig from the bottle, "well, I've no complaints Mrs. Hillard. I've enjoyed working for you and Mr. Hillard. He treated me like a son." Mrs. Hillard shuffled in her chair and pulled up her apron to wipe away a tear, "it's nice of you to say that Jesse, but it's not all bad news for you." Jesse was puzzled by this and turned quickly to face Mrs. Hillard, "what do you mean?" he asked. Mrs. Hillard smiled and then said, "My husband, God bless his soul, said you were a good honest chap who worked hard and deserved a reward for that, so he's left you the horse and both carts. You can carry on delivering the hay and straw with them." Jesse looked across at Mrs. Hillard, "well there no good to me, I can't drive them!" she said. Jesse was exceptionally pleased with the gifts and said, "thank you." to Mrs. Hillard.

The pleasure, however, was a bit short lived as Mrs. Hillard began to pull herself out of the chair, she said, "yes, it is a generous offer alright, and you can take them away before the end of the week." Jesse hadn't realized that Mrs. Hillard was intending to shut the shop so quickly, "ah..." he said. Mrs. Hillard turned. "That might give me a bit of a problem." Jesse said, as he stood up. After a moment's pause Mrs. Hillard hobbled towards Jesse and asked. "Why? The horse is in good health. And as far as I know both the carts are in good working order." Jesse rubbed his chin and quickly said, "oh no, it's not that. The problem is that I don't have anywhere to put them." Mrs. Hillard lifted her head and said, "Oh, I see, well if you don't want them, I'll...." Jesse quickly interrupted Mrs. Hillard and said quickly, "oh, I'll still have them, and don't you worry Mrs. Hillard. I'll find somewhere for them." Jesse plopped his cap on and left by the back door.

The following day Jesse was sat with Eunice and Emily at the breakfast table. The children were busy playing in the corner of the room with some old drawers. The room was a little dark, so Eunice got up and pulled open the curtains which let in the morning sunlight. Eunice, glancing out through the windows, saw Henry approaching the house, "you're Henry's here." she said, returning to the table. Jesse got up and went to let Henry in by the front door. "Thought you'd have been at work by now our Jesse," Henry said, walking straight past Jesse towards Emily, who he kissed on the cheek before sitting down at the table.

Jesse slammed the front door and quickly joined Henry, who had begun chewing on a chunk of bread which had been discarded by Emily. "Waste not; want not, eh our Jesse." Henry said laughing and nudging Jesse with his elbow. However, Jesse just nodded and gave a Neanderthal grunt in reply. Henry looked at Emily and silently worded, "what's wrong?" but Emily couldn't return an answer. Jesse suddenly perked up and said, "I've got no job. Mrs. Hillard is closing the shop." Jesse then spent the next twenty minutes telling Henry what had happened the previous day and how he'd been left the horse and carts by Mr. Hillard. He finished by saying, "so you see I need somewhere to stable the horse and to store the carts, otherwise...."

A silence descended as everybody tried to think of different places that the horse and carts could be stored. Emily suggested number three's backyard, and Eunice said, whilst still thinking. "You only need a small shed or shack for the horse, don't you?" The moment Eunice mentioned shack Jesse knew instantly what he was going to do. "That's it!" he shouted, banging his fist on the table, which startled both Emily and Eunice. "There's a shack at the back of The Black Bull in Mirfield. It's just the job, and it's up for sale." Jesse quickly turned to Eunice and asked, "How much did your Benny leave you then?" Eunice's face changed, "that's for our wedding. Remember!" she said. Jesse, who was by now eager to buy the shack, quickly reminded Eunice of what she'd said earlier. "You said it was for our wedding and a new start! Well, this is the new start." Jesse said, whilst Eunice thought about it for a moment and then went up stairs.

Eunice returned some minutes later with a small lacquered box and placed it on the table. Slowly, she opened the box to reveal a crisp white five pound note. Jesse and Henry had never seen a five pound note before and when Eunice lifted it up, and the five pound note turned out to be three, one on top of each other, both of them gasped. Eunice spread the three notes out on the table. She then pointed them in the direction of Jesse and said, "Here you go, pick one. You can have five pounds and only five pounds if it's anymore, you've had it!" Jesse quickly grabbed the middle note of the three and watched as Eunice returned the others to the box. Once the notes were safely inside the box Eunice slammed down the lid and said, "Go on then, get on with it. Go and buy your shack." Jesse folded the note and put it in his waistcoat pocket, "come on our Henry, we've got work to do." Henry groaned and got up from the table. He then followed Jesse out of the front door shrugging his shoulders at Emily as he went.

In Mirfield Jesse hadn't been able to buy the shack out right but the Leading Mason had taken the five pounds as a deposit and after explaining what he was going to use the shack for, had allowed Jesse to pay the rest in monthly one pound instalments until the full price of twelve pounds was paid off. To seal the deal Jesse and the mason had spat and shook hands. The mason then gave Jesse a bunch of keys, two of which would open the door that Jesse hadn't been able to budge previously. Jesse became so excited that he completely forgot to introduce Henry to the mason and left the lodge without even saying goodbye. Henry, who had waited patiently for the deal to be done, apologized to the mason and with a small grin on his face, explained that Jesse became very excitable at times. Henry and the mason walked slowly back to the front door of the lodge, they looked down the street just in time to see Jesse disappearing off the end of the street. "I'd better go and slow him down." Henry said to the mason. The mason nodded in agreement and gave Henry a reluctant smile before returning to the lodge.

Jesse had nearly reached the shack before Henry had caught up with him. "Steady on our Jesse. Your shack will still be there. It isn't going to disappear because you own it." Henry said, wheezing as he pulled Jesse back by his elbow. Jesse nodded and his pace slowed slightly. They walked the rest of the way at a reasonable pace and Jesse chatted about his plans to change the shack into a stable come store for the hay and straw.

It wasn't long before they arrived at the shack and Jesse was pushing open the front door. Jesse was surprised at the inside, it was as if it had been designed for a stable and store. There was a wall dividing the shack into two equal parts. "Remove those boxes and this side will make an ideal stable." Jesse said patting the dividing wall with the palm of his hand. Henry agreed and said, "What are we going to do with all these boxes? Some still have bowls in them." "Don't worry about them just now; we've got other things to do first." Jesse snapped. He then said, "times getting on and I need to get the horse and carts over here today." Jesse walked towards the door and pushing Henry out first, he locked it and said, "Come on!"

Jesse spent all week stocking the shack with hay and straw, it was hard work, but by the end of the week Jesse had a business and what's more, he'd made money. Tired and exhausted, but pleased with how things had gone, Jesse arrived home late on Saturday evening. He flopped down into the chair and bent down to untie his boots as Eunice entered the room. "Oh you're here. I was going to send out a search party for you." she said fetching Jesse a plate of food and placing it on the table. "I've been thinking." Jesse said scratching his head and walking bootless towards the table. "Is that your feet?" Eunice asked grabbing Jesse's boots. She then, keeping the boots at arm's length, took them outside and placed them on the doorstep. She quickly returned to the table and calmly asked Jesse, "thinking about what?" "Well it would save me a lot of time and effort if I didn't have to walk backwards and forwards to Mirfield everyday." Eunice sat down and linked Jesse's arm, she cuddled up to him and said, "Funny you should mention that, but we've got to leave here anyway." Jesse stopped eating for a moment and asked, "Why's that? I thought you liked it here." "I do but...." Just then Henry and Emily came in from the kitchen, "have you told him yet?" Jesse threw down his fork and said, "What the hell's going on?" Henry laughed and said, "Can't you guess?" Jesse shook his head and then Henry blurted out, "Emily and I are going to live together in Dewsbury. We'll take Florence of course." Jesse stood up and grinned, he held out his hands and shook Henry's hand hard. "I'm glad for you our Henry, you deserve a bit of luck." he said smiling and placing a small kiss on Emily's cheek.

However, as Jesse sat back down he realized that meant he was out of house and home. "Hang on a minute!" he said banging on the table for silence, "If you're leaving, where are we going to go?" He asked, looking toward Eunice, who smiled and said, "Don't you worry your pretty little face about that. I've sorted everything." Jesse quickly grabbed Eunice and pulled her down onto his lap. He threw his arms around her and said, "Oh yes, and who gave you permission to do that?" He then began to tickle Eunice around the waist. After a time of general messing around Eunice had to tell Jesse what she had arranged. "I've arranged for us to move back to Stevenson's Row." she said. "The house where Benny lived is free, and I've paid a week's rent starting Saturday." Jesse couldn't pretend he was happy about the arrangement, but since Eunice had already arranged it, he shrugged his shoulders and said, "Well, I suppose it's better than nothing." He continued to eat his food from the plate and was comforted by Henry, who kept saying, "You'll be alright. Think of all the time you'll save by not having to walk to Mirfield everyday."

Over the next two days, in between delivering straw and hay, Jesse spent time moving Emily and her things to Dewsbury. Eventually, all Emily's things had been moved and Jesse returned to the house on Quarry Terrace. He was greeted by Eunice, who was stood waiting patiently at the door. "Where's the cart?" she asked expectantly. Jesse smirked and just pushed past Eunice saying, "You're joking, aren't you?" Jesse knew by the look on Eunice's face that she was deadly serious and he was followed into the front room by an irate Eunice, "but I've packed everything ready to go." She screamed. Jesse looked around the room and could see boxes of all sizes ready to go. "I'm tired love. Can't we do it first thing in the morning?" Jesse asked collapsing into a chair. "We can if you don't mind sleeping on the floor." Eunice pointed to the collapse bed frame leaning against the wall. Jesse thought for a moment and asked, "Where's the mattress?" Eunice angrily answered by saying, "it's in the bedroom against the wall. It was too big for me to bring down the stairs." Jesse climbed the stairs, grabbed the mattress and in one swift movement, he threw it down the stairs, "there, that's the way to move a mattress." He said to himself following the mattress down the stairs.

At the bottom of the stairs Jesse picked up the mattress and rolled it into the front room where he allowed it to fall flat across the room floor. "There, that'll do us for tonight." Eunice laughed and pointed to the girls playing in among the packed boxes, "and what about them?" she asked. Jesse looked across at the girls and replied, "oh, they'll be alright, they can sleep between us. It's only for one night." Eunice opened a box, sighed and pulled out two sheets. "Come on you two into bed." she said to the girls, who moaned at first as children do when told to go to bed. But eventually, Eunice persuaded them to get between the sheets. However, they didn't sleep, partly because they were downstairs in a different environment, but mainly because Jesse had started to play a peek-a-boo game where the girls kept disappearing below the sheets. After about half an hour Eunice had to call a halt to the game. "Come on Jesse let the girls go to sleep now." She said handing Jesse some pork and bread on a plate.

It didn't take long for Jesse to devour the food. He watched the girls fall asleep. Eunice blew out the candle to reveal a faint beam of light which was coming through the un-curtained window from the street lamp outside. "Awe... isn't that romantic?" Jesse said lying down on the mattress beside the children. Eunice got in the otherside of the mattress, threw her hand across the children which Jesse clasped gently and kissed before falling asleep.

Chapter 12: Returning to Mirfield and Old Friends.

The next morning Jesse was awoken by Harriet and Emily pulling open his eye lids. "What time is it?" he asked, but received no reply. "Eunice, are you awake?" again there was no reply. So quietly, Jesse crept out of the sheets. He told the children to be quiet by putting his index finger over his lips. The girls started to giggle as Jesse crept around to Eunice's side of the mattress. Slowly, he beckoned the girl's forwards towards Eunice and then when they were all ready and in place. Jesse let out a scream of, "chaarrrr...ge...." immediately Jesse and both the girls jumped on top of Eunice. From under a pile of bodies the weary Eunice awoke to be greeted by Jesse's nose poking her in the eye. "Get off me!" squealed Eunice has she tried to wriggle free.

Quickly, everybody stood up and made a line at the side of the mattress. Jesse then led the girls off in a circle around the room shouting, "left right left right." Eventually, the line came to a crashing halt at the bottom of the mattress and all waited for Eunice to sit up. There was a moments silence and then Eunice, blurry eyed, sat up. Jesse belted out, "all present and correct ma'am," he then flung his hand to his forehead and gave a sloppy salute. The girls began to giggle as they set off around the room again with Jesse leading them. About half way around Jesse looked towards Eunice, winked and began pulling a peculiar ape like face. His marching turned into a monkey like walk, all of which made the girls fall about laughing. "You're all mad you lot." Eunice said as she leaped from beneath the sheets.

Breakfast consisted of a couple of raw turnips, a potato and a glass of cold murky water, which Eunice said, "would put hairs on your chest if you drank it down in one go." Jesse lifted the glass, held it up to the light and then swigged it off. Moments later he started making monkey sounds whilst looking down at his chest. Eunice grinned and then started to make up excuses why breakfast wasn't more substantial. "Everything's packed away." she said, becoming annoyed at Jesse's antics, who decided that he'd better go and get the cart before he got into anymore trouble. Jesse grabbed a turnip and put on his jacket before starting towards the door saying, "Right, I won't be long."

However, Jesse hadn't reached the front door before Harriet was flickering her large eye lashes at him and asking, "Can I come too daddy?" Jesse quickly turned and snapped angrily, "no!" thinking he'd be quicker on his own. Harriet was so stunned at her daddy's reply that her eyes soon filled with hurtful tears. Ignoring her, Jesse reluctantly started to open the front door, but just before closing it behind him he made the fatal mistake of looking back at Harriet. Who had by now, with both hands, lifted the hem of her tatty skirt and was weeping tragically into it. Occasionally Harriet would craftily lift her head slightly above the hem of her skirt and looked directly at Jesse. Her lip became prominent, it then began to quiver, but just before she broke out into a full blown tantrum, Jesse's heart melted, as it always did. "Oh alright, get your coat." he said, whilst walking back into the room. Eunice arrogantly smiled and handed him Harriet's coat. "What about Emily?" she asked, pointing towards Emily, who didn't seem interested in going anywhere and was busy playing with the potatoes and turnips on the floor. Jesse stood up straight after fastening Harriet's coat and said, "Look, why don't we make it a family trip? Why don't you come as well?" Eunice leant back and put her hands on the base of her back and said, "No, not today. Baby's kicking just now." Jesse reluctantly smiled and realized that that would mean he would have to drag both girls to Mirfield. "I can't manage them both love." He said, half expecting Eunice to say, "Alright, leave Emily." But she didn't, instead all she said was, "you'll manage. I'm sure."

Jesse slowly put Emily's coat on and began leading the girls towards the front door, "come on then girls let's go." He said still looking hopefully at Eunice, who came to the door. Jesse kissed Eunice and quietly said, "We might be a little longer." He then pointed to the girls with his head and smiled. Eunice nodded and then her face changed to pain, "ohhh...." she yelped as she sat down quickly on the door step. Jesse, showing concern, quickly knelt down and asked, "Are you alright love?" Eunice nodded her head and then Jesse made a quick decision, "we'll wait for a while." He took hold of Eunice's hand, which she quickly shook free and said, "No, no, you go. I'll be alright!" Jesse reluctantly got to his feet and was just about to say something when he was stopped by Harriet, who began to egg him on by shouting, "come on daddy, come on let's go." Jesse slowly walked towards the girls, turning his head occasionally to see where Eunice was. At the bottom of the street he looked back a final time and saw Eunice closing the door; she gave a little wave before actually closing it.

Halfway to Mirfield the girls began to slow up and Jesse could see they were beginning to tire. He removed a turnip from his jacket pocket and sat down at the side of the road. "Come on girls, take a rest." He said cutting small chunks from the turnip with his pen knife. Harriet took a chunk and asked, "Are we there yet?" Jesse pretended that they were. "Just down this road and we'll be there." He said, chomping on a piece of turnip. This seemed to perk the girls up for a bit and they set off again at a brisk pace, which didn't last long. "Can you carry me? I'm tired and my legs are hurting." Harriet complained. "Mine too!" came a cry from Emily has she tugged on Jesse's trousers. Jesse tried to put them off by again saying that it wasn't much further, but in truth it was another five miles.

The girls walked on a little further, but eventually, Jesse had no option but to give each girl in turn a piggy back, but it wasn't long before his neck began to ache and the girls did nothing but moan when it was their turn to walk. Jesse, eventually, just had to sit down and take a rest. They ate more turnip and then Emily, who was nosily peeping over the top of a dry brick wall, asked, "What are those buildings over there?" she pointed to farm buildings in the distance. Jesse stood up and turned quickly to see Woodside Farm. "Oh that's Woodside Farm!" he said folding away his penknife and dropping it back into his pocket. "I get most of my straw and hay from there," the moment the words had left his lips Jesse stuck out his chest, he felt quite proud that he knew the farm. A thought then quickly occurred to Jesse; perhaps the farm has a cart he could borrow. Quickly, Jesse began to march towards the farm, "come on girls. Follow me!" he said.

246

The trio walked quickly down a dirt track which led to the farm buildings. The farmer, who had seen Jesse and the girls coming down the track, came out to meet them, "now then Jesse, what can I do for you?" Jesse smiled and held out his hand which the farmer shook, "I need to borrow a small cart." The farmer laughed and said jokingly, "you won't get many bales of hay on that." Jesse didn't see what was so funny and quickly said, "No, no. I need it for the girls. I've been carrying them for the last two miles and we've got to get to Mirfield." Realizing that Jesse had no time for jokes the farmer thought for a moment and then said, "I haven't a small cart, never had the use for one!" Disappointed, Jesse thanked the farmer and began walking back up the track with the girls closely in tow. They hadn't gone far when the farmer shouted after them. "Wait a minute Jesse. Will this do ya?" Jesse turned and was so pleased to see the farmer pushing a large wooden wheel barrow towards him. "We use it for mucking out!" the farmer said. Jesse and the girls took a sniff at the barrow, "phew!" they all said together. But then Jesse said wearily, "Well it's better than nothing." The girls

agreed and clambered aboard. Jesse again thanked the farmer and said that he would drop the barrow off on his way back to Cleckheaton. The girls loved riding in the barrow, especially when Jesse made the barrow wobble by tipping it from side to side.

They arrived in Mirfield tired and smelly, but happy. Jesse brought out the horse from the shack; he patted it gently on the neck and said, "there, there my beauty." Hastily he spread a little hay over the yard floor for the horse to eat so he could begin to prepare the cart. He cautiously looked around to see where the girls were and found them sitting peacefully on the small back wall that separated the shack from the Bowling Green. They were laughing and joking with each other. Reassured that they were alright Jesse walked down the side of the shack to where the flat cart was stored. He took hold of the carts harnessing arms and began preparing the cart whilst still keeping one ear on the girls. Occasionally, to reassure himself that the girls were still alright, he would stop and listen to the girlish screams being generated by a game. It was a small two persons game, but screamingly loud, it was a sort of catch me if you can game. The loudness of the game reassured Jesse that all was well and the girls were safe and whilst ever he could hear them, he knew they were alright. But suddenly, the sounds began to change. The girlish screams turned into a much angrier, deeper sound.

Jesse dropped what he was doing and quickly walked to the back of the shack. There he was greeted by several angry men from the bowling club; all were shouting and waving their fist at the girls, who were by now quivering behind the shacks front door. "Look what your horse and children have done to our bowling green!" one man screamed. Jesse stared over the small wall at the smooth green grass and sure enough there were muddy skid marks and hoof prints all over the beautiful lawned turf. Jesse quickly jumped the wall and ran towards the horse, which was by now munching on more of the delicate grass. But as he turned the horse towards the sanctity of the shack, things were about to take a turn for the worse.

Suddenly, there was a farting sound and then a series of long thudding noises as the horse unloaded its breakfast all over the bowling green. Jesse knew instantly what the horse had done, but pretended he hadn't heard the noises and to give his pretence credibility, Jesse didn't look back. Instead, he kept his eyes focused on the shack and kept on pulling the horse slowly back towards it. As Jesse approached the men, he tried in vain to keep his face straight, but the closer Jesse got to the irate bowlers, the harder it became.

Eventually, Jesse just had to grin, which slowly turned into a small laugh and then into an explosion of laughter. The bowlers were at first a little stunned, but began to see the funny side of the matter and joined in with the laughter. Jesse, still laughing and shaking his head, walked past the men and tied the horse to the front door handle of the shack. The girls, on hearing all the laughter, emerged from behind the door and they too joined in the laughter, although they didn't know what the laughter was about. It was a good few minutes before all the laughter had subsided and Jesse could apologize to the bowlers, which he did by shaking their hands. The bowlers all returned the gesture willingly and Jesse thought that they weren't such a bad lot after all, and they didn't seem too bothered about the mess. Especially after Jesse had cleaned up all the horse muck and offered it free to a rose loving bowler. But then, just as the men were returning to their bowling, one of them turned to Jesse and said, "I think you need a gate lad." Jesse smiled reluctantly, but agreed by nodding.

On the way back to Cleckheaton Jesse dropped the wheel barrow off at the farm and arrived back in Quarry Terrace just in time for lunch. There was only potatoes and turnip again, but it was better than nothing. Jesse shouted, "We're back love!" as he entered the house. Eunice instantly replied, "Up here love." Jesse quickly climbed the stairs to the bedroom door, leaving the girls eating turnips on the front room floor. He pushed open the bedroom door to find Annie Naylor walking up and down the room with a small bundle held close to her chest, "well!" she said holding out the bundle towards Jesse. "This one certainly surprised everybody by dropping in early." A large grin appeared on Annie's face. On realizing what had happened Jesse's heart instantly missed a beat and he began to panic inside, "where's Eunice?" he screamed with a look of horror on his face. However, he needn't have panicked because seconds later from the otherside of the room came a quiet reply, "over here." Jesse turned quickly to see Eunice sat by the window sipping tea. "You took ya time." She remarked taking another sip of the tea. Jesse totally ignored the remark and walked straight towards Eunice. After grinning, he remarked, "Well aren't we full of surprises then?" Jesse slowly lifted Eunice's head up by the chin, she smiled lovingly at him. They kissed and then Eunice tried to take another sip of the tea. But before she could, Jesse had planted another tender kiss on her lips. He promptly smiled and then allowed Eunice to drop her head so she could continue sipping the tea.

248

After a moment Jesse turned towards Annie and asked excitedly, "what did we get this time then?" Annie opened up the bundle to reveal the child's sex and replied, "A boy! Have you decided on a name?" Jesse shook his head and took a peek at the child. "Not bad eh, considering he's two months early!" Annie said as she covered the child back up. Jesse was absolutely delighted it was a boy; he punched the air and shouted, "Yes! The name lives on," but as he looked again at the child he realized the child wasn't well. "He's only tiny, isn't he?" he asked showing some concern. Annie nodded her head. "Will he live?" Jesse asked quietly as he pulled back the child's blanket to take another look. "That's in the hands of the good lord." Annie replied, who placed the child into a blanket lined drawer. Jesse knelt down at the side of the drawer and leant over the child to take yet another look, but a closer look this time. He smiled at the child and kissed it gently on the forehead before saying under his breath, "welcome, welcome little Joseph." Meanwhile Annie was getting ready to leave. She pulled on her shawl and said, "Well he's certainly strong enough!" she looked across at Eunice and said, "The child should be alright in that drawer. I'll have to go now, are you going to be alright?" Eunice nodded her head and thanked Annie before she left.

It took two trips to move everything to Stevenson's Row and on the return trip Jesse decided to change carts to the smaller one. He thought it would be safer for baby Joseph and the girls to ride in, who were excitedly waiting for

him when he arrived back at Quarry Terrace. "Come on then!" Jesse shouted to the girls, who giggled as he pretended to throw them across the cart. Then, after a couple of attempts, he managed to hitch Eunice up onto the back of the cart. "Will you be alright with your legs dangling?" Jesse asked. Eunice nodded and then Jesse picked up the drawer containing Joseph

from where Eunice had left it on the front doorstep. Jesse, using one hand, checked the front door before carefully leaning past Eunice with the drawer. He placed the drawer into the bottom of the cart, smiled at the child and then said, "There you go young Joseph." As soon as he'd said the word 'Joseph' he knew he was in trouble. Trying to pretend nothing was wrong Jesse tapped the side of the drawer and gave Eunice a reluctant grin. Jesse quickly stood back up and started for the front of the cart, but he wasn't quick enough. Eunice grabbed him by the elbow and asked, "What do you mean? Joseph!" A red faced Jesse reluctantly replied, "oh yes, I've decided to call him Joseph, after my Grandad." He then pulled his elbow free and walked around to the horse, which he encouraged onward by pulling on its mouth piece and clicking his tongue. Eunice wasn't happy that Jesse had named the child without consulting her and remained silent for the rest of the journey, even when Jesse had asked, "Is everybody alright?" Eunice didn't answer.

Jesse dropped the family off in front of the house on Stephenson's Row and then started off back towards the shack along a very lonely dark Eastthorpe

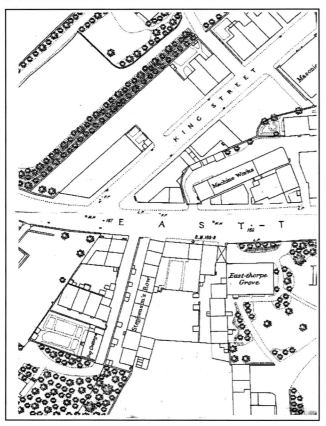

Lane. As he approached The Black Bull Hotel dusk was well gone, but through the dimly lit darkness of the night Jesse could just make out the silhouettes of two men stood on the pavement on the opposite side of the road. At first Jesse thought nothing of it. He gave them a wide berth and just drove on past and up the yard towards the shack. Jesse unhooked the horse and led it into the shack. He gave it enough water and hay for the night and then brought the small cart up the side of the shack and chained it to a wall hook. Whilst doing this Jesse looked back down the yard from behind the cart and making sure the men couldn't see him, he took a good long look at them. For a moment and it was just a moment in the lamp light, Jesse thought he saw one of the men wearing a mucky red and black spotted neckerchief, but at the time Jesse couldn't think why this should be significant, so he ruled it out as a figment of his imagination.

It wasn't long before the men began to move towards the shack. Jesse decided to make one of his decisions, and that was to move off quickly. He quickly walked around the shack and left by legging it across the bowling green. From behind a wall at the otherside of the bowling green Jesse, difficult though it was with the darkness, watched as the men looked around the shack, one of them tugged at the chains holding the carts whilst the other looked across the green in the direction of Jesse. For a moment Jesse thought the man had spotted where he was hiding, but he hadn't. Eventually, both men turned and left. Jesse quickly walked across to King Street. This street led back to Eastthorpe Lane. Jesse slowly walked out into Eastthorpe Lane and discretely looked back towards The Black Bull Hotel. The men were again stood on the pavement opposite The Black Bull. He could occasionally see their cigarettes glowing in the darkness as the men drew on them.

Jesse watched for a while before returning home. It was a black pudding supper and two hours later before Jesse had stopped thinking about the men and felt sleepy enough to climb the stairs to bed. His mind though wouldn't let him sleep, he spent an hour just tossing and turning, which eventually woke Eunice. Annoyed, Eunice complained, she thought that Jesse was still upset about her not talking to him earlier. So reluctantly, and trying to ease his mind and thereby his restlessness, she said, "I don't mind the name Joseph, but ask me next time!" Jesse nodded in the darkness and as Eunice felt the gesture, she turned over and pulled on the sheets before saying sternly, "goodnight." Jesse didn't say anything he just stared out through the gap in the curtains until he fell asleep.

The sleep was restless to say the least and continued until the early hours of the morning. Then suddenly, Jesse was awoken by a realization. He quickly sat bolt upright in bed screaming, "Tom Moore!" Eunice was startled at first but then realizing it was only Jesse dreaming, she asked Jesse sympathetically, "was it a bad one love." She began stroking Jesse's back to relax him, "No, no, no!" he screamed. "I've just realized where I've seen that mucky red and black neckerchief before. It was on Tom Moore, it was covering the hangman's mark." Eunice, tired and confused said, "What on earth are you talking about?" Jesse spent the next two hours explaining who and what Tom Moore was, and how he murdered the two kids on the canal. Eunice thought for a moment and then asked, "But how can it be Tom Moore if he was arrested for murder?" she paused and then said, "Surely he'd have been hung by now? Wouldn't he...?" Jesse agreed by nodding his head, but then said, "Aye, but he might have escaped!" the pair sat silently in bed for a moment as dawn's light pushed its way through the gap in the curtains. Suddenly there was a small whimper from a nearby draw. Jesse jumped out of bed and handed Joseph to Eunice, who promptly began breast feeding him. Jesse, shivering, got back into bed and said, "I need to see our Henry first thing tomorrow, he'll know if Tom Moore is dead or not." This was followed by a silence and then the sound of a child suckling. Eunice turned and was just about to ask Jesse, "How will your Henry know?" When she noticed Jesse had fallen asleep. Irritated at being left alone, Eunice quietly thanked Jesse, "thanks, thanks a lot Jesse!" she said disgruntled. Eunice continued to feed Joseph before eventually falling asleep herself with Joseph still attached to her breast.

Due to the restless night Jesse was late up the next morning and even then it was the girls playing in the next bedroom that had awoken him. He slowly lifted himself out of the bed, put on his trousers and walked towards the gap in the curtains. Gently he pulled back the right curtain and squinted out into the morning sunlight. After a moment of sight adjustment Jesse looked towards Eastthorpe Grove, known locally as the Grove. The Grove was a large house that overshadowed the small cottages in and around Stevenson's Row. The Grove was set in its own grounds and was owned by some well-to-do family who Jesse had only glimpsed in passing the front gate. After scratching his head and pulling up his trousers through a large thick leather belt, Jesse noticed a lot of activity around the small cottages next to the Grove. He watched for sometime and was just about to inform Eunice of the activity, when Eunice asked, "what are you looking at?" Jesse returned to the bed and quickly pulled out his boots from where he kept them under the bed. "There something going on over the way." He said, bending down to tie his boots. "There are a lot of people milling about. I'm going to see what's going on." Eunice, excited, quickly put Joseph down on top of the bed and ran towards the window. "Maybe it's a murder!" she said with a smirk on her face. Jesse wasn't amused and instantly snapped, "Very funny." He then left the room.

Jesse left by the backdoor and walked across the yard towards the outside toilets. After using the toilet he looked over the wall into the small alley which ran down the back of the toilets. The alley was full of police. They were busily searching the cottages and dragging out the occupants. Jesse watched in amazement as the police lined the occupants of each cottage up against the front wall of their own cottages. Just then a voice from behind Jesse asked, "What's going on?" Jesse turned to find a bearded man in a mucky black apron bearing down on him. "Search me!" Jesse replied shrugging his shoulders. Both men stood there watching the events and trying their best to listen in to what was being said. "Don't know anything about it," one man growled at a police officer as he was pushed up against a cottage wall. Just then a shawl clad woman, who was shivering, spoke up and said, "There were two of them. I saw them both from my upstairs window." She then, with a bony finger, pointed at a small dirty window in the apex of a cottage.

Straight away this grabbed the attention of an officer, who, trying to intimidate the woman quickly grabbed her and pulled her in towards him, "oh you did, did you?" he said placing his face right up against the woman's. But then suddenly the officer pulled back and began gipping. "What on earth have you been eating woman?" he asked, wiping some drool from his chin. The officer began wafting his hand in front of his nose and quickly let go of the woman. Jesse and other on lookers began to laugh, but a growl from the officer soon made everyone straighten their faces again. Just then a tall sergeant appeared from behind one of the cottages. "Here, tell the sergeant what you saw." The officer said, nudging the woman with his truncheon towards the sergeant whilst keeping a discreet distance. The sergeant knew the woman and knew how she smelt, "now then Hilda." The sergeant said, keeping the woman at arm's length, "can you describe these men to me?" Hilda didn't answer the sergeant; she just stood there against the wall of the cottage. The sergeant half grinned to himself and slowly took out a flask from his hip pocket. "Here you go Hilda, something to warm you up, and hopefully make you remember." Hilda frantically grabbed at the flask and began guzzling its contents. After a few moments the sergeant pulled back the flask and said, "Well! What did the men look like?" Hilda wiped away some liquid from her lips and with a toothless smiled cackled, "one of them was wearing a red and black spotted neckerchief!" Jesse knew instantly who the men were. It was obviously the same men he had seen the previous night opposite the Bull. His heart began to pound, and at this point he decided that he'd better leave before he got caught up in what was going on.

"Sounds like someone's been burgled," Jesse said out loud. Everyone around Jesse agreed either by saying, "Aye!" or by nodding their heads. The man in the black apron rubbed his beard, looked at Jesse and then also agreed. Just

252

then the police began to break up, what was by now, a considerable crowd. "Come on, on your way. There's nothing to see." The officers began pushing people towards Eastthorpe Lane with his truncheon. Jesse didn't mind moving, in fact, he welcomed the officer's intervention and to show that he wasn't bothered, he said out loud, "well... can't stand around here all day doing nothing, I've got good money to earn." The bearded man again agreed and said, "Aye me and all!" and with that both men headed out along Eastthorpe Lane.

Whilst walking along the lane Jesse realized that the man was walking in the same direction. "Do you work far?" Jesse enquired. There was a pause and the man said, "Not far. Just by The Black Bull Hotel. In fact, my place is in the Bull's yard." "That a bit of a coincidence," Jesse replied. "I work in the Bull's yard as well." Both men stopped and looked at each other. "Are you the chap who's bought the old shack?" the man asked. Jesse nodded and both men laughed. They then, in turn, introduce themselves, "I'm the blacksmith, my shops across from the shack." The man held out his hand and said sharply, "Bill Carters the name and smithying is my game." Jesse returned the handshake and said, "I've just started my own business in the shack, straw and hay. You can call me Jesse." Bill looked pleased and quickly replied, "straw and hay is it. Well there's certainly a need for that around here. The amount of customers I get moaning about having to go to Dewsbury or Cleckheaton for straw and hay is unbelievable!"

The men continued to walk along Eastthorpe Lane talking as they went. Jesse discovered that Bill was also his neighbour in Stevenson's Row and unknown to Jesse at that time, the relationship he had just struck up with Bill was going to prove to be a very profitable one. All that day customers kept arriving at the shack saying, "Bill says you can provide me with straw and hay." Jesse had at least ten customers wanting supplies of straw and hay. One customer even asked for the best quality hay saying, "He didn't want any cow fodder for his thoroughbred horses." This meant more profit per bale for Jesse. All day Jesse was in and out collecting and delivering straw and hay. Business was so good that he decided on his next delivery to call home and tell Eunice of his good fortune.

Jesse entered the house and was greeted by the girls as usual. Harriet pulled at Jesse's trousers and asked for her usual sweets, strawberry twist rock. Jesse had to explain that he would bring the rock at teatime as he hadn't been to the sweetie shop yet. The girls, although disappointed, ran back into the kitchen and continued playing their game of hide and seek whilst Jesse looked for Eunice. He eventually found her in the cellar doing some washing in a barrel. "You're home early!" she said pushing and pulling on an old splintered dolly in different directions. Jesse couldn't wait to tell Eunice of the business he'd done and how there was a great need for straw and hay in the area. However, before he could get his story out, Eunice had wiped her hands on her apron, removed a splinter from her hand with her teeth and had begun telling him the morning's events. It took her at least ten minutes to tell Jesse about the police and why they had been searching the cottages that morning, "Well!" she said, pointing a finger at Jesse, "it turns out that the Grove was robbed and the butler was knocked clean out by two burglars he'd interrupted." Eunice went on and on explaining every little detail about the burglary, never giving Jesse a chance to say why he was there.

Eventually, Jesse turned off and just stood there waiting for Eunice to finish prattling on. It wasn't until Eunice began describing the burglars and the words, "Mucky red and black spotted neckerchief!" escaped from Eunice's mouth that Jesse switched back on again, "Stop! Say that again." Jesse grabbed hold of Eunice's elbow. A pause descended and Eunice pulled her elbow free from Jesse's grip, "what, mucky red and black neckerchief!" she said. "It's him. I know it's him. It's Tom Moore!" Jesse began ranting and holding his forehead as he started to walk up and down the cellar. He'd stop occasionally to think about what he should do next. All Eunice could say was, "you'll have to tell the police. You'll have to tell em what you know." Jesse kept shushing Eunice and wagged his finger at her before rudely saying, "Quiet woman, let me think for a moment." Eunice tutted and went quiet.

Suddenly, the silence and Jesse's thoughts were interrupted by Joseph, who started to cry. Eunice turned sharply and picked up Joseph from his basket, which was nearby; she then sat on the bottom of the cellar steps and began

feeding him. Jesse continued walking up and down the cellar and was still ranting aimlessly to himself, when he suddenly stopped. He looked towards Eunice and asked, "Did anybody say anything about the second man? What he looked like? What he was wearing?" Eunice shook her head and said, "Why! What are you thinking about?" Jesse waved Eunice off for a moment and began walking up and down again. "If it is Tom Moore, you'll have to report your suspicions to the police!" pleaded Eunice. Annoyed, Jesse quickly walked towards Eunice, took a deep breath and said, "Don't you understand? I can't do that until I know who the second man was... now can I?" This left Eunice with a baffled expression on her face, which Jesse quickly removed by simply, saying, "our Henry." "But I thought you'd seen these men last night, your Henry wasn't the second man, was he?" asked Eunice. Jesse was quick to reply, "It was bloody dark, and I couldn't see a right lot. I don't really know who either man was." Jesse then quickly kissed Eunice and said, "I'll have to go. I'll see you later." He quickly stepped over Eunice and Joseph before climbing the rest of the cellar steps. The front door slammed as Jesse left.

On returning to the shack Jesse began loading his next delivery. He'd got about half the load onto the flat cart when a voice from behind him said, "hello our Jesse!" Jesse quickly looked up to find Henry stood over him, "oh it's you our Henry." Jesse said half-heartedly. This reception took Henry by surprise, so he tried to make light of it by saying, "oh, please to see ya our Henry!" but it had no effect on Jesse. He just continued to load the cart. Instantly, Henry knew there was something wrong, but undeterred Henry continued to talk, "there's someone here who wants to meet you." Henry said pointing to

254

someone out of sight around the side of the shack. There was a pause and Jesse took a sharp breath, he was expecting the worst. But then a Scottish voice echoed from around the corner, "hello Jesse. How ya doing lad?" it was old Mr. McCullum, who had a large grin on his face and an out stretched hand which Jesse gladly shook.

After the formalities Mr. McCullum sat on a bale of straw, which was laid at the side of the shack. He drew out his clay pipe from the inside pocket of his coat, filled it with tobacco and took a few puffs whilst trying to light it. The smell was a favourite of Jesse's, so he took a deep breath to inhale the fumes, "ah... that smells good." Jesse said throwing another bale onto the cart. At this point Mr. McCullum stood up and walked across to Jesse; he removed his pipe from the side of his mouth and said, "now then Jesse, young Henry here tells me we can do some business together. I need hay and straw for the Ship Inn and the canal horses, whilst you need supplies of horse corn." Jesse laughed and said, "And why do I need supplies of horse corn?" Henry became annoyed and angrily spoke out, "this is a good business opportunity our Jesse, can't you see that?" Jesse gave Henry a cold look and snapped, "We need to talk before you go arranging business deals for me!" At this point Mr. McCullum began to slip away. "You two have obviously got some problems to sort out, so I'm going to leave you to it. When you're ready to deal, let me know." He waved his hand and walked away leaving a blue trail of smoke floating in the air behind him.

As soon as Mr. McCullum had disappeared from sight Henry blurted out, "what the bloody hell's the matter with you?" Jesse continued loading the cart before asking, "Did you know Tom Moore was alive?" Henry rubbed his un-shaven chin and thought carefully before replying, "Yes, I'd heard he'd gotten off with the kid's murder at Liverpool Assizes, so what?" Jesse, trying to catch Henry out, quickly asked, "Where were you last night?" By this time Henry was beginning to get really annoyed with Jesse's attitude and quickly yelled back, "at home with Em and Flo, why? What's it to ya?" Jesse waited for a moment and then slipped in the words, "are you sure?" Henry lunged at Jesse and grabbed him by his jacket lapels; he pushed him back against the shack wall and screamed, "What do you mean are you sure? Of course I'm bloody sure. Now tell me what's going on." Jesse pulled his lapels free from Henry's gripped fists and blurted out, "Tom Moore did a job last night across at the Grove." There was a silence before Henry, who was still puzzled, said, "And..." Jesse side stepped Henry and was about to release his next sentence, when he was interrupted by Eunice, "and there were two of them!" she said smugly. Henry quickly turned to face Jesse and said angrily, "and you think it was me, don't you?" Jesse was going to reply but Henry was having none of it and instantly began shouting, "Well! If that's what you think of me, then you're no brother of mine!" he screamed before flapping his hand in disgust at Jesse and barging past Eunice, nearly knocking her off her feet as he passed.

Eunice looked critically at Jesse for a moment. Jesse, guilt ridden, just shrugged his shoulders in reply as much as to say, he'll be back. "Anyway what do you want?" Jesse asked politely, realizing that Eunice must have wanted something. He then angrily threw the last bale onto the back of the cart. Whilst Eunice coughed to clear her throat, she then replied, "The Reverend Maud has been to see me this morning. He wants to see us about setting a date for the wedding." Jesse smiled and quickly said, "Bye, that lad doesn't waste any time, does he?" Eunice took a deep breath and said, "I told him you were too busy at the moment and that the first Sunday of next month would be alright. That will give him time to call the banns." Jesse nodded his head in agreement and said, "That means, I've got to make up with our Henry, he's going to be the best man." Eunice grinned and began to walk away, "that's your problem." She said, "I'll see you tonight." Jesse nodded and Eunice disappeared down the yard towards a very busy Eastthorpe Road, where she finally gave a little wave before disappearing behind a row of carriages lining the otherside of the road.

The weeks passed and Jesse was beginning to tire of being nagged by Eunice about the wedding situation and the fact that he hadn't been to make up with Henry. Every Sunday after the banns were called in church Jesse would be bombarded by Eunice all the way home from the church. Until eventually, one Sunday, he gave up and promised Eunice he would visit Henry in Dewsbury the very next day. Anyway he said, "I've to invite Emily and Florence to the wedding so I can kill two birds with one stone." Eunice agreed, linked Jesse's arm and didn't say another word the rest of the way home.

Jesse was up early the following morning and snuck out of the house without waking anybody. His walk along Eastthorpe Lane towards the shack was cold

 and uneventful. As he arrived at the shack Jesse blew gently into his hands to warm them, he then took a moment to look around. There weren't many people up and about, even the mills were quiet, which made a pleasant change thought Jesse, as he began quickly harnessing the small cart. Jesse was keen to get started so without further ado he clicked the horse on and headed off towards Dewsbury. He was hoping to catch Henry up before he left for work. Henry had told Jesse that he lived in a small terrace house in the middle of Dewsbury. The house was rented from a nameless landlord and wasn't very much to look at, but as Henry always said about the house, "it was cheap and cheerful." In reality, it was poor housing, which was situated in one of the most deprived areas of Dewsbury.

It wasn't long before Jesse entered the area and instantly he was overcome by a feeling of unease. It was an area where you kept looking over your shoulder to make sure there was nobody coming up behind you. Jesse eased himself towards the middle of the cart and decided it would be safer to stay on

the cart until he arrived at Henry's house. The horse trotted on slowly past rows of terrace houses, the odd curtain would twitch and occasionally Jesse would catch a glimpse of a dirty faced occupant. Sometimes, if he listened carefully, he could hear the door bolts being slowly drawn to a lock.

Eventually, Jesse arrived at the alley where Henry's house was. He didn't want to leave the horse and cart at the bottom of the alley, so he slowly turned the horse into the alley. At first the horse hesitated and Jesse had to push him on by saying, "I know lad, but get on." He then clicked his tongue and the horse pulled forward. Jesse slowly began counting the houses as he made his way up the alley, eventually arriving at number fourteen. Which was Henry's house or so Jesse thought? Jesse jumped down and tied up the horse to a drain pipe, he gave the horse its nose bag and all seemed well as he checked both ways up and down the alley. He pulled up his trousers, wiped his nose with the back of his hand and approached the door. Jesse knocked twice and waited, he could hear movement on the inside. A bolt was pulled back and the door opened slightly, just enough for a wrinkly old face to peer around the door edge. "Yes, what do you want?" an old lady asked. Jesse stunned at first replied, "I'm looking for my brother Henry and his wife."

There was a moment's silence and then the old woman opened the door further, "you'd better come in then." She said. Jesse reluctantly entered the house and instantly, he was amazed. He had never seen as much stuff in one place, boxes piled high to the ceiling, bags of all descriptions littered the little floor space that there was. "There up there!" the old woman snapped pointed to some turning stairs at the other corner of the room. Jesse began slowly weaving his way across the room taking care not to stand on anything. About half way across the room Jesse had to push an old armchair forward so he could pass it. The movement of the chair quickly released an aroma into the room. The air was instantly filled with a strong smell of cat urine, so strong, it took Jesse's breath away. "That's the cat's chair, she'll not be pleased you've moved it!" cried the old woman from the front door. Jesse couldn't answer the old woman because he was still trying to get his breath back. The old woman hobbled towards Jesse and enquired if he was alright. Jesse nodded and the old woman then said, "Henry's room is at the front. Turn right at the top of the stairs."

Jesse looked at the old woman for a moment and nodded again before once more starting off towards the stairs. However, his progress was soon blocked by a dark coloured sack, which was laid across the bottom of the steps and was unseen by Jesse. The sack clanked as Jesse fell forward over it. "Watch where you're going," the old woman shouted as she rushed across the room to inspect the contents of the sack for damage. Jesse apologized and then laughingly joked, "What's in there, the family silver?" The old woman was not amused and quickly took the sack back across to the otherside of the room snapping, "Mind your own business!" Jesse thought the old woman's behaviour 'a little odd,' but then thought that she must be a little senile, her being of an old age.

Jesse continued up the stairs towards the bedroom door and before knocking, he paused for a moment to straighten his hair. After knocking gently Jesse heard a groaning noise from within and then the sound of bed springs releasing the weary body of someone coming to answer the door. "What is it now?" a voice said as the door swung open. "It's only me," Jesse replied, as he entered the room. Henry, seeing it was Jesse, quickly turned around and walked back towards the bed. "Oh, it's you our Jesse. And pray tell what do you want at this ungodly hour?" Henry asked scratching his backside before sitting back down on the edge of the bed. He yawned and began to shake Emily, who was still covered by gray grimy sheets. "Em, Em. Are you awake? It's our Jesse. He's come to visit." Emily quickly sat up and pulled up the sheet to cover her virtue, "Oh Jesse! Can you give us a minute?" She said turning red with embarrassment. Jesse nodded his head, coughed and then returned to the otherside of the door closing it behind him.

After a couple of minutes Emily came to the door and whilst pushing her hair back off her face said, "you caught us on the hop Jesse, arriving so early." Jesse came back into the room and answered Emily by saying, "I thought you'd all be up and ready to go to work." Henry was quick to reply, "there's not much work around here our Jesse and what there is as already been taken." Jesse looked around the place and asked, "Well how do you live if neither of you do any work?" "Oh, we survive. This and that you know." Emily replied.

Jesse then began to explain why he was there, "let's not beat about the bush, you know why I'm here. I've come to apologise for what I said the other week. I was a bit rash, and I should have trusted you." Henry jumped off the bed quickly and without thought, said, "Ok, apology accepted. Now let bygones be bygones." He put out his hand for Jesse to shake which Jesse did gladly. After a good session of shaking hands and hugging the release came and Jesse decided to strike whilst the iron was hot by quickly saying, "There is of course another matter." The room suddenly became silent. Em and Henry both looked straight towards Jesse. "What's that then?" they both asked together. "Oh it's nothing to worry about, it's just the wedding, it's next Sunday. Are you still going to be my best man?" Henry pretended to think about it by rubbing his hand on his cheek; he smiled, lifted his eyes and said, "of course I am. I wouldn't miss it for the world!" Jesse was so relieved that a grin appeared almost instantly on his face. He then asked, "Where's Florence?" as he began looking around the room. Henry mumbled his words, but eventually managed to say, "She's across the stairs in the other bedroom. We rent both the rooms." Jesse lifted his head to acknowledge Henry before sitting at the other end of the bed.

Jesse stopped for about thirty minutes catching up on all the gossip, but eventually, he had to say, "Well I must be off. I've work to do and customers waiting." Henry nodded and started to show Jesse to the door. On reaching the top of the stairs Jesse thought he could hear deep coughing coming from the bedroom opposite, the bedroom where Florence was supposed to be. Jesse stopped for a moment to listen, but Henry, who was quick to approach Jesse from behind, began coughing. "That's a bad cough you've got there our Henry." Jesse said. Henry nodded and said, "Aye. I will have to get a tonic for it later." Jesse descended the stairs and said his goodbyes at the front door before leaving. Outside he looked up and waved to Emily, who was watching through the bedroom window. Taking a last glance up at the window, a saddened faced Florence appeared and Jesse blew her a kiss which she did not return. Jesse couldn't help himself but all the way back to Mirfield the appearance of Florence at the window bothered him. She certainly wasn't happy he thought. The deep coughing coming from Florence's bedroom was also on Jesse's mind. The cough was too deep to have been made by Florence. Maybe it was actually Henry coughing all along? Did the coughing even come from Florence's room? Jesse was beginning to question his own judgment by the time he'd arrived back at the shack.

The following Sunday morning everyone rose early and dressed in their Sunday best ready for the wedding. Eunice's sisters, Caroline, Agnes and Ellen had arrived early carrying the three traditional cakes. After placing the cakes on the table in the front parlour they began busily preparing food with Eunice in the kitchen ready for the reception at the house after church. Jesse, worrying himself to death, had been walking up and down the entrance hall, occasionally opening the front door to look for Henry. But by the time Eunice's brother, Samuel, had arrived with a small open top coach being drawn by two white horses to take Jesse and his supposedly best man to the church, there was still no sign of either Henry or Em, not to mention Florence. Annoyed, Jesse climbed into the coach and said, "Where can they be?" "I don't know but we've got to go, otherwise you're going to be late. The Reverend Maud wouldn't like that." Samuel replied.

Just then Eunice came to the front door with Harriet and Emily, she was dressed in a scruffy dressing gown and her hair was all over the place. "Here don't forget these two," she said through a mouth full of clips and pins. Jesse dismounted and literally threw the girls onto the front seat of the coach. He was just about to get back into the coach when Eunice shouted, "Eh!" she then pointed to her cheek inviting Jesse to plant a kiss. Jesse tutted and reluctantly planted the kiss. Eunice quickly became annoyed at Jesse's attitude and snapped, "Here you!" Jesse looked straight at Eunice, who hesitated before speaking, "don't take it out on us because of your Henry!" she said pointing a finger at Jesse, who quickly relented and gently kissed Eunice before apologizing. "That's better." Eunice said before waving and closing the door.

Jesse arrived at Saint Mary's Church bang on time and was greeted by the Reverend Maud. "No best man?" the reverend enquired whilst looking around the coach. This made Jesse squirm uncomfortably and pulling on his shirt collar, he replied, "oh he'll be along presently." The girls then quickly jumped down from the coach and entered the church. Jesse shook the reverend's hand, nodded and then crept past the reverend to take his place at the front of the empty church. However, it didn't stay empty for long as people began to arrive for the service. Everytime someone entered the church Jesse's head would flick around to see who it was. It wasn't long before the church was full and Jesse began receiving the usual secretive waves from people he knew. However, there was still no sign of Henry.

The reverend appeared from the vestibule and stood at the front ready to perform the service. The organist took his seat and was just about to strike up the first chords when there was a loud clattering noise from the back of the church. The whole congregation turned to witness a large candle stick being knocked over by Henry, who in his haste to enter the church, had opened the

door fully and with such ferocity that he'd knocked the candle clean off it stand. The stand then hit the stone floor and rolled over a number of times causing the clattering sound to reverberate around a by now silent church.

Jesse was probably the only person not to look around in the church. He seemed to know instantly that it could only be one thing causing the noise, 'Henry' he thought. Henry picked up the candle stand and the candle. Trembling, he stood the stand back up and placed the candle back in position. He then turned to the congregation and reluctantly smiled as he made his way down the central aisle to the front. The girls giggled as Henry took his place at Jesse's side. After a brief silent moment Henry leant across to Jesse's ear and quietly whispered, "Slept in, sorry." He then quickly stood up straight as the reverend looked leeringly over his glasses at him. The service began and Eunice walked down the aisle with her eldest brother Joshua, who gave her away. It wasn't long before the bells were ringing out over the roof tops of Mirfield and the bride and groom were making their way back up the aisle towards the door.

As tradition dictated everybody filed out behind the happy couple and began to throw the traditional rice as they all flowed out into a damp churchyard. The Reverend Maud with Jesse and Eunice formed a small line outside the church door where they began busily shaking hands and receiving congratulations from family and friends. They'd nearly finished and the last remnants of the congregation had nearly stepped through the door and out into, what was by now becoming a drizzly sort of a day. When there was such a rumpus and a sharp short scream from amidst the grave stones.

Jesse turned quickly to see Henry being bundled off by two burly policemen whilst Em and Florence stood by helplessly watching. Jesse instantly went to his brother's aid, but by the time he'd reached Henry the police were throwing him into the back of a horse drawn Black Maria. The door of which was slammed firmly shut by an officer who then had the arrogance to push Jesse back away from the Maria. "That's my brother!" Jesse said angrily. The police officer looked at Henry and laughed, he then looked at Jesse and said, "what, him? He's just a thief!"

Just then the drizzle changed to rain and the rain turned into a torrential down pour accompanied by thundering and lightening. Most of the congregation headed back into the church out of the rain including Eunice and the Reverend Maud, but not Jesse. He waited for the officer to mount the front of the Maria, and then quickly he grabbed hold of the bars of the rear window and pulled himself up so he could look into the Maria. "Henry! Henry!" Jesse called as the rain began to run down his face and into his eyes. Jesse had no

260

choice, if he wanted to see into the Maria clearly he would have to clear the rain from his eyes. Reluctantly, Jesse took one hand off the bars so he could wipe his eyes clear of the rain. He then gazed into the back of the Maria and

 sure enough, with clear eyes, there, sat in the front corner of the Maria was Henry. Henry didn't say anything he just stared back at Jesse.

There was then a deep cough and Jesse's heart fell as he realized that Henry wasn't alone in the Maria. Jesse quickly glanced towards the opposite corner and to his stunned amazement, there sat Tom Moore, coughing and wearing his red and black spotted neckerchief. Jesse quickly looked back towards Henry, who quietly said, "sorry our Jesse, sorry." Jesse slid down the bars, stunned at what he'd just seen. As he let go of the bars and stood back on the floor, the officer told the horse to walk on. Jesse stood there helpless in the rain, watching the Black Maria disappear down the road into a mist of heavy rain.

Chapter 13: Poor, Poor Joseph.

Henry had been sent to prison for 20 years, but Jesse, who was disgusted, had said, "good riddance" to him at his trial after hearing what Henry and his mate Tom Moore had done to the butler. Both were lucky that the butler had survived their horrid attack, if he hadn't, then both would have surely been hung for their troubles. However, Jesse still missed Henry and often thought of him and how he might be doing.

The years passed and Jesse continued to eek out a living from his hay and straw business. It wasn't brilliant, but he'd gained the confidence of enough customers to make it worthwhile. Jesse referred to these customers as his regulars, and he did everything within his powers to ensure they were kept happy by doing things like, delivering on time and at a price that they could afford. The days were long and had become quite busy for Jesse and the business. It seemed that everybody wanted their deliveries all at the same time. Jesse had thought of using Sunday to relieve the pressure but since most people would be in church, including himself on Sundays, that was a bad idea. Anyway, he thought, the Reverend Maud wouldn't have liked that either. So to relieve the pressure Jesse made one of his decisions and bought a small hand cart. He then enlisted the help of Joseph, who was only sat around the house being too ill to go and work in the mill. Joseph was ever so pleased to start work with his dad.

However, Joseph, who had been weakened by every childhood disease you could mention, wasn't a very strong lad and was a rather fragile looking character for a lad of sixteen. To Jesse, he always seemed to be complaining about one pain or another. Jesse had put this down to him being mothered too much by Eunice, who was always ensuring that he was wrapped up right and had he'd put on his vest and other such things mother's witter on about. Despite these drawbacks Jesse was determined he was going to make a man of Joseph. Joseph, on the other hand, was always ready to take on new challenges and was determined to try his best and not let Jesse down. On his very first day Joseph began pushing the small  hand cart around Mirfield delivering hay and straw to the nearby regulars. The hand cart only carried one large bale, which was just as well, because Joseph usually ran out of breathe if he had to climb any hills, but no-one seemed to be bothered so long as the hay and straw was delivered on time.

The first three or four weeks went well, but then Joseph began to cough badly, "It's the dust from these wretched bales," he moaned, choking, coughing and holding his shirt sleeve over his mouth to prevent more inhalation of the dust. Jesse became annoyed and quickly snapped, "It's only a bit of dust lad. It won't hurt you." Jesse placed his hands on his hips and began shaking his head, he then calmly said, "I don't know lad. What are you going to do, if you don't work with me?" Joseph hesitated before replying, "I can't work any longer in this dust dad. It's no good for my chest. Maybe I should work in the mill after all?" Joseph could see Jesse wasn't happy about his comments, so quickly, he pulled out a handkerchief from his pocket and tied it around his nose and mouth before throwing another bale onto the hand cart and beating a hasty retreat down the yard, leaving Jesse fuming at the shack door.

Jesse watched as Joseph disappeared. Then a voice from across the yard shouted, "Hey up Jesse, have you got a minute?" Jesse strolled across the yard to where Bill Carter the smithy was stood wiping sweat from his blackened face. "What's up Jesse? You don't look happy." Bill said from behind a sweat stained handkerchief. Jesse began explaining about Joseph; he finally finished by saying, "Anyway, enough of my problems. What can I do for you?" Bill turned to face Jesse, wiped the inside brim of his flat cap and said, "I noticed Joseph wasn't too happy with his lot either and wondered..." Bill paused for a moment whilst he rubbed his chin, he then continued, "well, I might have a solution for you. I need a lad, maybe your Joseph would like to try smithying? It might change his outlook on things and cheer him up a bit." Jesse hesitated and was just about to speak when Bill began to talk again, "I'll make him my apprentice mind." Jesse again hesitated and scratched his cheek. He then told Bill, "You might be better with my other son, Thomas, rather than Joseph. Thomas is a strong lad and quite able." "But your Thomas is only twelve, isn't he still at school?" asked Bill. Jesse nodded his head and said, "Aye, that's the problem." There was a moment silence between the two men whilst both gave thought to the problem and then Jesse spoke up and said, "oh, what the hell! I was ploughing fields younger than that!" He then held out his hand and said, "take Thomas, he'll learn more with you than he would at school anyway." Reluctantly Bill held out his hand and said, "If you're sure now?" Jesse nodded and replied, "oh, I'm sure, but I'm not sure if his mother will be." Jesse reluctantly grinned, winked and made his way back across the yard to the shack.

Darkness had arrived and Jesse and Joseph began locking up the shack after making sure that the horse was watered and fed for the night. They wearily walked back along Eastthorpe Road towards Stevenson's Row talking as they went. Jesse apologized to Joseph for being a little sharp earlier that day and said, "If you really want to go into the mill. Then go!" Astonished Joseph replied, "Really, what about the business?" Jesse placed his arm around Joseph's shoulders, gave him a smacker of a kiss on his cheek and whispered, "Let me worry about that, alright!" Joseph nodded in agreement.

Later that night Jesse climbed into bed and snuggled up against Eunice. "And what are you after?" she asked, pushing Jesse back onto his side of the bed. "Oh nothing," replied Jesse, turning the other way in a rather poor attempt at playing uninterested in anything. Eunice quickly grabbed Jesse's shoulder and pulled him around to face her. "Come on then, let's hear it!" she said. Jesse quickly turned the rest of his body towards Eunice, put his hand between the side of his face and the pillow and snuggled up. "How do you feel about our Thomas leaving school?"Jesse asked politely. "What! You've already taken

Joseph. Surely you can manage without Thomas?" Jesse sat bolt upright and said, "it's not for me. It's for Bill! He needs a lad in the smithy shop." "It was you who said that schooling was the most important thing in life. You not having a great deal of it yourself." Eunice replied angrily. Jesse thought for a moment and then said. "Yes, but the money will come in useful." A silence descended on the bed. Eunice pulled up the sheets and said, "We have enough money coming in at the moment, what with both the girls bringing in wages from the mill. So you can't use that as an excuse." On the word mill Jesse remembered that Joseph wanted to join the girls in the mill, and thought he'd best tell Eunice now and get all the flack over and done with in one go. "Talking of mills," he said sheepishly, "our Joseph wants to go into the mill. He can't stand the dust working with me." Eunice yawned and wearily asked, "Can we discuss these things in the morning? I'm tired and need to get my beauty sleep." Jesse nodded, kissed Eunice goodnight and turned over to his side of the bed.

The next morning Eunice was noticeably quiet, she'd made boiled eggs for breakfast and was sat dipping small chunks of bread into hers at the table. Jesse, who was sat opposite, was engrossed in gently spooning out his egg with a teaspoon, when Thomas arrived at the table. Thomas looked at both of them and quietly said, "it's awfully quiet around here this morning, has someone died?" He then plonked himself down at the table between Jesse and Eunice before taking an egg from the bowl, which was sat steaming in the middle of the table. He was just about to knock the top off his egg, when Eunice angrily stood up and announced, "Well, it looks like you're going to work!" Thomas was startled by this sudden announcement and to say the least a little baffled. Thomas turned his head slowly towards Jesse hoping he could shed light on the announcement, but instead, Jesse just sat there silently spooning his egg.

Eventually, Jesse gave Thomas a half smile and signalled to him to be silent by putting his index finger to his lips. Eunice disappeared into the kitchen saying, "and you two can clean the table before you leave." Both Jesse and Thomas replied by nodding their heads at the same time. There was then the sound of rattling crockery before Eunice bounded back into the room. She passed the table and opened the front door, but before leaving, perhaps to get her own back on Jesse, said, "Oh, and by the way, you're daughters pregnant!" Jesse leaped from his chair and grabbed hold of Eunice by the elbow. "What do you mean my daughters pregnant?" Eunice pulled Jesse's hand off her elbow and slammed it down towards the floor. "You heard your darling daughter is pregnant!" Jesse began to shake with anger, "How! I mean, who? I mean, when!" Eunice grinned and said, "I thought that might get a reaction from you." She shut the front door and sat back down at the table.

Jesse who was still recovering from the shock, rubbed his forehead in disbelieve. "I'm going to be a Grandad!" he said, flopping back down into his chair opposite Eunice. Then as reality struck home, Jesse screamed, "Who's the father?" Requiring an immediate answer from Eunice, Jesse looked straight at her, "oh, he's an overlooker in the mill where she works." She stammered. Jesse quickly stood back up and shouted, "I'll have him! I know what those overlookers are like in the mill. They take advantage of young girls." Eunice waved her hand at Jesse and told him to sit back down. "Calm down, it's nothing like that," she said. "They've been walking out together for months." Jesse froze for a moment and then said, "Well, how come I don't know anything about this chap, and why hasn't he been to ask me if he could walk out with our Harriet?" Eunice smiled pleasantly at Jesse and said, "You've been too busy with the business for him to ask you. You were never here when he came." Jesse started to rant. "Oh so this has been going on for months behind my back. It's a fine thing when the father is the last to know."

On and on Jesse went until Eunice began to grin, which quickly broke out into laughter. Thomas also began to laugh at Jesse ranting on to himself. Slowly Jesse began to stop. He looked across at Eunice and began laughing at himself. It was a good few minutes before the laughter abated and then suddenly the sound of the mill's claxon could be heard. Eunice stood up and said, "oh my God! I'm going to be late." She quickly kissed Jesse on the cheek and said, "He's a really nice lad, and they're going to be married, so all you have to do is put your hand in your pocket and pay for the wedding." She then gently tapped Jesse on the cheek, winked and smiled lovingly at him. "I'm off!" she said as she left by the front door. "Hang on a minute!" Jesse shouted. Eunice returned by poking her head back around the front door. Annoyed at being shouted back, she quickly snapped, "what now!" Jesse paused for a moment and then with a smug  look on his face, asked, "and where are these young lovers going to live?" he crossed his arms and winked at Thomas, who grinned and said nothing. "Oh, don't worry about that. It's all been sorted. They're going to have the front bedroom."

Eunice quickly slammed the door before Jesse could say anything more on the subject. She walked quickly out onto Stevenson's Row, where if truth be known she had a right good giggle about the morning's events. Still livid with Eunice, Jesse looked across the table at Thomas and said, "Come on lad. We've work to go to. I'll explain what you're going to be doing on the way." Jesse got up and ambled towards the bottom of the stairs where he shouted for Joseph. "He's not up there!" Thomas said. "He went with the girls for the early shift in the mill. He said you said he could!" Jesse nodded his head as he returned to the room. He pulled his jacket off the back of his chair and slid into it in one swift movement, "aye, I suppose I did." He then grinned to himself before saying, "come on then lad. Let's get started." Thomas stood up and they both left for work by the front door, making sure the door was locked by giving it a good tug before leaving. They hadn't gone far before Jesse started to tell Thomas what he was going to do. Thomas was ever so pleased to learn that he was going to be apprentice to Bill Carter the blacksmith. So pleased in fact, that when they arrived at The Black Bull Yard, Thomas didn't even say, see you later or goodbye to Jesse, he just skipped his way into The Blacksmiths Shop and wasn't seen until teatime.

A month later the banns for Harriet's marriage were read out in church and the happy couple were only too pleased to learn that they were to be spared the wrath of the Reverend Maud about sex before marriage. The right reverend had been replaced by the Reverend Frederick Grenside, who was a more lenient type of vicar, some said too lenient. The Reverend Grenside performed the wedding ceremony without criticism or favour on a very pleasant spring day in May 1888. It wasn't a very lavish affair, just a few close friends and family attended, and even they had to intermingle with the usual congregation to save money. However, it was all Jesse could afford due to business being a bit slow and everyone made the best of it. Bill Carter had even taken on the role of usher and as tradition dictated Harriet had pinned favours on Bill's shoulders of white ribbon and flowers, some with silver leaves entwined in them before he had left for the church. Jesse had also dressed up the horse and small cart with favours. He and Harriet had fastened them on that morning. These were removed when Mr. and Mrs. Henry Howarth arrived back at the bride's home and were placed in a decorated corner in the front parlour of the house, which Eunice had spent three hours earlier that morning making sure it was up to scratch.

Harriet and Henry stood proudly in front of the decorated corner waiting for their guest to arrive. Jesse was the first to congratulate the couple by shaking Henry's hand and giving Harriet a long kiss on her cheek. He then went and stood by the front door, so he could direct the guest through to the front parlour. Most of the guests were walking from the church, so Jesse kept looking up the row to see if there was any sign, eventually there was. It was Eunice's three sisters, Caroline, Agnes and Ellen, who were first to appear followed by their husbands who were busy chatting to Eunice's brothers Joshua and Samuel, "their coming!" Jesse shouted to the happy couple, who were by now pinching kisses from one another in the front parlour and getting very excited about receiving their guests.

"Welcome, welcome!" Jesse said as he began removing coats and gloves from people. "Where's our Eunice?" a voice said from the back of a small group of guest. Jesse looked over to see Caroline smiling at him. "She's in the kitchen cooking the wedding breakfast." Caroline acknowledged Jesse's answer by nodding and rolling up her sleeves. "Come on girls, many hands make light work." The three sisters barged past Jesse and entered the kitchen instead of the front parlour. It wasn't long before hearty breakfasts were being served by the sisters and guests were stood around eating. Eunice came in from the kitchen and handed Jesse and Thomas a plate of food then she began to look around for Joseph. "Where's our Joseph?" she asked. Jesse shrugged his shoulders and Thomas didn't say anything until Eunice gave him a quick dig in his side with her elbow. Thomas let out a yelp and rubbing his side, angrily replied, "How should I know? I'm not his keeper!" Jesse could see Eunice was worried and said, "I'll find him love. He won't be far." Eunice smiled nervously at Jesse, who began searching the house. Eventually, he ended up in the back bedroom where he found Joseph sat on the edge of his bed. "What's the matter lad?" Jesse asked sitting down on the bed at the side of Joseph. "Oh nothing, I'll be alright in a minute!" replied Joseph, as he began coughing into a small piece of cloth he'd fashioned into a handkerchief. Jesse put his arm around Joseph and said, "Still got that cough I see." Joseph nodded his head and coughed again, this time longer and deeper than before. When he'd finished, he glanced into the cloth to see what it was he'd coughed up. Whatever it was, it was red and bloody, and to prevent Jesse from seeing it, Joseph quickly folded the cloth in half and pushed it quickly into his jacket pocket.

Jesse grinned and with his arm around Joseph's shoulder he gave him a one armed hug. "Come on then lad," he said. "Let's get back to the party." Jesse started towards the door, "you need to see a doctor about that cough." He said showing concern and opening the door. Joseph shook his head and replied, "No, it'll pass. Give it time. Anyway, we can't afford it just now with business being slow and the cost of the wedding and all." Jesse didn't disagree with that, but replied, "Nevertheless, tomorrow, I'll ask Doctor Parker to call. He might be able to give you a tonic." Jesse made his way back downstairs to the front parlour closely followed by Joseph. At the door of the parlour Jesse turned to look at Joseph and said, "But for today my lad, you've got to attend your sister's wedding. So come on, look sprightly." He then pushed Joseph into the front parlour where Eunice was waiting for him with his plate of food. Joseph took the plate from Eunice and decided he would sit in the backyard and enjoy the fresh air, whilst he ate the food. Secretly however, he really wanted to see what it was he'd coughed up into the cloth. Joseph slowly ate the food, it was a really nice breakfast with all the trimmings, but the bacon rind had started Joseph coughing again and after that no matter how hard he tried, his appetite had gone.

Joseph put the plate down on the stone wall that ran around the yard, burped and then punched his chest with the end of a clinched fist. After this he slowly pulled out the cloth from his jacket pocket. With quivering hands, he slowly opened the cloth to reveal a large circle of bright red blood with a large amount of blood-tinged sputum covering the middle of the cloth which was slightly green in colour. At this point, Joseph knew enough about the dreaded consumption to know that he needed to see the doctor quickly.

Just then a voice from behind Joseph asked, "Have you finished?" Joseph quickly placed the cloth back in his pocket as Eunice approached him from the direction of the kitchen. She picked the plate up from the top of the wall and looked down at it. The plate still had its half eaten breakfast sat on it. Even the fat had solidified holding its contents in one lump. Eunice was just about to start preaching at Joseph on the morals of wasting food when she realized that Joseph wasn't well. "Are you alright?" she asked, gently stroking Joseph's hair. "I worry so much about you." Eunice continued to say whilst showing more motherly affection in the form of a small kiss on his cheek. Joseph made his excuses and said he was tired and would like to go to bed. Eunice nodded and watched as Joseph headed towards the stairs. Jesse passed him in the kitchen and blocked Eunice's view for a moment. "What's wrong with him then?" Jesse asked as he took a swig from a small tankard of ale. Eunice, who looked worried, quickly replied, "He says he's alright, but he's not kidding me. He's ill!" Jesse grinned and said, "Stop mothering him, he'll be alright!" Eunice wasn't amused by Jesse's comments and stomped back into the kitchen where she began viciously rattling pots and pans as she washed up.

The rest of the day went well and time seemed to go by without anybody noticing that the bride and groom had changed into their travelling clothes and were stood on the door step waiting to set off on their honeymoon. Harriet was going to be escorted by Emily who had been her chief bridesmaid. Jesse brought the small cart to the front of the house and helped Harriet into it. She shook off her left shoe as she entered the cart for luck. Henry obligingly picked it up and replaced it gently back onto Harriet's foot whilst looking moon faced at her, "Doesn't it make you want to gip?" Emily said climbing into the cart. Jesse laughed and said, "Aye, it happens to the best of em, love!" he started to shake his head as Henry jumped aboard the cart and quickly grabbed Harriet's hand as he sat down between the girls in the back of the cart. Everybody then began throwing rice at the happy couple as Jesse pulled away and headed towards Mirfield's train station.

Eunice, with a tear in her eye, watched the cart disappear from sight, she then returned to the house which seemed so quiet after the day's events. Call it mother's instinct, but the silence seemed to draw her straight towards Joseph's bedroom where she opened the door slowly. Her heart nearly missed a beat when she realized Joseph was laid flat in the bed like a corpse that had been laid out. She quickly moved towards the bed and sat on the edge, where she gently grabbed Joseph's hand and clasped it between hers before whispering, "Joseph." At first Joseph didn't answer, but then as he realized who it was, he opened his eyes and said, "Aye ya mum." Eunice smiled at Joseph and calmly placed her hand on his forehead to feel his temperature. Her hand was instantly repelled by the heat being generated by Joseph. "You're
burning up," she said. Panic set in and Eunice quickly soaked a towel with cold water from the jug and bowl which was sat on the dresser in the corner of the room. She brought the bowl and the wet towel back to the bedside where she placed the bowl on the bed and tenderly placed the wet towel on Joseph's forehead. The lack of speech from Joseph showed that he was tired and very weak. So weak, in fact, that Eunice shouted for Thomas, who appeared instantly at the door. "Go and fetch Doctor Parker. Go on, quickly!" she screamed. "Why what's the matter?"" Thomas asked, not realizing that Eunice was in no mood for his questions. "Don't ask such stupid questions, go and

get the doctor!" Eunice snapped pushing Thomas back out of the room to encourage his departure.

Thomas flew like the wind towards the doctor's house and soon returned with the doctor in tow, "upstairs doctor." Thomas stammered whilst sitting down on the bottom of the stairs to regain his breath. The doctor didn't say a right lot. He just put his hat on the hallway desk and walked calmly past Thomas pushing his black medical bag before him up the stairs. Moments later Eunice appeared red eyed at the top of the stairs. At this point Thomas realized that it must be serious and went to assist his mother back down the stairs. They both sat quietly at the bottom of the stairs, the silence was deafening, only to be broken by the occasional footsteps sounds from the bedroom. But then the front door opened and Jesse entered. Eunice got up quickly and ran towards Jesse, she began to cry. "It's the consumption, I know it is!" she cried, flinging her arms around Jesse's neck. Jesse pulled Eunice down to his chest by undoing her arms. "Now... now..." Jesse said, trying to get Eunice to stop crying. "Don't take on so Eunice. Let's hope and pray that it isn't." All three returned to the bottom of the stairs and waited for the doctor to emerge.

After about half an hour the bedroom door clattered open and the doctor appeared, he didn't let his face slip for a moment, he just rubbed his rather long sideburns and asked if there was somewhere where they could talk. Jesse showed the doctor into the front parlour. He allowed Eunice to enter after the doctor and then entered himself leaving Thomas sat on the stairs. However, Thomas wasn't going to be left out and quickly placed his ear on the door to listen in. The first sound to be heard was that of the doctor coughing. Eunice, beginning to cry, asked quickly, "Is it the consumption doctor?" The doctor paused before answering, "I'm not sure at this point. I need to take the sputum and analyse it to be sure." The doctor then reached into his bag and pulled out a brown jar and a dark green bottle. "Rub this on his chest at regular intervals," he said, handing Eunice the jar. The doctor then began to read the label on the bottle before saying, "Twice a day with a little water." He handed Eunice the bottle and then looked for the way out. Jesse stepped back and opened the door for the doctor. Outside the door was Thomas who was waiting with the doctor's hat. The doctor snatched the hat from Thomas and walked towards the front door. "Two bales of straw for my horse, that's my fee." Jesse quickly walked past the doctor to open the front door and replied, "Yes doctor, I'll deliver them in the morning." Jesse thanked the doctor who left saying, "I'll be back in a couple of days."

The following day Jesse was delivering the straw to the doctor's house. He'd already dropped the first bale in the stable and was returning with the second when he was stopped by the doctor. "Now then Jesse!" the doctor said. Jesse dropped the second bale and said, "good morning doctor." "Have you a moment?" the doctor enquired. Jesse knew instantly by the doctor's tone that it wasn't going to be good news. He wiped his hands on the back of his trousers, straightened his cap and walked into the doctor's house, making sure he wiped his feet before entering. "Come in, come in!" the doctor shouted from behind a large desk in a room to the left of the doorway. Jesse removed his cap and entered the room before sitting down on a red velvet chair that the doctor had pointed to. "I'm not going to beat about the bush Jesse. It's not good news. Joseph has Phthisis Pulmonalis!" Jesse looked at the doctor puzzled. "Oh, that's tuberculosis to the uninitiated." Jesse, under his breath, whispered to himself, "Oh, so it was the consumption after all." The doctor heard Jesse's whisper and agreed by nodding his head. Jesse's head began to spin and he became somewhat confused at the news, he didn't really know what to say next, he just stammered out a rough sentence of questions, "what now? How long has the lad got? What shall I tell the wife?" The doctor waited until Jesse had calmed down and composed himself. He then calmly said, "Firstly, we must get Joseph to the hospital so no one else in the family can become infected." The doctor paused for a moment whilst he poured two large whiskeys from a crystal decanter, which was languishing on the end of the large desk. "Here drink this!" the doctor said handing Jesse one of the glasses. Jesse, at first, only took a small sip from the glass, not wishing to appear greedy. "Get it down you man!" the doctor snapped using his hand to

encourage Jesse to drink the liquid. Jesse wiped his lips with his tongue as his pallet received the ten year old malt for the second time. It was as smooth as nectar.

Jesse returned home with the bad news and two days later Joseph was received at the new Mirfield Memorial Hospital suffering from severe weight loss and a small fever, his coughing had got slightly better due to the tonic the doctor had prescribed and this had given hope to both him and Eunice. Jesse, however, wasn't so convinced nor was Harriet and both continued to show concern for Joseph until he died an agonizing nine weeks later at the tender age of seventeen. Eunice, as you would expect, was devastated at the loss of Joseph, but little did she know that the situation and her feelings, were going to get much worse as that black day wore on.

After a silent walk, the family was returning to a dark cold house on Stevenson's Row. Bill Carter was stood at his front door and was going to ask how Joseph was, but on seeing the posture and faces of the family, he realized instantly that there was no point. He just quietly nodded his head at Jesse and went back inside, before closing the door quietly.

Jesse lit two candles and then sat at the table. Harriet went into the kitchen and began to bring items to the table. Firstly, a cheese board, then a round loaf of bread followed by a large carving knife. Eunice, who was by now sitting opposite Jesse, said, "I don't think I could manage anything just now, but you lot eat. I'll just sit here for a while before bed." Harriet began carving slices off the loaf with the knife whilst Thomas tore off a piece of cheese from the front of a triangular piece sat in the middle of the cheese board.

Nobody ate much and there wasn't much conversation either, in fact, the only sound to be heard was bread and cheese being swallowed and washed down by brown ale. Jesse, realising that everybody was at the table and had nearly finished eating, thought it was the appropriate time to say something about Joseph's funeral. "Well I don't know what we're going to do now?" He said looking for a response from Eunice, who was by now, just staring red eyed at a flickering candle in the middle of the table. After an unresponsive moment from Eunice, Harriet replied, "whatever do you mean dad?" Jesse looked across at Eunice and cringingly said, "How are we going to pay for the funeral?" Again there was no response from Eunice. Harriet continued to fill in for Eunice and asked, "Why are we skint?" Jesse nodded his head. "How can that be? I thought we had plenty of money." Thomas whimsical announced whilst putting another piece of cheese into his mouth. Jesse became angry at Thomas for butting in and quickly replied, "We had, but Harriet's wedding took most of it!" As soon as the words had left Jesse's mouth, he realized his mistake. Harriet looked straight at him and asked, "What! We can't afford Joseph's funeral because of my wedding?" Harriet began to fill up and Jesse stood up, "I didn't mean it like that love," he said.

Trying to make things better, Jesse sat back down and said, "The funerals not the problem, it's the plot, plots are five guineas and that's not to mention the headstone. Have you and Henry got any money?" Harriet looked at Henry, who just shook his head and reluctantly answered, "We spent what money we had on your bottom drawer." Jesse's voice became quieter as he said, "we've no choice then...." everybody around the table looked towards Jesse and waited for him to complete the sentence. It was a solemn moment which ended in Jesse announcing. "He'll have to have a pauper's grave then." At the mention of a pauper's grave Eunice let out a loud wail and her forehead fell to the table. Jesse quickly rounded the table and lifted Eunice's head gently up off the table. The wailing continued and no-one, no matter what they said, could stop Eunice's out pouring of grief and the thought of a pauper's grave for Joseph only served to make matters worse.

Seeing her mother upset and believing she was to blame for Joseph's deathly demise, Harriet began to cry and was led away from the table by Henry. Thomas left and went to his bedroom saying he couldn't stand to see people crying, but Jesse suspected he just wanted to be on his own. This left Jesse sat with Eunice, who was desperately trying to stop crying. However, everytime she tried, the thought of a pauper's grave would enter her mind and the crying would restart. Three hours later the snivelling began to cease and Jesse started talking calmly and quietly to Eunice. "Are you alright?" he asked. Eunice looked up and nodded her head; she wiped her nose and asked, "Are you sure we can't afford a plot Jesse?" Jesse sighed and trying not to upset Eunice again, said, "I'm sorry love, but we just haven't got the money right now." Eunice wiped her nose again and nodded her head as she finally accepted their predicament.

After a restless night both Eunice and Jesse were up early. The breakfast was quiet, only to be interrupted by the odd snivel. After breakfast Eunice grabbed her coat from off the wall peg and began to put it on. "Why don't you take the day off love? I'm sure the mill won't mind!" Jesse said helping her on with her coat. "No I'd rather be busy. Work will take my mind off of things." Eunice replied as she fastened her coat buttons. Jesse nodded and said, "Ok then, I'll walk you on." Jesse grabbed his jacket, plonked on his cap whilst Eunice linked his arm. They walked slowly along Eastthorpe Lane towards the mill. As they walked Jesse explained that he would visit the Reverend Grenside that very morning and work out the arrangements for the funeral. Eunice nodded and gave Jesse a kiss before disappearing across the mill yard towards a pair of double doors. She waved before entering.

Jesse loaded up the cart with his first load of the day and set off across The Black Bull's Yard towards Eastthorpe Lane. On passing the smithy shop, he noticed Thomas, who was hard at work with Bill, "morning, morning Bill." Jesse said from the front of his cart. Jesse pulled back on the horse as Bill walked towards him. "I'm sorry to hear about Joseph." "Aye, I'm just going to see the reverend about the arrangements." Bill nodded and then said, "My condolences to the family then." He then wiped his hands on his apron and returned to the anvil where he was shaping a horse shoe. Jesse acknowledged Bill's condolences by thanking him.

It wasn't long before Jesse arrived at the church and found the reverend pruning his roses in the vicarage garden. Jesse removed his cap and waited whilst the reverend played with various stems, he cut a little here and then a little there. Eventually, Jesse, who was getting fed up of waiting decided to cough. "I know you're there. Just give me a moment." The reverend said as he continued to inspect the roses. After trimming a few more bushes the reverend had made his way around to the otherside of one particular bush and was now facing Jesse. "Ah! So it's you Jesse. I suppose you've come about Joseph." Jesse was very surprised that the reverend even knew about Joseph, but then he realized that the reverend attended the hospital regularly to give out the last rights and things.

Jesse began to reluctantly explain his situation to the reverend: who seemed uninterested in what Jesse had to say and just continued to prune and inspect his roses. After more pruning Jesse stopped speaking and the reverend looked up. "Go on I'm listening," he said, but Jesse wasn't convinced and waited for more attention. It took a moment for the reverend to realize that Jesse was waiting, but eventually, he put down the pruners and stood before Jesse. "Well!" he asked. Jesse hesitated and had to pluck up the courage before asking, "Is it possible for our Joseph to be placed into a pauper's grave?" The reverend thought for a moment, "We only have two and their right at the top of the graveyard up against the wall." The reverend said pointing over a rose bush towards a black wall at the top end of the graveyard. Before Jesse could say anything else the reverend had resumed his pruning and had turned his back on Jesse once again.

Jesse decided to ignore the reverend for a moment and put his hand over his eyebrows. He looked towards the black wall at the top of the graveyard and thought the area was a little out of the way, a little untidy and he would have preferred to have had Joseph buried a little nearer the church, but then, he thought, beggars can't be choosers! "Is that place up there consecrated ground reverend?" The reverend replied, with a couple of nods. Jesse waited for the reverend to go around to the otherside of the bush before repeating his request, "Would it be possible then for my lad to be placed there?" Again the reverend thought, "Well one of them is full to bursting." The reverend paused and thought again, "fifty eight in that one, I think!" he said. Jesse was shocked and startled by this number and blurted out, "how many?" "Fifty eight!" the reverend replied. "Oh, don't worry there's plenty of room in the other. We might have to do a bit of shuffling and dig a bit more out, but we'll get him in." Jesse felt sick to his stomach at the thought of Joseph having to share his final resting place with unknown others and after arranging the following Monday at two in the afternoon for the funeral, he began to wonder if he was doing the right thing.

Jesse bid the reverend, "good morning!" to which the reverend smiled and said, "See you on Monday then." Jesse nodded, replaced his cap and set off to deliver his load. As usual, things began to spin around inside Jesse's head and the usual sorts of questions began to materialize as the ride back seemed longer than usual. By the time he'd arrived back at the shack the only thing to come from his spinning thoughts, was that Eunice should not find out about the paupers graves and the amount of people in them. It would break her heart, especially if she thought that there were criminal types in the graves.

Jesse visited the pauper's graves a couple of times over the next few days and gradually became use to the idea of Joseph being buried there. On one warm evening visit, he brought Eunice along to show her where Joseph was to be buried. As soon as she saw the unmarked pauper's grave Eunice began to fill up. "Oh my God!" she said pulling a handkerchief from her skirt pocket. Jesse quickly tried to comfort Eunice by placing his arm around her shoulders and saying, "Come on now, you promised you wouldn't start." "I know I did, but I didn't realize he was going to end up here, up against the wall!" Eunice snivelled as she wiped her nose and looked towards the church. "And he's so far away from the church!" Jesse pulled Eunice away from the graves and said, "Listen, when things pick up and the business begins to turn a profit again. And it will, mark my words! We'll buy our own plot and have Joseph transferred into it. How's that sound?" Eunice looked at Jesse with a runny nose and red eyes. She grabbed hold of his arm tightly and desperately squealed, "Promise, promise me Jesse, promise me you'll do that!" Jesse nodded his head and Eunice seemed to take some solace from the promise. They slowly walked back towards home without speaking another word.

The family managed to club together enough money to pay for a coffin and the hearse. The hearse would be pulled by a lone horse and the coffin was to be made of cheap unshaven wood with wooden handles. Bill Carter had said he would fashion a plaque for the top of the coffin, which would have Joseph's name and date of death on it. With all preparations complete the family arrived at the church yard being led by the hearse, which was all rigged out in black ostrich feathers and lace. The hearse came to an abrupt halt in front of the graveyard gates. Slowly, Jesse, Bill, Henry along with Thomas pulled the coffin from the hearse and lifted it up onto their shoulders. They walked slowly through the gates of the graveyard with the coffin aloft towards the pauper's graves followed by a tearful Eunice, who was being comforted by Emily and by now a very pregnant Harriet. Bill's wife and other neighbours brought up the rear of the small darkly dressed procession as it began to rain and the large droplets could be heard drumming on the wooden coffin.

It took a couple of minutes for the procession to arrive at the graveside, but when they did, the whole procession was shocked by the ungodly sight that their eyes fell upon. There at the side of the grave was a pile of newly dug earth with two perspiring grave diggers stood hovering above it, behind them, stacked two high, was a line of muddy wooden coffins, some with handles some without. Jesse and the other men gently put down Joseph's coffin and smiled nervously at the grave diggers, one of them doffed his cap in reply.

A silence descended on the procession as they patiently waited for the reverend to appear, which he eventually did under a black umbrella. "What's going on here then reverend?" Jesse asked pointing to the row of muddy coffins. "Well I did tell you we would have to do a bit of re-arranging in order to get Joseph into the grave. Well, we've had to remove some of the coffins, so that we could dig the grave another couple of foot or so deeper." The reverend then grinned and said, "we can get at least another ten coffins into the grave now." On hearing this Eunice began to wail, it was the last thing Jesse wanted her to here, but since she'd seen the coffins and the reverend had already spoken, there was very little he could do about it. The reverend's grin turned into a pleasant smile and he began using one hand to spatter holy water on Joseph's coffin, whilst trying to read some words from a small black book, which he held in the other hand with the umbrella. Whilst the words were being said Eunice had no option but to calm down to a small whimper so she could hear what was being said by the reverend. After the words were said, which Eunice felt were only too brief, the women in the procession turned and headed back towards the graveyard gates which left just the men to complete the internment.

The coffin was dragged to the edge of the grave. Jesse and Bill jumped down into the bottom of the grave and landed with a squelch into thick mud. The grave was quickly becoming a quagmire in the rain and deep puddles were forming in the bottom of the cold grave. Jesse pulled the coffin along the ground towards him and Bill grabbed a handle which helped to ease the coffin into the bottom of the grave. "Put him up that end of the grave!" the reverend said pointing further up the grave. Jesse and Bill lifted the coffin, one at each end and placed it at the top end of the grave. As Jesse laid his end of the coffin down and with tears in his eyes, he knelt down and kissed the coffin where he thought Joseph's face would be. "Goodnight son," he said quietly before jumping back out of the grave, he then turned to pull Bill out of the grave with a one handed yank.

The four men stood at the side of the grave in a moment of respect, the moment came to an end with a little bow of their heads. They then quietly and solemnly left the grave and joined the path which led back to the gate, at this point, Jesse couldn't resist; he had to take a final look back at the grave. The grave diggers had already started to load the grave with the muddy coffins, first a coffin, then a dividing plank. Then another coffin on top of that and so on until it reached two feet below the top of the grave. This sight distressed Jesse and he began to fill up. Bill could see that Jesse was becoming upset so he pulled him on by his elbow saying, "come on Jesse let the lad rest in peace." To which Jesse replied, "What, with all that lot on top of him!"

Chapter 14: Death becomes you.

Over the next three months Jesse was forced by Eunice to save quickly. As soon as he had enough money saved, he went with Eunice to the vicarage to put a small deposit down on a plot in the graveyard. Jesse knocked gently on the vicarage door and after some movement, the reverend answered in his dressing gown. Quickly pulling the dressing gown to a close, and rapidly tying up its dangling cord around his waist, the reverend said, "I'll be with you in a minute. You go on and I'll meet you in the graveyard." Jesse and Eunice turned and began walking back down the vicarage path towards the graveyard when suddenly, a shout from an open upstairs window bellowed, "don't forget the cheaper plots are down at the bottom of the embankment, under the trees!" Jesse nodded and the reverend closed the window and disappeared back inside.

Whilst waiting for the reverend, Eunice and Jesse began walking around the graveyard looking for the best positions. Eventually, they decided on one of the cheaper plots at the bottom of the embankment. The plot didn't occupy the best position in the yard, but Eunice seemed pleased with it because it was closer to the church than the pauper's grave occupied by Joseph. To get to the plot one had to walk down the small embankment in front of the church where the large elm trees grew. These elms rustled in the wind and in autumn they would release their leaves to cover the plot. Jesse pointed this out to Eunice, who remarked, "that's alright! They'll keep its occupants warm during the cold winter months." The Reverend Grenside had heard this remark as he approached and hadn't found the comment amusing. The reverend frowned at Eunice as Jesse quickly straightened his face. "Made your minds up then?" he asked, whilst rubbing his hands to warm them. Eunice and Jesse quickly answered together a resounding, "Yes!" and pointed to a piece of earth in front of a large elm. "Good!" said the reverend. "Come on then, let's mark it on the map." He turned and began walking briskly back towards the church with Eunice and Jesse following closely behind him.

The trio arrived in front of the church and Jesse pulled the deposit from his pocket, he quickly handed it to the reverend who counted the coins from one hand to the other. Suddenly, after the money had been counted and checked, the reverend seemed to quickly lose interest in Jesse and Eunice and began to say his goodbyes. "Don't worry," he said. "I'll mark you on the map." The reverend entered the vestibule of the church and was just about to open the large oak door with a large rough iron key, which he kept on a chain in his pocket, when Eunice let out a loud cough. This got the reverend's attention. The reverend slowly turned, and realizing his business was not yet finished, he walked back to the entrance of the vestibule. "Was there something else?" he asked.

After a moment's hesitation, Eunice gave Jesse a nudge and egged him on with her head to speak to the reverend. "Go on then, ask him!" she said. Jesse was very reluctant to say anything and had to be goaded again by Eunice, "you promised, so go on, ask him!" she said angrily. Jesse, after blushing for a moment removed his cap and quietly began to speak. However, before he could say anything worthwhile, Eunice intervened by angrily saying, "Oh, I don't know!" she pushed her way in front of Jesse and blurted out. "We want our Joseph moving into our plot!" Jesse cringed at the way Eunice was behaving and expected the reverend to explode. Instead he calmly said, "That won't be possible." Eunice turned to look at Jesse, her eyes turned red as tears began to appear. Jesse pulled Eunice back from the reverend and asked calmly, "why not? We thought you were allowed to move people." The reverend thought for a moment as Eunice began to weep on Jesse's shoulder. Jesse looked over Eunice's shoulder towards the reverend and waited for an answer. Eventually, rubbing his chin and trying not to make the situation any worse, the reverend calmly answered, "As you know we had to remove coffins from the grave to make it deeper." Jesse nodded his head. "Well, Joseph is now at the bottom of the grave with about four rows of coffins above him and to retrieve him would mean removing all those coffins. It's just not practical!" Eunice turned her face away from the reverend and further into Jesse's shoulder, she began to wail. Jesse pulled her closer towards him and hugged her tightly with his right arm whilst his left arm was extended in a help me please gesture to the reverend.

The reverend, seeing the gesture and that Eunice was deeply upset, invited them both into the church. Eunice sat down on a pew at the back of a stone cold church and was given a small glass of sherry by the reverend, who kept a bottle hidden for just such occasions. The sherry did the trick and it wasn't long before Eunice began to reconcile herself. Jesse then gave the reverend the nod and both quietly walked to the back of the church. Before Jesse could say anything the reverend began to apologise and said, "Nothing can be done." Frustrated, Jesse said loudly, "Are you sure?" Eunice quickly looked around and Jesse instantly lowered his voice. "Surely, it's only a matter of removing four coffins, the ones above Joseph." Jesse whispered. The reverend grabbed Jesse's elbow and led him into a small office at the back of the church, saying, "It's not that easy." Swiftly the reverend rounded an old oak desk that was sat in the middle of the office and pulled out a large bunch of keys from a side drawer. Slamming the drawer closed the reverend, irritated, said, "follow me!" he then began to fiddle with the keys to find the right one. Jesse followed the reverend through a half frosted glass door at the back of the office and down a thin corridor. At the end of the corridor there was a set of spiral stairs leading down to a cold and dark place where Jesse didn't really want to go, but he followed. At the bottom of the stairs, the reverend lit a candle and unlocked a small door. Again, they walked down another long corridor, which seemed to be going further down and under the church; it was like walking down a long ramp to hell. Eventually the corridor stopped and yet another door had to be unlocked.

This door led to a small white washed chamber and in the corner, where the white wash had fallen to the floor was a stack of coffins, five high. Their brass handles flickered in the candle light as the reverend approached them, "Like I was saying Jesse. It isn't that easy, look!" Jesse looked across at the reverend who was pointing to some laths separating the layers of coffins. He then started to explain. "As you can see the coffins are in layers and the layers are divided by long planks of wood, like this!" he said pointing to two planks at the same time. "These planks, laths if you like, would have to be removed. The problem with that is that some of the laths are twenty feet long and support maybe five or six coffins, like you see here and before a lath can be removed all the coffins on top of that particular lath have to be removed

first." Jesse nodded his head and rubbed his chin as he entered into deep thought about the situation. The reverend then began babbling on about where the church got the laths from. "The laths come from the barge building yards around Mirfield. They use them for barge keels. We of course get them for nothing because they've got knots in them and they're not strong enough to make keels from." The reverend then patted a lath gently and looked across at Jesse, who was still deep in thought and had switched off from what the reverend was saying. On realizing the reverend had stopped speaking, Jesse quickly spoke out loudly, "well it's not impossible then!" he said.

There was a moment's silence and then the reverend realizing what Jesse was talking about said, "What, oh, getting Joseph out. No not impossible, but to get Joseph out we would have to take out maybe ten to fifteen coffins or more. Remember, the set up you see here is underground and that means digging, and when there's digging involved, there's always a cost and money involved, which you don't seem to have right now." The reverend rattled the warm coins that Jesse had given him earlier before heading towards the door. At the door the reverend waited for a moment as Jesse came out of the chamber and walked half way back up the corridor. The reverend locked the door and then led a silent Jesse back to the office where he tried to console him by saying, "Take my advice Jesse and let the lad rest in peace." Jesse realizing he had no alternatives just nodded his head in disappointment and returned to Eunice, who was still sat waiting patiently on the pew, "well!" she said arrogantly. Jesse didn't answer; he just put on his cap and walked out of the church.

Eunice managed to catch up with Jesse about half way down Church Lane, "are you going to answer me?" she said, pulling Jesse to a stop by his elbow. Jesse pulled himself free and began walking again whilst stating bluntly, "no! We can't move our Joseph!" Eunice ran after Jesse and screamed, "What do you mean? We can't move Joseph. That's my son you're talking about, and I want him moving." Jesse grabbed Eunice by the arms and pulled her close into him, "well we can't, and do you want to know why?" A silence descended on the pair which was broken by Jesse screaming into Eunice's face, "money, that's right, bloody money as usual!" he shook Eunice viciously and then with a tear in his eye said, "we can't afford to have him dug out of that pauper's grave because we're skint as usual! So there he lies, and there he'll have to stay!"

The next two months were very difficult for Jesse and Eunice, their relationship was at breaking point. There were so many silent breakfasts and cold dark evening spent staring into the embers of the kitchen fire, it became almost unbearable. Until one evening when Henry burst into the kitchen screaming, "Harriet's waters have broken." Eunice quickly ran upstairs and shouted back, "Boil some water Jesse, and send Thomas for the doctor." Jesse gave Thomas the nod and off he went. He then hastily filled a large black pot with water and put it over the fire, it hissed as the spilt water evaporated from the sides of the pot. "Come on lad, sit down." Jesse said to Henry who was just about to follow Eunice up the stairs. "There's nothing up there that concerns you. Our job is to stay out of the way and wait." Henry reluctantly returned to the kitchen and sat opposite Jesse who was beginning to settle back into his chair. "I suppose you're an old hand at this type of thing?" Henry said to Jesse, who just grinned. However, Jesse may have appeared to be calm and collected on the outside, but inside, he was worried to death, as he always was when he didn't know what the outcome of the birth was going to be. The thoughts and experiences of child birth did not hold well with Jesse and his thoughts always flashed back to Percilla and that tragic outcome.

Doctor Parker arrived and placed his top hat on the hallway desk as he had done when he came to visit Joseph. Thomas was just about to say, "Up the stairs doctor!" when the doctor stopped him by saying, "I know, up the stairs!" Thomas nodded and then joined Jesse and Henry by the kitchen fire. "Before you sit down," Jesse said, pointing to a large chest of drawers at the back of the kitchen. "Get some of those old sheets out of that bottom drawer and start tearing them into strips." Thomas opened the drawer and took out a pile of old linen sheets, he threw one at Henry. "Come on mate, it's your baby!" he said as he began to rip up a sheet. Puzzled, Henry asked, "What do we need these for?" Jesse stood up and walked towards Henry. He grinned, pulled up his trousers through his belt and said, "I'm buggered if I know lad, but any minute now they'll be asking for them, it's one of the mysteries of child birth, hot water and plenty of linen strips." All three of them began to laugh as Jesse shrugged his shoulders and pulled a long face whilst beginning to rip up a sheet.

The hours passed and Eunice had been down twice for the hot water and strips of linen. Thomas had fallen asleep in the fire hearth and Jesse was nodding in his chair. The only one to be wide awake and alert was Henry who was listening intently to every sound coming from the bedroom. Each sound had him up and out of the chair in anticipation of receiving his newly born child.

Dawn broke and the bedroom door handle began to rotate. The sound, although only small, squeaked its way down the stairs and into the kitchen where it found Jesse's ears. It might have been the silence or the absence of a baby's cry, but instinctively, Jesse knew something was wrong. He quickly

279

rushed to the bottom of the stairs and began climbing, Henry followed keen to meet his child. Thomas continued to sleep and was oblivious to what was about to unfold. Halfway up the stairs Jesse was suddenly stopped in his tracks by the doctor, who was descending the stairs. Eunice, who was close behind the doctor, was carrying a small bundle of linen. The doctor shook his head and said, "I'm sorry Jesse, but we couldn't save the child. It was still born." Jesse's heart missed a beat and hurriedly he asked, "And Harriet?" "She's alright, tired, but alright." Eunice replied from behind the doctor. Jesse and Henry began to retreat back down the stairs to allow the doctor to retrieve his hat from the hallway table before leaving.

The door slammed and then Eunice turned to Jesse and Henry and asked, "well, do you two want to meet the child or not?" Both replied with a nod and Eunice approached them whilst removing the linen cover from the child's blue grey face. "Meet Annie Howarth!" she said quietly. The two men stood there in floods of tears as each man in turn took hold of the child and gave it a hug and a delicate kiss on its forehead. Eunice, after the men had finished, retrieved the child, placed the linen cover over its face again and placed it in the bottom drawer where Thomas had removed the linen sheets from the night before. She gently closed the draw and told Jesse adamantly, "this time we're going to bury our granddaughter in our own plot. There's going to be no more paupers' graves for this family." Jesse nodded in agreement and replied, "I'll see the reverend later on today."

That day, whilst on a delivery, Jesse pulled up outside the vicarage. He tied the horse to some railings and strapped on its nose bag before walking down the path towards the vicarage's front door. On seeing Jesse approaching the reverend opened the door and cried, "Oh! It's not about Joseph again! Please, I beg of you, let the lad rest in peace!" Jesse removed his cap and replied, "No reverend, it's not our Joseph I'm here about. It's our new granddaughter, born early this morning." Jesse began to get upset at this point so the reverend invited him into the vicarage. "Come on in Jesse, sit down," he said. "We're just about to have some tea." The reverend's wife, who entered from the kitchen, issued them both with some sweet milky tea and a small biscuit, which she served from an old wooden tray she'd placed on the sideboard.

After recomposing himself Jesse said, "The child was still born, and we need to bury her in our plot." The reverend put on his glasses and said, "Hang on a minute Jesse!" he opened a large black book which was sat on his desk and after a moment of contemplation and a couple of swigs from his tea cup, the reverend began informing Jesse about his plot. "Your plot will only hold three coffins Jesse. You do know that, don't you?" Jesse hesitated and then replied, "Well that's enough room for me, the wife and a spare for our Harriet or Thomas if we should need it." The reverend nodded in agreement and then asked, "But what about your granddaughter? Do you want to put her in a pauper's grave?" Jesse shuddered at the thought and was quick to reply, "No, no! My wife would go crazy if I said yes to that." Jesse scratched his head and thought for a moment. He was just about to ask something else when the reverend's wife, who was sat quietly in the corner of the room, said, "You are allowed foot graves for children." Jesse instantly looked across at the reverend for an explanation. The reverend looked towards his wife and with a raised eyebrow, said, "Yes dear. I'd forgotten all about that." The reverend explained to Jesse that small coffins were allowed across the bottom of the grave, at the foot end. This pleased Jesse who instantly said, "Problem solved

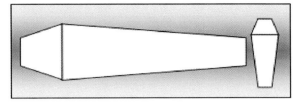

then. We'll bury her in a foot grave in our plot." Jesse stood up and was about to leave when the reverend said, "Wait a minute Jesse, one thing at a time. We first need to baptize the child." Jesse slowly sat back down and said, "But the child's dead reverend," the reverend looked sternly at Jesse and said, "nevertheless Jesse, the child still has to be baptized before it can be buried in consecrated ground." The reverend slammed the book closed and continued sipping his tea in little delicate sips.

A week later the child was christened and then buried silently in the plot at Saint Mary's graveyard. They say time is a great healer, but do mothers ever come to terms with the loss of a child? Henry and Jesse did everything possible to comfort Harriet over the next few weeks. Unfortunately, whilst doing this Jesse had forgotten that Eunice had also recently lost a child, and when she took to her bed complaining of pains in the lower regions of her stomach. Jesse thought it was attention seeking and jealousy. He made Eunice aware of his feelings early one morning before leaving for work. However, when he returned home later that day things hadn't improved much and Eunice was still in bed.

On entering the kitchen Jesse could see that the sink was still full of dishes, the fire ash was still laid in the hearth and there was no sign of any food being prepared. Jesse sighed and slowly walked towards the cellar head. He opened the door and reached down into a cold corner of the cellar head where he kept a crate of brown ale. The crate should have been full of bottles but there was only three left and these were taking up the back row of the crate. He pulled one clear of the crate and returned to the kitchen where he sat down, pulled out the cork with his teeth and put his weary feet on the hearth rail. As he sat there swigging the cool brown ale from the bottle, his thoughts turned to who had drunk his ale?

After some moments of thought Jesse reached a decision, "Thomas!" he said to himself. "It must be him, it can't be anyone else!" just then Thomas slammed the front door. "Is that you Thomas?" Jesse screamed. Thomas popped his head around the corner and was greeted by a barrage of abuse from Jesse. It took Thomas at least five minutes to calm Jesse down, he then explained to him that it was Eunice who had drunk his ale and that she had a thirst she couldn't quench. A sceptical Jesse growled at Thomas, he threw his empty bottle into the bottom of the hearth where it smashed. He then screamed, "Wait here!" Thomas shrugged his shoulders before sitting down in his usual place by the hearth.

Jesse dashed upstairs and entered a darkened bedroom where Eunice was sleeping. He walked towards the bed and accidentally kicked over a load of empty bottles which rattled and scattered their way across the bedroom floor waking Eunice from her sleep. Yawning, she asked, "Is that you Jesse?" Jesse replied with a grunt. "Light a candle love." Jesse lit a candle that was on the bedside table and looked towards Eunice. Instantly, Jesse could see Eunice wasn't well and his attitude changed immediately. Quietly, he then asked, "how do you feel love? Feeling any better?" Eunice fluffed up a pillar and sat up in bed, placing the pillar behind her for support. She then said without hesitation, "Bring me a bottle of brown ale Jesse, I'm thirsty." Jesse again looked closely at Eunice and replied, "You'd be better off with water." Eunice wasn't pleased with Jesse's reply and angrily growled, "Don't be difficult. I want brown ale, it tastes better." Jesse returned to the cellar head and brought Eunice the last two bottles of brown ale. However, before handing them over, Jesse calmly said, "that's the last two." Eunice grabbed at the first bottle and almost swigged it off in one go. She was then overcome with pain and squirmed whilst her hand quickly disappeared below the sheets to the area of pain. She gently rubbed her stomach easing the pain and her face returned to normal as the pain dissipated slowly.

By this time Jesse had dragged a wooden chair from the corner of the room and was sat at the side of the bed. Showing concern, Jesse tilted his head to one side and asked, "Shall I send Thomas for the doctor?" Eunice adjusted her position in the bed and replied, "No! It's just a little wind. It'll go with time." An awkward silence descended on the room and neither of them knew what to say next. After a couple of minutes Jesse began drumming his fingers on the bedside table, still trying to think of something to say and to break the silence, Jesse uneasily asked, "are you hungry?" Eunice smiled and replied, "No not really." She then adjusted her position once more in the bed before asking, "Is Harriet home yet?" Jesse was puzzled by this question and quickly asked, "Why, what do you want Harriet for?" Eunice sighed and replied sternly, "it's a woman's thing Jesse." Jesse lifted his head and nodded knowing he wouldn't get to know anymore about what was wrong. Jesse got up and walked towards the bedroom door, he shouted for Harriet, who appeared at the bottom of the stairs almost instantly. "What is it?" she asked, rubbing her hands on Eunice's apron which she'd put on to cook tea in. "Your mother wants you." Jesse replied as he descended the stairs. Harriet tutted and stormed up the stairs towards the bedroom.

Jesse entered the kitchen and was approached by Thomas, "is mother alright?" he asked. Jesse sat down and replied, "Your guess is as good as mine Thomas lad!" Thomas went back to sit in the fire hearth whilst Jesse tried to poke some life into a flagging fire which Harriet had just lit. Just then Harriet returned and went straight to the drawer where the old linen was kept. "Come on, tear this into strips!" she said, throwing Thomas a folded linen sheet. Jesse and Thomas both looked at each other in bemusement, but not wishing to aggravate Harriet, they both began tearing the sheets into strips. Suddenly, Thomas exclaimed, "mother's not going to have a baby, is she?" Harriet laughed and pinched Thomas on the cheek before saying, "don't be silly, she's far too old for that! But we'll still need plenty of hot water, so put on the large pan, and Father, make some of those strips a bit wider." Jesse started to tear the strips a little wider whilst Harriet disappeared back up the stairs armed with arms full of linen strips. Jesse grinned at Thomas's facial expressions and then shrugged his shoulders, which really meant, 'I'm buggered if I know!' It wasn't long before Harriet returned for the hot water which she took upstairs. There was then a silence as Jesse settled back into his chair. The wait was only about ten minutes, but when you're the one doing the waiting, it always seems longer.

Eventually, Harriet appeared at the bottom of the stairs with a bloody pile of wet linen strips. "You can go up now," she said. Jesse and Thomas both stood up and headed for the stairs. Harriet allowed Jesse to pass her but blocked Thomas's way to the stairs by standing in front of him. Thomas tried in vain to pass Harriet, but she was adamant that he wasn't going to pass her and angrily said, "not you, sit down!" she pushed Thomas back into the kitchen and waited for a couple of seconds allowing Jesse to reach the top of the stairs and enter the bedroom, which was out of earshot of what she was about to say. Harriet put her finger over her lips signalling to Thomas not to talk loud, she then whispered, "Go and get the doctor, mothers not well!" Thomas started towards the door, but just before leaving he asked quietly, "Is it bad?" Harriet didn't know what to say and just shrugged her shoulders whilst smiling nervously at Thomas. It was sometime before Thomas arrived back at the house and when he did, he found Harriet sat in Jesse's chair by the fire. Henry was sat at the table. "Where's the doctor?" Harriet asked. Thomas shook his head and said, "He's out on a call, up Hopton somewhere. We just have to wait, it might be tomorrow."

The doctor didn't appear until the following teatime and when he did he wasn't very helpful. As usual everybody had left the bedroom and had congregated in the kitchen waiting for the doctor to emerge with the results of his examination. After some considerable time the doctor entered the silent kitchen shaking his head. Jesse was the first to speak, "well, what's the matter with her doctor?" The doctor raised his head, stroked his sideburns and thought for a moment, then, still deep in thought replied, "I'm not sure at the moment Jesse. It's definitely woman troubles with all the bleeding, it points to the womb. All we can do is to wait. Keep her comfortable and change her regularly, I'll return in a couple of days." Jesse nodded his head and then the doctor handed him a large brown bottle from his bag, "If she has anymore stomach pains give her two large spoonfuls of this." Jesse again nodded and the doctor left.

Over the next few days the family took it in turn to baby sit Eunice. Harriet of course did most of the changing returning home from the mill at dinnertime to change Eunice during the day. The doctor did eventually return on the fourth day claiming he had been very busy. Thankfully, the bleeding had stopped two days previously and Eunice was beginning to regain some of her strength. The doctor smiled on seeing Eunice sat up in bed and began taking her pulse. After a moment of holding Eunice's wrist and peering down at his pocket watch, he exclaimed, "everything appears to be back to normal." The doctor then tucked his watch back into his waistcoat pocket and asked, "How's your stomach? Are you still getting the pains?" His voice changed and then he continued to say in a whisper, "down there." Eunice hesitated before coughing. She then quietly said, "Well they're not as bad as they have been." The doctor placed Eunice's hand back under the bed sheets. He then began strutting up and down the bedroom, "good, good!" he said feeling proud that the patient seemed much improved. Jesse walked the doctor to the door and before leaving the doctor gave him his final judgement, "please continue using the tonic," he said. "And if she gets anymore pains, let me know." Jesse nodded and thanked the doctor.

Over the next few months Eunice remained in bed. She experienced more discharges and the pain returned from time to time, but as Jesse kept on saying, "at least she's still alive and still with us." This encouraged the family to carry out their duties and all of them remained vigilant with one member of the family always present at Eunice's bedside to administer the tonic and to help with other matters of hygiene.

With Eunice being bedridden the pressure on Harriet, the only female in the family, was horrendous. As well as trying to hold down a job in the mill, cook and clean for the family, not to mention shopping and changing her mother in between these everyday tasks, the pressure, as you might expect, began to tell on Harriet. So much so that it became noticeable, and one evening whilst sitting with her mother, the question was asked, "you look pale, are you alright?" Eunice said peering at Harriet through the dim candle light. Eunice patted the bed and beckoned Harriet to her, "come closer," she said. Harriet sat on the bed and her mother placed her hand underneath Harriet's chin, she tilted her head towards the candle light and took a good look at Harriet's face. After a moment of inspection Eunice instinctively knew something wasn't quite right. "Have you got something to tell me?" Eunice enquired. The silence Eunice received to her question was all she needed to confirm that something was wrong. "There's nothing wrong!" Harriet exclaimed politely, pulling herself free from Eunice's grip. "Nothing at all, I'm sure." Harriet said, trying to appear nonchalant. She then began straightening the bed sheets and wiping away some crumbs, which were from the bread and cheese Eunice had had for tea. Eunice however, wasn't deceived by Harriet's pretence and quickly said, "Stop!" Harriet looked her mother in the eye, she then approached her slowly and realizing that Eunice wasn't going to be fobbed off by her pretence, she had to admit to her deception. Quietly she said, "I'm pregnant again."

Eunice smiled nervously and then said, "Oh my God, don't tell your father. Well not until he needs to know. He's got enough problems at the moment, and you know what he thinks about pregnancies." Harriet nodded her head and began tucking in the sheets, ensuring that they were nice and tight. Just as she'd finished and was about to say goodnight a gentle knock came on the bedroom door and Henry's head appeared around the corner of the door. He yawned and said, "Ready for bed love." Harriet replied with a short nod and started towards the door. However, before Henry could withdraw, Eunice called him into the bedroom. "You, young man, make sure you look after her when I'm gone." Harriet was horrified at what her mother had said and quickly approached her. "Don't speak like that mother." Harriet said quietly. Eunice grabbed Harriet's hand and shook it gently. "Listen here my girl. It's my time, and you must get use to that. When you've got to go, you've got to go!" Harriet began to cry and bent down to hug her mother. Eunice pushed Harriet back and said, "Look after my grandchild as well," pointing to Harriet's tummy. Just then Jesse entered the room and said, "come on you lot. Out! I'm tired and need my bed." Thomas shouted, "Goodnight!" from the landing and everyone retired to their appropriate bedrooms, leaving Jesse none the wiser.

More months passed and Harriet began to show, she began wearing baggy clothing, in particular large coats, which were always good for covering up the bump, either way Jesse hadn't noticed. However, this may have been because he was more concerned with Eunice's health, which had begun to deteriorate rapidly. Jesse was so concerned that he sent for the doctor early one evening and when the doctor arrived, he went straight upstairs into the bedroom and didn't say a word to anyone. After about an hour with Eunice the doctor descended the stairs and entered the kitchen where he found the family waiting patiently for his prognosis. The doctor shook his head and looked at Jesse, he then quietly asked, "Is there somewhere where we can talk?" Jesse replied instantly and said, "There's no-one here that isn't family, so whatever you've got to say, you can say it in front of them." The doctor was shocked for a moment. But after recomposing himself and straightening his jacket by the lapels, he coughed to clear his throat, "well!" he said, "its not good news, I'm afraid." He paused for a moment and then slowly peered around the room at all the unhappy faces. Their eyes were all concentrated on him and every word he spoke, which unnerved the doctor slightly.

Eventually, Jesse had to persuade the doctor to speak again. The doctor acknowledged Jesse and began to speak once more, "I have extensively examined the patient. The examination revealed much internal disease probably due to child bearing and at the moment your mother is suffering from severe asthenia." At this point, Harriet coughed to interrupt the doctor. "Suffering from what?" she asked, looking confused and puzzled. She shrugged her shoulders at the doctor who looked directly at Harriet. Realizing Harriet didn't understand the word 'asthenia' the doctor quickly explained, "Oh, tired, weak and basically worn out." Harriet nodded showing that she understood and the doctor continued, "I have administered one drachm of Laudanum for her pain and your wife is now sleeping." The doctor handed Jesse a small green glass bottle saying, "If the pain gets worse, then give her a teaspoon full of this. It will also help her to sleep if she should wake." The doctor then started to say his goodbyes, shaking everybody by the hand, leaving Jesse until last. Jesse quickly got up to receive his handshake and then began to escort the doctor towards the front door, "This way doctor." Jesse said leading the doctor down the hall with a candle, but before opening the front door Jesse held the candle aloft so he could see the doctor's face, and then, he challenged the doctor to tell him the truth. "Alright doctor, how long has my wife got?" Jesse asked. There was a silence and the candle flickered before the doctor, who was a little unsure of what Jesse's reaction was going to be, replied, "two months, maybe three!" He then nervously smiled and began walking sideways as Jesse opened the door for him to leave. As the doctor reached the door, Jesse closed it slightly, freezing the doctor between the wall and the door. Jesse then gratefully whispered, "thank you doctor." The doctor nodded and said, "You're welcome Jesse, you're welcome."

It was six weeks later before Jesse decided to tell the rest of the family that Eunice was dying. His reason for not doing it before was that he'd decided that there was enough pain in the family already without adding more. But then he thought it was unfair that they didn't know. Jesse took sometime to think about how he should tell the family and decided that he should convene a family meeting that very week in the kitchen.

On the day of the meeting Jesse locked the shack early and walked across to the Blacksmith's Shop. He popped his head around the corner of the door and shouted across the shop to Thomas, who was braying a hammer down on a red hot piece of metal, "Don't forget to be home early for the meeting." Thomas nodded and continued hammering the piece of metal. Jesse withdrew and began slowly walking along Eastthorpe Lane towards home. As usual, he had a lot on his mind and the thoughts were going around and around in his head. It wasn't until he reached Stevenson's Row when Henry brought him back into this world by saying, "evening Jesse, evening Jesse!" Jesse lifted his head and said, "Oh it's you Henry." They walked the rest of the way together talking about what sort of a day they'd had as they went. When they reached the house, Harriet was stood by the front door waiting for them. She greeted them both with a small kiss on the cheek. "Thomas won't be long." Jesse said entering the house and walking down the hall towards the kitchen. He then enquired about Eunice, "how's your mother?" Harriet flinched and replied, "Not good, she's so weak father." Jesse nodded and poked the fire in the hearth before sitting in his usual chair. Henry sat opposite Jesse and Harriet began pouring some tea out from an old black teapot on the table.

After handing out the tea all three sat in the kitchen silently sipping tea from their cups. Harriet could see from her position at the table that Jesse was becoming more annoyed as time when on. Eventually, infuriated, Jesse jumped out of his chair and screamed, "Where's that little bugger now?" Harriet, trying to ease Jesse's rage, said, "Oh he won't be long father, I'm sure, sit down and finish your tea." Jesse began grumbling to himself as he sat back down. He then took the last few gulps to empty his tea cup and wiped away the dribble from his chin with a trembling palm. Just as his rage was about to leave him the front door slammed and in came Thomas. Harriet quickly reacted and stood up. She walked quickly towards Thomas, this put her between Thomas and the annoyed Jesse. She kissed Thomas in the way she had done earlier when receiving Jesse and Henry. Jesse made an angry dash towards Thomas. Harriet screamed and Henry had to pull Jesse back to prevent him from punching Thomas. However, the raised voices and the swearing drifted up the stairs and could be heard by the awakened Eunice, who brought the argument to a sudden stop by banging on the floor with a walking stick Harriet had left at the side of the bed. Immediately, Harriet left the stunned family and raced up the stairs to find Eunice out of bed and trying to crawl across the floor towards the door. Harriet frantically tried to lift Eunice back into bed but couldn't, so she shouted for Jesse, who came immediately to assist. Eunice was devastated by what she'd heard and was sobbing uncontrollably sat up in bed. It took Jesse nearly an hour to settle her back down. Promising that he would not argue with Thomas seemed to do the trick. Jesse administered the laudanum and made sure Eunice was asleep before returning to the kitchen where Harriet, Henry and a very nervous Thomas were sat quietly waiting.

Thomas was the first to talk, he stood up and desperately tried to tell Jesse why he'd been late, but Jesse wasn't interested and just raised his hand. This stopped Thomas in mid sentence and from giving his excuse, "There are more important things to discuss." Jesse told Thomas as he fell quiet. Jesse stood in front of the fire which was beginning to crackle and spit sparks as the fire took hold. Jesse took a moment and then cleared his throat by spitting into the fire. "There's no easy way of saying this," he said, "so I'll just say it." He then announced the pending death of Eunice, which didn't seem to surprise either Henry or Thomas. However, Harriet was a different matter. She was absolutely devastated and began crying instantly. She reached out for her father with both arms. Jesse threw his arms around Harriet and pulled her into him, but the embrace was a mistake. The moment their stomachs met Jesse knew instantly that Harriet was pregnant and he quickly pushed her away, but he didn't let go of her arms. Glaring into Harriet's eyes, Jesse ferociously screamed at her, "You're pregnant, aren't you?" With large tears pouring down her face Harriet gave a simple nod and turned to Henry. Jesse flopped down into his chair and began shaking his head. "What a time to get pregnant. How stupid could you be?" Jesse said angrily. Harriet quickly turned in the arms of Henry and screamed back at Jesse, "we didn't plan it you know, and how did we know that mother was going to...." Harriet couldn't finish the sentence; she just blew her nose before returning to face Henry.

At this point, Thomas intervened and quietly said, "You two are going to wake mother again if you don't calm down." Jesse nodded in agreement and then, with a much reduced tone, asked, "When's the baby due?" The answer came from Henry, who was still comforting Harriet, he looked over her shoulder and replied, "three weeks, maybe sooner." Jesse tutted and spat again into the fire before turning his attentions to Thomas. "Did you know?" he growled. Thomas shook his head and sharply replied, "No! Oh I'm off to bed!" he then departed as sharply as his reply had been. Henry and Harriet had also had enough and began to make their way to the bottom of the stairs, "aye, we're off as well father." Harriet said as Henry disappeared up the stairs, but just before Harriet took her first step, Jesse stopped her. "Harriet!" Harriet froze at the bottom of the stairs and looked back at Jesse, she waited. Jesse poked the fire a little and then stood up to blow out the candle on the mantel. There was a pause and then turning his head towards Harriet, he asked, "Does your mother know?" Harriet lifting her skirts and angrily replied, "What do you think?" She started off up the stairs and about half way up the stairs she said, "of course she bloody does, she's my mother, isn't she?" Jesse sat back down and grumbled to himself, "always the last to know, as usual." He then continued to poke more life out of the fire. He sat there in its red glow staring into its embers until he began to lose the heat and his consciousness.

The following night, whether it was the thought of losing her mother or the fact that Jesse had ignored her the whole day. Harriet went to bed feeling the pain that all expectant mothers feel at times. Holding her stomach she slid off to sleep, but was awoken two hours later by Henry complaining that the bed was wet. Harriet sat up and told Henry to go for the doctor. She then shouted for Thomas, who was already awake and seemed to appear at the bedroom door as if by magic, said, "I know, hot water and strips of linen, and plenty of both!" Harriet grinned at Thomas who made his way down the stairs towards the kitchen. Jesse wasn't amused on hearing the commotion, it had woken Eunice. Eunice quickly calmed Jesse down and told him to bring her a bowl so she could be sick in it. Jesse, who had a face like stone, lifted the water jug out of the bowl and placed the bowl on the bed, his attitude and the way he had done this infuriated Eunice who quickly became angry. "Listen to me Jesse." She said, pulling the bowl onto her lap, "I'm not long for this world and the only thing I desire is to see is my grandchild before I go." She began to be sick into the bowl and as it slapped its way around the bottom of the bowl. Eunice continued to wrench, bringing up more of the bloody liquid. Jesse instantly on hearing the sound, sat on the bed, put his arm around Eunice and tried to assist her to be sick.

Eventually, the sickness subsided and Jesse suggested that Eunice took some more laudanum to try and ease the pain, but Eunice refused, saying, "My daughter requires more attention than I do this night." Her answer didn't please Jesse and his face dropped once more. "Ah!" she said, "there's the Jesse I've learned to love so much." Eunice handed Jesse the bowl back and cheekily grinned at him. Then, from behind her, she pulled on her shoal, using the corner of it to wipe her mouth free from vomit. She slowly beckoned Jesse. "Come here love," she said tenderly. Jesse put the bowl on the floor, and again he had to be encouraged to sit on the bed by Eunice, who patted the bed gently. Jesse was slow, but eventually, he hitched himself up on to the bed, leant over and tenderly kissed Eunice on the lips, whilst taking hold of her hand. Eunice slowly caressed Jesse's hand and began speaking quietly and tenderly to him, "now then Jesse," she said. "I know how you hate this pregnancy lark, and you've had some bad experiences in the past, but it's a necessary part of life." Eunice shook Jesse's hand and he nodded, "so for tonight can you please accept it and try your best to help Harriet get through it." Jesse had no option but to agree with Eunice and gave her another kiss. He got up from the bed and said, "I'd better go and give Thomas a hand with the hot water." Jesse started towards the bedroom door, "Oh and Jesse." Jesse stopped and turned towards Eunice, who smiled at him and said, "When the child's born be sure and bring it to me, won't you?" Jesse nodded and unlatched the door. He closed it quietly and joined Thomas in the kitchen. An hour passed and Jesse was getting worried that the doctor hadn't arrived, but his heart eased when Henry came through the front door with the doctor in close pursuit. Henry started to lead the doctor up the stairs, but he paused briefly to ask Jesse how Eunice was doing. Jesse replied, "as good as could be expected." After leading the doctor to Harriet's bedroom, Henry returned to the kitchen, where he found Jesse and Thomas tearing up linen sheets. After

288

Thomas had run out of sheets, Jesse suggested that he go and fetch Bill Carters wife, Annie.

Annie arrived in her dressing gown. Her hair was platted and tied with small pink ribbons at the ends. Jesse thanked her for coming. She was about to ascend the stairs when she noticed Henry, who was sat by the fire with a pile of linen strips in front of him. "I'll take those," she said, snatching the linen away from Henry, who was only too glad to release it into Annie's knowledgeable care. Annie grinned at Henry and then quickly vanished upstairs into the bedroom, the linen trailing behind her. As the hours passed Annie returned to the kitchen a number of times for both hot water and linen. It seemed the more screaming and groaning coming from the bedroom the more water and linen was required.

But at last a deadly silence descended on the bedroom and everybody in the kitchen held their breath. The door unlatched and footsteps could be heard descending the stairs. It was Annie holding a small bundle of linen. As she entered the kitchen she looked at Henry and said politely, "you have a son." She handed the child to Henry, who immediately smiled and said, "Arthur my son." He then tearfully exposed the child to Jesse, who was beaming from ear to ear and beginning to cry with joy himself. Just then Henry realized something was wrong, he quickly turned to see the doctor stood at the bottom of the stairs. "Harriet!" he said quietly. The doctor shook his head and medically stated, "She had a weak heart. The labour proved too difficult for her." He then put on his hat and nodded apprehensively before turning to leave. Annie quietly opened the door to let the doctor out. She then smiled nervously across the room at Jesse before leaving herself.

Henry handed the child to Jesse and walked solemnly up the stairs to see the body of his wife. The tears were streaming down his face as he entered a darkened bedroom. After entering, he slowly closed the bedroom door behind him, the latch dropping being the last sound to come from the room. Jesse looked at the child then at Thomas. "I'd better go and introduce young Arthur here to your mother," he said. Thomas nodded and Jesse began to climb the stairs. However, before he had reached the top of the stairs, Thomas quickly rushed to the bottom of the stairs and said, "Father!" Jesse turned to see Thomas desperately looking up the stairs at him. "Don't tell mother about Harriet, not just yet!" he said. Jesse solemnly nodded and entered the bedroom. Eunice had fallen asleep sat up in bed. The candle had nearly burnt itself out and Jesse, using one arm, took a new candle from the window sill and lit it using the old candle. He then dripped some hot wax from the new candle onto the chair at the side of the bed where the old candle was and sat the new candle on it. Jesse held the candle in place for a second for the hot wax to solidify before letting go of the candle.

The room glowed yellow from the new candle and Jesse sat down on the bed next to Eunice. He gently began nudging and calling Eunice back from her deep sleep, "Eunice, Eunice love." He said quietly. Eunice slowly opened her eyes and then began to wake at the same pace. Eventually, her eyes focused on Jesse and the new baby, she smiled and asked, "Is this my new grandchild?" Jesse nodded and then tenderly passed the child to Eunice announcing, "meet Arthur Howarth!" However, Eunice was so weak that she was unable to hold the child without the fear of dropping it. She was so weak in fact, that Jesse had to wrap Eunice's arms around the child so she could hold him. He then steadied Eunice by holding her hands together. After a moment of settling down, Eunice pulled back the linen that the child was wrapped in. A teardrop fell from her cheek and landed upon the child's face. Eunice gently wiped it away with her thumb and said, "There, there my little one." She looked up at Jesse and said, "He's like Harriet, isn't he?" Jesse agreed and then Eunice asked, "Talking of which, how is she?" Jesse became very nervous and hesitated to answer Eunice, but eventually he managed to say, "Oh she's alright, she's sleeping just now." Eunice smiled and continued to cuddle the child.

After about ten minutes of lovingly cuddling the child, Eunice couldn't bear the pain or the weight of the child any longer and had to ask Jesse to remove the child which he did saying, "Well! What do you think of him then?" But there was no answer from Eunice. Jesse instantly looked towards Eunice, who was by now slumped forward, she'd gone, in seconds, she'd slipped away to join Harriet. Jesse put the child back down on the bed and let out a horrific scream, "nooooo..." he screamed. The scream was so loud and painful that it brought Thomas and Henry rushing into the room. Thomas on seeing the position of his mother went straight to his father and flung his arms around him. They both began sobbing together. Henry, meanwhile, lifted Arthur off the bed and walked back into Harriet's bedroom leaving the grieving pair to grieve over Eunice. At this point, you may wonder how this scene of death could become any worse. But alas, it could, and it did, the child died an hour later.

Chapter 15: Life after sixty.

With typhus, tuberculosis and dyphereor rampant, it was not unusual for three members of one family to die on the same day. However, Jesse had, with his business, become an important upstanding member of the Mirfield community and to reflect this, the whole of Stevenson's Row, as a mark of respect, had pinned black ribbons to their front doors. On the day of the funerals, the procession slowly left Stevenson's Row and to Jesse's surprise, there were customers and friend's lining the road all the way to the church. Each person joining the procession after it had past them and by the time the procession had arrived at the church it was quite a length. The  Reverend Grenside even commented from the pulpit on the number of people who were in church for the funeral service and said, "That it proved how well respected Jesse and his family had become in the Mirfield community."

The respect, however, over the next few months, started to deteriorate as Jesse began to spend more time in The Black Bull than at work. Things came to a head one evening when Jesse had been thrown out of The Black Bull and had arrived home smelling of drink. The very moment he walked into the kitchen, he began ranting at Thomas. "Get out of my way!" he growled, pushing Thomas to the floor and stumbling towards the cellar head. He took two bottles of brown ale from the full crate and pulled out the cork on one of them whilst placing the other safely on the table. Jesse dragged a chair from under the table and flopped down into it. He began guzzling the ale from the bottle whilst Thomas and Henry looked on in revulsion, "Is this how it's going to be then?" Thomas asked Jesse, who guzzled some more of the ale and then wiped his chin with his sleeve before answering. "Why! This is my house and I'll do what I want, and if you and his nibs over there," pointing at Henry, "don't bloody like it. Then you can both bugger off and live somewhere else!" Jesse took another swig from the bottle. Henry looked at Thomas and calmly said, "that's enough for me mate, I'm off!" and with that Henry walked out of the kitchen and straight up the stairs only to appear ten minutes later with a small bundle. "I'm off then," he said from the bottom of the staircase. Thomas nodded and Jesse, still being abusive, stood up and lifted up the second bottle of ale in celebration at Henry's departure. There was a wobble, which took a moment to steady. Then Jesse focused on Henry and with dribble running down his chin announced with a slurred voice, "and it's a good riddance to you." He just managed the sentence before flopping back down into the chair with a large stupid grin on his face. He then took another swig from the bottle.

Thomas sat quietly in the hearth for over an hour watching Jesse drinking himself into a stupor. Eventually, Jesse's face fell flat on the table and the drunken snoring began. Thomas quietly walked over to Jesse and placed a linen sheet gently over his shoulders before collecting the empties and returning them to the crate at the top of the cellar head. He then blew out the candles which were scattered around the kitchen before retiring to his bed.

The following morning Thomas was up early, he slowly and silently crept down the stairs. From the bottom of the stairs he peered into the kitchen where Jesse's face was still laid flat out on the table. The sight of Jesse's fist gripping another half empty bottle of ale was enough to suggest to Thomas that he should leave and go to work, leaving Jesse undisturbed.

When Thomas arrived at work, Bill Carter could see by the bleak expression on Thomas's face that something was wrong and politely asked if everything was alright. Thomas had no option but to reply, "No!" Bill approached Thomas and lent him an understanding ear. "Come on then," he said, "tell your old Uncle Bill all about it." Bill rested his backside on an old shiny anvil whilst Thomas took sometime to compose himself. It wasn't long before Thomas was pouring his heart out to Bill, most of it about Jesse and how he was behaving. Just as Thomas had about finished assassinating Jesse's character a thin faced man wearing a small bowler hat and a pair of funny little wired spectacles, which were hanging halfway down his nose, peered into the shop through the window. "Looks like a customer." Bill said getting up off the anvil and opening the door, which allowed the man to enter. "I'm looking for the hayman, his place seems locked. Have you seen him this morning?" the man asked Bill, who looked towards Thomas for guidance as to what to say. After all he thought I don't wish to embarrass Thomas by saying the wrong thing. However, Thomas didn't respond favourably and wasn't very helpful in guiding Bill, he just gave a large sigh and turned away. Trying to resolve the situation Bill doffed his cap and said, "He's probably out on a delivery sir. Perhaps I can be of help?" The man hesitated and started to squirm. Bill again looked towards Thomas for a response. It took a moment, but Thomas decided he'd better respond. "I'm the hayman's son," he said holding out his hand. The man shook it and knowing that Thomas was the hayman's son seemed to put the man at ease. "Oh good!" he said. "I wish to purchase three bales of hay and two of straw." The man handed Thomas three half crowns, "I'll pay you the rest when you deliver the goods." In a flash the man produced a card from his inside jacket pocket, "My card and delivery address!" the man said, before leaving.

Thomas looked at the card and then at Bill, then back at the card. "What shall I do now?" he asked. Bill shrugged his shoulders and said, "I don't know, but you'd better go and get your father and have those bales delivered." Thomas nodded and put the card into his shirt pocket before setting off to fetch Jesse.

The journey proved to be a waste of time, Jesse was still drunk. Thomas entered the kitchen to find the table full of empty ale bottles. Jesse's head was laid in the middle of them and he was snoring like a pig. The whole kitchen smelt of stale ale and vomit. The stench was so bad that Thomas himself was nearly sick and had to open some windows so he could breathe fresh air for a moment or two before bringing his head back into the stinking kitchen. To prevent the smell reaching his nostrils Thomas placed his sleeve over his nose and then, just before leaving, he noticed a bundle of keys on the floor under the table where Jesse was sat. He slowly picked them up being careful not to disturb Jesse. They were the keys for the shack and Thomas knew exactly what he was going to do next.

Thomas opened the shack, hooked up the horse to the cart and began loading the bales onto the cart. After placing four bales onto the cart Bill Carter appeared on the otherside of the cart. "What's this then? Have you gone into business for yourself?" he asked placing an elbow on the end of the cart. Thomas stopped loading and hesitated before answering, "well, someone's got to do it and there's only me, isn't there?" Bill nodded in agreement and then said, "Well, if you've got a moment? I'd like a word." Thomas walked around the cart and stood facing Bill, "what's up Bill?" Thomas asked, looking concerned. Bill removed his cap and scratched his head and said, "Don't take this the wrong way Thomas, but it's like this. I'm paying you to work for me, not to run your father's business." Thomas thought for a moment and then replied, "What can I do? What options have I got?"

They both stood motionless in the middle of the yard thinking about the situation, when Thomas came up with, what he thought was the answer, "I've got it!" he said. "I'll take sometime off." Bill laughed and quickly said, "Aye but without pay." Thomas's face changed and then Bill said sympathetically, "you can't expect me to pay you, surely not!" Thomas straightened his face and thought about it for a moment. He had no option but to agree with Bill. "Ok Bill, without pay it is." Bill screwed up his face in desperation and said, "There's still the problem of how long? I mean it's been nearly three months since your mother and Harriet died. How long is it going to be before your father get's back on his feet and back to work?" Thomas finished putting the last bale onto the cart before replying. "How would I know?" he said grabbing the horse by the harness and turned it around. Thomas stepped up onto the front of the cart leaving Bill in the middle of the yard. "I just don't know Bill. Can you give me two weeks?" Bill lifted his hands and said, "Do I have a choice? Two weeks then and only two weeks mind." Thomas shouted, "Thanks Bill!" as he pulled out of the yard and into the road.

The first week passed without Jesse even leaving the house, all he'd done was drink and drink and become more argumentative as the week went on. He hadn't washed or eaten anything of substance and by the weekend Thomas was becoming worried. So much so that he decided he needed to get some help, but the question was, where from? He needed to find someone who could handle Jesse and his temper, which showed itself everytime Thomas tried to talk to him about his drinking. But, as  Thomas was to find out, talking about the drinking wasn't the only thing which sent Jesse into a rage. The simple act of refusing to fetch Jesse some more drink would do the trick. On one occasion of refusal, Jesse attacked Thomas with the empty ale bottles. Thomas managed to evade the first two that were thrown at him, but unfortunately, he wasn't quick enough to dodge the following two as they came crashing down on his head. More bottles were thrown by Jesse and went smashing to the floor. Thomas quickly skedaddled upstairs holding his cut head, where he stayed until he thought it was safe to come back down. After an hour and still bleeding Thomas had to make the decent to the kitchen to get some linen from the bottom drawer. He crept slowly down the stairs and cautiously looked around the corner of the kitchen door. Jesse was asleep in his chair next to a cooling hearth. Slowly, Thomas made his way to the drawers at the back of the kitchen.

He slowly and gently opened the bottom drawer of three with one hand whilst trying to control the bleeding with the other. The drawer was empty so Thomas tried the middle drawer which contained two pairs of old shoes wrapped in a holed scarf. By now the blood was running down Thomas's arm and onto the floor, he was desperate to find some linen to stop the bleeding. In desperation Thomas pulled open the top and last drawer, it squeaked and instantly Thomas's head spun towards Jesse, who just grunted and turned over in his chair. But just as Thomas thought things were alright, the drawer fell from his hand and hit the floor sending its contents scattering across the kitchen floor and waking Jesse from his stupor. Thomas ducked quickly under the table and waited. Jesse looked around suspiciously, but satisfied that all was well he got up and left slamming the kitchen door behind him. Thomas, relieved, exhaled and came out from under the table. He quickly grabbed a strip of linen, which was laid on the floor and bundled it up to make a dabber for his head cut. Thomas sat down and held the dabber on his cut until it stopped bleeding.

Whilst sitting there Thomas stared down at the drawer contents, which were now scattered all over the floor, he noticed a bible sticking out from beneath the upside down drawer. He leant over and slowly picked it up, he flicked it open to the first page and there, written in black handwriting was a citation. The bible had been presented to Jesse for his attendance at church, but more importantly the citation said, that if Jesse ever needed help, then the church would be there for him. It was signed at the bottom of the page by the Reverend Grenside. Thomas immediately said to himself, "that's it, the church, they'll help me." Thomas quickly collected the drawer contents and bundle them all back into the replaced drawer. He then pushed the bible into his jacket pocket and climbed the stairs to bed.

The following morning Thomas set off towards the church and hopefully to get some help from the Reverend Grenside, who Jesse had often spoken about and had a great deal of respect for. A half hour walk later Thomas arrived at the vicarage, he knocked hard on the door and waited, there was no reply, he knocked again and again, but there was still no reply. Thomas decided to take a look through the front room window, knowing it was considered rude by people he did it very discreetly, he could see no-one was at home, there was just a small fire glowing red in the hearth. Thomas sat down on the doorsteps and waited.

Just as his behind was becoming numb, he noticed a crowd of people coming out of the church. They were all dressed in their Sunday best, "of course, it's

Sunday!" Thomas said to himself, realizing that everybody had been in church. Thomas stood up and quickly and dusted off his behind with the palms of his hands as the reverend approached. The reverend had a black book under his arm and seemed to be leading what Thomas thought to be quite a crowd. The crowd came quickly to a halt when the reverend suddenly stopped and asked, "now then Thomas, what can we do for you?"

By now the crowd of people had huddled around the back of the reverend and were all staring at Thomas and waiting for his answer, which was a little baffling and to say the least, a little brief. "To see you sir," Thomas replied. The reverend who was by now towering over Thomas, laughed, but the crowd didn't say or do anything. They just continued to stare at Thomas, "to see me, Thomas, about what?" the reverend asked, trying to gain more information from Thomas, who was glued to the spot and by now beginning to feel quite intimidated by the reverend. Thomas answered, "Oh... eh... my father! I have his bible here!" The reverend lurched forward and put his arms around Thomas before saying, "welcome Thomas, welcome, even though we haven't seen much of you in church lately, welcome." Thomas squirmed and after a lingering moment the reverend open the vicarage door and said, turning to the crowd, "let me introduce some of the congregation. I'm the Reverend Grenside, but you know that!" he explained. Thomas smiled, thinking, well, I should do. The reverend then began scanning the congregational crowd. He eventually stopped and grabbed at a hand, which he gently pulled from the crowd. Attached to the hand was a placid faced lady who approached Thomas and quietly said, "Welcome Thomas." She curtsied and the reverend introduced her, "and this is my wife Eliza," he said. Eliza then disappeared into the vicarage. The reverend got hold of Thomas's wrist and began pointing out who the other members of the crowd were. "This is my eldest son Henry, and his wife Sarah, and those are their children Ada, Emma and...." the reverend searched around for a moment and then, spotting a little chap sat on a nearby wall, said proudly, "and that's little Fredrick over there, named after yours truly." The reverend had a big beam on his face and Thomas could have sworn his chest expanded three inches when he said who the child was named after.

It was sometime before Thomas had been introduced to the rest of the crowd. I'll never remember all this lot, he thought. After all, there was even another two Thomas's' amongst the crowd, which began to disperse saying that they were going home for their dinners. The reverend rubbed under his nose with an index finger and asked Thomas to stay for dinner. "Come on Thomas, Eliza will have ours on the table. You can then tell me how Jesse and his business are getting on." Thomas and the reverend entered the house to find Eliza in the front parlour using a small sewing machine. Thomas had never seen such an instrument and watched in amazement as the machine's needle when up and down and Eliza pushed the material underneath the machine with such accuracy. "Dinner will be about ten minutes," she said to Thomas and the reverend: who pulled out a chair from under the table, "sit down Thomas lad." Thomas walked around to the otherside of the table to a chair on the opposite side to where the reverend was sat. "Now then lad how's your father?" the reverend asked placing his elbows on the table. This act was soon reprimanded by Eliza, "Elbows Fredrick dear," she said, removing the machine from the table and straightening the table cloth with the flat of her hand. The reverend quickly removed his elbows and made a facial gesture to Thomas by lifting his eyebrows.

Thomas smiled, but he didn't answer the reverend's question, he was too busy looking around the room. Thomas had never seen so many items of interest in one room. He was most interested in a clock busily ticking away on the mantelpiece.

The reverend noticed Thomas's interest in the clock, "that clock was my Grandma Hannah's, it belonged to her father Tom. It's been handed down through the family. I suppose Henry will be next in line." The reverend told Thomas proudly whilst adjusting his position in the chair. A moment passed and the reverend then looked Thomas in the eye and repeated his question about Jesse. Thomas drew nearer the table and removed the bible from his jacket pocket once more. He placed it on the table and opened it so he could read the citation inside, when he was finished, he said, "well... father needs help now, its father I've come about." Thomas began shaking his head, "he's not well, he's drinking and not running the business." Thomas spent a good half hour telling the reverend and Eliza the whole story. Suddenly, Eliza interrupted Thomas by saying, "oh the dinner!" she quickly opened the oven door and was blasted by a torrid of black smoke from the oven. She quickly, with her apron, pulled a black pot from the oven and placed it on the top hob, where she began stirring the stew inside frantically. "Just in time!" she said wiping her forehead and pretending that she'd just about saved its contents.

Over dinner Thomas told more of his woeful story, the story finished with Thomas saying, "I don't really know what to do next reverend." Thomas began to fill up and Eliza handed him a handkerchief. The reverend thought for a moment and then said, "well there's only one thing for it, and that is for me to visit Jesse when he's least expecting it." Eliza agreed by nodding. The three of them then became silent as they finished the rest of the meal. Thomas finished first and placed his spoon down on his plate. After a quick smile he thanked Eliza for the dinner and said how wonderful the meal had been. Thomas then took a quick glance out through the window at the afternoon sky and said, "It's getting late, I'd best be off. It'll be dark in an hour." Courteously he stood up, placed the bible back in his pocket and rounded the table towards Eliza. He leant over and gently kissed her on the cheek. The reverend, realizing Thomas was leaving, quickly stood up and offered Thomas an outstretched hand whilst still clutching his serviette in the other. Thomas quickly rubbed his hand clean on his jacket before he shook the reverend's hand. "Aye lad, it's quite a trek back!" the reverend said, rounding the table and joining Thomas at the otherside. He gently put his arm around Thomas and said, "But a young lad like you should have no problem with that. Hey!" He nudged Thomas and placed his serviette on the table. Thomas quickly returned the lent handkerchief to Eliza before the reverend pulled him towards the front door. At the front door the reverend could see Thomas was still a little uncertain and told him sympathetically, "don't worry Thomas lad. I won't let you down, that bible is no false promise." Thomas smiled nervously and replied, "I know that, but don't leave it too long will you?" the reverend assured Thomas that he'd be there within the following week. Thomas nodded and set off down Church Lane towards home.

Thomas had walked about halfway back home when his feet began to hurt and darkness began to gain the better of the day. By the time he'd reached the bottom of Mirfield it was certainly dark and the only thing to guide him home was the poor gas lit lamps and what appeared to be shouting in the distance. The nearer Thomas got to the centre of Mirfield the louder and more aggressive the shouting became. Then just before he arrived at The Black Bull the shouting stopped as if it had never existed at all. Funny, thought Thomas, he stopped and listened. There was nothing, nothing at all, just a deadly silence. Thomas shrugged his shoulders and put it down to drunken locals leaving the pub. However, on passing The Black Bull Thomas happened to glance across the road towards the pub yard and the shack. In the darkness of the pub yard Thomas thought he saw something moving slowly along the floor, he wasn't sure at first, so he froze and waited for a moment and watched. "There it is again!" he said to himself. Thomas slowly, apprehensively, walked across the road towards the yard. As he approached he could hear faint groaning noises coming from what appeared to be a bundle of rags crawling across the yard floor.

Eventually, Thomas began to form an image in his mind of what it was that was crawling along the yard floor. It was Jesse, bleeding and dragging a badly damaged leg behind him, "father!" Thomas screamed as he ran the last yards to help Jesse. He quickly turned Jesse onto his back and then the stench hit Thomas full on in the face. It was a combination of ale and vomit which was plastered down the front of Jesse's waist coat. Thomas who was by now worried asked, "Are you alright?" But Jesse's reply was slurred and incomprehensible. At this point Thomas became annoyed, and instantly stood up, "drunk, drunk again!" he shouted. He started to walk away, but only managed ten paces before his conscience got the better of him. He returned to Jesse and angrily grabbed Jesse's by the arm. Using the arm, he pulled Jesse to his feet. Thomas then wrapped the arm around his neck and slowly began dragging Jesse towards home. At this point he didn't even care if he was hurting Jesse, he just dragged him physically towards home stopping occasionally to get his breath.

It took Thomas quite sometime and all his strength to drag Jesse home. But eventually, he turned into the front garden path on Stevenson's Row only to be confronted by the reverend. The reverend, after taking the short cut, had been sat waiting on the doorstep to see Jesse. On seeing Thomas he quickly ran to help Thomas with Jesse. "Told you I'd come when he was least expecting it, didn't I?" the reverend lifted Jesse off of Thomas who just nodded and said, in a disgusted tone, "Well here ya go, drunk again." The reverend carried Jesse up the steps and into the house, he laid him flat on the kitchen floor and said to Thomas, "Go to bed Thomas. I'll deal with this from here on in. And don't worry!" Thomas nodded as Jesse began to snore. Suddenly, Thomas began to hesitate and started thanking the reverend for coming, but the reverend, again trying to reassure Thomas that things would be alright said, "Go on lad, get yourself to bed, your father will be alright with me. I'll let him sleep it off!" The reverend started to light a fire in the hearth and Thomas looked pitifully towards Jesse before going to bed.

The next morning Thomas came down the stairs. The kitchen was warm and the reverend was sat enjoying a cup of tea at the kitchen table. "There's tea in the pot if you want one Thomas," the reverend said smiling at Thomas, who sighed and sat down at the table. Thomas looked towards Jesse, who was still asleep on the floor and was still making a horrendous snoring noise. "Has he been awake yet?" Thomas asked the reverend, who quickly replied, "Oh you're just in time for my awakening ceremony." He then pointed to a bucket full of ice cold water which was sat in the corner of the kitchen by the door. "In fact, it's time he was up for work!" the reverend stood up, grabbed the bucket by the handle and in one swift movement, he threw the lot over Jesse. Instantly, Jesse sat up and began swearing, he wiped his face free from water and angrily got to his feet. The moment he saw Thomas, he began blaming him for his drenching and made a furious dash towards him. The dash was accompanied by a flurry of punches. However, no punches landed as the reverend stood between Thomas and Jesse whilst saying calmly, "Now Jesse, behave yourself," this startled Jesse, because in his rage, he hadn't even noticed that the reverend was even in the room. "Oh it's you reverend. I didn't see you there!" Jesse said, guiltily adjusting his clothes in a vain attempt to look half decent, he then began patting down his unwashed hair with a bit of spit on his hand. The reverend looked towards Thomas and with a serious expression on his face said, "Your father and I need to talk, so you get yourself off to work and I'll see you later." Thomas grabbed his jacket, removed the bible from the pocket and threw it down on the table saying, "he's all yours, reverend." Thomas smirked at Jesse before leaving.

After Thomas had left, the atmosphere changed, it became more relaxed as the reverend and Jesse pulled out chairs from underneath the kitchen table. Whilst doing this there was a loud clanging noise as the chairs pulled over all the empty ale bottles which had been stored underneath the table. Jesse's eyes went skywards and he gave a large sigh as he sat down. The reverend handed him a cup of tea and said, "Ok Jesse, let's hear it." Jesse began telling the reverend all about the events of the past three or four months and how he missed Eunice, Harriet and Joseph. After the sad story was told the reverend realized that this was not the time to tell Jesse off, but to offer the hand of assistance. "You've certainly had a bad time of it Jesse," the reverend said sympathetically, he then paused before saying, "but you've got to put it behind you and get on with your life. God will take care of your dead family.

Your job is to keep the business going and to look after your living family, namely Thomas. And this drinking is not the answer, and neither is missing church every week." Jesse nodded his head and replied, "I didn't know what else to do reverend, and drinking makes me forget my troubles!" The pair finished their tea and began reminiscing how things use to be before the deaths of Joseph, Harriet and Eunice.

Three hours later the reverend had to round things off by saying, "I've got to get back Jesse, Eliza will be waiting." Jesse nodded and then began to say something else, but suddenly he stopped and thought for a moment. The reverend hadn't quite heard what Jesse had said, but he'd seen Jesse's facial gesture and asked, "What!" Jesse tried to cover up what he was saying by smiling and saying, "oh it's nothing! It doesn't really matter reverend." Jesse escorted the reverend to the front door and just before leaving the reverend took from his pocket a florin, "Here Jesse, something to see you on from the poor fund, give it me back when you're back on your feet." Jesse hesitated, but then gracefully accepted the money, after all he thought, I'm skint! The pair shook hands and patted each other on the back before the reverend set off back towards the church. Jesse decided to walk with the reverend as far as the shack where he pretended to go to work and waved to the reverend from the shack door. But as soon as the reverend had disappeared out of sight Jesse sleeked off to The Black Bull where he spent the two shillings on ale and chases.

The weeks passed and Jesse's behaviour didn't improve much. He worked, but only to feed his drinking habit of an evening and weekends. Not only the reverend, but the doctor and even Bill Carter had tried to persuade Jesse to alter his evil ways, but to no avail. The drinking came to a head when Thomas arrived home late one evening to find the doors locked and the house all in darkness. In his anger, he kicked the front door before walking back towards The Black Bull, where he was sure to find Jesse drinking with his crony's. Thomas entered the pub and was received by a thick band of choking tobacco smoke drifting in the air. He coughed and began scanning the tables for Jesse, but then came a tap on his shoulder. Thomas turned to find Jesse grinning at him. "And what do you want my lad?" asked Jesse, dribbling and stumbling into Thomas. Thomas pushed Jesse back off of him and said, "I can't get in the house, have you got a key? Mine doesn't seem to work!" Jesse laughed out loud and proudly announced to the entire pub, "everybody!" the pub fell silent and everybody looked towards Jesse. "This is my son Thomas, he's my only son, and I love him dearly." Everybody in the pub raised their glasses and welcomed Thomas. Jesse began staggering and was forced to lean on Thomas. The lean turned into an arm around the shoulders and a rather vain attempt to kiss Thomas on the cheek. Thomas was having none of it and pushed Jesse away before quickly unwrapping himself from Jesse's arm lock. Again, Thomas asked Jesse for his key. Jesse pulled an old well worn key from his pocket and dangled it in front of Thomas's face on a piece of string. "Is this what you want?" Thomas instantly grabbed the key and headed for the door, "Won't do you any good!" Jesse said, whilst laughing at the same time. Thomas stopped and turned around slowly, "why, what have you done now?" he asked. Jesse began to walk back to a stall at the rear of the pub, where a dreary dressed old lady was sat with two other scruffy looking old men. Jesse sat down next to the old lady. Thomas approached the stall and repeated his question, "why what have you done now?" "Oh precious son of mine, it's not what I've done. It's what I haven't done!" Jesse said sarcastically. The old woman looked at Jesse and began cackling like an old hen. Thomas was now getting really frustrated and exasperated, he asked, "Ok what haven't you done?" Jesse bellowed with laughter and more cackling came from the old woman. It took a moment and then a silent moment before Jesse could hold his drunken face straight. He then said, whilst bursting into laughter again, "I haven't paid the rent, and the landlords changed all the locks, we've been thrown out lad!" Jesse exploded into laughter and banged on the table in excitement at  telling Thomas the news. Thomas looked around the pub, and he seemed to be the only one in the pub that wasn't laughing. Thomas stomped out of the pub and walked back towards Stevenson's Row. He had no option but to stop at Bill Carter's house for the next few weeks, but eventually, to be fair to Bill Carter and his family, Thomas was forced to make a decision and decided to leave Mirfield.

On the morning that Thomas decided to leave it was clear and fine, there was very little wind and before leaving Thomas decided to work a last morning with Bill. They'd both set off for work early and arrived at The Black Bull Yard in bright sun light. Bill opened his shop and put out some ironwork advertising his skills. "Go on then!" he said to Thomas pointing to the shack with his hand. Thomas walked slowly towards the shack. He knocked quietly on the shack door and listened, he could hear a shuffling noise, which turned into certain movement from the inside of the shack. A bolt was drawn back and Jesse answered the door. "Oh it's you!" he said leaving the door half open and walking back into the darkness of the shack. Thomas pushed open the door to reveal two chairs in front of a small fire; one was occupied by the old lady from the pub. "You've met Mary haven't you?" Jesse asked, whilst sitting down in the second chair and throwing another large piece of wood onto the fire.

Thomas didn't beat about the bush; he came straight to the point and told Jesse that he was leaving and what he planned to do. Jesse didn't show much interest in what Thomas had to say, he just took another swig from an ale bottle and then handed it to the old woman before saying, "aye lad, if that's what you want to do." He then took the bottle back from the old lady and took another swig. An awkward silence descended on the shack which was broken by a single horse nay and the clomping of its hooves on the stone floor. "Horse needs feeding Jesse!" the old woman said poking at the fire. At this point Thomas felt that the time was right for him to leave, so he just said, "ok then, I'll be off." He left without so much as a hug or a kiss from his father, which left him with a feeling of destitution. The feeling stayed with Thomas for many a year, and it was years before Thomas felt like returning to Mirfield, in fact, twelve long years.

Thomas arrived back in Mirfield by train. He had brought his new wife Eva with him to meet Jesse. He'd warned Eva what they might find at the shack and decided to take the bull by the horns and go straight to the shack from the station. It took about ten minutes to walk up Station Road towards The Black Bull and when they eventually turned into the yard, there, stood in front of his shop, was Bill Carter. Bill immediately recognized Thomas and quickly walked forward to greet him with hand held out and a beaming smile, "Thomas lad, how ya doing?" Bill asked as he shook hands and hugged Thomas. After the clinch Thomas introduced Eva as his wife. Bill welcomed her and kissed her tenderly on the cheek, he then said to Thomas, "I suppose you've come to see ya father?" Thomas nodded his head and enquired, "Is he in?" Bill nodded and replied, "I think so." Thomas took hold of Eva's hand and shook it to reassure her. "Come on then, best foot forward." He said, as they approached the shack where they found Jesse brushing down the horse. Thomas spoke first from behind Jesse and said, "He's new!" Jesse turned around and saw Thomas, "aye the other died on me, but this one will do me for now." There was a cautious moment and then the pair hugged. "Hello father," Thomas said bravely. Jesse didn't say anything at first, but he had a small tear in his eye and had to pretend he'd gotten some bale dust in it as he wiped it away with a dirty rag he took off some nearby bales. Thomas turned and pulled Eva towards him. "This is my wife Eva!" he said proudly, giving Eva a small kiss on the lips. Jesse shook hands with Eva and then walked around the side of the shack returning a couple of seconds later with the old lady in tow. "And this is my wife Mary Ann." Jesse said, grinning. Thomas grinned back and approached Mary; he gave her a hug and asked quietly, "how's he been?" Mary smiled kindly and said, "We don't drink during the week now, we only have a couple of milk stouts on a Friday evening and a couple on Saturday." Thomas smiled with relief and thanked Mary, "oh it wasn't me. It was Jesse. He realized after you'd gone what he'd done. Driving you away like that. He'll be ever so pleased that you're back!" Thomas looked Mary in the eye for a moment; she then asked apprehensively, "You are back... aren't you?" Thomas squirmed for a moment and then replied, "not exactly, we have a house in Gainsborough, that's in Lincolnshire. It's quite a distance from here. Eva comes from out that way." Mary smiled and said, "It's not me you've to tell, it's him!" she pointed to an old man, who was sat on the shack wall telling his new daughter-in-law all about his childhood days in Shalbourne.

The reminiscing went on for about two hours. It ended with Thomas saying, "Well we've got to get back love." Eva nodded and stood up. Jesse asked, "When are you coming back?" Thomas had to explain gently that it wasn't convenient at the moment for him to move back to Mirfield. However, he did say that he would keep in touch by letter and would visit regularly now that Mirfield was linked by rail to Wakefield and Huddersfield. Jesse, not wanting to cause any more trouble between him and Thomas, stood up and gave Thomas a hug and whilst doing this, he whispered in Thomas's ear quietly, "don't stay away too long Thomas. I'm not getting any younger." Thomas grabbed Jesse's hands, and whilst gripping them tightly, he promised Jesse he'd be back soon. Jesse nodded and turned to kiss Eva whilst Thomas did the same to Mary. Jesse then put his arm around Mary and both of them watched as Thomas and Eva disappeared across the yard towards Station Road. Both couples gave a last wave and then they were gone.

The following day Jesse was up early and busied himself with cleaning out the horse and getting things ready for the day's deliveries. He'd just finish loading the last bale onto the cart when he turned around and noticed things were awfully quiet. He slowly walked down the yard, and at the bottom he looked along the road. There was not a soul in sight. After a pause, he placed his hands on his hips and looked the other way, and again, not a soul in sight. Funny! He thought to himself. He took his watch from his waistcoat pocket and quietly said to himself, "Well it's turned nine, wonder where everybody is?" Just then he noticed Bill Carter coming along the otherside of the road. "Morning Bill, it's awfully quiet this morning." Jesse said as Bill approached him. But then, Jesse noticed as Bill got closer, that he was dressed all in black and carrying a large black ribbon tied in a bow. Jesse's heart dropped at the

sight, and he quickly approached Bill. "Oh I'm sorry Bill!" Jesse said, thinking Bill had lost family. He then asked quietly, "who has died then Bill?" Bill stopped and stared at Jesse for a moment, but then he realized that Jesse didn't know. "Haven't you heard Jesse?" Jesse stood there looking helpless. "Heard what?" he said looking towards Bill for an answer. Bill came closer and said, "It's the old queen Jesse, she's dead, she passed away yesterday and the whole country is in mourning. Everybody's been told to wear black and put up black or purple ribbons." Stunned by this information Jesse sat down on The Black Bull's steps and said, "The old queen dead! She's been on the throne most of my life. I've never known any other monarch." Jesse paused for a moment and then with a sad tone in his voice, he said, "things won't be the same without the old queen." Bill agreed and they both slowly walked back up the yard together.

The mourning for Queen Victoria went on for three months, and if we are honest about the matter, the people of Mirfield had become tiresome of it. But then a morning came when everyone started to take down the black and purple ribbons and life began to return to normal. Jesse was beginning to build up his business again and confidence in him and his business had begun to return. The following year Thomas had visited three times and both Jesse and Mary had been invited to Gainsborough to meet Eva's parents, but there was a problem. Thomas was worried that Jesse and Mary would get lost on their way to Gainsborough, so on his last visit, he had told them both that he would come and fetch them and this Thomas did. He caught the early morning train from Gainsborough to Mirfield, changing at Wakefield. The trains were on time and Thomas had arrived early in Mirfield, which he was pleased about. This meant that Jesse and Mary would have the full day for the visit, or so he thought....

Thomas arrived at the shack to find Jesse sitting outside on the low wall. He was waiting patiently with a grin and crossed arms. As Thomas approached, Mary appeared from behind the shack clutching a large brown paper bag, she looked nervous. "Are we all ready then?" Thomas asked politely, giving Mary a kiss on the cheek. Jesse stood up and said, "As ready as we'll ever be!" but then he quickly grabbed Thomas by the elbow and said, "Just a minute lad, before we go, we've got a few things we need to ask you about these here trains." Jesse winked and grinned at Thomas. There was the usual silence and then Thomas asked, "What, what about them?" Jesse rubbed his freshly shaven chin and said, "Well, it's like this lad. Mary's a bit nervous about going on a train. We've been told that these trains travel at over seventy miles an hour, is this true?" Thomas thought for a moment and whilst nodding his head, said, "I suppose they do!" Jesse looked at Mary, who wasn't happy about Thomas's reply. "Isn't that faster than the human body can stand?" Thomas began to laugh, whilst Jesse had all on trying to keep a straight face. He began secretly signally to Thomas to stop laughing by shaking his head and waved his hand vigorously on Mary's blind side. Thomas realized what Jesse was trying to signal to him and looked across at Mary, who was by now looking even more nervous than before. Thomas quickly stopped laughing and stood up straight; he straightened his tie and gave a little cough. Jesse paused for a moment and then asked another question. "Won't we explode at that sort of speed?" Thomas was about to break into laughter again, but Jesse's frown was enough to stop him. Then, trying to keep his face straight, Thomas said reassuringly, "I've come here this morning by train, and I'm still alright, aren't I?" He then began prodding his body with an opened spanned hand.

Jesse looked across at a by now very distressed Mary and said, "Look! He's alright, isn't he?" He then joined in the prodding. Mary smiled nervously and quietly said, "I don't know Jesse, what if the thing flips over like it did the other year?" Jesse, in despair, began to get angry and growled, "Well then, it'll be up to the good lord then, won't it? Now are we going or aren't we?" Mary slowly stood up and linked Jesse's arm before politely saying, "If you're going to go, then we'll go together, and then if anything happens, it'll happen to the both of us, won't it?" Jesse shrugged his shoulders and looked bemused at Thomas, who was looking at his watch and getting worried about the time. "Come on then if you're ready," he said, starting off down the yard at a pace. Jesse and Mary, who were still linked together, hurriedly scurried after Thomas, "not so fast our Thomas lad. We're not as young as we used to be." Mary said gasping for breath and still grasping her large brown paper bag.

Thankfully, the journey was quite uneventful and both Jesse and Mary seemed to enjoy the new experience of train travel, although Thomas wasn't too sure about Mary, because when they'd arrived at Gainsborough, she seemed very keen to depart, what she described as, "the snorting beast!"

On arrival, Eva was waiting on the station platform for them; she smiled respectfully and greeted everybody with a small peck on the cheek. She hastily led everybody off the platform and out through a small archway to a horse and small cart which was tethered at the side of the station by a black iron railing. "Here we go!" Eva said, untying the horse and handing the rains to Thomas. Jesse helped Mary into the back of the cart and then hitched up Eva, "I'll sit with our Thomas up front," he said, mounting the cart and plonking himself down at the side of Thomas. "Off we go." Jesse said enthusiastically rubbing his hands together. Thomas cracked the whip and off they set. It wasn't long before the little cart had left Gainsborough and was heading out into the open countryside. Jesse began reminiscing about how the countryside reminded him of back home when he was a lad. He even took a deep breath and said, "Ah country air, ya can't beat it!" before exhaling. The horse trotted on for some miles, five in all before Mary asked, "can we stop for a moment?" Thomas nodded his head and pulled the cart over. Jesse jumped down and made his way around to the back of the cart saying, "There's a decent thick edge over there." But as he grabbed hold of Mary she looked at him bemused, "whatever, do you mean Jesse?" she asked as Jesse became embarrassed and said, "you know, to do your business." Both girls laughed and then Mary said, "We don't need the loo, ya fool!" Jesse, who was baffled, asked, "Well why have we stopped then?" Mary looked around and then pointed to a nice lush grass verge at the side of the road. "Over there will do just fine!" she said grabbing the large brown paper bag from the back of the cart.

Thomas dropped the rains over the horse's head which allowed it to begin munching on the fresh green grass of the verge. Jesse, on the other hand, was stood in amazement at the women, who were by now, sat down on the grass verge. Thomas walked around the back of the cart and joined Jesse before asking, "What's going on here then?" Jesse lifted his cap up at the front and quickly replied, "I was just about to ask you that!" With hands in their pockets, both men slowly ambled towards the women, who were by now busily digging out brown packages from deep inside the large brown paper bag that Mary had brought with her. "What's all this then?" Jesse asked sitting down at the side of Mary, who was reading the names on the packages. "Here is yours!" she told Jesse, handing him a package. Jesse opened the package to find a cheese sandwich. "You little bugger!" he said, grinning all over his face, "a bloody picnic!" Mary smiled and said, "Yes, you're always telling me of how you had picnics as a child and I thought this would be an ideal opportunity to have one!" Jesse leant across and gave Mary a sweet kiss on the lips before saying tenderly, "thanks love."

It wasn't long before they headed off again and Jesse asked, "I thought Eva's parents lived in Gainsborough?" Thomas looked at Jesse and replied, "They do. All these outlying villages come under Gainsborough Council." Jesse thought for a moment and then asked, "Well which of these villages do Eva's parents live in?" Thomas didn't answer, he just pointed to a village in the distance. "It looks like Shalbourne!" remarked Jesse. Thomas just smiled and pushed the horse on as they passed a village sign saying, "Scotter." Just after the sign Thomas turned left down a small steep hill which after about fifty yards flattened out into a small track leading across a field to a very smart farm house with a lawned front garden and a small vegetable garden to the rear. Thomas pulled up in front of a gravel path leading to the front door. The door was set in its own vestibule, which protruded from the front of the main house. Before everybody had dismounted from the cart Eva's Father, a portly bald man, appeared at the door. "Mother they're here!" he shouted back into the house, but then, he seemed to be pushed out through the door by a gaggle of giggling girls. "Don't push me dears," he said being pushed down the path towards the cart.

Introductions were made on the gravel path. The last person to be introduced was Eva's mother, Maria, who appeared at the door with a tray containing a jug of lemonade and some crystal glasses. She placed the tray down on the lawn and shook hands with everybody. Eva handed out the glasses and her sister Mabel poured the lemonade, stating that, "it was homemade!" everytime she poured out another glass full.

Jesse, Maria, Mary and Eva's father, James, walked across the lawn together whilst sipping their lemonade. Jesse began talking with James about farming and hay making. They compared northern methods with southern methods of stacking the stooks, it all baffled the ladies, and they were soon heading towards the front door as spots of rain began to hit their faces. Inside the door was a hallway laden with thick red velvet carpet. The carpet led directly to a stairway leading up to a colourful stained glass window. To the right of the hallway was a luxurious lounge, to the left, a large dining room with a table set for tea.

A maid suddenly appeared from the direction of the kitchen and curtsied, she told Maria that, "tea was ready mam," and then she disappeared as suddenly as she had appeared. Maria began busily ushering everybody into the dining room and pointing out where everybody was to be seated. It took a couple of minutes to arrange everybody, but eventually, all were seated and busily making light chitchat. Maria rang a small silver bell which was on the table, and the maid with an elderly butler began serving the meal, which Jesse thought was quite a feast.

Towards the end of the meal James stood up and coughed. This got everyone's attention and a silence descended over the table. After a brief moment James cordially invited the men into the lounge for what he described as, "the best cigars and brandy in Lincolnshire." But before anyone had time to move, Thomas stood up and announced, "Eva and I have something to say before anybody moves." James slowly sat back down in his chair and looked across at Maria to see if she knew what Thomas was talking about. Her answer was very short and swift so as not to be seen by the others around the table. She quickly shrugged her shoulders whilst shaking her head very slightly. James's eyes then turned to focus on Eva, who was moving swiftly around the table to join Thomas, she then happily grabbed Thomas's arm and linked him whilst waiting for Thomas to make the announcement. The room fell silent and all eyes were on Thomas, who cleared his throat and then, with his chest stuck out, proudly announced, "You're going to be grandparents." Everybody looked at each other whilst Eva and Thomas stood there smirking. Jesse was the first to his feet and with a large clap of his hands he shouted at the top of his voice, "bloody marvellous, absolutely, bloody marvellous!" he grabbed Thomas and shook his hand whilst patting him on the back and congratulating him. He then turned to Eva and whilst lifting her off her feet and smothering her in kisses he screamed, "you little beauty!" Jesse spun her around and around sending Eva into dizzy oblivion. He was eventually stopped by Mary saying, "Put her down Jesse, and let someone else congratulate the mother-to-be." Eva's father James ordered the butler to break out a bottle of the best wine to celebrate the good news.

The celebrations went on well into the evening and more than one bottle of the best wine was drunk before Jesse, who was probably the happiest person at the celebration, and Mary had to return to the train station in the rain for the journey home.

The platform was cold and damp. The rain, which was heavy and blowing across the bottom end of the platform, was whipped up into a spray which slowly made its way up the rest of the platform. To try and keep dry, Jesse and Mary took shelter up against the wall of the ticket office. Whilst Thomas, who had escorted them to the station, was explaining to Jesse where to change trains in Wakefield and which platform they should be on to catch their connecting train to Mirfield. Jesse, who was squinting from the spray wetting his face, nodded his head as the train pulled into the station amongst clouds of steam and small lumps of soot being blown from its dirty chimney. Thomas quickly gave Mary a kiss goodbye on her wet cheek, and shook Jesse's hand as they both boarded the train. Thomas slammed the train door shut and then Jesse pulled the window down from the inside. The rain drops got larger as Jesse stuck his head out through the open window. He grabbed Thomas by the back of his neck and pulled him nearer the train door. Quickly, Jesse leant over until his lips were parallel with Thomas's ear, he then quietly whispered, "listen lad, I'm not getting any younger and the one thing that I wish for in my life is to see my grandson, so when he's born, bring him to see me." A tear from Jesse's eye joined the rain which was hitting his face and it made its way downwards. Looking Thomas in the eye, Jesse said, "Promise me Thomas. Promise me!" he shook Thomas's hand and repeated his request "Promise me you will, promise." Thomas had no option but to reply, "I will father, I will. I promise. I'll bring the child to see you." Jesse smiled and nodded, he began waving as the train began to pull away. But just before Jesse was out of ear shot Thomas shouted, "But father, what if it's a girl?" Jesse shrugged his shoulders and shouted back, "that's alright, bring her anyway." And with that he waved again, and pulled up the window as the train disappeared into the damp darkness of the night.

Everyday Jesse thought about his pending grandchild, wondering and worrying, as he always did on these occasions, if everything was alright. Mary had taunted Jesse about his worrying, "you'll worry yourself into an early grave." She told Jesse, who just grinned and sang, "It won't be long now, it won't be long now." He then did a little dance and a wiggle as he walked the horse to the cart. Mary laughed to herself and said, "Silly sod."

Jesse began loading the cart with his first order of the day. Mary had to help Jesse do the loading; the bales were now getting the better of Jesse at his age. "Come on then, the last one!" Mary cried, waiting for Jesse to grab his end of the bale. Jesse straightened the last bale onto the cart and then bent over to grab his end of the last bale. But then he started to cough and was forced to straighten up, he used the wall of the shack to steady himself. Mary quickly stood up and caringly asked, "Are you alright?" Jesse waved her off and said between coughs, "I'll be alright, give me a minute." Mary waited patiently as Jesse coughed even more. She decided to fetch Jesse some water, which seemed to stem the cough long enough for them to load the last bale. Mary became worried and decided to join Jesse on the delivery, so she hitched up alongside him on the cart. "There's no need Mary. I'm alright lass!" Jesse said, but Mary was having none of it, and stayed put. Jesse glared at her and then tutted before setting off.

Eventually, Jesse had to see the doctor and received a tonic for his cough, which he took when he felt a coughing bout coming on. The bouts seemed to visit him more at night and the early hours of the morning. Jesse put this down to the cold air which circulated around the shack after the fire had gone out. And as you can imagine, coughing at that time of day kept him well in with Mary, who was often woken by the coughing. It was early one morning when Mary had scolded Jesse for waking her that the cough seemed particularly bad. Jesse took the tonic twice before it began to subside. After tossing and turning in bed for half an hour Jesse decided to get up and looked out through the shack window. Dawn had broken and so Jesse decided to start work instead of going back to bed as he usually did. He swigged down a gulp of the tonic and replaced the cap before he coughed his way outside, where he harnessed the horse to the wall ring and began grooming it.

Later that day, with Jesse getting up at dawn, he felt tired and weary. There were no outstanding orders, so he told Mary that he was going to take a nap inside. He told her to wake him in two hours or if anything of interest happened. Mary smiled and nodded her head before returning to the sunny part of the small wall outside, where she'd placed an old cloth to make the wall more comfortable whilst sunning herself. Mary had sat there for maybe an hour when she was interrupted by a shadow blocking out the sunlight from her face. She slowly opened her eyes, and at first she could only see a bluish silhouette of a man leaning over her. She placed her hand over her eyebrows and strained to see who it was, but then a voice said, "hello Mary, where's father?" Mary recognized the voice instantly and quickly jumped up saying, "Thomas! What a surprise!" As Mary's eyes cleared from the glare of the sun, she realized that Eva was stood a little further back behind Thomas, "oh you've brought Eva with you as well." Eva was carrying a little blue bundle, "and it's a boy!" Mary cried excitedly. "Your father will be pleased." Mary approached Eva, who peeled back the child's blanket to reveal a perfectly formed baby boy. "Oh he's beautiful, give us a hold." Eva handed the baby over to Mary, who sat on the wall and began cuddling him, making sure the sun didn't go in the child's eyes by sitting slightly at an angle to the sun. After a couple of, "coo's" and "he has your eyes." Thomas said, "Well where is he then?" Mary handed the baby back to Eva and said, "I'll go and fetch him, your father was tired and went for a lie down." Mary went back into the shack followed by Thomas and Eva, who was getting the baby ready to meet his grandad. The place was quiet and Mary shouted, "Jesse! Jesse! Thomas is here with the new baby, and it's a boy!" There was no reply. Mary pulled back the sheet that hung down the centre of the shack; it separated the bedroom from the horses' stable. "Jesse, are you awake?" Mary said nudging a pile of blankets on the bed, but it didn't move. Thomas, realizing that something was wrong, entered the bedroom and pulled back the sheets to reveal Jesse, who had sadly passed away in that past hour whilst Mary was sunning herself outside.

This you may think is a sudden and sad end to our story, but unfortunately, that's how death visits us all from time to time. Jesse died at the age of seventy two in 1904 and his new grandson was named after him, as family tradition dictated.

You must be made aware that whilst writing this story I took great pains and efforts not to mention the surname of the people you have been reading about, Jesse, Eunice, Henry, Charles, Percilla, Joseph, Thomas and all the others in the story. The reason for this is because their surname appears on the front of this book. That's right; they were my ancestors and the story. Well it's almost true....

Thomas: -   Thomas survived the First World War and sadly died of his wounds in 1921 after three years of agony.

Eva: -   Eva lived to a ripe old age and after nursing her great grandchild, me, she died in 1959 at the age of eighty nine.

Mary Ann: -   Out lived Jesse by seven years and died in 1911 leaving the shack to her son by her first marriage.

Jesse: -   Jesse's grandson (Jesse) was registered as a girl at birth (Jessie). This affected his life in all sorts of ways, but then that's another story.

Jesse. "A Different Man."